Global Investment Performance Standards (GIPS®) Handbook

SECOND EDITION
2007

Guidance and Interpretations for the GIPS Standards

GIPS Secretariat
CFA Institute
560 Ray C. Hunt Drive
P.O. Box 3668
Charlottesville, VA
22903-0668 USA
www.cfainstitute.org

ISBN 978-1-932495-44-7
Printed in the United States of America
August 2007

Table of Contents

1. INTRODUCTION

1-1 PREFACE

Because the Global Investment Performance Standards (GIPS®) are updated and expanded through interpretations, Guidance Statements, and new provisions, the GIPS Handbook has been created as a companion to complement this dynamic nature of the Standards. This version of the Handbook captures the additions, eliminations, and changes resulting from the recent revisions to the GIPS standards (effective 1 January 2006).

Proposals of new interpretive guidance that are not yet formally adopted by the GIPS Executive Committee have been included in this Handbook in Chapter 5. Although these proposed guidelines have not been finalized or adopted, they have been included because they provide valuable information on the application of the Standards in specific situations. The proposals are clearly marked to easily identify and distinguish them from the adopted guidance and provisions that must be considered when complying with the Standards. As each proposal is adopted, it will be published on the CFA Institute website, and ultimately, the final provisions and/or guidance will be printed in the next update of this Handbook.

The Investment Performance Standards section of the CFA Institute website (www.cfainstitute.org/cfacentre/ips/) is a resource for the most current information on the Standards. The website includes recent interpretations, proposals, and reports on the activities of the committees that oversee the GIPS standards, as well as information on webcasts, conferences, workshops, and other educational opportunities related to the Standards. Additionally, CFA Institute circulates a bi-monthly e-mail update detailing current events relating to the GIPS standards. To receive the e-mail alerts, please write to standards@cfainstitute.org and provide name, postal address, and e-mail address in the body of the message.

1-2 OBJECTIVES OF THE GIPS STANDARDS

The Global Investment Performance Standards were developed by CFA Institute (formerly the Association for Investment Management and Research) in partnership with many other organizations worldwide and with experts from a variety of fields within the global investment industry. The Standards were developed in order to provide an ethical framework for the calculation and presentation of the investment performance history of an investment management firm. The GIPS standards are a voluntary set of standards based on the fundamental principles of full disclosure and fair representation. Through voluntary compliance, firms can build an environment of credibility and trust in the investment industry.

Having one global standard for performance measurement and evaluation benefits two major groups: investment management firms and their clients and prospective clients. Investment management firms that comply with the GIPS standards allow clients, prospective clients, and consultants the best opportunity to fairly evaluate the past performance of the firm. Compliance enables a firm to fairly compete against other firms throughout the world. The Standards also provide a realistic, standardized framework and outline of internal controls necessary to ensure performance figures are directly comparable.

Prospective clients have a greater level of confidence in the integrity of performance presentations and are able to more easily compare the track records of compliant firms. Compliance with the GIPS standards demonstrates a firm-wide commitment to ethical best practices and that the firm employs strong internal control processes. Additionally, current clients attempting to evaluate their managers' performance also benefit by being able to compare their actual results to the firm's analogous product "average" as defined by the Standards. However, compliance with the Standards does not obviate the need for due diligence on the part of prospective or current clients or consultants in evaluating performance data and other important qualitative research on investment managers.

1-3 HISTORY OF THE GIPS STANDARDS

In the past, the investment community had great difficulty obtaining meaningful comparisons of accurate investment performance data. Making apples-to-apples comparisons of investment performance was problematic, and the existence of country-specific guidelines for performance presentation further complicated matters. This need for a practitioner-driven set of ethical principles and a standardized, industry-wide approach to calculating and reporting investment results led the Association for Investment Management and Research (AIMR®, now known as CFA Institute) to sponsor, develop, and publish a minimum global standard by which firms could calculate and present their investment results.

The foundation for the GIPS standards was first laid in 1987, with the creation of the AIMR Performance Presentation Standards (AIMR-PPS®), voluntary performance guidelines for the North American investment management industry

The GIPS committee began work in 1995 with the goal of developing one globally accepted set of standards. AIMR published the GIPS standards for public comment in February 1998 after circulating several preliminary drafts among industry participants to obtain their acceptance of the concepts of the Standards. After an extensive period of public comment, AIMR's Board of Governors formally endorsed the GIPS standards in February 1999.

Since their introduction in 1999, the GIPS standards have gathered momentum with investment management firms in more than 25 countries adopting these voluntary, ethical standards for calculating and presenting historical investment performance. As of 1 January 2006, the GIPS standards experienced their first major revision, which facilitated the move to one truly global Standard. All of the former country versions of GIPS standards (CVGs) are now in the process of transitioning to a single standard so that by the time firms calculate 2006 performance figures, they will claim compliance *only* with the GIPS standards.

The success of the Standards is the result of an alliance among experts from a variety of fields within the global investment industry. The GIPS standards represent the culmination of the effort of a diverse group of investment professionals representing a number of global investment organizations.

1-4 THE GIPS EXECUTIVE COMMITTEE

With the release of the GIPS standards in 1999, the GIPS committee was replaced by the Investment Performance Council (IPC), which served as the committee responsible for maintaining the Standards. It consisted of approximately 36 members from a variety of fields within the global investment industry representing 15 countries. From 1999 to 2006, the IPC focused on its principle goal: to have all countries adopt the GIPS standards as *the* standard for investment firms seeking to present historical investment performance.

In February 2005, the IPC took the final step toward global uniformity when it revised the GIPS standards and created a single global standard for investment performance reporting that increased minimum standards worldwide. It was the most comprehensive and significant upgrade to the Standards since their inception in 1999.

In order to facilitate involvement from all industry stakeholders and provide a necessary conduit for the collaboration of ideas and mutual engagement in the process, the IPC was transformed in 2006 into the more nimble GIPS Executive Committee (EC). The EC serves as the effective decision-making authority for the GIPS standards.

The EC meets at least three times each year either in person or by conference call, with other conference calls scheduled as needed. Both in-person meetings and conference calls are open to the public. The agendas and materials for each meeting as well as the findings of each meeting are published on the CFA Institute website (see www.cfainstitute.org/cfacentre/ips/).

The EC recognizes that the investment industry is constantly evolving and, therefore, the GIPS standards must be flexible to remain effective, useful, and relevant. The EC has created four standing subcommittees: the GIPS Council, the Interpretations Subcommittee, the Verifier/Practitioner Subcommittee, and the Investor/Consultant Subcommittee to contribute to the development of the GIPS standards.

The GIPS Council engages and works directly with all Country Sponsors in the development, promotion, and maintenance of the GIPS standards. The Interpretations Subcommittee clarifies the GIPS standards through interpretations that effectively respond to new issues presented by the global investment industry. The Practitioners/Verifiers Subcommittee is composed of third-party service providers, including verifiers, software developers, and custodians, that assist investment management firms in the implementation and application of the Standards. This Subcommittee provides a forum to discuss the application, implementation, and impact of the Standards. The Investors/Consultants Subcommittee is composed of investors (and those representing investors), regulators and consultants from the investment industry, including clients, plan sponsors, retail investors, and others, to create a forum for the end user of investment performance information; this subcommittee will be responsible for assisting in the development and direction of the GIPS standards.

The subcommittees' proposals are circulated for public comment prior to their adoption and incorporation into the GIPS standards, allowing further involvement from industry practitioners.

1-5 GLOBAL IMPLEMENTATION

One objective of the GIPS standards is to obtain worldwide acceptance of a standard for the calculation and presentation of investment performance in a fair, comparable format that provides full disclosure. In order to achieve this goal, the strategy in the past has been to (1) transition the existing local standards to the GIPS standards and (2) evolve the GIPS standards to incorporate local best practices from all regional standards so as to form one globally accepted standard for investment performance calculation and reporting.

Transitioning Existing Local Standards
To effectively transition existing local standards, some countries needed to adopt certain long-standing requirements in addition to the GIPS standards. Since 1999, some countries have employed the "Country Version of GIPS" (CVG) approach, whereby those that had existing performance standards could adopt the GIPS standards as the core. This core was only supplemented to satisfy local regulatory or legal requirements and well-established practices. Any other differences were to be transitioned out of the CVG so that the CVG would ultimately converge with the GIPS standards.

By revising the GIPS standards, the EC hopes that CVGs will no longer be necessary. Instead, all CVG-compliant firms will be granted reciprocity for periods prior to 1 January 2006. Their CVG-compliant history will satisfy the GIPS requirement to show at least a five-year track record.

The EC strongly encourages countries without an investment performance standard in place to accept the GIPS standards as the local standard and translate them into the native language when necessary, thus promoting a "translation of GIPS" (TG).

As of December 2005, 25 countries throughout North America, Europe, Africa, and the Asia Pacific region had adopted the GIPS standards (1999 version). Out of these 25 countries, 9 had an endorsed CVG (Australia, Canada, Ireland, Italy, Japan, South Africa, Switzerland, United Kingdom, and United States). The remaining endorsed standards were either GIPS (in English) or translations of GIPS (German, Danish, French, Hungarian, Dutch, Norwegian, Polish, and Spanish).

Evolving the GIPS Standards
In addition to improving the 1999 version of the GIPS standards, the 2006 version includes new sections to address real estate and private equity investments as well as new

provisions to address fees. It also includes guidelines for claiming compliance with the GIPS standards in advertisements and formalizes positions resulting from the development of guidance statements (such as firm definition, composite definition, and portability) and incorporates local best practices for performance measurement and reporting from around the world. The GIPS standards as revised in 2006 are no longer a *minimum* worldwide standard. Instead, this version reflects global performance measurement and presentation best practices and eliminates the need for separate local standards.

As a result, firms from all countries can comply with one standard, the GIPS standards, from 1 January 2006, and the industry will ultimately achieve convergence of all standards.

The Role of Local Country Sponsors

The presence of a local sponsoring organization for investment performance standards, known as a "Country Sponsor," is essential for effective implementation of the Standards and ongoing operation within a country. Such Country Sponsors also provide an important link between the EC, the governing body for the GIPS standards, and the local markets in which investment managers operate. Country Sponsors ensure broad local representation and inclusion so all interested parties are permitted the opportunity to participate at the local level.

The Country Sponsor, by actively supporting the Standards and the work of the EC, will ensure that the country's interests can and will be taken into account as the GIPS standards are developed going forward. Compliance with the GIPS standards is voluntary. Local market support and competitive pressures will ultimately determine how successfully the GIPS standards will be embraced in different countries and regions around the world.

The EC has formalized a process by which the Country Sponsors and their adoption of the GIPS standards will be reviewed and assessed for endorsement by the EC as GIPS compatible. It is therefore important to clarify the role that the Country Sponsor will take in contributing to and interfacing with this process. These guidelines endeavor to answer some frequently asked questions with regard to Country Sponsors and to outline and recommend the particular responsibilities and functions which they should consider undertaking.

Who typically acts as a Country Sponsor?

Country Sponsors have tended to be a local association representing fund managers, pension funds, or professional societies (e.g., banking or asset management associations, financial analysts associations, CFA Institute societies), or a joint undertaking between these associations. One of the objectives of Country Sponsors, invariably similar to that of the EC and CFA Institute, is to advance the interests of the local investment community by establishing and maintaining the highest standards of professional excellence and ethical integrity in regard to the calculation and reporting of performance information.

What are the responsibilities or functions of a Country Sponsor?

As a general rule the most likely responsibilities accepted or functions undertaken by the GIPS Country Sponsor fall into the following categories:

Within the country:

1. Nominate a representative to serve on the Regional Investment Performance Subcommittee (RIPS) and GIPS Council who is responsible to voice local issues and concerns and serve as a conduit between GIPS Council and Country Sponsor.
2. Promulgate locally the GIPS standards and maintain their integrity.
3. Provide local market support for the GIPS standards by:
    - Encouraging local investment managers to comply.
    - Enhancing public awareness.
    - Seeking support from all investors, in particular by endorsing compliance.
    - Determining the need for education programs and endorsing and contributing to GIPS educational initiatives.

4. Commit to and ensure that a country's TG will incorporate all future additions or improvements to the GIPS standards and ongoing interpretations of existing GIPS provisions.

5. Determine whether translations of the GIPS standards, guidance statements and/or interpretations would be beneficial, and if so, undertake the process according to EC guidance. Ensure, as far as possible, consistency in the application of the Standards despite potential language differences.

6. Provide interpretation and support to answer country-specific, historical standards issues.

7. Actively cooperate with the EC to market the GIPS standards within the country.

8. Ensure appropriate local market expertise and issues (i.e., clients, consultants, verifiers, plan sponsor, software, etc.) are represented by members of the Country Sponsor.

Outside the country:

9. Interface with the EC to:
   - Nominate appropriate EC candidates and technical subcommittee members.
   - Provide relevant response to requests for public comment.

10. Undertake the interactive relationship with the EC to:
    - Submit to the EC either their *GIPS in English* or *TG*.
    - Represent local issues and concerns.

11. Provide interpretations support to:
    - Interface between the EC's Interpretations Subcommittee and the local market for questions and answers related to the core GIPS standards (which could include, for instance, providing translation where necessary).

12. Participate in cross-border activities to:
    - Provide a country representative who will serve on the appropriate RIPS and GIPS Council
      - to represent local issues and views and to exchange cross border considerations;
      - to provide input to further develop the GIPS standards as the "gold standard" (e.g., identifying local "best practices" for possible incorporation into the GIPS standards).
    - Promote and support fair "right of access" competition for all investment managers.
    - Liaise to promote uniformity in verification services.

Relationship with Regulators

It is important that Country Sponsors appreciate the relationship among all parties involved in the promulgation of the Standards, including local regulators with whom Country Sponsors should forge supportive and productive relationships.

The self-regulatory nature of the GIPS standards necessitates a strong commitment to ethical integrity. Self-regulation also facilitates local regulators in exercising their responsibility for ensuring the fair disclosure of information to and within the financial markets in general. Country Sponsors—who are actively involved in looking at performance reporting—can encourage local regulators to:

- recognize the benefit of voluntary compliance with standards which represent global best practices,
- give consideration to adopting a function implemented by some regulators, to enforce sanctions upon false claims of compliance as fraudulent advertising, and
- recognize and encourage independent verification services.

1-6 INTERPRETIVE GUIDANCE

Firms that claim compliance with the GIPS standards must comply with all the requirements of the GIPS standards, including any updates, reports, or clarifications published by the EC, as well as the most recent version of the GIPS Handbook. All clarification and update information is made available to the public via the CFA Institute website (see www.cfainstitute.org/cfacentre/ips/) and must be considered when determining a firm's claim of compliance.

Along with promoting the adoption of the GIPS standards on a worldwide basis, one of the key challenges in applying a global standard is ensuring a consistent understanding and application of those standards across multiple markets and disciplines. The Interpretations Subcommittee of the EC often identifies key issues on which to provide proactive guidance and answers to questions raised by the global investment industry as firms face challenges in applying the GIPS standards in different legal, structural, and cultural frameworks.

The fundamental aspect of these processes is engaging the public in opportunities to participate in the development of practical guidance through public comment. CFA Institute and the EC strongly believe that industry comment is critical in establishing pragmatic standards acceptable to the global investment industry.

CFA Institute receives hundreds of questions each year at the GIPS Helpdesk (gips@cfainstitute.org). Many of the questions are straightforward and have been answered in existing guidance already published and available. Others are more complex or pose new challenges on the application of the Standards to a firm's investment processes.

The Interpretations Subcommittee responds to requests for guidance by issuing answers to questions that have not already been answered in existing guidance. If the question involves either a fundamental or complex issue, the Subcommittee may choose to issue a Guidance Statement. Guidance Statements incorporate all applicable existing interpretations that have been published on a subject in an effort to consolidate all relevant information and existing interpretations. The Interpretations Subcommittee may also refer questions of a technical nature to an EC technical subcommittee (such as Real Estate or Leverage & Derivatives) for guidance.

Prior to adoption, all Guidance Statements are available for public comment (via the CFA Institute website) for a 60- to 90-day period (depending on the complexity of the Guidance Statement). After the public comment period, the Interpretations Subcommittee reviews the comments, modifies the Guidance Statement as needed, and presents the Guidance Statement to the EC for formal adoption.

All EC-approved Guidance Statements are then published on the CFA Institute's website in the GIPS Interpretations Library (www.cfainstitute.org/cfacentre/ips/gipslibrary.html) and included in the next update of this Handbook. It is important to note that Guidance Statements on the GIPS standards are applicable to all firms claiming GIPS compliance.

The adopted EC Guidance Statements are included in this Handbook in Section 4 and the proposed Guidance Statements are clearly marked as such and are included in Section 5. Excerpts of EC-adopted Guidance Statements are also included in the Discussion section of each applicable provision in Section 3 of this book.

Global Investment Performance Standards (GIPS®)

Approved February 2005

GLOBAL INVESTMENT PERFORMANCE STANDARDS (GIPS®)

As Revised by the Investment Performance Council 7 December 2004 and Adopted by the CFA Institute Board of Governors 4 February 2005

Developed by CFA Institute, in Partnership with the Following Local Sponsors:

Australia — Performance Analyst Group of Australia
Austria — Österreichischen Verreinigung für Finanzanalyse und Asset Management und der Vereinigung Österreichischer Investmentgesellschaften
Belgium — Belgian Association for Pension Institutions
Denmark — The Danish Society of Investment Professionals, The Danish Society of Financial Analysts
France — Société Francaise des Analystes Financiers and Association Francaise de la Gestion Financière
Germany — BVI Bundesverband Investment und Asset Management e.V., Deutsche Vereinigung für Finanzanalyse und Asset Management, and German CFA Society
Hong Kong — The Hong Kong Society of Financial Analysts
Hungary — Hungarian Society of Investment Professionals
Ireland — Irish Association of Investment Managers
Italy — Italian Investment Performance Committee
Japan — The Security Analysts Association of Japan
Luxembourg — Association Luxembourgeoise des Fonds d'Investissement and Association Luxembourgeoise des gestionnaires de portefeuilles et analystes financiers
Netherlands — Beroepsvereniging van Beleggingsdeskundigen
New Zealand — CFA Society of New Zealand
Norway — The Norwegian Society of Financial Analysts
Poland — Polski Komitet Wyników Inwestycyjnych
Portugal — Associação Portuguesa de Analistas Financeiros
Singapore — Investment Management Association of Singapore
Spain — CFA Spain
South Africa — Investment Management Association of South Africa
Sweden — Swedish Society of Financial Analysts
Switzerland — Swiss Bankers Association
United Kingdom — National Association of Pension Funds Ltd
United States and Canada — CFA Institute

INVESTMENT PERFORMANCE COUNCIL (IPC) 2004–2005

Chair
James E. Hollis III, CFA
Cutter Associates, Inc.
United States

Consultants
Brian Henderson
Hymans Robertson
United Kingdom

Ron Surz
PPCA, Inc.
United States

Derivatives/Performance Measurement
Yoshiaki Akeda
Nomura Funds Research and Technologies
Japan

Bruce J. Feibel, CFA
Eagle Investment Systems
United States

Europe, Middle East, and Africa (EMEA)
Hans-Jörg von Euw
Swisscanto Asset Management Ltd.
Switzerland

Lesley A. Harvey
Ernst & Young
South Africa

Jean-François Hirschel
Societe Generale Asset Management
France

Europe
Stefan Illmer
Credit Suisse Asset Management
Switzerland

Erik Sjöberg
Erik Sjöberg Finanskonsult
Sweden

Individual/Private Investor
Terry Pavlic, CFA
Pavlic Investment Advisors, Inc.
United States

Max Roth
Banque Cantonale Vaudoise
Switzerland

Maria E. Smith-Breslin
Smith Affiliated Capital Corp.
United States

Institutional Investors (1)
David Gamble
United Kingdom

Deborah Reidy
Hewitt & Becketts
Ireland

Institutional Investors (2)
Lynn A. Clark
LA Clark Consulting
Canada

Ehsan Rahman
Washington Metropolitan Area Transit Authority
United States

Insurance
Glenn Solomon
Australia

Todd A. Jankowski, CFA
The Northwestern Mutual Life Company
United States

Japan
Shinichi Kawano
Merrill Lynch Investments Managers Co., Ltd.
Japan

Shigeo Ishigaki
KPMG Japan (KPMG AZSA & Co.)
Japan

Yoh Kuwabara
ChuoAoyama PricewaterhouseCoopers
Japan

Mutual Funds
Alain Ernewein
Stratégie Investissement Performance
France

Neil E. Riddles, CFA
Hansberger Global Investors, Inc.
United States

North America
Karyn D. Vincent, CFA
Vincent Performance Services LLC
United States

Iain W. McAra
JP Morgan Fleming Asset Management
United States

David Spaulding
The Spaulding Group Inc.
United States

Pacific Basin
Louis Boulanger, CFA
New Zealand

Tunku Afwida Malek
Commerce Asset Fund Managers Sdn Bhd
Malaysia

Cheng Chih Sung
Government of Singapore Investment Corporation
Singapore

Venture Capital/Real Estate/Other
Carol Anne Kennedy
Pantheon Ventures Limited
United Kingdom

Paul S. Saint-Pierre
Wall Street Realty Capital
United States

Verification
Carl R. Bacon
Statpro
United Kingdom

Herbert M. Chain
Deloitte & Touche LLP
United States

Louise Spencer
PricewaterhouseCoopers
United Kingdom

CFA Institute Staff
Alecia L. Licata
Cindy S. Kent
Carol A. Lindsey

Table of Contents

PREFACE: BACKGROUND OF THE GIPS STANDARDS

Investment practices, regulation, performance measurement, and reporting of performance results have historically varied considerably from country to country. Some countries have established performance calculation and presentation guidelines that are domestically accepted, and others have few standards for presenting investment performance. These practices have limited the comparability of performance results between firms in different countries and have hindered the ability of firms to penetrate markets on a global basis.

CFA Institute (formerly known as the Association for Investment Management and Research or AIMR) recognized the need for a global set of performance presentation standards, and in 1995, it sponsored and funded the Global Investment Performance Standards (GIPS®) Committee to develop a single standard for presenting investment performance. In February 1999, the GIPS committee finalized the GIPS standards and presented them to the AIMR Board of Governors, who formally endorsed them.

The success of the Standards is the result of an alliance among experts from a variety of fields within the global investment industry. The following key industry groups have been involved in and contributed significantly to promoting and developing the GIPS standards:

Australia — Performance Analyst Group of Australia
Austria — Österreichischen Verreinigung für Finanzanalyse und Asset Management und der Vereinigung Österreichischer Investmentgesellschaften
Belgium — Belgian Association for Pension Institutions
Denmark — The Danish Society of Investment Professionals, The Danish Society of Financial Analysts
France — Société Francaise des Analystes Financiers and Association Francaise de la Gestion Financière
Germany — BVI Bundesverband Investment und Asset Management e.V., Deutsche Vereinigung für Finanzanalyse und Asset Management, and German CFA Society
Hong Kong — The Hong Kong Society of Financial Analysts
Hungary — Hungarian Society of Investment Professionals
Ireland — Irish Association of Investment Managers
Italy — Italian Investment Performance Committee
Japan — The Security Analysts Association of Japan
Luxembourg — Association Luxembourgeoise des Fonds d'Investissement and Association Luxembourgeoise des gestionnaires de portefeuilles et analystes financiers
Netherlands — Beroepsvereniging van Beleggingsdeskundigen
New Zealand — CFA Society of New Zealand
Norway — The Norwegian Society of Financial Analysts
Poland — Polski Komitet Wyników Inwestycyjnych
Portugal — Associação Portuguesa de Analistas Financeiros
Singapore — Investment Management Association of Singapore
Spain — CFA Spain
South Africa — Investment Management Association of South Africa
Sweden — Swedish Society of Financial Analysts
Switzerland — Swiss Bankers Association
United Kingdom — National Association of Pension Funds Ltd
United States and Canada — CFA Institute

With the release of the GIPS standards in 1999, the GIPS committee was replaced by the Investment Performance Council (IPC), which serves as the global committee responsible for the Standards. It consists of 36 members from 15 countries. The IPC's members have diverse and in-depth investment experience. They come from firms of all sizes and specialize in mutual funds, private wealth management, insurance, pension funds, private equity and venture capital, real estate, investment consulting services, and performance measurement and verification.

The principal goal of the IPC is to have all countries adopt the GIPS standards as the standard for investment firms seeking to present historical investment performance. The IPC envisions GIPS compliance acting as a "passport" that allows firms to enter the arena of investment management competition on a global basis and to compete on an equal footing. The GIPS passport will level the playing field and promote global competition among investment firms, which will, in turn, provide prospective clients with a greater level of confidence in the integrity of performance presentations as well as the general practices of a compliant firm.

In order to achieve this goal, over the past 5 years, the IPC has used a dual approach convergence strategy to (1) transition the existing local standards to the GIPS standards and (2) evolve the GIPS standards to incorporate local best practices from all regional standards so as to form one improved standard for investment performance calculation and reporting.

The IPC strongly encourages countries without an investment performance standard in place to accept the GIPS standards as the local standard and translate them into the native language when necessary, thus promoting a "translation of GIPS" (TG). However, to effectively transition existing regional standards, the IPC acknowledges that some countries need to adopt certain long-standing requirements in addition to the GIPS standards.

Since 1999, the IPC has promoted the "Country Version of GIPS" (CVG) approach, whereby countries that had existing performance standards could adopt the GIPS standards as the core. This core was only to be supplemented to satisfy local regulatory or legal requirements and well-established practices. Any other differences were to be transitioned out of the CVG so that the CVG would converge with the GIPS standards. The CVG model has facilitated the movement of the industry toward one standard for the calculation and presentation of investment performance.

Today, 25 countries throughout North America, Europe, Africa, and the Asia Pacific Region have adopted the GIPS standards, encouraging investment management firms to follow the Standards when calculating and reporting their performance results. Out of these 25 countries, 9 have an IPC-endorsed CVG (Australia, Canada, Ireland, Italy, Japan, South Africa, Switzerland, United Kingdom, and United States). The remaining IPC-endorsed standards are either translations of GIPS (German, Danish, French, Hungarian, Dutch, Norwegian, Polish, and Spanish) or GIPS (in English).

In addition to improving the original GIPS standards, this version includes new sections to address real estate and private equity investments as well as new provisions to address fees. It also includes guidelines for claiming compliance with the GIPS standards in advertisements and formalizes positions resulting from the development of guidance statements (such as firm definition, composite definition, and portability) and incorporates local best practices for performance measurement and reporting from around the world. A glossary and several examples have been included to assist with the application of the GIPS standards. (Words appearing in CAPITAL letters are defined in the GIPS Glossary in Appendix E.) The GIPS standards are no longer a minimum worldwide standard. Instead, this version promotes the highest performance measurement and presentation practices and eliminates the need for separate local standards.

We are now entering the second phase of the convergence strategy to the GIPS standards—namely to evolve the GIPS standards to incorporate local best practices from all regional standards. To effectively move toward one globally accepted standard for investment performance calculation and presentation, the IPC strongly encourages countries without an investment performance standard in place to accept the GIPS standards in English or translate them into the local language, adopting a TG approach.

By revising the GIPS standards, it is the IPC's hope that CVGs will no longer be necessary. Instead, all CVG-compliant firms will be granted reciprocity for periods prior to 1 January 2006. Their CVG-compliant history will satisfy the GIPS requirement to show at least a 5-year track record. In this way, firms from all countries will comply with one standard, the GIPS standards, from 1 January 2006 and the industry will achieve convergence of all standards.

I. INTRODUCTION

A. PREAMBLE — WHY IS A GLOBAL STANDARD NEEDED?

1. The financial markets and the investment management industry are becoming increasingly global in nature. Given the variety of financial entities and countries involved, this globalization of the investment process and the exponential growth of assets under management demonstrate the need to standardize the calculation and presentation of investment performance.

2. Prospective clients and investment management firms will benefit from an established standard for investment performance measurement and presentation that is recognized worldwide. Investment practices, regulation, performance measurement, and reporting of performance results vary considerably from country to country. Some countries have guidelines that are widely accepted within their borders, and others have few recognized standards for presenting investment performance.

3. Requiring investment management firms to adhere to performance presentation standards will help assure investors that the performance information is both complete and fairly presented. Investment management firms in countries with minimal presentation standards will be able to compete for business on an equal footing with investment management firms from countries with more developed standards. Investment management firms from countries with established practices will have more confidence that they are being fairly compared with "local" investment management firms when competing for business in countries that have not previously adopted performance standards.

4. Both prospective and existing clients of investment management firms will benefit from a global investment performance standard by having a greater degree of confidence in the performance numbers presented by the investment management firms. Performance standards that are accepted in all countries enable all investment management firms to measure and present their investment performance so that clients can readily compare investment performance among investment management firms.

B. VISION STATEMENT

5. A global investment performance standard leads to readily accepted presentations of investment performance that (1) present performance results that are readily comparable among investment management firms without regard to geographical location and (2) facilitate a dialogue between investment managers and their prospective clients about the critical issues of how the investment management firm achieved performance results and determines future investment strategies.

C. OBJECTIVES

6. To obtain worldwide acceptance of a standard for the calculation and presentation of investment performance in a fair, comparable format that provides full disclosure.

7. To ensure accurate and consistent investment performance data for reporting, record keeping, marketing, and presentations.

8. To promote fair, global competition among investment management firms for all markets without creating barriers to entry for new investment management firms.

9. To foster the notion of industry "self-regulation" on a global basis.

D. OVERVIEW

10. The Global Investment Performance Standards ("GIPS standards" or "Standards") have several key characteristics:

    a. For the purpose of claiming compliance with the GIPS standards, investment management FIRMS MUST define an entity that claims compliance ("FIRM"). The FIRM MUST be defined as an investment FIRM, subsidiary, or division held out to clients or potential clients as a DISTINCT BUSINESS ENTITY.

    b. The GIPS standards are ethical standards for investment performance presentation to ensure fair representation and full disclosure of a FIRM'S performance.

    c. The GIPS standards REQUIRE FIRMS to include all actual fee-paying, discretionary PORTFOLIOS in COMPOSITES defined according to similar strategy and/or investment objective and REQUIRE FIRMS to initially show GIPS-compliant history for a minimum of five (5) years or since inception of the FIRM or COMPOSITE if in existence less than 5 years. After presenting at least 5 years of compliant history, the FIRM MUST add annual performance each year going forward up to ten (10) years, at a minimum.

    d. The GIPS standards REQUIRE FIRMS to use certain calculation and presentation methods and to make certain disclosures along with the performance record.

    e. The GIPS standards rely on the integrity of input data. The accuracy of input data is critical to the accuracy of the performance presentation. For example, BENCHMARKS and COMPOSITES SHOULD be created/selected on an EX-ANTE basis, not after the fact.

    f. The GIPS standards consist of provisions that FIRMS are REQUIRED to follow in order to claim compliance. FIRMS are encouraged to adopt the RECOMMENDED provisions to achieve best practice in performance presentation.

    g. The GIPS standards MUST be applied with the goal of full disclosure and fair representation of investment performance. Meeting the objectives of full disclosure and fair representation will likely require more than compliance with the minimum REQUIREMENTS of the GIPS standards. If an investment FIRM applies the GIPS standards in a performance situation that is not addressed specifically by the Standards or is open to interpretation, disclosures other than those REQUIRED by the GIPS standards may be necessary. To fully explain the performance included in a presentation, FIRMS are encouraged to present all relevant ADDITIONAL INFORMATION and SUPPLEMENTAL INFORMATION.

    h. All requirements, clarifications, updated information, and guidance MUST be adhered to when determining a FIRM'S claim of compliance and will be made available via the *GIPS Handbook* and the CFA Institute website (www.cfainstitute.org).

i. In cases where applicable local or country-specific law or regulation conflicts with the GIPS standards, the Standards REQUIRE FIRMS to comply with the local law or regulation and make full disclosure of the conflict.

j. The GIPS standards do not address every aspect of performance measurement, valuation, attribution, or coverage of all asset classes. The GIPS standards will evolve over time to address additional aspects of investment performance. Certain RECOMMENDED elements in the GIPS standards may become REQUIREMENTS in the future.

k. Within the GIPS standards are supplemental REAL ESTATE and PRIVATE EQUITY provisions that MUST be applied to these asset classes. (See sections II.6 and II.7.)

E. SCOPE

11. Application of the GIPS Standards: FIRMS from any country may come into compliance with the GIPS standards. Compliance with the GIPS standards will facilitate a FIRM'S participation in the investment management industry on a global level.

12. Historical Performance Record:

a. FIRMS are REQUIRED to present, at a minimum, 5 years of annual investment performance that is compliant with the GIPS standards. If the FIRM or COMPOSITE has been in existence less than 5 years, the FIRM MUST present performance since the inception of the FIRM or COMPOSITE; and

b. After a FIRM presents 5 years of compliant history, the FIRM MUST present additional annual performance up to 10 years, at a minimum. For example, after a FIRM presents 5 years of compliant history, the FIRM MUST add an additional year of performance each year so that after 5 years of claiming compliance, the FIRM presents a 10-year performance record.

c. FIRMS may link a non-GIPS-compliant performance record to their compliant history so long as no noncompliant performance is presented after 1 January 2000 and the FIRM discloses the periods of noncompliance and explains how the presentation is not in compliance with the GIPS standards.

d. FIRMS previously claiming compliance with an Investment Performance Council-endorsed Country Version of GIPS (CVG) are granted reciprocity to claim compliance with the GIPS standards for historical periods prior to 1 January 2006. (See "Background of GIPS Standards" for more details on CVGs). If the FIRM previously claimed compliance with a CVG, at a minimum, the FIRM MUST continue to show the historical CVG-compliant track record up to 10 years (or since inception).

Nothing in this section shall prevent FIRMS from initially presenting more than 5 years of performance results.

F. COMPLIANCE

13. Effective Date: The GIPS standards were amended by the IPC on 7 December 2004 and adopted by the CFA Institute Board of Governors on 4 February 2005. The effective date of the revised Standards is 1 January 2006. All presentations that include performance results for periods after 31 December 2005 MUST meet all the REQUIREMENTS of the revised GIPS standards. Performance presentations that

include results through 31 December 2005 may be prepared in compliance with the 1999 version of the GIPS standards. Early adoption of these revised GIPS standards is encouraged.

14. REQUIREMENTS: FIRMS MUST meet all the REQUIREMENTS set forth in the GIPS standards to claim compliance with the GIPS standards. Although the REQUIREMENTS MUST be met immediately by a FIRM claiming compliance, the following REQUIREMENTS do not go into effect until a future date:

    a. For periods beginning 1 January 2008, REAL ESTATE investments MUST be valued at least quarterly.

    b. For periods beginning 1 January 2010, FIRMS MUST value PORTFOLIOS on the date of all LARGE EXTERNAL CASH FLOWS.

    c. For periods beginning 1 January 2010, FIRMS MUST value PORTFOLIOS as of the calendar month-end or the last business day of the month.

    d. For periods beginning 1 January 2010, COMPOSITE returns MUST be calculated by asset weighting the individual PORTFOLIO returns at least monthly.

    e. For periods beginning 1 January 2010, CARVE-OUT returns are not permitted to be included in single asset class COMPOSITE returns unless the CARVE-OUTS are actually managed separately with their own cash balances.

    Until these future REQUIREMENTS become effective, these provisions SHOULD be considered RECOMMENDATIONS. FIRMS are encouraged to implement these future REQUIREMENTS prior to their effective dates. To ease compliance with the GIPS standards when the future REQUIREMENTS take effect, the industry should immediately begin to design performance software to incorporate these future REQUIREMENTS.

15. Compliance Check: FIRMS MUST take all steps necessary to ensure that they have satisfied all the REQUIREMENTS of the GIPS standards before claiming compliance with the GIPS standards. FIRMS are strongly encouraged to perform periodic internal compliance checks and implement adequate business controls on all stages of the investment performance process—from data input to presentation material—to ensure the validity of compliance claims.

16. Third-Party Performance Measurement and COMPOSITE Construction: The GIPS standards recognize the role of independent third-party performance measurers and the value they can add to the FIRM'S performance measurement activities. Where third-party performance measurement is an established practice or is available, FIRMS are encouraged to use this service as it applies to the FIRM. Similarly, where the practice is to allow third parties to construct COMPOSITES for FIRMS, FIRMS can use such COMPOSITES in a GIPS-compliant presentation only if the COMPOSITES meet the REQUIREMENTS of the GIPS standards.

17. Sample Presentations: Sample presentations, shown in Appendix A, provide examples of what a compliant presentation might look like.

G. IMPLEMENTING A GLOBAL STANDARD

18. In 1999, the Investment Performance Council (IPC) was created and given the responsibility to meet the ongoing needs for maintaining and developing a high-quality global investment performance standard. The IPC provides a practical and effective implementation structure for the GIPS standards and encourages wider public participation in an industry-wide standard.

19. One of the principal objectives of the IPC is for all countries to adopt the GIPS standards as the common method for calculating and presenting investment performance. As of December 2004, more than 25 countries around the world had adopted or were in the process of adopting the GIPS standards. The IPC believes the establishment and acceptance of the GIPS standards are vital steps in facilitating the availability of comparable investment performance history on a global basis. GIPS compliance provides FIRMS with a "passport" and creates a level playing field where all FIRMS can compete on equal footing.

20. The presence of a local sponsoring organization for investment performance standards is essential for their effective implementation and on-going operation within a country. Such country sponsors also provide an important link between the IPC, the governing body for the GIPS standards, and the local markets where investment managers operate.

    The country sponsor, by actively supporting the GIPS standards and the work of the IPC, will ensure that the country's interests can and will be taken into account as the GIPS standards are developed going forward. Compliance with the GIPS standards is voluntary, but support from the local country sponsor will help drive the success of the GIPS standards.

21. The IPC strongly encourages countries without an investment performance standard in place to accept the GIPS standards as the local standard and translate them into the local language when necessary, thus promoting a "translation of GIPS" (TG).

22. Compliance with the GIPS standards will provide FIRMS with a "right of access" to be considered alongside all investment managers, thereby allowing all FIRMS to be evaluated on equal terms.

23. Although the GIPS standards may be translated into many languages, if a discrepancy arises between the different versions of the Standards (e.g., TGs), the English version of GIPS standards is controlling.

24. The IPC will continue to develop the GIPS standards so that they maintain their relevance within the changing investment management industry and has committed to evaluating the Standards every 5 years.

25. The self-regulatory nature of the GIPS standards necessitates a strong commitment to ethical integrity. Self-regulation also assists regulators in exercising their responsibility for ensuring the fair disclosure of information to and within the financial markets in general. Regulators are encouraged to:

    - recognize the benefit of voluntary compliance with standards that represent global best practices,
    - give consideration to adopting a function favored by some regulators, namely to enforce sanctions upon false claims of compliance with the GIPS standards as fraudulent advertising, and
    - recognize and encourage independent verification services.

26. Where existing laws or regulations already impose performance presentation standards, FIRMS are strongly encouraged to comply with the GIPS standards in addition to those local requirements. Compliance with applicable law or regulation does not necessarily lead to compliance with the GIPS standards. When complying with the GIPS standards and local law or regulation, FIRMS MUST disclose any local laws and regulations that conflict with the GIPS standards.

II. PROVISIONS OF THE GLOBAL INVESTMENT PERFORMANCE STANDARDS

The GIPS standards are divided into eight sections that reflect the basic elements involved in presenting performance information: fundamentals of compliance, input data, calculation methodology, COMPOSITE construction, disclosures, presentation and reporting, REAL ESTATE, and PRIVATE EQUITY.

The provisions for each section are divided between REQUIREMENTS, listed first in each section, and RECOMMENDATIONS. FIRMS MUST meet all the REQUIREMENTS to claim compliance with the GIPS standards. FIRMS are strongly encouraged to adopt and implement the RECOMMENDATIONS to ensure that the FIRM fully adheres to the spirit and intent of the GIPS standards. Examples of GIPS-compliant presentations are included as Appendix A. A Glossary is included as Appendix E to serve as a reference and provide brief descriptions of key words and terms in the GIPS standards. Words appearing in CAPITAL letters are defined in the GIPS Glossary.

0. Fundamentals of Compliance: Critical issues that a FIRM MUST consider when claiming compliance with the GIPS standards are defining the FIRM, documenting FIRM policies and procedures, maintaining compliance with updates to the GIPS standards, and properly using the claim of compliance and references to verification. The definition of the FIRM is the foundation for FIRM-wide compliance and creates defined boundaries whereby TOTAL FIRM ASSETS can be determined. Once a FIRM meets all of the REQUIREMENTS of the GIPS standards, it MUST appropriately use the claim of compliance to state compliance with the GIPS standards.

1. Input Data: Consistency of input data is critical to effective compliance with the GIPS standards and establishes the foundation for full, fair, and comparable investment performance presentations.

2. Calculation Methodology: Achieving comparability among FIRMS' performance presentations requires uniformity in methods used to calculate returns. The Standards mandate the use of certain calculation methodologies for both PORTFOLIOS and COMPOSITES. [corrected January 2006]

3. Composite Construction: A COMPOSITE is an aggregation of one or more PORTFOLIOS into a single group that represents a particular investment objective or strategy. The COMPOSITE return is the asset-weighted average of the performance results of all the PORTFOLIOS in the COMPOSITE. Creating meaningful, asset-weighted COMPOSITES is critical to the fair presentation, consistency, and comparability of results over time and among FIRMS.

4. Disclosures: Disclosures allow FIRMS to elaborate on the raw numbers provided in the presentation and give the end user of the presentation the proper context in which to understand the performance results. To comply with the GIPS standards, FIRMS MUST disclose certain information about their performance presentation and policies adopted by the FIRM. Disclosures are to be considered static information that does not normally change from period to period. Although some disclosures are REQUIRED of all FIRMS, others are specific to certain circumstances and thus may not be REQUIRED. No "negative assurance" language is needed for nonapplicable disclosures.

5. Presentation and Reporting: After gathering the input data, calculating returns, constructing the COMPOSITES, and determining the necessary disclosures, the FIRM MUST incorporate this information in presentations based on the REQUIREMENTS set out in the GIPS standards for presenting the investment performance returns. No finite set of provisions can cover all potential situations or anticipate future developments in investment industry structure, technology, products, or practices. When appropriate, FIRMS have the responsibility to include other information not necessarily covered by the Standards in a GIPS-compliant presentation.

6. Real Estate: These provisions apply to all investments where returns are primarily from the holding, trading, development, or management of REAL ESTATE assets. REAL ESTATE includes land, buildings under development, completed buildings, and other structures or improvements held for investment purposes. The provisions apply regardless of the level of control the FIRM has over management of the investment. The provisions apply irrespective of whether a REAL ESTATE asset or investment is producing revenue. They also apply to REAL ESTATE investments with leverage or gearing.

7. Private Equity: These provisions apply to all PRIVATE EQUITY investments other than OPEN-END or EVERGREEN FUNDS (which MUST follow the main GIPS provisions). PRIVATE EQUITY investments MUST be valued according to the GIPS PRIVATE EQUITY Valuation Principles found in Appendix D. PRIVATE EQUITY refers to investments in nonpublic companies that are in various stages of development and encompasses venture investing, buyout investing, and mezzanine investing. Fund-of-funds investing as well as secondary investing are also included in PRIVATE EQUITY. Investors typically invest in PRIVATE EQUITY assets either directly or through a fund of funds or LIMITED PARTNERSHIP.

0. FUNDAMENTALS OF COMPLIANCE

0.A Definition of the Firm — Requirements

0.A.1 The GIPS standards MUST be applied on a FIRM-wide basis.

0.A.2 FIRMS MUST be defined as an investment firm, subsidiary, or division held out to clients or potential clients as a DISTINCT BUSINESS ENTITY.

0.A.3 TOTAL FIRM ASSETS MUST be the aggregate of the MARKET VALUE of all discretionary and nondiscretionary assets under management within the defined FIRM. This includes both fee-paying and non-fee-paying assets.

0.A.4 FIRMS MUST include the performance of assets assigned to a subadvisor in a COMPOSITE provided the FIRM has discretion over the selection of the subadvisor.

0.A.5 Changes in a FIRM'S organization are not permitted to lead to alteration of historical COMPOSITE results.

0.B Definition of the Firm — Recommendations

0.B.1 FIRMS are encouraged to adopt the broadest, most meaningful definition of the FIRM. The scope of this definition SHOULD include all geographical (country, regional, etc.) offices operating under the same brand name regardless of the actual name of the individual investment management company.

0.A Document Policies and Procedures — Requirements

0.A.6 FIRMS MUST document, in writing, their policies and procedures used in establishing and maintaining compliance with all the applicable REQUIREMENTS of the GIPS standards.

0.A Claim of Compliance — Requirements

0.A.7 Once a FIRM has met all the REQUIRED elements of the GIPS standards, the FIRM MUST use the following compliance statement to indicate that the FIRM is in compliance with the GIPS standards:

> "[Insert name of FIRM] has prepared and presented this report in compliance with the Global Investment Performance Standards (GIPS®)."

0.A.8 If the FIRM does not meet all the REQUIREMENTS of the GIPS standards, the FIRM cannot represent that it is "in compliance with the Global Investment Performance Standards except for...".

0.A.9 Statements referring to the calculation methodology used in a COMPOSITE presentation as being "in accordance [or compliance] with the Global Investment Performance Standards" are prohibited.

0.A.10 Statements referring to the performance of a single, existing client as being "calculated in accordance with the Global Investment Performance Standards" are prohibited except when a GIPS-compliant FIRM reports the performance of an individual account to the existing client.

0.A Firm Fundamental Responsibilities — Requirements

0.A.11 FIRMS MUST make every reasonable effort to provide a compliant presentation to all prospective clients. That is, FIRMS cannot choose to whom they want to present compliant performance. (As long as a prospective client has received a compliant presentation within the previous 12 months, the FIRM has met this REQUIREMENT.)

0.A.12 FIRMS MUST provide a COMPOSITE list and COMPOSITE DESCRIPTION to any prospective client that makes such a request (a sample list and COMPOSITE DESCRIPTION are included in Appendix B). FIRMS MUST list "discontinued" COMPOSITES on the FIRM'S list of COMPOSITES for at least 5 years after discontinuation.

0.A.13 FIRMS MUST provide a compliant presentation for any COMPOSITE listed on the FIRM'S list and a COMPOSITE DESCRIPTION to any prospective client that makes such a request.

0.A.14 When the FIRM jointly markets with other FIRMS, the FIRM claiming compliance with the GIPS standards MUST be sure that it is clearly defined and separate relative to any other FIRMS being marketed and that it is clear which FIRM is claiming compliance.

0.A.15 FIRMS are encouraged to comply with the RECOMMENDATIONS and MUST comply with all applicable REQUIREMENTS of the GIPS standards, including any updates, reports, guidance statements, interpretations, or clarifications published by CFA Institute and the Investment Performance Council, which will be made available via the CFA Institute website (www.cfainstitute.org) as well as the *GIPS Handbook.*

0.B Verification — Recommendations

0.B.2 FIRMS are encouraged to undertake the verification process, defined as the review of a FIRM'S performance measurement processes and procedures by an independent third-party verifier. A single verification report is issued in respect to the whole FIRM; verification cannot be carried out for a single COMPOSITE. The primary purpose of verification is to establish that a FIRM claiming compliance with the GIPS standards has adhered to the Standards.

0.B.3 FIRMS that have been verified are encouraged to add a disclosure to COMPOSITE presentations or advertisements stating that the FIRM has been verified. FIRMS MUST disclose the periods of verification if the COMPOSITE presentation includes results for periods that have not been subject to FIRM-wide verification. The verification disclosure language SHOULD read:

> "[Insert name of FIRM] has been verified for the periods [insert dates] by [name of verifier]. A copy of the verification report is available upon request."

1. INPUT DATA

1.A Input Data — Requirements

1.A.1 All data and information necessary to support a FIRM'S performance presentation and to perform the REQUIRED calculations MUST be captured and maintained.

1.A.2 PORTFOLIO valuations MUST be based on MARKET VALUES (not cost basis or book values).

1.A.3 For periods prior to 1 January 2001, PORTFOLIOS MUST be valued at least quarterly. For periods between 1 January 2001 and 1 January 2010, PORTFOLIOS MUST be valued at least monthly. For periods beginning 1 January 2010, FIRMS MUST value PORTFOLIOS on the date of all LARGE EXTERNAL CASH FLOWS.

1.A.4 For periods beginning 1 January 2010, FIRMS MUST value PORTFOLIOS as of the calendar month-end or the last business day of the month.

1.A.5 For periods beginning 1 January 2005, FIRMS MUST use TRADE DATE ACCOUNTING.

1.A.6 ACCRUAL ACCOUNTING MUST be used for fixed-income securities and all other assets that accrue interest income. MARKET VALUES of fixed-income securities MUST include accrued income.

1.A.7 For periods beginning 1 January 2006, COMPOSITES MUST have consistent beginning and ending annual valuation dates. Unless the COMPOSITE is reported on a noncalendar fiscal year, the beginning and ending valuation dates MUST be at calendar year-end (or on the last business day of the year).

1.B Input Data — Recommendations

1.B.1 ACCRUAL ACCOUNTING SHOULD be used for dividends (as of the ex-dividend date).

1.B.2 When presenting NET-OF-FEES RETURNS, FIRMS SHOULD accrue INVESTMENT MANAGEMENT FEES.

1.B.3 Calendar month-end valuations or valuations on the last business day of the month are RECOMMENDED.

2. CALCULATION METHODOLOGY

2.A Calculation Methodology — Requirements

2.A.1 Total return, including realized and unrealized gains and losses plus income, MUST be used. [corrected September 2005]

2.A.2 TIME-WEIGHTED RATES OF RETURN that adjust for EXTERNAL CASH FLOWS MUST be used. Periodic returns MUST be geometrically linked. EXTERNAL CASH FLOWS MUST be treated in a consistent manner with the FIRM'S documented, COMPOSITE-specific policy. At a minimum:

a. For periods beginning 1 January 2005, FIRMS MUST use approximated rates of return that adjust for daily-weighted EXTERNAL CASH FLOWS.

b. For periods beginning 1 January 2010, FIRMS MUST value PORTFOLIOS on the date of all LARGE EXTERNAL CASH FLOWS.

2.A.3 COMPOSITE returns MUST be calculated by asset weighting the individual PORTFOLIO returns using beginning-of-period values or a method that reflects both beginning-of-period values and EXTERNAL CASH FLOWS.

2.A.4 Returns from cash and cash equivalents held in PORTFOLIOS MUST be included in TOTAL RETURN calculations.

2.A.5 All returns MUST be calculated after the deduction of the actual TRADING EXPENSES incurred during the period. Estimated TRADING EXPENSES are not permitted.

2.A.6 For periods beginning 1 January 2006, FIRMS MUST calculate COMPOSITE returns by asset weighting the individual PORTFOLIO returns at least quarterly. For periods beginning 1 January 2010, COMPOSITE returns MUST be calculated by asset weighting the individual PORTFOLIO returns at least monthly.

2.A.7 If the actual direct TRADING EXPENSES cannot be identified and segregated from a BUNDLED FEE:

a. when calculating GROSS-OF-FEES RETURNS, returns MUST be reduced by the entire BUNDLED FEE or the portion of the BUNDLED FEE that includes the direct TRADING EXPENSES. The use of estimated TRADING EXPENSES is not permitted.

b. when calculating NET-OF-FEES RETURNS, returns MUST be reduced by the entire BUNDLED FEE or the portion of the BUNDLED FEE that includes the direct TRADING EXPENSES and the INVESTMENT MANAGEMENT FEE. The use of estimated TRADING EXPENSES is not permitted.

2.B Calculation Methodology — Recommendations

2.B.1 Returns SHOULD be calculated net of nonreclaimable withholding taxes on dividends, interest, and capital gains. Reclaimable withholding taxes SHOULD be accrued.

2.B.2 FIRMS SHOULD calculate COMPOSITE returns by asset weighting the member PORTFOLIOS at least monthly.

2.B.3 FIRMS SHOULD value PORTFOLIOS on the date of all LARGE EXTERNAL CASH FLOWS.

3. COMPOSITE CONSTRUCTION

3.A Composite Construction — Requirements

3.A.1 All actual, fee-paying, discretionary PORTFOLIOS MUST be included in at least one COMPOSITE. Although non-fee-paying discretionary PORTFOLIOS may be included in a COMPOSITE (with appropriate disclosures), nondiscretionary PORTFOLIOS are not permitted to be included in a FIRM'S COMPOSITES.

3.A.2 COMPOSITES MUST be defined according to similar investment objectives and/or strategies. The full COMPOSITE DEFINITION MUST be made available on request.

3.A.3 COMPOSITES MUST include new PORTFOLIOS on a timely and consistent basis after the PORTFOLIO comes under management unless specifically mandated by the client.

3.A.4 Terminated PORTFOLIOS MUST be included in the historical returns of the appropriate COMPOSITES up to the last full measurement period that the PORTFOLIO was under management.

3.A.5 PORTFOLIOS are not permitted to be switched from one COMPOSITE to another unless documented changes in client guidelines or the redefinition of the COMPOSITE make it appropriate. The historical record of the PORTFOLIO MUST remain with the appropriate COMPOSITE.

3.A.6 Convertible and other hybrid securities MUST be treated consistently across time and within COMPOSITES.

3.A.7 CARVE-OUT segments excluding cash are not permitted to be used to represent a discretionary PORTFOLIO and, as such, are not permitted to be included in COMPOSITE returns. When a single asset class is carved out of a multiple asset class PORTFOLIO and the returns are presented as part of a single asset COMPOSITE, cash MUST be allocated to the CARVE-OUT returns in a timely and consistent manner. Beginning 1 January 2010, CARVE-OUT returns are not permitted to be included in single asset class COMPOSITE returns unless the CARVE-OUT is actually managed separately with its own cash balance.

3.A.8 COMPOSITES MUST include only assets under management within the defined FIRM. FIRMS are not permitted to link simulated or model PORTFOLIOS with actual performance.

3.A.9 If a FIRM sets a minimum asset level for PORTFOLIOS to be included in a COMPOSITE, no PORTFOLIOS below that asset level can be included in that COMPOSITE. Any changes to a COMPOSITE-specific minimum asset level are not permitted to be applied retroactively.

3.B Composite Construction — Recommendations

3.B.1 CARVE-OUT returns SHOULD not be included in single asset class COMPOSITE returns unless the CARVE-OUTS are actually managed separately with their own cash balance.

3.B.2 To remove the effect of a significant EXTERNAL CASH FLOW, the use of a TEMPORARY NEW ACCOUNT is RECOMMENDED (as opposed to adjusting the COMPOSITE composition to remove PORTFOLIOS with significant EXTERNAL CASH FLOWS).

3.B.3 FIRMS SHOULD not market a COMPOSITE to a prospective client who has assets less than the COMPOSITE'S minimum asset level.

4. DISCLOSURES

4.A Disclosures — Requirements

4.A.1 FIRMS MUST disclose the definition of "FIRM" used to determine the TOTAL FIRM ASSETS and FIRM-wide compliance.

4.A.2 FIRMS MUST disclose the availability of a complete list and description of all of the FIRM'S COMPOSITES.

4.A.3 FIRMS MUST disclose the minimum asset level, if any, below which PORTFOLIOS are not included in a COMPOSITE. FIRMS MUST also disclose any changes to the minimum asset level.

4.A.4 FIRMS MUST disclose the currency used to express performance.

4.A.5 FIRMS MUST disclose the presence, use, and extent of leverage or derivatives (if material), including a sufficient description of the use, frequency, and characteristics of the instruments to identify risks.

4.A.6 FIRMS MUST clearly label returns as GROSS-OF-FEES or NET-OF-FEES.

4.A.7 FIRMS MUST disclose relevant details of the treatment of withholding tax on dividends, interest income, and capital gains. If using indexes that are net-of-taxes, the FIRM MUST disclose the tax basis of the BENCHMARK (e.g., Luxembourg based or U.S. based) versus that of the COMPOSITE.

4.A.8 FIRMS MUST disclose and describe any known inconsistencies in the exchange rates used among the PORTFOLIOS within a COMPOSITE and between the COMPOSITE and the BENCHMARK.

4.A.9 If the presentation conforms with local laws and regulations that differ from the GIPS REQUIREMENTS, FIRMS MUST disclose this fact and disclose the manner in which the local laws and regulations conflict with the GIPS standards.

4.A.10 For any performance presented for periods prior to 1 January 2000 that does not comply with the GIPS standards, FIRMS MUST disclose the period of noncompliance and how the presentation is not in compliance with the GIPS standards.

4.A.11 For periods prior to 1 January 2010, when a single asset class is carved out of a multiple asset PORTFOLIO and the returns are presented as part of a single asset COMPOSITE, FIRMS MUST disclose the policy used to allocate cash to the CARVE-OUT returns.

4.A.12 FIRMS MUST disclose the FEE SCHEDULE appropriate to the presentation.

4.A.13 If a COMPOSITE contains PORTFOLIOS with BUNDLED FEES, FIRMS MUST disclose for each annual period shown the percentage of COMPOSITE assets that is BUNDLED FEE PORTFOLIOS.

4.A.14 If a COMPOSITE contains PORTFOLIOS with BUNDLED FEES, FIRMS MUST disclose the various types of fees that are included in the BUNDLED FEE.

4.A.15 When presenting GROSS-OF-FEES RETURNS, FIRMS MUST disclose if any other fees are deducted in addition to the direct TRADING EXPENSES.

4.A.16 When presenting NET-OF-FEES RETURNS, FIRMS MUST disclose if any other fees are deducted in addition to the INVESTMENT MANAGEMENT FEE and direct TRADING EXPENSES.

4.A.17 FIRMS MUST disclose that ADDITIONAL INFORMATION regarding policies for calculating and reporting returns is available upon request.

4.A.18 Beginning 1 January 2006, FIRMS MUST disclose the use of a subadvisor(s) and the periods a subadvisor(s) was used.

4.A.19 FIRMS MUST disclose all significant events that would help a prospective client interpret the performance record.

4.A.20 FIRMS MUST disclose the COMPOSITE DESCRIPTION.

4.A.21 If a FIRM is redefined, the FIRM MUST disclose the date and reason for the redefinition.

4.A.22 If a FIRM has redefined a COMPOSITE, the FIRM MUST disclose the date and nature of the change. Changes to COMPOSITES are not permitted to be applied retroactively.

4.A.23 FIRMS MUST disclose any changes to the name of a COMPOSITE.

4.A.24 FIRMS MUST disclose the COMPOSITE CREATION DATE.

4.A.25 FIRMS MUST disclose if, prior to 1 January 2010, calendar month-end PORTFOLIO valuations or valuations on the last business day of the month are not used.

4.A.26 FIRMS MUST disclose which DISPERSION measure is presented.

4.B Disclosures — Recommendations

4.B.1 If a parent company contains multiple defined FIRMS, each FIRM within the parent company is encouraged to disclose a list of the other FIRMS contained within the parent company.

4.B.2 FIRMS SHOULD disclose when a change in a calculation methodology or valuation source results in a material impact on the performance of a COMPOSITE return.

4.B.3 FIRMS that have been verified SHOULD add a disclosure to their COMPOSITE presentation stating that the FIRM has been verified and clearly indicating the periods the verification covers if the COMPOSITE presentation includes results for periods that have not been subject to FIRM-wide verification.

5. PRESENTATION AND REPORTING

5.A Presentation and Reporting — Requirements

5.A.1 The following items MUST be reported for each COMPOSITE presented:

a. At least 5 years of performance (or a record for the period since FIRM or COMPOSITE inception if the FIRM or COMPOSITE has been in existence less than 5 years) that meets the REQUIREMENTS of the GIPS standards; after presenting 5 years of performance, the FIRM MUST present additional annual performance up to 10 years. (For example, after a FIRM presents 5 years of compliant history, the FIRM MUST add an additional year of performance each year so that after 5 years of claiming compliance, the FIRM presents a 10-year performance record.)

b. Annual returns for all years.

c. The number of PORTFOLIOS and amount of assets in the COMPOSITE, and either the percentage of the TOTAL FIRM ASSETS represented by the COMPOSITE or the amount of TOTAL FIRM ASSETS at the end of each annual period. If the COMPOSITE contains 5 PORTFOLIOS or less, the number of PORTFOLIOS is not REQUIRED. [corrected September 2005]

d. A measure of DISPERSION of individual PORTFOLIO returns for each annual period. If the COMPOSITE contains 5 PORTFOLIOS or less for the full year, a measure of DISPERSION is not REQUIRED. [corrected September 2005]

5.A.2 FIRMS may link non-GIPS-compliant returns to their compliant history so long as the FIRMS meet the disclosure REQUIREMENTS for noncompliant performance and only compliant returns are presented for periods after 1 January 2000. (For example, a FIRM that has been in existence since 1995 and that wants to present its entire performance history and claim compliance beginning 1 January 2005 MUST present returns that meet the REQUIREMENTS of the GIPS standards at least from 1 January 2000 and MUST meet the disclosure REQUIREMENTS for any noncompliant history prior to 1 January 2000.)

5.A.3 Returns of PORTFOLIOS and COMPOSITES for periods of less than 1 year are not permitted to be annualized.

5.A.4 a. Performance track records of a past FIRM or affiliation MUST be linked to or used to represent the historical record of a new FIRM or new affiliation if:

i. Substantially all the investment decision makers are employed by the new FIRM (e.g., research department, PORTFOLIO managers, and other relevant staff),
ii. The staff and decision-making process remain intact and independent within the new FIRM, and
iii. The new FIRM has records that document and support the reported performance.

b. The new FIRM MUST disclose that the performance results from the past FIRM are linked to the performance record of the new FIRM,

c. In addition to 5.A.4.a and 5.A.4.b, when one FIRM joins an existing FIRM, performance of COMPOSITES from both FIRMS MUST be linked to the ongoing returns if substantially all the assets from the past FIRM'S COMPOSITE transfer to the new FIRM.

d. If a compliant FIRM acquires or is acquired by a noncompliant FIRM, the FIRMS have 1 year to bring the noncompliant assets into compliance.

5.A.5 Beginning 1 January 2006, if a COMPOSITE includes or is formed using single asset class CARVE-OUTS from multiple asset class PORTFOLIOS, the presentation MUST include the percentage of the COMPOSITE that is composed of CARVE-OUTS prospectively for each period.

5.A.6 The total return for the BENCHMARK (or BENCHMARKS) that reflects the investment strategy or mandate represented by the COMPOSITE MUST be presented for each annual period. If no BENCHMARK is presented, the presentation MUST explain why no BENCHMARK is disclosed. If the FIRM changes the BENCHMARK that is used for a given COMPOSITE in the performance presentation, the FIRM MUST disclose both the date and the reasons for the change. If a custom BENCHMARK or combination of multiple BENCHMARKS is used, the FIRM MUST describe the BENCHMARK creation and re-balancing process. [corrected January 2006]

5.A.7 If a COMPOSITE contains any non-fee-paying PORTFOLIOS, the FIRM MUST present, as of the end of each annual period, the percentage of the COMPOSITE assets represented by the non-fee-paying PORTFOLIOS.

5.B Presentation and Reporting — Recommendations

5.B.1 It is RECOMMENDED that FIRMS present the following items:

a. COMPOSITE returns gross of INVESTMENT MANAGEMENT FEES and ADMINISTRATIVE FEES and before taxes (except for nonreclaimable withholding taxes),

b. Cumulative returns for COMPOSITE and BENCHMARKS for all periods,

c. Equal-weighted mean and median returns for each COMPOSITE,

d. Graphs and charts presenting specific information REQUIRED or RECOMMENDED under the GIPS standards,

e. Returns for quarterly and/or shorter time periods,

f. Annualized COMPOSITE and BENCHMARK returns for periods greater than 12 months,

g. COMPOSITE-level country and sector weightings.

5.B.2 It is RECOMMENDED that FIRMS present relevant COMPOSITE-level risk measures, such as beta, tracking error, modified duration, information ratio, Sharpe ratio, Treynor ratio, credit ratings, value at risk (VaR), and volatility, over time of the COMPOSITE and BENCHMARK. [corrected September 2005]

5.B.3 After presenting the REQUIRED 5 years of compliant historical performance, the FIRM is encouraged to bring any remaining portion of its *historical* track record into compliance with the GIPS standards. (This does not preclude the REQUIREMENT that the FIRM MUST add annual performance to its track record on an *on-going* basis to build a 10-year track record.)

6. REAL ESTATE

Following are provisions that apply to the calculation and presentation of REAL ESTATE assets. The REAL ESTATE provisions supplement all the REQUIRED and RECOMMENDED elements of the GIPS standards (outlined in Section II.0. through Section II.5.), except the REAL ESTATE provisions that override the existing GIPS provisions for valuation: II.6.A.1, II.6.A.2, II.6.B.1, and II.6.B.2. Investment types not considered as REAL ESTATE and, therefore, addressed elsewhere in the general provisions of the GIPS standards include: [corrected January 2006]

- Publicly traded REAL ESTATE securities, including any listed securities issued by public companies,
- Commercial mortgage-backed securities (CMBS),
- Private debt investments, including commercial and residential loans where the expected return is solely related to contractual interest rates without any participation in the economic performance of the underlying REAL ESTATE.

If a PORTFOLIO includes a mix of REAL ESTATE and other investments that are not REAL ESTATE, then these REQUIREMENTS and RECOMMENDATIONS only apply to the REAL ESTATE portion of the PORTFOLIO, and when the FIRM CARVES-OUT the REAL ESTATE portion of the PORTFOLIO, the GIPS CARVE-OUT provisions (see II.3.A.7) MUST also be applied.

6.A Real Estate Input Data — Requirements

6.A.1 REAL ESTATE investments MUST be valued at MARKET VALUE at least once every 12 months. For periods beginning 1 January 2008, REAL ESTATE investments MUST be valued at least quarterly.

6.A.2 REAL ESTATE investments MUST be valued by an external PROFESSIONALLY DESIGNATED, CERTIFIED, OR LICENSED COMMERCIAL PROPERTY VALUER/APPRAISER at least once every 36 months. In markets where neither professionally designated nor appropriately sanctioned valuers or appraisers are available and valuers or appraisers from other countries bearing such credentials do not commonly operate, then the party responsible for engaging such services locally shall take necessary steps to ensure that only well-qualified property valuers are used.

6.B Real Estate Input Data — Recommendations

6.B.1 REAL ESTATE investments SHOULD be valued at least quarterly.

6.B.2 REAL ESTATE investments SHOULD be valued by an external valuer or appraiser at least once every 12 months.

6.B.3 If calculating the INTERNAL RATE OF RETURN, FIRMS SHOULD use quarterly cash flows at a minimum.

6.A Real Estate Disclosures — Requirements

6.A.3 In addition to the other disclosure REQUIREMENTS of the GIPS standards, performance presentations for REAL ESTATE investments MUST disclose:

a The calculation methodology for component returns—that is, component returns are (1) calculated separately using chain-linked TIME-WEIGHTED RATES OF RETURN, or (2) adjusted such that the sum of the INCOME RETURN and the CAPITAL RETURN is equal to the TOTAL RETURN, [corrected September 2005]

b. The FIRM'S description of discretion,

c. The valuation methods and procedures (e.g., discounted cash flow valuation model, capitalized income approach, sales comparison approach, the valuation of debt payable in determining the value of leveraged REAL ESTATE),

d. The range of performance returns for the individual accounts in the COMPOSITE,

e. The source of the valuation (whether valued by an external valuer or INTERNAL VALUATION or whether values are obtained from a third-party manager) for each period,

f. The percent of total MARKET VALUE of COMPOSITE assets (asset weighted not equally weighted) to total REAL ESTATE assets valued by an EXTERNAL VALUATION for each period, and [corrected September 2005]

g. The frequency REAL ESTATE investments are valued by external valuers.

6.B Real Estate Disclosures — Recommendations

6.B.4 If since-inception INTERNAL RATE OF RETURN performance results are shown, the FIRM SHOULD disclose the time period that is covered as well as the frequency of the cash flows used in the calculation.

6.A Real Estate Presentation and Reporting — Requirements

6.A.4 The income and capital appreciation component returns MUST be presented in addition to TOTAL RETURN.

6.B Real Estate Presentation and Reporting — Recommendations

6.B.5 When available, the capital and income segments of the appropriate REAL ESTATE BENCHMARK SHOULD be presented.

6.B.6 It is RECOMMENDED that FIRMS present the since-inception INTERNAL RATE OF RETURN for the COMPOSITE.

6.B.7 It is RECOMMENDED that the following items be presented, especially in those circumstances when the investment manager has the ability to control the timing of investor capital call tranches during the fund's or PORTFOLIO'S initial acquisition period:

a. GROSS- and NET-OF-FEES (including incentive allocations) annualized since inception TIME-WEIGHTED RATE OF RETURN and INTERNAL RATE OF RETURN (terminal value based on ENDING MARKET VALUE net assets of the COMPOSITE) to the last year reported for the COMPOSITE.

b. GROSS- and NET-OF-FEES (including incentive allocations) annualized since inception TIME-WEIGHTED RATE OF RETURN and INTERNAL RATE OF RETURN (based on realized cash flows only, excluding unrealized gains) to the last year reported for the COMPOSITE.

c. In addition, other performance measures may provide additional useful information for both prospective and existing investors. The GIPS PRIVATE EQUITY Provisions (See GIPS standards II.7) provide guidance with regard to such additional measures as investment and REALIZATION MULTIPLES and ratios relating to PAID-IN-CAPITAL.

7. PRIVATE EQUITY

Following are provisions that apply to the calculation and presentation of PRIVATE EQUITY investments other than OPEN-END or EVERGREEN FUNDS (which MUST follow the main GIPS provisions). The PRIVATE EQUITY provisions supplement all the REQUIRED and RECOMMENDED elements of the GIPS standards (outlined in Section II.0. through Section II.5), except these PRIVATE EQUITY provisions that override the existing GIPS provisions for valuation (II.7.A.1 and II.7.B.1), calculation methodology (II.7.A.2 and II.7.A.3), fees (II.7.A.4 and II.7.A.5), and presentation and reporting of returns (II.7.A.20). [corrected January 2006]

7.A Private Equity Input Data — Requirements

7.A.1 PRIVATE EQUITY investments MUST be valued (preferably quarterly but at least annually) according to the GIPS PRIVATE EQUITY Valuation Principles provided in Appendix D.

7.B Private Equity Input Data — Recommendations

7.B.1 PRIVATE EQUITY investments SHOULD be valued quarterly.

7.A Private Equity Calculation Methodology — Requirements

7.A.2 FIRMS MUST calculate the annualized since-inception INTERNAL RATE OF RETURN (SI-IRR).

7.A.3 The annualized SI-IRR MUST be calculated using either daily or monthly cash flows and the period-end valuation of the unliquidated remaining holdings. Stock DISTRIBUTIONS MUST be valued at the time of DISTRIBUTION.

7.A.4 NET-OF-FEES RETURNS MUST be net of INVESTMENT MANAGEMENT FEES, CARRIED INTEREST, and TRANSACTION EXPENSES.

7.A.5 For INVESTMENT ADVISORS, all returns MUST be net of all underlying partnership and/or fund fees and CARRIED INTEREST. NET-OF-FEES RETURNS MUST, in addition, be net of all the INVESTMENT ADVISOR'S fees, expenses, and CARRIED INTEREST.

7.A. Private Equity Composite Construction — Requirements

7.A.6 All CLOSED-END PRIVATE EQUITY investments, including, but not limited to, fund of funds, partnerships, or DIRECT INVESTMENTS, MUST be included in a COMPOSITE defined by strategy and VINTAGE YEAR.

7.A.7 Partnership/fund investments, DIRECT INVESTMENTS, and OPEN-END PRIVATE EQUITY investments (e.g., EVERGREEN FUNDS) MUST be in separate COMPOSITES.

7.A. Private Equity Disclosures — Requirements

7.A.8 FIRMS MUST disclose the VINTAGE YEAR of the COMPOSITE.

7.A.9 For all closed (discontinued) COMPOSITES, FIRMS MUST disclose the final realization (liquidation) date of the COMPOSITE.

7.A.10 FIRMS MUST disclose the unrealized appreciation/depreciation of the COMPOSITE for the most recent period.

7.A.11 FIRMS MUST disclose the total COMMITTED CAPITAL of the COMPOSITE for the most recent period.

7.A.12 For the most recent period, FIRMS MUST disclose the valuation methodologies used to value their PRIVATE EQUITY investments. If any change occurs in either valuation basis or methodology from the prior period, the change MUST be disclosed.

7.A.13 If the presentation complies with any local or regional valuation guidelines in addition to the GIPS PRIVATE EQUITY Valuation Principles, FIRMS MUST disclose which local or regional guidelines have been used.

7.A.14 FIRMS MUST document the FIRM'S valuation review procedures and disclose that the procedures are available upon request.

7.A.15 FIRMS MUST disclose the definition of the COMPOSITE investment strategy (e.g., early stage, development, buy-outs, generalist, turnaround, mezzanine, geography, middle market, and large transaction).

7.A.16 If a BENCHMARK is used, FIRMS MUST disclose the calculation methodology used for the BENCHMARK.

7.A.17 If a valuation basis other than FAIR VALUE is used to value investments within the COMPOSITE, FIRMS MUST disclose for the most recent period presented their justification for why FAIR VALUE is not applicable. Additionally, FIRMS MUST disclose the following:

a. The carrying value of non-FAIR-VALUE-basis investments relative to total fund.

b. The number of holdings valued on a non-FAIR-VALUE basis.

c. The absolute value of the non-FAIR-VALUE-basis investments.

7.A.18 FIRMS MUST disclose whether they are using daily or monthly cash flows in the SI-IRR calculation.

7.A.19 If a FIRM does not use a calendar year period-end, a disclosure MUST be made indicating the period-end used.

7.A Private Equity Presentation and Reporting — Requirements

7.A.20 FIRMS MUST present both the NET-OF-FEES and GROSS-OF-FEES annualized SI-IRR of the COMPOSITE for each year since inception.

7.A.21 For each period presented, FIRMS MUST report:

a. PAID-IN CAPITAL to date (cumulative DRAWDOWN),

b. Total current INVESTED CAPITAL, and

c. Cumulative DISTRIBUTIONS to date.

7.A.22 For each period presented, FIRMS MUST report the following multiples:

a. TOTAL VALUE to PAID-IN CAPITAL (INVESTMENT MULTIPLE or TVPI),

b. Cumulative DISTRIBUTIONS to PAID-IN CAPITAL (REALIZATION MULTIPLE or DPI),

c. PAID-IN CAPITAL to COMMITTED CAPITAL (PIC MULTIPLE), and

d. RESIDUAL VALUE TO PAID-IN CAPITAL (RVPI).

7.A.23 If a BENCHMARK is shown, the cumulative annualized SI-IRR for the BENCHMARK that reflects the same strategy and VINTAGE YEAR of the COMPOSITE MUST be presented for the same periods for which the COMPOSITE is presented. If no BENCHMARK is shown, the presentation MUST explain why no BENCHMARK is disclosed.

7.B Private Equity Presentation and Reporting — Recommendations

7.B.2 FIRMS SHOULD present the average holding period of the investments (PORTFOLIO companies) over the life of the COMPOSITE.

III. VERIFICATION

The primary purpose of verification is to establish that a FIRM claiming compliance with the GIPS standards has adhered to the Standards. Verification will also increase the understanding and professionalism of performance measurement teams and consistency of presentation of performance results.

The verification procedures attempt to strike a balance between ensuring the quality, accuracy, and relevance of performance presentations and minimizing the cost to FIRMS of independent review of performance results. FIRMS SHOULD assess the benefits of improved internal processes and procedures, which are as significant as the marketing advantages of verification.

The goal of the IPC in drafting the verification procedures is to encourage broad acceptance of verification.

Verification is strongly encouraged and is expected to become mandatory at a future date. The IPC will re-evaluate all aspects of mandatory verification by 2010 and provide the industry sufficient time to implement any changes.

A. SCOPE AND PURPOSE OF VERIFICATION

1. Verification is the review of an investment management FIRM'S performance measurement processes and procedures by an independent third-party "verifier." Verification tests:

   a. Whether the FIRM has complied with all the COMPOSITE construction REQUIREMENTS of the GIPS standards on a FIRM-wide basis, and

   b. Whether the FIRM'S processes and procedures are designed to calculate and present performance results in compliance with the GIPS standards.

   A single verification report is issued in respect of the whole FIRM; verification cannot be carried out for a single COMPOSITE.

2. Third-party verification brings credibility to the claim of compliance and supports the overall guiding principles of full disclosure and fair representation of investment performance.

3. The initial minimum period for which verification can be performed is 1 year of a FIRM'S presented performance. The RECOMMENDED period over which verification is performed is that part of the FIRM'S track record for which GIPS compliance is claimed.

4. A verification report must confirm that:

   a. The FIRM has complied with all the COMPOSITE construction REQUIREMENTS of the GIPS standards on a FIRM-wide basis, and

   b. The FIRM'S processes and procedures are designed to calculate and present performance results in compliance with the GIPS standards.

Without such a report from the verifier, the FIRM cannot state that its claim of compliance with the GIPS standards has been verified.

5. After performing the verification, the verifier may conclude that the FIRM is not in compliance with the GIPS standards or that the records of the FIRM cannot support a complete verification. In such situations, the verifier must issue a statement to the FIRM clarifying why a verification report was not possible.

6. A principal verifier may accept the work of a local or previous verifier as part of the basis for the principal verifier's opinion.

7. The minimum GIPS verification procedures are described in section III.B Required Verification Procedures.

B. REQUIRED VERIFICATION PROCEDURES

The following are the minimum procedures that verifiers must follow when verifying an investment FIRM'S compliance with the GIPS standards. Verifiers must follow these procedures prior to issuing a verification report to the FIRM:

1. Pre-verification Procedures

   a. Knowledge of the FIRM: Verifiers must obtain selected samples of the FIRM'S investment performance reports and other available information regarding the FIRM to ensure appropriate knowledge of the FIRM.

   b. Knowledge of GIPS Standards: Verifiers must understand all the REQUIREMENTS and RECOMMENDATIONS of the GIPS standards, including any updates, reports, guidance statements, interpretations, and clarifications published by CFA Institute and the Investment Performance Council, which will be made available via the CFA Institute website (www.cfainstitute.org) as well as the *GIPS Handbook.* All clarification and update information must be considered when determining a FIRM'S claim of compliance.

   c. Knowledge of the Performance Standards: Verifiers must be knowledgeable of country-specific laws and regulations applicable to the FIRM and must determine any differences between the GIPS standards and the country-specific laws and regulations.

   d. Knowledge of FIRM Policies: Verifiers must determine the FIRM'S assumptions and policies for establishing and maintaining compliance with all applicable REQUIREMENTS of the GIPS standards. At a minimum, verifiers must determine the following policies and procedures of the FIRM:

      i. Policy with regard to investment discretion. The verifier must receive from the FIRM, in writing, the FIRM'S definition of investment discretion and the FIRM'S guidelines for determining whether accounts are fully discretionary;
      ii. Policy with regard to the definition of COMPOSITES according to investment strategy. The verifier must obtain the FIRM'S list of COMPOSITE DEFINITIONS with written criteria for including accounts in each COMPOSITE;
      iii. Policy with regard to the timing of inclusion of new accounts in the COMPOSITES;
      iv. Policy with regard to timing of exclusion of closed accounts in the COMPOSITES;
      v. Policy with regard to the accrual of interest and dividend income;
      vi. Policy with regard to the market valuation of investment securities;

vii. Method for computing the TIME-WEIGHTED-RATE OF RETURN for the portfolio;
viii. Assumptions on the timing of capital inflows/outflows;
ix. Method for computing COMPOSITE returns;
x. Policy with regard to the presentation of COMPOSITE returns;
xi. Policies regarding timing of implied taxes due on income and realized capital gains for reporting performance on an after-tax basis;
xii. Policies regarding use of securities/countries not included in a COMPOSITE'S BENCHMARK;
xiii. Use of leverage and other derivatives; and
xiv. Any other policies and procedures relevant to performance presentation.

e. Knowledge of Valuation Basis for Performance Calculations: Verifiers must ensure that they understand the methods and policies used to record valuation information for performance calculation purposes. In particular, verifiers must determine that:

i. The FIRM'S policy on classifying fund flows (e.g., injections, disbursements, dividends, interest, fees, and taxes) is consistent with the desired results and will give rise to accurate returns;
ii. The FIRM'S accounting treatment of income, interest, and dividend receipts is consistent with cash account and cash accruals definitions;
iii. The FIRM'S treatment of taxes, tax reclaims, and tax accruals is correct and the manner used is consistent with the desired method (i.e., gross- or net-of-tax return);
iv. The FIRM'S policies on recognizing purchases, sales, and the opening and closing of other positions are internally consistent and will produce accurate results; and
v. The FIRM'S accounting for investments and derivatives is consistent with the GIPS standards.

2. Verification Procedures

a. Definition of the FIRM: Verifiers must determine that the FIRM is, and has been, appropriately defined.

b. COMPOSITE Construction. Verifiers must be satisfied that:

i. The FIRM has defined and maintained COMPOSITES according to reasonable guidelines in compliance with the GIPS standards;
ii. All the FIRM'S actual discretionary fee-paying PORTFOLIOS are included in a COMPOSITE;
iii. The FIRM'S definition of discretion has been consistently applied over time;
iv. At all times, all accounts are included in their respective COMPOSITES and no accounts that belong in a particular COMPOSITE have been excluded;
v. COMPOSITE BENCHMARKS are consistent with COMPOSITE DEFINITIONS and have been consistently applied over time;
vi. The FIRM'S guidelines for creating and maintaining COMPOSITES have been consistently applied; and
vii. The FIRM'S list of COMPOSITES is complete.

c. Nondiscretionary Accounts. Verifiers must obtain a listing of all FIRM PORTFOLIOS and determine on a sampling basis whether the manager's classification of the account as discretionary or nondiscretionary is appropriate by referring to the account's agreement and the FIRM'S written guidelines for determining investment discretion.

d. Sample Account Selection: Verifiers must obtain a listing of open and closed accounts for all COMPOSITES for the years under examination. Verifiers may check compliance with the GIPS standards using a selected sample of a FIRM'S accounts. Verifiers SHOULD consider the following criteria when selecting the sample accounts for examination:

   i. Number of COMPOSITES at the FIRM;
   ii. Number of PORTFOLIOS in each COMPOSITE;
   iii. Nature of the COMPOSITE;
   iv. Total assets under management;
   v. Internal control structure at the FIRM (system of checks and balances in place);
   vi Number of years under examination; and
   vii Computer applications, software used in the construction and maintenance of COMPOSITES, the use of external performance measurers, and the calculation of performance results.

This list is not all-inclusive and contains only the minimum criteria that SHOULD be used in the selection and evaluation of a sample for testing. For example, one potentially useful approach would be to choose a PORTFOLIO for the study sample that has the largest impact on COMPOSITE performance because of its size or because of extremely good or bad performance. The lack of explicit record keeping or the presence of errors may warrant selecting a larger sample or applying additional verification procedures.

e. Account Review: For selected accounts, verifiers must determine:

   i. Whether the timing of the initial inclusion in the COMPOSITE is in accordance with policies of the FIRM;
   ii. Whether the timing of exclusion from the COMPOSITE is in accordance with policies of the FIRM for closed accounts;
   iii. Whether the objectives set forth in the account agreement are consistent with the manager's COMPOSITE DEFINITION as indicated by the account agreement, PORTFOLIO summary, and COMPOSITE DEFINITION;
   iv. The existence of the accounts by tracing selected accounts from account agreements to the COMPOSITES;
   v. That all PORTFOLIOS sharing the same guidelines are included in the same COMPOSITE; and
   vi. That shifts from one COMPOSITE to another are consistent with the guidelines set forth by the specific account agreement or with documented guidelines of the FIRM'S clients.

f. Performance Measurement Calculation: Verifiers must determine whether the FIRM has computed performance in accordance with the policies and assumptions adopted by the FIRM and disclosed in its presentations. In doing so, verifiers SHOULD:

   i. Recalculate rates of return for a sample of accounts in the FIRM using an acceptable return formula as prescribed by the GIPS standards (e.g., TIME-WEIGHTED RATE OF RETURN); and

ii. Take a reasonable sample of COMPOSITE calculations to assure themselves of the accuracy of the asset weighting of returns, the geometric linking of returns to produce annual rates of returns, and the calculation of the DISPERSION of individual returns around the aggregate COMPOSITE return.

g. Disclosures: Verifiers must review a sample of COMPOSITE presentations to ensure that the presentations include the information and disclosures REQUIRED by the GIPS standards.

h. Maintenance of Records: The verifier must maintain sufficient information to support the verification report. The verifier must obtain a representation letter from the client FIRM confirming major policies and any other specific representations made to the verifier during the examination.

C. DETAILED EXAMINATIONS OF INVESTMENT PERFORMANCE PRESENTATIONS

Separate from a GIPS verification, a FIRM may choose to have a further, more extensive, specifically focused examination (or performance audit) of a specific COMPOSITE presentation.

FIRMS cannot make any claim that a particular COMPOSITE has been independently examined with respect to the GIPS standards unless the verifier has also followed the GIPS verification procedures set forth in section III.B. FIRMS cannot state that a particular COMPOSITE presentation has been "GIPS verified" or make any claim to that affect. GIPS verification relates only to FIRM-wide verification. FIRMS can make a claim of verification only after a verifier has issued a GIPS verification report.

To assert a verification report has been received, a detailed examination of a COMPOSITE presentation is not REQUIRED. Examinations of this type are unlikely to become a REQUIREMENT of the GIPS standards or become mandatory.

APPENDIX A — SAMPLE GIPS-COMPLIANT PRESENTATIONS

EXAMPLE 1:

Sample 1 Investment Firm
Balanced Composite
1 January 1995 through 31 December 2004

Year	Gross-of-Fees Return (percent)	Net-of-Fees Return (percent)	Benchmark Return (percent)	Number of Portfolios	Internal Dispersion (percent)	Total Composite Assets (CAD Million)	Total Firm Assets (CAD Million)
1995	16.0	15.0	14.1	26	4.5	165	236
1996	2.2	1.3	1.8	32	2.0	235	346
1997	22.4	21.5	24.1	38	5.7	344	529
1998	7.1	6.2	6.0	45	2.8	445	695
1999	8.5	7.5	8.0	48	3.1	520	839
2000	–8.0	–8.9	–8.4	49	2.8	505	1014
2001	–5.9	–6.8	–6.2	52	2.9	499	995
2002	2.4	1.6	2.2	58	3.1	525	1125
2003	6.7	5.9	6.8	55	3.5	549	1225
2004	9.4	8.6	9.1	59	2.5	575	1290

Sample 1 Investment Firm has prepared and presented this report in compliance with the Global Investment Performance Standards (GIPS®).

Notes:

1. Sample 1 Investment Firm is a balanced portfolio investment manager that invests solely in Canadian securities. Sample 1 Investment Firm is defined as an independent investment management firm that is not affiliated with any parent organization. For the periods from 2000 through 2004, Sample 1 Investment Firm has been verified by Verification Services Inc. A copy of the verification report is available upon request. Additional information regarding the firm's policies and procedures for calculating and reporting performance results is available upon request.
2. The composite includes all nontaxable balanced portfolios with an asset allocation of 30% S&P TSX and 70% Scotia Canadian Bond Index Fund, which allow up to a 10% deviation in asset allocation.
3. The benchmark: 30% S&P TSX; 70% Scotia Canadian Bond Index Fund rebalanced monthly.
4. Valuations are computed and performance reported in Canadian dollars.
5. Gross-of-fees performance returns are presented before management and custodial fees but after all trading expenses. Returns are presented net of nonreclaimable withholding taxes. Net-of-fees performance returns are calculated by deducting the highest fee of 0.25% from the quarterly gross composite return. The management fee schedule is as follows: 1.00% on first CAD25M; 0.60% thereafter.
6. This composite was created in February 1995. A complete list and description of firm composites is available upon request.
7. For the periods 1995 and 1996, Sample 1 Investment Firm was not in compliance with the GIPS standards because portfolios were valued annually.
8. Internal dispersion is calculated using the equal-weighted standard deviation of all portfolios that were included in the composite for the entire year.

EXAMPLE 2:

Sample 2 Asset Management Company
Equities World BM MSCI Active Mandates Direct

Reporting Currency CHF **Creation Date 01 July 1999**

Period	Total Return (%)	MSCI World (ri) in CHF Benchmark Return (%)	Number of Portfolios	Composite Dispersion (Range)	Total Composite Assets (millions)	Percentage of Firm Assets (%)
2004	18.0	19.6	6	0.2	84.3	<0.1
2003	–35.3	–33.0	8	0.7	126.6	0.1
2002	–16.0	–14.5	8	1.5	233.0	0.2
2001	–13.5	–11.8	7	1.3	202.1	0.2
2000	60.2	46.1	<5	N/A	143.7	0.2
1999	21.3	17.5	<5	N/A	62.8	<0.1
1998	22.5	26.3	<5	N/A	16.1	<0.1

Compliance Statement
Sample 2 Asset Management Company has prepared and presented this report in compliance with the Global Investment Performance Standards (GIPS®).

Definition of the Firm
Sample 2 Asset Management Company is an independent investment management firm established in 1997. Sample 2 Asset Management Company manages a variety of equity, fixed income, and balanced assets for primarily Swiss and European clients. Additional information regarding the firm's policies and procedures for calculating and reporting performance returns is available upon request.

Benchmark
Sources of foreign exchange rates may be different between the composite and the benchmark.

Fees
Performance figures are presented gross of management fees, custodial fees, and withholding taxes but net of all trading expenses.

List of Composites
A complete listing and description of all composites is available on request.

Verification
Sample 2 Asset Management Company has been verified by an independent verifier on an annual basis from 1998 through 2003.

Fee Schedule
The standard fixed management fee for accounts with assets under management of up to CHF50 million is 0.35% per annum.

Minimum Account Size
The minimum portfolio size for inclusion in Equities World BM MSCI composite is CHF1 million.

EXAMPLE 3:

Schedule of Performance Results
Sample 3 Realty Management Firm
Core Real Estate Composite

1 January 1995 through 31 December 2004

	Gross-of-Fees Returns					NCREIF		Year-End Composite				
Year	Income Return	Capital Return	TOTAL	Range of Returns	Composite Dispersion	Property Index Benchmark	Number of Portfolios	Net Assets (USD Million)	Percent Leveraged	External Valuation	Firm Total Net Assets (USD Million)	Percent of Firm Assets
1995	5.1%	-4.0%	0.8%	0.7-1.0	NA	-5.6%	<5	$ 79	43%	100%	$ 950	8%
1996	5.5%	-0.9%	4.5%	4.0-5.0	NA	-4.3%	<5	$ 143	49%	100%	$ 989	14%
1997	6.9%	-1.5%	5.3%	5.0-5.4	NA	1.4%	<5	$ 217	56%	100%	$ 1,219	18%
1998	8.1%	0.9%	9.1%	8.9-9.7	NA	6.4%	<5	$ 296	54%	100%	$ 1,375	22%
1999	8.9%	1.7%	10.8%	9.9-11.0	NA	7.5%	<5	$ 319	50%	100%	$ 1,425	22%
2000	9.0%	0.5%	9.6%	9.1-10.9	0.7	10.3%	5	$ 367	45%	100%	$ 1,532	24%
2001	9.1%	1.2%	10.5%	10.0-10.7	0.3	13.9%	5	$ 349	39%	100%	$ 1,712	20%
2002	7.9%	1.8%	9.9%	9.8-10.5	0.3	16.3%	6	$ 398	31%	100%	$ 1,796	22%
2003	8.5%	2.9%	11.5%	10.9-12.0	0.5	11.1%	6	$ 425	28%	100%	$ 1,924	22%
2004	8.2%	2.5%	10.8%	9.9-11.8	0.8	12.0%	7	$ 432	22%	100%	$ 1,954	22%
Annualized Since Inception Time-Weighted Returns:												
	7.7%	0.5%	8.0%			6.7%						
Annualized Since Inception Internal Rate of Return:												
			7.8%									

Example 3: Sample 3 Realty Management Firm

DISCLOSURES

Compliance Statement
Sample 3 Realty Management Firm has prepared and presented this report in compliance with the Global Investment Performance Standards (GIPS®).

The Firm
Sample 3 Realty Management Firm (the "Firm"), a subsidiary of ABC Capital, Inc., is a registered investment adviser under the Investment Advisors Act of 1940. The Firm exercises complete discretion over the selection, capitalization, asset management, and disposition of investments in wholly-owned properties and joint ventures. A complete list and description of the Firm's composites is available upon request.

The Composite
The Core Real Estate Composite (the "Composite") comprises all actual fee-paying discretionary portfolios managed by the Firm with a core investment and risk strategy with an income focus having a minimum initial portfolio size of $10 million. Portfolios that initially qualify are excluded later from the composite if their asset size decreases below the minimum requirement due to capital distributions. The Composite was created in 1998. Composite dispersion is measured using an asset-weighted standard deviation of returns of the portfolios.

Valuation
Assets are valued quarterly by the Firm and appraised annually by an independent Member of the Appraisal Institute. Both the internal and external property valuations rely primarily on the application of market discount rates to future projections of free cash flows (unleveraged cash flows) and capitalized terminal values over the expected holding period for each property. Property mortgages, notes, and loans are marked to market using prevailing interest rates for comparable property loans if the terms of existing loans preclude the immediate repayment of such loans. Loan repayment fees, if any, are considered in the projected year of sale.

Calculation of Performance Returns
Returns presented are denominated in United States dollars. Returns are presented net of leverage. Composite returns are calculated on an asset-weighted average basis using beginning-of-period values. Returns include cash and cash equivalents and related interest income. Income return is based on accrual recognition of earned income. Capital expenditures, tenant improvements, and lease commissions are capitalized and included in the cost of the property, are not amortized, and are reconciled through the valuation process and reflected in the capital return component. Income and capital returns may not equal total returns due to chain-linking of quarterly returns. Annual returns are time-weighted rates of return calculated by linking quarterly returns. For the annualized since-inception time-weighted return, terminal value is based on ending market value of net assets of the Composite. For the since-inception internal rate of return, contributions from and distributions to investors since 1 January 1995, and a terminal value equal to the composite's ending market value of net assets as of 31 December 2004, are used. The IRR is calculated using monthly cash flows. Additional information regarding policies for calculating and reporting returns in compliance with the GIPS standards is available upon request.

Investment Management Fees
Some of the portfolios pay incentive fees ranging between 10% and 20% of IRR in excess of established benchmarks. Current annual investment advisory fees are as follows:

Up to $30 million:	1.6%
$30 – $50 million:	1.3%
over $50 million:	1.0%

NCREIF Property Index Benchmark
The National Council of Real Estate Investment Fiduciaries (NCREIF) Property Index benchmark has been taken from published sources. The NCREIF Property Index is unleveraged, includes various real estate property types, excludes cash and other nonproperty related assets and liabilities, income, and expenses. The calculation methodology for the index is not consistent with calculation methodology employed for the Composite because the benchmark computes the total return by adding the income and capital appreciation return on a quarterly basis.

EXAMPLE 4:

Sample 4 Private Equity Partners
Buy-Out Composite
1 January 1995 through 31 December 2002

Year	Annualized SI-IRR Gross-of-Fees (%)	Annualized SI-IRR Net-of-Fees (%)	Benchmark Return (%)	Composite Assets (USD$ mil)	Total Firm Assets (USD$ mil)
1995	(7.5)	(11.07)	(9.42)	4.31	357.36
1996	6.2	4.53	2.83	10.04	402.78
1997	13.8	10.10	14.94	14.25	530.51
1998	13.1	9.28	14.22	25.21	613.73
1999	53.2	44.53	37.43	54.00	871.75
2000	40.6	26.47	32.97	24.25	1,153.62
2001	29.9	21.86	27.42	8.25	1,175.69
2002	25.3	17.55	25.24	10.25	1,150.78

Year	Paid-In Capital (USD$ mil)	Invested Capital (USD$ mil)	Cumulative Distributions (USD$ mil)	Investment Multiple (TVPI)	Realization Multiple (DPI)	PIC	RVPI
1995	4.68	4.68	0.00	0.92	0.00	0.19	0.92
1996	9.56	9.56	0.00	1.05	0.00	0.38	1.05
1997	14.54	12.91	2.55	1.16	0.18	0.58	0.98
1998	23.79	22.15	2.55	1.17	0.11	0.95	1.06
1999	25.00	19.08	15.78	2.79	0.63	1.00	2.16
2000	25.00	17.46	27.44	2.07	1.10	1.00	0.97
2001	25.00	14.89	39.10	1.89	1.56	1.00	0.33
2002	25.00	13.73	41.25	2.06	1.65	1.00	0.41

TVPI = Total Value to Paid-In Capital
DPI = Distributed Capital to Paid-In Capital
PIC = Paid-In Capital to Committed Capital
RVPI = Residual Value to Paid-In Capital

Sample 4 Private Equity Partners has prepared and presented this report in compliance with the Global Investment Performance Standards (GIPS®).

Example 4: Sample 4 Private Equity Partners

DISCLOSURES

Sample 4 Private Equity Partners is an independent private equity investment firm, having offices in London, New York, and San Francisco. The Sample 4 Buy-Out Composite invests in private equity buyouts and was created in January 1995.

The Sample 4 Buy-Out Composite complies with the XYZ Venture Capital Association's valuation guidelines. Valuations are prepared by Sample 4's valuations committee and reviewed by an independent advisory board. Sample 4 follows the fair value basis of valuation as recommended in the GIPS Private Equity Valuation Principles. All investments within the Sample 4 Buy-Out Composite are valued either using a most recent transaction or an earnings multiple. Sample 4's valuation review procedures are available upon request.

The GP-BO index is used as the benchmark and is constructed as the QRS index return plus 500 basis points. The benchmark return is calculated using monthly cash flows. There is only one fund in the composite for all time periods, and the dispersion of portfolio returns within the composite, therefore, is zero for all years.

The vintage year of the Sample 4 Buy-Out Fund is 1995, and total committed capital is USD$25 million. The total composite assets (unrealized gains) are USD$10.25 million as of 31 December 2002.

The fund's SI-IRR calculation incorporates monthly cash flows.

The standard fee schedule currently in effect is as follows: 1.00% of assets under management. In addition, there is a 20% incentive fee for all assets. The incentive fee is applied to the value added in excess of fees, expenses, and the return of the GP-BO Index. [corrected October 2006]

A complete list of firm composites and composite performance results is available upon request. Additional information regarding the firm's policies and procedures for calculating and reporting performance results is available upon request.

APPENDIX B — SAMPLE LIST AND DESCRIPTION OF COMPOSITES

Sample Asset Management Firm

List and Description of Composites

The **Small Cap Growth Composite** includes all institutional portfolios invested in U.S. equities with strong earnings and growth characteristics and small capitalizations. The benchmark is the Russell 2000® Growth Index.

The **Large Cap Growth Composite** includes all institutional portfolios invested in U.S. equities with strong earnings and growth characteristics and large capitalizations. The benchmark is the Russell 1000® Growth Index.

The **Core Fixed Income Composite** includes all institutional portfolios invested in fixed securities. Portfolios within the composite will have a duration that is plus or minus 20 percent of the benchmark. The benchmark is the Lehman Brothers Aggregate Bond Index.

The **Intermediate Fixed Income Composite** includes all institutional portfolios invested in fixed securities. Portfolios within the composite will have a duration that is plus or minus 20 percent of the benchmark. The benchmark is the Lehman Brothers Intermediate Aggregate Bond Index.

The **High Yield Fixed Income Composite** includes all institutional portfolios invested in high yield debt securities. The benchmark is the Lehman Brothers U.S. Corporate High Yield Bond Index.

The **Balanced Growth Composite** includes all institutional balanced portfolios that have a 50–70% allocation to growth equities, with a typical allocation between 55–65%. The benchmark is 60% S&P 500® and 40% Lehman Brothers Aggregate Bond Index. Only portfolios greater than $5 million are included in the composite.

Terminated Composites

The **GARP Equity Composite** includes all institutional portfolios invested in growth stocks that are reasonably priced and valued "cheap" compared with their peers. The benchmark is the S&P 500® Index. The composite terminated in November 2003.

The **Small-Mid Cap Growth Composite** includes all institutional portfolios invested in U.S. equities with strong earnings and growth characteristics. The benchmark is the Russell 2500® Growth Index. The composite terminated in February 2004.

APPENDIX C — GIPS ADVERTISING GUIDELINES

A. PURPOSE OF THE GIPS ADVERTISING GUIDELINES

The Global Investment Performance Standards provide the investment community with a set of ethical standards for FIRMS to follow when presenting their performance results to potential clients. The Standards serve to provide greater uniformity and comparability among investment managers without regard to geographical location and to facilitate a dialogue between FIRMS and their prospective clients about the critical issues of how the FIRM achieved historical performance results and determines future investment strategies.

The GIPS Advertising Guidelines attempt to serve as industry global best practice for the advertisement of performance results. The GIPS Advertising Guidelines do not replace the GIPS standards nor do they absolve FIRMS from presenting performance presentations that adhere to the REQUIREMENTS of the full GIPS standards. The guidelines only apply to FIRMS that already satisfy all the REQUIREMENTS of the Standards on a FIRM-wide basis and claim compliance with the Standards. FIRMS that claim compliance can choose to advertise that claim using the GIPS Advertising Guidelines.

The guidelines are mandatory for FIRMS that include a claim of compliance with the GIPS Advertising Guidelines in their advertisements. The guidelines are voluntary for FIRMS that do not include a claim of compliance in their advertisements. All FIRMS are encouraged to abide by these ethical guidelines.

Definition of Advertisement

For the purposes of these guidelines, an advertisement includes any materials that are distributed to or designed for use in newspapers, magazines, FIRM brochures, letters, media, or any other written or electronic material addressed to more than one prospective client. Any written material (other than one-on-one presentations and individual client reporting) distributed to maintain existing clients or solicit new clients for an advisor is considered an advertisement.

Relationship of GIPS Advertising Guidelines to Regulatory Requirements

The GIPS Advertising Guidelines are guidelines that promote an ethical framework for advertisements. They do not change the scope of the activities of local regulatory bodies regarding the regulation of advertisements. FIRMS advertising performance results MUST also adhere to all applicable regulatory rules and requirements governing advertisements. FIRMS are encouraged to seek legal or regulatory counsel because it is likely that additional disclosures are REQUIRED. In cases where applicable law or regulation conflicts with the GIPS Advertising Guidelines, the guidelines REQUIRE FIRMS to comply with the law or regulation. FIRMS MUST disclose any conflicts between laws/regulations and the GIPS Advertising Guidelines.

The calculation and advertisement of pooled unitized products, such as mutual funds and open-ended investment companies, are regulated in most markets. These advertising guidelines are not intended to replace the regulations when a FIRM is advertising performance solely for a pooled unitized product. However, should a GIPS-compliant FIRM choose to advertise performance results, the FIRM MUST apply all applicable laws and regulations as well as the GIPS Advertising Guidelines in order to include a claim of compliance with the GIPS standards.

B. REQUIREMENTS OF THE GIPS ADVERTISING GUIDELINES

All advertisements that include a claim of compliance with the GIPS Advertising Guidelines MUST include the following:

1. A description of the FIRM.

2. How an interested party can obtain a presentation that complies with the REQUIREMENTS of GIPS standards and/or a list and description of all FIRM COMPOSITES.

3. The GIPS Advertising Guidelines compliance statement:
   [Insert name of firm] claims compliance with the Global Investment Performance Standards (GIPS®).

All advertisements that include a claim of compliance with the GIPS Advertising Guidelines and that present performance results MUST also include the following information (the relevant information MUST be taken/derived from a presentation that adheres to the REQUIREMENTS of the GIPS standards):

4. A description of the strategy of the COMPOSITE being advertised.

5. Period-to-date COMPOSITE performance results in addition to either:

   a. 1-, 3-, and 5-year cumulative annualized COMPOSITE returns with the end-of-period date clearly identified (or annualized period since COMPOSITE inception if inception is greater than 1 and less than 5 years). Periods of less than 1 year are not permitted to be annualized. The annualized returns MUST be calculated through the same period of time as presented in the corresponding compliant presentation; or

   b. 5 years of annual COMPOSITE returns with the end-of-period date clearly identified (or since COMPOSITE inception if inception is less than 5 years). The annual returns MUST be calculated through the same period of time as presented in the corresponding compliant presentation.

6. Whether performance is shown gross and/or net of INVESTMENT MANAGEMENT FEES.

7. The BENCHMARK TOTAL RETURN for the same periods for which the COMPOSITE return is presented and a description of that BENCHMARK. (The appropriate COMPOSITE BENCHMARK return is the same BENCHMARK TOTAL RETURN as presented in the corresponding GIPS-compliant presentation.) If no BENCHMARK is presented, the advertisement MUST disclose why no BENCHMARK is presented.

8. The currency used to express returns.

9. The description of the use and extent of leverage and derivatives if leverage or derivatives are used as an active part of the investment strategy (i.e., not merely for efficient PORTFOLIO management) of the COMPOSITE. Where leverage/derivatives do not have a material effect on returns, no disclosure is REQUIRED.

10. When presenting noncompliant performance information for periods prior to 1 January 2000 in an advertisement, FIRMS MUST disclose the period(s) and which specific information is not compliant as well as provide the reason(s) the information is not in compliance with the GIPS standards.

Additional and Supplemental Information
FIRMS are encouraged to present SUPPLEMENTAL INFORMATION or ADDITIONAL INFORMATION (in addition to the information REQUIRED under the GIPS Advertising Guidelines) provided the SUPPLEMENTAL INFORMATION is clearly labeled as such and shown with equal or lesser prominence than the information REQUIRED under the guidelines. Where such SUPPLEMENTAL INFORMATION is included for noncompliant periods, these periods MUST be disclosed together with an explanation of what information is not compliant and why it is not in compliance with the GIPS standards.

SUPPLEMENTAL and ADDITIONAL INFORMATION is the subject of the "Guidance Statement on the Use of Supplemental Information" and users should refer to that guidance for further clarification on how to disclose such data.

SAMPLE ADVERTISEMENTS

Sample Advertisement without Performance Returns

Sample 4 Investments

Sample 4 Investments is the institutional asset management division of Sample 4 Plc and is a registered investment advisory firm specializing in qualitative, growth-oriented investment management.

Sample 4 Investments claims compliance with the Global Investment Performance Standards (GIPS®).

To receive a complete list and description of Sample 4 Investments' composites and/or a presentation that adheres to the GIPS standards, contact John Doe at (800) 555-1234, or write to Sample 4 Investments, 123 Main Street, Resultland 12345, or e-mail jdoe@sample4investments.com

Sample Advertisement Including Performance Returns (1-, 3-, and 5-year annualized)

Sample 4 Investments: Global Equity Growth Composite Performance				
	Ending 31 Mar 04	Ending 31 Dec 03		
Results shown in US $ before fees	Period to Date (3 mths)	1 Year	3 Years per annum	5 Years per annum
Global Equity Growth	–3.84%	–19.05%	–14.98%	0.42%
MSCI World Index	–4.94%	–19.54%	–16.37%	–1.76%

Sample 4 Investments is the institutional asset management subsidiary of Sample 4 plc and is a registered investment advisor specializing in qualitative, growth-oriented investment management. The Global Equity Growth Composite strategy focuses on earnings, growth of earnings, and key valuation metrics.

Sample 4 Investments claims compliance with the Global Investment Performance Standards (GIPS®).

To receive a complete list and description of Sample 4 Investments' composites and/or a presentation that adheres to the GIPS standards, contact Jean Paul at +12 (034) 5678910, or write Sample 4 Investments, One Plain Street, Resultland 12KJ4, or jpaul@sample4inv.com.re.

OR the firm may present:

Sample Advertisement Including Performance Returns (5 years of annual returns)

Sample 4 Investments: Global Equity Growth Composite Performance						
Results are shown in US $ before fees	Period to Date (3 mths to 31 Mar 04)	31 Dec 2003	31 Dec 2002	31 Dec 2001	31 Dec 2000	31 Dec 1999
Global Equity Growth Composite	–3.84%	–19.05%	–17.05%	–8.47%	31.97%	25.87%
MSCI World Index	–4.94%	–19.54%	–16.52%	–12.92%	25.34%	24.80%

Sample 4 Investments is the institutional asset management subsidiary of Sample 4 plc and is a registered investment advisor specializing in qualitative, growth-oriented investment management. The Global Equity Growth Composite strategy focuses on earnings, growth of earnings, and key valuation metrics.

Sample 4 Investments claims compliance with the Global Investment Performance Standards (GIPS®).

To receive a complete list and description of Sample 4 Investments' composites and/or a presentation that adheres to the GIPS standards, contact Jean Paul at +12 (034) 5678910, or write Sample 4 Investments, One Plain Street, Resultland 12KJ4, or jpaul@sample4inv.com.re.

APPENDIX D — PRIVATE EQUITY VALUATION PRINCIPLES

INTRODUCTION

Opinions among INVESTMENT ADVISORS, practitioners, and investors differ regarding the valuation of PRIVATE EQUITY assets. The margin of error for a particular valuation methodology may often be greater than the difference between alternative methodologies. The volatility of asset values is also often high, increasing the perception that a historical valuation was "wrong." Although cash-to-cash returns are the principal metric, PRIVATE EQUITY funds raise capital in part based on unrealized interim returns. The valuation of unrealized assets underpinning these interim returns is critical to this analysis.

Although many points are contested, some common ground exists:

- The PRIVATE EQUITY industry must strive to promote integrity and professionalism in order to improve investor confidence and self-regulation.
- Consistency and comparability are important in reporting to investors, and many aspects of valuation SHOULD be transparent. More information, however, does not always equal greater transparency, and there are legal and practical constraints on the dissemination of information.
- Each PRIVATE EQUITY investment is based on a set of assumptions. It is reasonable for investors to expect interim valuations to reflect factors that, at a minimum, adversely impact these assumptions.
- When a PRIVATE EQUITY asset becomes publicly traded, arguments against interim valuations fall away, although practical considerations may remain where there are restrictions on trading or trading volumes are low.

Beyond these issues are the debates on valuation basis and methodology. The move toward a FAIR VALUE basis has been gathering momentum in most areas of financial reporting. Particularly for early stage venture investments that may not achieve profitability for a number of years, practical problems remain and the utility of the FAIR VALUE basis must garner greater support before a consensus on detailed guidelines is likely to be possible.

GUIDELINES FOR VALUATION

The following MUST be applied to all forms of investment vehicles making PRIVATE EQUITY investments. These principles do not apply to OPEN-END or EVERGREEN FUNDS.

1. Valuations MUST be prepared with integrity and professionalism by individuals with appropriate experience and ability under the direction of senior management.

2. FIRMS MUST document their valuation review procedures.

3. FIRMS MUST create as much transparency as deemed possible in relation to the valuation basis used to value fund investments. For the latest period presented, the valuation methodologies used to value PRIVATE EQUITY investments MUST be clearly disclosed, including all key assumptions.

4. The basis of valuation MUST be logically cohesive and applied rigorously. Although a FAIR VALUE basis is RECOMMENDED, all valuations MUST, at a minimum, recognize when assets have suffered a diminution in value. (Please see the Additional Considerations section for further guidance on diminution circumstances.)

5. Valuations MUST be prepared on a consistent and comparable basis from one reporting period to the next. If any change is deemed appropriate in either valuation basis or method, the change MUST be explained. When such a change gives rise to a material alteration in the valuation of the investments, the effect of the change SHOULD also be disclosed.

6. Valuations MUST be prepared at least annually. (Quarterly valuations are RECOMMENDED.)

FAIR VALUE RECOMMENDATION

It is RECOMMENDED that the FAIR VALUE basis, which is consistent with international financial reporting principles, be used to value PRIVATE EQUITY investments. This valuation SHOULD represent the amount at which an asset could be acquired or sold in a current transaction between willing parties in which the parties each acted knowledgeably, prudently, and without compulsion.

The accuracy with which the value of an individual PRIVATE EQUITY asset can be determined will generally have substantial uncertainty. Consequently, it is RECOMMENDED that a valuation method that involves the least number of estimates is preferred over another method that introduces additional subjective assumptions. However, if the latter method results in more accurate and meaningful valuation, then it SHOULD be used instead of the former method.

Valuation Hierarchy

The following hierarchy of FAIR VALUE methodologies SHOULD be followed when valuing PRIVATE EQUITY investments:

1. Market Transaction
   Where a recent independent third-party transaction has occurred involving a material investment as part of a new round of financing or sale of equity, it would provide the most appropriate indication of FAIR VALUE.

2. Market-Based Multiples
   In the absence of any such third-party transactions continuing to have relevance, the FAIR VALUE of an investment may be calculated using earnings or other market-based multiples. The particular multiple used SHOULD be appropriate for the business being valued. Market-based multiples include, but are not limited to, the following: price to earnings, enterprise value to EBIT, enterprise value to EBITDA, and so on.

3. Discounted Expected Future Cash Flows
   This method SHOULD represent the present value of risk-adjusted expected cash flows, discounted at the risk-free rate.

Additional Considerations

1. Where a third-party transaction has taken place other than at arm's length, or where the new investor's objectives in making the investment are largely strategic in nature (i.e., the new investor was not acting solely as a financial investor), the manager SHOULD consider ignoring the valuation or applying an appropriate discount to it.

2. A material diminution in the value of an investment may result from, among other things, a breach of covenant, failure to service debt, a filing for creditor protection or bankruptcy, major lawsuit (particularly concerning intellectual property rights), or a loss or change of management. Other events may include fraud within the

company, a material devaluation in an investment currency that is different from the fund currency, substantial changes in quoted market conditions, or any event resulting in profitability falling significantly below the levels at the time of investment or the company performing substantially and consistently behind plan. Estimating the extent of the diminution in most cases will generally involve both quantitative and qualitative analysis and SHOULD be performed with as much diligence as possible.

3. The FIRM SHOULD have policies in place for informing clients/prospects when a material diminution has taken place within the PORTFOLIO. Waiting until a quarterly update may often not provide the prospective investor with this critical information soon enough to make an informed decision.

4. Within the valuation hierarchy there will be certain industries where very specific valuation methodologies become applicable. Within the correct industry, either of these methods could be considered the primary valuation methodology in the absence of an applicable third-party transaction. Whenever one of these methods is used, the FIRM MUST justify the measure as representing the most appropriate and accurate method for calculating a FAIR VALUE.

    a. Net Assets: For FIRMS that derive a majority of their value from their underlying assets rather than the company's earnings, this method may be preferred.

    b. Industry BENCHMARKS: In particular industries, there are metrics, such as "price per subscriber", that can be used to derive the value of a FIRM. These measures are very specialized to the industries they represent and must not be carried over to more diversified FIRMS.

5. It is RECOMMENDED that valuations be reviewed by a qualified person or entity that is independent from the valuer. Such parties would include third-party experts, an independent advisory board, or a committee independent of the executives responsible for the valuations.

6. As stated in the Valuation Hierarchy section of this document, FAIR VALUE allows for the use of a recent transaction as the primary methodology for valuation. Accordingly, when an investment is first made, this "cost" represents the most recent transaction and, therefore, the FAIR VALUE. In this case, the cost is permitted to be used not because it represents the cost of the investment but, rather, because it represents the value of the most recent transaction.

Cost as a basis of valuation is only permitted when an estimate of FAIR VALUE cannot be reliably determined. Although a FAIR VALUE basis SHOULD always be attempted, the PRIVATE EQUITY Provisions do recognize that there may be situations when a non-FAIR-VALUE basis is necessary. Ultimately, FIRMS must keep in mind that investors make decisions based on FAIR VALUES, not out-of-date historical cost-based measures.

In any case, when a non-FAIR-VALUE basis is used, the FIRM MUST disclose its justification for why a FAIR VALUE basis cannot be applied. In addition, for each COMPOSITE, the FIRM MUST disclose the number of holdings to which a non-FAIR-VALUE basis is applied, the TOTAL VALUE of those holdings, and the value of those holdings as a percentage of the total COMPOSITE/fund assets.

7. Where companies have activities that span more than one sector, making it impractical to find comparable companies or sectors, each earnings stream may be valued independently. Sector average multiples, based on companies of comparable size, can be used where it is not practical or possible to identify a sufficient number of directly comparable companies.

8. The entry multiple(s) for an investment SHOULD only be used as a last resort when comparable quoted companies are not available.

9. All quasi-equity investments SHOULD be valued as equity unless their realizable value can be demonstrated to be other than the equity value.

10. When a PRIVATE EQUITY FIRM has invested in loan stock and preference shares alongside an equity investment, these instruments SHOULD not generally be valued on the basis of their yield. They SHOULD be valued at cost plus any premium or rolled up interest only to the extent it has fully accrued, less any provision/discount where appropriate.

APPENDIX E — GIPS GLOSSARY

The following definitions are solely for the purpose of interpreting the GIPS standards.

ACCRUAL ACCOUNTING The system of recording financial transactions as they come into existence as a legally enforceable claim, rather than when they settle.

ADDITIONAL INFORMATION Information that is REQUIRED or RECOMMENDED under the GIPS standards and is not considered as "SUPPLEMENTAL INFORMATION" for the purposes of compliance.

ADMINISTRATIVE FEES All fees other than the TRADING EXPENSES and the INVESTMENT MANAGEMENT FEE. ADMINISTRATIVE FEES include CUSTODY FEES, accounting fees, consulting fees, legal fees, performance measurement fees, or other related fees. These ADMINISTRATIVE FEES are typically outside the control of the investment management FIRM and are not included in either the GROSS-OF-FEES RETURN or the NET-OF-FEES RETURN. However, there are some markets and investment vehicles where ADMINISTRATIVE FEES are controlled by the FIRM. (See the term "BUNDLED FEE.")

BENCHMARK An independent rate of return (or hurdle rate) forming an objective test of the effective implementation of an investment strategy.

BUNDLED FEE A fee that combines multiple fees into one "bundled" fee. BUNDLED FEES can include any combination of management, transaction, custody, and other ADMINISTRATIVE FEES. Two specific examples of BUNDLED FEES are the wrap fee and the all-in fee.

All-In Fee Due to the universal banking system in some countries, asset management, brokerage, and custody are often part of the same company. This allows banks to offer a variety of choices to customers regarding how the fee will be charged. Customers are offered numerous fee models in which fees may be bundled together or charged separately. All-in fees can include any combination of INVESTMENT MANAGEMENT, TRADING EXPENSES, CUSTODY, and other ADMINISTRATIVE FEES.

Wrap Fee Wrap fees are specific to a particular investment product. The U.S. Securities and Exchange Commission (SEC) defines a wrap fee account (now more commonly known as a separately managed account or SMA) as "any advisory program under which a specified fee or fees not based upon transactions in a client's account is charged for INVESTMENT ADVISORY services (which may include PORTFOLIO management or advice concerning the selection of other investment advisers) and execution of client transactions." A typical separately managed account has a contract or contracts (and fee) involving a sponsor (usually a broker or independent provider) acting as the INVESTMENT ADVISOR, an investment management firm typically as the subadvisor, other services (custody, consulting, reporting, performance, manager selection, monitoring, and execution of trades), distributor, and the client (brokerage customer). Wrap fees can be all-inclusive, asset-based fees (which may include any combination of management, transaction, custody, and other ADMINISTRATIVE FEES).

CAPITAL EMPLOYED (REAL ESTATE) The denominator of the return expressions, defined as the "weighted-average equity" (weighted-average capital) during the measurement period. CAPITAL EMPLOYED SHOULD not include any income or CAPITAL RETURN accrued during the measurement period. Beginning capital is adjusted by weighting the cash flows (contributions and distributions) that occurred during the period. Cash flows are typically weighted based on the actual days the flows are in or out of the PORTFOLIO. Other weighting methods are acceptable; however, once a methodology is chosen, it SHOULD be consistently applied.

CAPITAL RETURN (REAL ESTATE) The change in the MARKET VALUE of the REAL ESTATE investments and cash/cash equivalent assets held throughout the measurement period (ENDING MARKET VALUE less beginning MARKET VALUE) adjusted for all capital expenditures (subtracted) and the net proceeds from sales (added). The return is computed as a percentage of the CAPITAL EMPLOYED through the measurement period. Synonyms: capital appreciation return, appreciation return.

CARRIED INTEREST (PRIVATE EQUITY) The profits that GENERAL PARTNERS earn from the profits of the investments made by the fund (generally 20–25%). Also known as "carry."

CARVE-OUT A single or multiple asset class segment of a multiple asset class PORTFOLIO.

CLOSED-END FUND (PRIVATE EQUITY) A type of investment fund where the number of investors and the total COMMITTED CAPITAL is fixed and not open for subscriptions and/or redemptions.

COMMITTED CAPITAL (PRIVATE EQUITY) Pledges of capital to a VENTURE CAPITAL fund. This money is typically not received at once but drawn down over three to five years, starting in the year the fund is formed. Also known as "commitments."

COMPOSITE Aggregation of individual PORTFOLIOS representing a similar investment mandate, objective, or strategy.

COMPOSITE CREATION DATE The date when the FIRM first groups the PORTFOLIOS to create a COMPOSITE. The COMPOSITE CREATION DATE is not necessarily the earliest date for which performance is reported for the COMPOSITE. (See COMPOSITE INCEPTION DATE.)

COMPOSITE DEFINITION Detailed criteria that determine the allocation of portfolios to COMPOSITES. COMPOSITE DEFINITIONS MUST be documented in the FIRM'S policies and procedures.

COMPOSITE DESCRIPTION General information regarding the strategy of the COMPOSITE. A description may be more abbreviated than the COMPOSITE DEFINITION but includes all salient features of the COMPOSITE.

COMPOSITE INCEPTION DATE The earliest date for which performance is reported for the COMPOSITE. The COMPOSITE INCEPTION DATE is not necessarily the date the PORTFOLIOS are grouped together to create a COMPOSITE. Instead, it is the initial date of the performance record. (See COMPOSITE CREATION DATE.)

CUSTODY FEES — The fees payable to the custodian for the safekeeping of the PORTFOLIO'S assets. CUSTODY FEES typically contain an asset-based portion and a transaction-based portion of the fee. The total CUSTODY FEE may also include charges for additional services, including accounting, securities lending, or performance measurement. CUSTODY FEES that are charged per transaction SHOULD be included in the CUSTODY FEE and not included as part of the TRADING EXPENSES.

DIRECT INVESTMENTS (PRIVATE EQUITY) — An investment made directly in VENTURE CAPITAL or PRIVATE EQUITY assets (i.e., not via a partnership or fund).

DISPERSION — A measure of the spread of the annual returns of individual PORTFOLIOS within a COMPOSITE. Measures may include, but are not limited to, high/low, inter-quartile range, and standard deviation (asset weighted or equal weighted).

DISTINCT BUSINESS ENTITY — A unit, division, department, or office that is organizationally and functionally segregated from other units, divisions, departments, or offices and retains discretion over the assets it manages and should have autonomy over the investment decision-making process. Possible criteria that can be used to determine this include:

- being a legal entity
- having a distinct market or client type (e.g., institutional, retail, private client, etc.)
- using a separate and distinct investment process

[corrected August 2005]

DISTRIBUTION (PRIVATE EQUITY) — Cash or the value of stock disbursed to the LIMITED PARTNERS of a venture fund.

DRAWDOWN (PRIVATE EQUITY) — After the total COMMITTED CAPITAL has been agreed upon between the GENERAL PARTNER and the LIMITED PARTNERS, the actual transfer of funds from the LIMITED PARTNERS' to the GENERAL PARTNERS' control in as many stages as deemed necessary by the GENERAL PARTNER is referred to as the drawdown.

ENDING MARKET VALUE (PRIVATE EQUITY) — The remaining equity that a LIMITED PARTNER has in a fund. Also referred to as net asset value or RESIDUAL VALUE.

EVERGREEN FUND (PRIVATE EQUITY) — An OPEN-END FUND that allows for on-going investment and/or redemption by investors. Some EVERGREEN FUNDS reinvest profits in order to ensure the availability of capital for future investments.

EX-ANTE — Before the fact. (See EX-POST.)

EX-POST — After the fact. (See EX-ANTE.)

EXTERNAL CASH FLOW — Cash, securities, or assets that enter or exit a PORTFOLIO.

EXTERNAL VALUATION (REAL ESTATE)
An EXTERNAL VALUATION is an assessment of MARKET VALUE performed by a third party who is a qualified, PROFESSIONALLY DESIGNATED, CERTIFIED, OR LICENSED COMMERCIAL PROPERTY VALUER/APPRAISER. EXTERNAL VALUATIONS MUST be completed following the valuation standards of the local governing appraisal body.

FAIR VALUE
The amount at which an asset could be acquired or sold in a current transaction between willing parties in which the parties each acted knowledgeably, prudently, and without compulsion.

FEE SCHEDULE
The FIRM'S current INVESTMENT MANAGEMENT FEES or BUNDLED FEES for a particular presentation. This schedule is typically listed by asset level ranges and should be appropriate to the particular prospective client. [corrected September 2005]

FINAL REALIZATION DATE (PRIVATE EQUITY)
The date when a COMPOSITE is fully distributed.

FIRM
For purposes of the GIPS standards, the term "FIRM" refers to the entity defined for compliance with the GIPS standards. See the term "DISTINCT BUSINESS ENTITY."

GENERAL PARTNER (PRIVATE EQUITY)
(GP) a class of partner in a partnership. The GP retains liability for the actions of the partnership. In the PRIVATE EQUITY world, the GP is the fund manager and the LIMITED PARTNERS (LPs) are the institutional and high-net-worth investors in the partnership. The GP earns a management fee and a percentage of profits. (See the term "CARRIED INTEREST.")

GROSS-OF-FEES RETURN
The return on assets reduced by any TRADING EXPENSES incurred during the period.

GROSS-OF-FEES RETURN (PRIVATE EQUITY)
The return on assets reduced by any TRANSACTION EXPENSES incurred during the period.

INCOME RETURN (REAL ESTATE)
The investment income accrued on all assets (including cash and cash equivalents) during the measurement period net of all nonrecoverable expenditures, interest expense on debt, and property taxes. The return is computed as a percentage of the CAPITAL EMPLOYED through the measurement period.

INTERNAL VALUATION (REAL ESTATE)
An INTERNAL VALUATION is an advisor's or underlying third-party manager's best estimate of MARKET VALUE based on the most current and accurate information available under the circumstances. An INTERNAL VALUATION could include industry practice techniques, such as discounted cash flow, sales comparison, replacement cost, or a review of all significant events (both general market and asset specific) that could have a material impact on the investment. Prudent assumptions and estimates MUST be used, and the process MUST be applied consistently from period to period, except where a change would result in better estimates of MARKET VALUE.

INTERNAL RATE OF RETURN (PRIVATE EQUITY) (IRR) is the annualized implied discount rate (effective compounded rate) that equates the present value of all the appropriate cash inflows (PAID-IN CAPITAL, such as drawdowns for net investments) associated with an investment with the sum of the present value of all the appropriate cash outflows (such as DISTRIBUTIONS) accruing from it and the present value of the unrealized residual PORTFOLIO (unliquidated holdings). For an interim cumulative return measurement, any IRR depends on the valuation of the residual assets.

INVESTED CAPITAL (PRIVATE EQUITY) The amount of PAID-IN CAPITAL that has been invested in PORTFOLIO companies.

INVESTMENT ADVISOR (PRIVATE EQUITY) Any individual or institution that supplies investment advice to clients on a per fee basis. The INVESTMENT ADVISOR inherently has no role in the management of the underlying PORTFOLIO companies of a partnership/fund.

INVESTMENT MANAGEMENT FEE The fee payable to the investment management FIRM for the ongoing management of a PORTFOLIO. INVESTMENT MANAGEMENT FEES are typically asset based (percentage of assets), performance based (based on performance relative to a BENCHMARK), or a combination of the two but may take different forms as well.

INVESTMENT MULTIPLE (TVPI MULTIPLE) (PRIVATE EQUITY) The ratio of TOTAL VALUE to PAID-IN-CAPITAL. It represents the TOTAL RETURN of the investment to the original investment not taking into consideration the time invested. TOTAL VALUE can be found by adding the RESIDUAL VALUE and distributed capital together.

LARGE EXTERNAL CASH FLOW The Standards do not contain a specified amount of cash or percentage that is considered to be a LARGE EXTERNAL CASH FLOW. Instead, FIRMS MUST define the COMPOSITE-specific size (amount or percentage) that constitutes a LARGE EXTERNAL CASH FLOW.

LIMITED PARTNER (PRIVATE EQUITY) (LP) an investor in a LIMITED PARTNERSHIP. The GENERAL PARTNER is liable for the actions of the partnership and the LIMITED PARTNERS are generally protected from legal actions and any losses beyond their original investment. The LIMITED PARTNER receives income, capital gains, and tax benefits.

LIMITED PARTNERSHIP (PRIVATE EQUITY) The legal structure used by most venture and PRIVATE EQUITY funds. Usually fixed life investment vehicles. The GENERAL PARTNER or management firm manages the partnership using the policy laid down in a partnership agreement. The agreement also covers terms, fees, structures, and other items agreed between the LIMITED PARTNERS and the GENERAL PARTNER.

MARKET VALUE The current price at which investors buy or sell securities at a given time. [corrected August 2005]

MARKET VALUE (REAL ESTATE)
The most probable price that a property SHOULD bring in a competitive and open market under all conditions requisite to a fair sale, the buyer and seller each acting prudently and knowledgeably, and assuming the price is not affected by undue stimulus. Implicit in this definition is the consummation of a sale as of a specified date and the passing of title from seller to buyer under conditions whereby:

a. Buyer and seller are typically motivated.
b. Both parties are well informed or well advised and each acting in what they consider their own best interests.
c. A reasonable time is allowed for exposure in the open market.
d. Payment is made in terms of currency or in terms of financial arrangements comparable thereto.
e. The price represents the normal consideration for the property sold unaffected by special or creative financing or sales concessions granted by anyone associated with the sale.

MUST
A REQUIRED provision for claiming compliance with the GIPS standards. (See the term "REQUIRE.")

NET-OF-FEES RETURN
The GROSS-OF-FEES RETURN reduced by the INVESTMENT MANAGEMENT FEE.

OPEN-END FUND (PRIVATE EQUITY)
A type of investment fund where the number of investors and the total COMMITTED CAPITAL is not fixed (i.e., open for subscriptions and/or redemptions). (See the term "EVERGREEN FUND.")

OPEN MARKET VALUE (REAL ESTATE)
[corrected January 2006]
An opinion of the best price at which the sale of an interest in the property would have been completed unconditionally for cash consideration on the date of valuation, assuming:

a. a willing seller;
b. that prior to the date of valuation there had been a reasonable period (having regard to the nature of the property and the state of the market) for the proper marketing of the interest, for the agreement of the price and terms, and for the completion of the sale;
c. that the state of the market, level of values, and other circumstances were on any earlier assumed date of exchange of contracts the same as on the date of valuation;
d. that no account is taken of any additional bid by a prospective purchaser with a special interest; and
e. that both parties to the transaction had acted knowledgeably, prudently, and without compulsion.

PAID-IN CAPITAL (PRIVATE EQUITY)
The amount of COMMITTED CAPITAL a LIMITED PARTNER has actually transferred to a venture fund. Also known as the cumulative DRAWDOWN amount.

PIC MULTIPLE (PRIVATE EQUITY)
The ratio of PAID-IN-CAPITAL to COMMITTED CAPITAL. This ratio gives prospective clients information regarding how much of the total commitments has been drawn down.

PORTFOLIO
An individually managed pool of assets. A PORTFOLIO may be a subportfolio, account, or pooled fund.

PRIVATE EQUITY	PRIVATE EQUITY includes, but is not limited to, organizations devoted to VENTURE CAPITAL, leveraged buyouts, consolidations, mezzanine and distressed debt investments, and a variety of hybrids, such as venture leasing and venture factoring.
PROFESSIONALLY DESIGNATED, CERTIFIED, OR LICENSED COMMERCIAL PROPERTY VALUER/APPRAISER (REAL ESTATE)	In Europe, Canada and parts of southeast Asia, the predominant professional designation is that of the Royal Institution of Chartered Surveyors (RICs). In the United States, the professional designation is Member [of the] Appraisal Institute (MAI). In addition, each state regulates REAL ESTATE appraisers, and based on one's experience, body of work, and test results, is then registered, licensed, or certified.
REAL ESTATE	REAL ESTATE Investments include: • Wholly owned or partially owned properties, • Commingled funds, property unit trusts, and insurance company separate accounts, • Unlisted, private placement securities issued by private REAL ESTATE investment trusts (REITs) and REAL ESTATE operating companies (REOCs), and • Equity-oriented debt, such as participating mortgage loans or any private interest in a property where some portion of return to the investor at the time of investment is related to the performance of the underlying REAL ESTATE.
REALIZATION MULTIPLE (PRIVATE EQUITY)	The REALIZATION MULTIPLE (DPI) is calculated by dividing the cumulative DISTRIBUTIONS by the PAID-IN-CAPITAL.
RECOMMEND/ RECOMMENDATION	Suggested provision for claiming compliance with the GIPS standards. A RECOMMENDATION is considered to be best practice but is not a REQUIREMENT. (See the term "SHOULD.")
REQUIRE/ REQUIREMENT	A provision that MUST be followed for compliance with the GIPS standards. (See the term "MUST.")
RESIDUAL VALUE (PRIVATE EQUITY)	The remaining equity that a LIMITED PARTNER has in the fund. (The value of the investments within the fund.) Also can be referred to as ENDING MARKET VALUE or net asset value.
RESIDUAL VALUE TO PAID-IN-CAPITAL (RVPI) (PRIVATE EQUITY)	RESIDUAL VALUE divided by the PAID-IN-CAPITAL.
SETTLEMENT DATE ACCOUNTING	Recognizing the asset or liability on the date when the exchange of cash, securities, and paperwork involved in a transaction is completed. Impact on performance: Between TRADE DATE and SETTLEMENT DATE, an account does not recognize any change between the price of the transaction and the current MARKET VALUE. Instead, on SETTLEMENT DATE, the total difference between the price of the transaction and the current MARKET VALUE is recognized on that day. (See TRADE DATE ACCOUNTING.)
SHOULD	Encouraged (RECOMMENDED) to follow the RECOMMENDATION of the GIPS standards but not REQUIRED. (See the term "RECOMMEND.")

SUPPLEMENTAL Any performance-related information included as part of a compliant performance presentation that supplements or enhances the REQUIRED and/or RECOMMENDED disclosure and presentation provisions of the GIPS standards.

TEMPORARY NEW ACCOUNT A tool that FIRMS can use to remove the effect of significant cash flows on a PORTFOLIO. When a significant cash flow occurs in a portfolio, the FIRM may treat this cash flow as a "TEMPORARY NEW ACCOUNT," allowing the FIRM to implement the mandate of the PORTFOLIO without the impact of the cash flow on the performance of the PORTFOLIO.

TIME-WEIGHTED RATE OF RETURN Calculation that computes period-by-period returns on an investment and removes the effects of EXTERNAL CASH FLOWS, which are generally client-driven, and best reflects the FIRM'S ability to manage assets according to a specified strategy or objective.

TOTAL FIRM ASSETS TOTAL FIRM ASSETS are all assets for which a FIRM has investment management responsibility. TOTAL FIRM ASSETS include assets managed outside the FIRM (e.g., by subadvisors) for which the FIRM has asset allocation authority.

TOTAL RETURN (REAL ESTATE) The change in the MARKET VALUE of the PORTFOLIO, adjusted for all capital expenditures (subtracted), net proceeds from sales (added), and investment income accrued (added) during the measurement period expressed as a percentage of the CAPITAL EMPLOYED in the PORTFOLIO over the measurement period.

TOTAL VALUE (PRIVATE EQUITY) RESIDUAL VALUE of the PORTFOLIO plus distributed capital.

TRADE DATE ACCOUNTING The transaction is reflected in the PORTFOLIO on the date of the purchase or sale, and not on the SETTLEMENT DATE. Recognizing the asset or liability within at least 3 days of the date the transaction is entered into (Trade Date, T+ 1, T+2 or T+3) all satisfy the TRADE DATE ACCOUNTING REQUIREMENT for purposes of the GIPS standards. (See SETTLEMENT DATE ACCOUNTING.)

TRADING EXPENSES The costs of buying or selling a security. These costs typically take the form of brokerage commissions or spreads from either internal or external brokers. CUSTODY FEES charged per transaction SHOULD be considered CUSTODY FEES and not direct transaction costs. Estimated TRADING EXPENSES are not permitted.

TRANSACTION EXPENSES (PRIVATE EQUITY) Include all legal, financial, advisory, and investment banking fees related to buying, selling, restructuring, and recapitalizing PORTFOLIO companies.

VENTURE CAPITAL (PRIVATE EQUITY) Risk capital in the form of equity and/or loan capital that is provided by an investment institution to back a business venture that is expected to grow in value.

VINTAGE YEAR (PRIVATE EQUITY) The year that the VENTURE CAPITAL or PRIVATE EQUITY fund or partnership first draws down or calls capital from its investors.

AUSTRALIA	Performance Analyst Group of Australia
AUSTRIA	Österreichischen Vereinigung für Finanzanalyse und Asset Management und der Vereinigung Österreichischer Investmentgesellschaften
BELGIUM	Belgian Association for Pension Institutions
DENMARK	The Danish Society of Investment Professionals, The Danish Society of Financial Analysts
FRANCE	Société Francaise des Analystes Financiers and Association Francaise de la Gestion Financière
GERMANY	BVI Bundesverband Investment und Asset Management e.V., Deutsche Vereinigung für Finanzanalyse und Asset Management, and German CFA Society
HONG KONG	The Hong Kong Society of Financial Analysts
HUNGARY	Hungarian Society of Investment Professionals
IRELAND	Irish Association of Investment Managers
ITALY	Italian Investment Performance Committee
JAPAN	The Security Analysts Association of Japan
LUXEMBOURG	Association Luxembourgeoise des Fonds d'Investissement and Association Luxembourgeoise des gestionnaires de portefeuilles et analystes financiers
NETHERLANDS	Beroepsvereniging van Beleggingsdeskundigen
NEW ZEALAND	CFA Society of New Zealand
NORWAY	The Norwegian Society of Financial Analysts
POLAND	Polski Komitet Wyników Inwestycyjnych
PORTUGAL	Associação Portuguesa de Analista Financeiros
SINGAPORE	Investment Management Association of Singapore
SPAIN	CFA Spain
SOUTH AFRICA	Investment Management Association of South Africa
SWEDEN	Swedish Society of Financial Analysts
SWITZERLAND	Swiss Bankers Association
UNITED KINGDOM	National Association of Pension Funds Ltd
UNITED STATES AND CANADA	CFA Institute

3. EXPLANATION OF THE PROVISIONS OF THE GIPS STANDARDS AND VERIFICATION

FUNDAMENTALS OF COMPLIANCE — DEFINITION OF THE FIRM REQUIREMENTS

0.A.1 The GIPS standards MUST be applied on a FIRM-wide basis.

Discussion: The GIPS standards provide an ethical framework for the calculation and presentation of the investment performance history of an investment management firm. The definition of the firm is the foundation for firm-wide compliance and creates defined boundaries for determining the assets of the firm. Only investment firms with actual assets under management can claim compliance with the Standards.

A firm must comply with all of the required provisions of the Standards to claim compliance. Compliance cannot be met on a per-composite or per-product basis but can only be met on a firm-wide basis. Once the firm determines its boundaries, all actual, fee-paying, discretionary portfolios that have been within that defined entity at any time during the period for which the firm claims compliance must be placed in firm-defined composites. Composite presentations including the claim of compliance are then created for prospective clients.

In addition to creating composite presentations in compliance with the Standards, the firm must abide by additional requirements when claiming compliance. For example, the firm must document, in writing, the policies and procedures used in establishing and maintaining compliance with the requirements of the Standards.

Cross Reference: Guidance Statement on Definition of the Firm (Section 4-4), Provision 0.A.2, Provision 0.A.3, Provision 0.A.4, Provision 0.A.7, Provision 0.A.15, Provision 0.B.1, Provision 3.A.8, Provision 4.A.1

Application:

1. *Our firm definition includes both equity and fixed-income products. Can we present only our equity products (strategies) in compliance with the Standards?*

No, the claim of compliance is a firm-wide claim declared on the composite presentations and, if the firm chooses, in advertisements. The firm described above has been defined to include both equity and fixed-income products. As such, the firm must make the claim of compliance based on all actual, fee-paying, discretionary portfolios within the firm's defined boundaries—both the equity and the fixed-income products—in composites. Additionally, the firm must ensure it has adhered to all the applicable requirements of the Standards prior to making the claim of compliance.

0.A.2 FIRMS MUST be defined as an investment firm, subsidiary, or division held out to clients or potential clients as a DISTINCT BUSINESS ENTITY.

Discussion: It is the firm's responsibility to ensure that it is fairly and appropriately defined. The Standards recommend that the firm adopt the broadest, most meaningful definition of the firm. The firm's definition will reflect the specific circumstances at each firm and must reflect how the entity (firm) is held out to clients or potential clients as a distinct business entity. A distinct business entity is a unit, division, department, or office that is organizationally and functionally segregated from other units, divisions, departments, or offices, that retains discretion over the assets it manages, and that should have autonomy over the investment decision-making process.

Possible criteria for determining these points include, but are not limited to the following:

- being a legal entity;
- having a distinct market or client type (e.g., institutional, retail, private client, etc.);
- using a separate and distinct investment process.

A firm is permitted to be redefined if the changes within the firm are so significant that it is held out to clients or potential clients as a new firm. The new firm must determine if there is a continuation from the prior firm or if the restructuring is so substantial that it is essentially a new entity. In some cases, a firm definition may change without the firm losing its performance history.

Cross Reference: Guidance Statement on Definition of the Firm (Section 4-4), Provision 0.A.1, Provision 0.A.3, Provision 0.A.5, Provision 0.A.6, Provision 0.A.14, Provision 0.B.1, Provision 4.A.1, Provision 4.A.21, Provision 4.B.1

Application:

Note: Some of the answers below represent only possible solutions to the issues presented based on the information provided. Other solutions may also be possible.

1. *Company A is located in New York and has offices in Los Angeles, Chicago, and Dallas that service its U.S. clients and offices in London, Zurich, and Hong Kong to service its non-U.S. clients. All of the U.S. offices are registered as one investment entity and the non-U.S. offices are each registered with the appropriate national investment regulators. How could Firm A define itself as a firm according to the GIPS standards?*

The GIPS standards encourage companies/entities to adopt the broadest, most meaningful definition of a firm. If possible, Company A should consider defining itself to include the assets managed by all of its offices for the purposes of GIPS compliance. However, Company A could define itself as smaller entities based on whether the different regional branches (e.g., United States, London, Zurich, and Hong Kong) or combination of branches (e.g., London/Zurich or London/Hong Kong) are held out to clients or potential clients as separate entities.

2. *Company B is a multinational investment firm with offices around the world, including in Japan, Australia, the United Kingdom, and the United States. Although all offices are part of the global parent, each office is registered with the appropriate national regulatory authority. Company B (Japan) is ready to comply with the GIPS standards. However, Company B (U.S.) cannot claim compliance at this time. Can Company B (Japan) claim compliance with the GIPS standards?*

Company B (Japan) may be able to claim compliance with the GIPS standards if it can be defined as a separate "firm" for the purposes of the GIPS standards, even though it is part of a multinational firm. Company B (Japan) can define itself as a firm if it is held out to clients or potential clients as a distinct business entity. Company B (Japan) must include on its presentations how the firm is defined. This definition should clearly state that the composite returns shown are those of Company B (Japan) so that no one could assume that any other part of Company B is claiming compliance (see Provision 4.A.1). Company B (Japan) would also be encouraged to disclose that the defined firm is a subsidiary of a larger parent company.

3. *Company C manages money for both retail and institutional clients. There are two autonomous group within Company C: "Company C Institutional Investment Management," which manages institutional assets, and "Company C Retail Investors," which manages retail assets. How should Company C define itself as a firm to comply with the GIPS standards?*

The GIPS standards encourage firms to adopt the broadest, most meaningful definition of a firm. Company C should consider defining itself to include the assets managed by both the institutional entity and the retail entity for the purposes of claiming compliance with the GIPS standards. However, Company C could define the two autonomous entities as separate firms if each subsidiary is held out to clients and potential clients as a distinct business unit.

4. *Company D has offices in London and Edinburgh. Although the individual investment managers in each office make the investment decisions, all the research and security trading are based in London. The Edinburgh office wants to define itself as a firm, "Firm D: Edinburgh," and claim compliance with the GIPS standards. Can that office define itself as a firm separate from the rest of Company D and claim compliance with the GIPS standards?*

If the Edinburgh office of Company D is not held out to clients or potential clients as a separate entity, the Edinburgh office cannot define itself as a firm for the purposes of the GIPS standards.

0.A.3 TOTAL FIRM ASSETS MUST be the aggregate of the MARKET VALUE of all discretionary and nondiscretionary assets under management within the defined FIRM. This includes both fee-paying and non-fee-paying assets.

Discussion: Total firm assets:

- include assets for which a firm has either conditional or unconditional authority to trade the assets;
- include fee-paying assets (where a fee is payable to the investment management firm for the ongoing management of a portfolio's assets) and non-fee-paying assets (where no fee is payable to the investment management firm for the ongoing management of a portfolio's assets);
- include assets managed outside the firm (e.g., by subadvisors) for which the firm has asset allocation (assignment) authority (i.e., the firm has discretion over the selection of the subadvisor);
- are equal to the market value of all discretionary and nondiscretionary assets under management within the defined firm;
- exclude assets within advisory-only relationships;
- include cash and cash equivalents (substitutes).

Assets to which the Standards cannot be applied (e.g., museum pieces and art) are not to be considered by firms when claiming compliance and are not to be included in total firm assets.

Cross Reference: Guidance Statement on Definition of the Firm (Section 4-4), Provision 0.A.1, Provision 0.A.2, Provision 0.A.4, Provision 1.A.2, Provision 3.A.1, Provision 3.A.8, Provision 4.A.1, Provision 5.A.1

Application:

1. *Firm A has the following assets under management. Under the GIPS standards, which of these assets are to be included in the definition of "total firm assets" and disclosed?*

Asset	Included?	Reason
Discretionary Assets in all asset classes: Firm has unconditional trading authority to implement its strategy	Yes	Firm controls investment decisions and the Standards can be applied.
Nondiscretionary Assets in all asset classes: Firm has conditional trading authority; strategy implementation restricted	Yes	Client-imposed restrictions result in firm having limited control of investment decisions.
Assets within advisory-only client relationships	No	Firm has no control of implementation of investment decisions and no trading authority for the assets.

Real Estate Assets	Yes	Assets can be valued according to real estate provisions.
Venture capital and private equity assets	Yes	Assets can be valued according to private equity provisions.
Assets directed to a subadvisor by the firm	Yes	Firm retains investment authority and discretion of subadvisor selection.
Assets directed to a subadvisor by client	No	Firm does not select the subadvisor and does not retain discretion or investment authority of assets.
Non-fee-paying assets	Yes	Firm controls investment decisions and the Standards can be applied.
Overlay Assets: Firm manages underlying portfolio and overlay	Yes	Underlying portfolio and overlay assets are included in firm assets.
Overlay Assets: Firm does not manage underlying portfolio; only implements overlay	Yes	Underlying portfolio is not included in firm assets; amount allocated to implement overlay strategy included in firm assets.
Products to which the Standards do not apply (e.g., pieces of art)	No	Varies. For example, for some assets, the market value is not determinable; other assets are not within the domain of investment management, etc.

2. *We do not include non-fee-paying portfolios in our composites. Do we have to include non-fee- paying portfolios in our firm assets?*

Yes, both fee-paying and non-fee-paying portfolios must be included in total firm assets.

3. *A client hires Manager A to implement a tactical asset allocation futures overlay on a $100 million portfolio managed by another firm. Manager A is given $10 million to implement the overlay strategy. What must Manager A report as firm assets?*

Manager A is required to include the $10 million in the total firm assets; the firm may choose to also report the $100 million separately as overlay assets.

4. *How do we determine what is considered a non-fee-paying portfolio?*

If a portfolio pays no management fee, it is considered a non-fee-paying portfolio. Some firms may manage portfolios that have a minimal management fee that is meant to cover operating or transaction costs. If a portfolio has a very minor management fee that is not representative of a management fee a client portfolio would pay, the firm should consider such portfolios as non-fee-paying portfolios.

5. *An investment management firm has a Euro-zone fixed-income composite that contains the following three portfolios:*

   1. *A fund that is invested in European bonds with net assets of 20.*
   2. *A fund that is invested in bonds of one country of the Euro-zone with net assets of 30.*
   3. *A private portfolio invested entirely in the two above-mentioned funds. Net assets of this portfolio are 10.*

   a. *Is it correct to say that the number of portfolios of the composite described above is three?*
   b. *Is it correct to say that the amount of assets in the composite is 20 + 30 + 10 = 60?*
   c. *Is it correct to say that the firm's total assets are 50 or that the firm's total assets are 60 (in this case, the firm only owns that one composite)?*

The question is that of eliminating double counting assets. Is it correct to say that showing the above composite's asset level as 60 is not misleading to the reader? (The firm will also disclose what percent the composite represents of the firm's assets, therefore, showing 110 percent of the firm's assets means that some assets are counted more than once. That is, the management of the private portfolio above is not geared toward choosing the securities in the portfolio but rather toward realizing the proper asset allocation between both funds.)

The GIPS standards are based on the principles of fair representation and full disclosure. Double counting assets would not fairly represent the firm's assets. The composite would have 3 portfolios and have net assets of 50. If there are no other assets within the firm, then total firm assets would be 50.

0.A.4 FIRMS MUST include the performance of assets assigned to a subadvisor in a COMPOSITE provided the FIRM has discretion over the selection of the subadvisor.

Discussion: Some firms utilize a subadvisor to manage part or all of a particular strategy. For example, if a firm specializes in managing equities, it might hire a subadvisor to manage the fixed-income portion of its balanced portfolios.

If a firm has discretion over the selection of the subadvisor (i.e., can hire and/or fire), the firm must claim the subadvisor's performance as part of its performance history and include the assets in the firm's total assets. Because the subadvisor has discretion over the actual investment of the assets and the firm has discretion over the selection of the subadvisor, both the firm and the subadvisor are able to claim the performance of the assets as their own. The firm is able to claim this performance because the subadvised portion of the portfolio is essentially viewed as an asset (similar to purchasing a mutual fund within the portfolio) and the firm must be held responsible for its decision to utilize a subadvisor. The firm can only include the subadvisor's performance record relevant to those assets assigned by the firm. If a firm does not have discretion over subadvisor selection, it must not include the subadvisor's performance in its performance history and must not include the assets in total firm or composite assets.

Firms must disclose the use of subadvisors for periods beginning 1 January 2006.

Cross Reference: Guidance Statement on Definition of the Firm (Section 4-4), Provision 0.A.1, Provision 0.A.3, Provision 3.A.8, Provision 4.A.18

0.A.5 Changes in a FIRM'S organization are not permitted to lead to alteration of historical COMPOSITE results.

Discussion: Once the boundaries for the firm definition have been determined, the historical composite performance remains as part of the firm's history until those boundaries are redefined. Changes in legal status, investment style, or personnel are not valid reasons for redefining the firm, unless the changes are such that the firm is held out to clients or potential clients in a significantly different way. A simple name change is not sufficient reason to redefine the firm and restart the performance record. In some cases, a firm definition may change without the firm losing its performance history. Please refer to the Guidance Statement on Performance Record Portability for related guidance.

Firms are permitted to be redefined if the changes within the firm are so significant that it is held out to clients or potential clients as a new firm. The new firm must determine if there is a continuation from the prior firm or if the restructuring is so substantial that it is essentially a new firm.

Cross Reference: Guidance Statement on Definition of the Firm (Section 4-4), Guidance Statement on Performance Record Portability (Section 4-7), Provision 0.A.2, Provision 4.A.1, Provision 4.A.19, Provision 4.A.21, Provision 5.A.4

Application:

1. *Firm A changed its legal status from a partnership to a corporation. As of what date should the new firm start reporting performance?*

A change in legal status typically will not result in a new firm for purposes of compliance with the Standards. If the boundaries for Firm A remain unchanged, the performance history remains unchanged. If, however, the change in legal status results in new boundaries for Firm A, the firm will disclose the date and reason for the redefinition (see Provision 4.A.21). The firm must also review Provision 5.A.4 for applicability.

FUNDAMENTALS OF COMPLIANCE — DOCUMENT POLICIES AND PROCEDURES REQUIREMENTS

0.A.6 FIRMS MUST document, in writing, their policies and procedures used in establishing and maintaining compliance with all the applicable REQUIREMENTS of the GIPS standards.

Discussion: Written policies and procedures are essential to implementing adequate business controls on all stages of the investment performance process—from data input to presentation material—to ensure the validity of compliance claims. The Standards delineate a number of policies firms are to establish. A firm must document all the policies and procedures it follows for meeting the requirements of the GIPS standards. Items that should be considered for documentation include but are not limited to the following:

- criteria used to define the firm;
- criteria for defining discretion;
- valuation policies;
- calculation methodologies;
- how the firm handles large cash flows;
- how it handles new and terminated portfolios;
- policies for using a minimum portfolio size;
- composite definitions.

A complete checklist of policies and procedures required for compliance with the Standards does not exist, and will likely be different for each firm. However, a basic discussion of minimally expected documented policies and procedures can be found in the Verification section of the Standards.

Cross Reference: Verification (Section 3-9), Provision 0.A.15, Provision 4.A.17

FUNDAMENTALS OF COMPLIANCE — CLAIM OF COMPLIANCE REQUIREMENTS

0.A.7 Once a FIRM has met all the REQUIRED elements of the GIPS standards, the FIRM MUST use the following compliance statement to indicate that the FIRM is in compliance with the GIPS standards:

"[Insert name of FIRM] has prepared and presented this report in compliance with the Global Investment Performance Standards (GIPS®)."

Discussion: Only investment management firms with actual assets under management can claim compliance with the GIPS standards. Plan sponsors using third-party investment managers, consultants, and software vendors cannot make the claim of compliance unless they manage actual, discretionary investment assets. These groups are encouraged to endorse the Standards. Plan sponsors may require that third-party investment managers of the Plan's assets comply with the Standards. Software firms can state that their product helps or assists with the compliance process, but no software product can itself claim compliance (i.e., software cannot comply with the Standards).

To claim compliance, a firm must meet all the requirements of the GIPS standards on a firm-wide basis, as well as abide by all interpretations and guidance issued. Firms are also strongly encouraged to follow all recommended provisions of the Standards.

Strict adherence to the basic requirements of the Standards does not necessarily guarantee fair and adequate performance reporting. The requirements of the GIPS standards do not cover the specific situations of every firm. In preparing performance reports, firms must keep in mind the spirit and objectives of the Standards: fair representation and full disclosure. Meeting the intent of the Standards will likely require actions beyond those that simply meet the minimum requirements. Furthermore, compliance with the Standards also requires adherence to all applicable laws and regulations.

A firm meeting all the requirements MUST use the following "Compliance Statement" on its composite presentations to indicate that the firm is in compliance with the GIPS standards:

[Insert name of firm] has prepared and presented this report in compliance with the Global Investment Performance Standards (GIPS®).

Consultant questionnaires often require managers to fill in quarterly performance charts. The questionnaires then ask the manager to indicate whether or not the numbers presented in the chart have been prepared in accordance with the GIPS standards. Questions regarding whether returns "are prepared" in compliance with the Standards demonstrate a misunderstanding of the meaning of compliance. However, if the performance information used to answer a questionnaire is from a GIPS-compliant presentation (or an update to the presentation), the firm can indicate the information provided is in compliance. The firm must provide a full presentation that satisfies the requirements of the Standards to the consultant at the time of completing the initial questionnaire and, at a minimum, every 12 months thereafter.

Enforcement: CFA Institute (owner of these marks) may take appropriate action against any firm that misuses the mark "GIPS®" or the claim of compliance statement, including false claims of compliance with the GIPS standards.

CFA Institute members, CFA charterholders, and CFA candidates who misuse the term "GIPS" or the claim of compliance statement, misrepresent their performance history or the performance history of their firm, or falsely claim compliance with the Standards are also subject to disciplinary sanctions under the CFA Institute Code of Ethics and Standards of Professional Conduct. Possible disciplinary sanctions include public censure, suspension of membership, and revocation of the CFA designation.

Regulators with jurisdiction over firms claiming compliance with the Standards may also issue sanctions if they deem false claims of compliance as misrepresentations.

Cross Reference: Provision 0.A.1, Provision 0.A.8, Provision 0.A.9, Provision 0.A.10, Provision 0.A.15

0.A.8 If the FIRM does not meet all the REQUIREMENTS of the GIPS standards, the FIRM cannot represent that it is "in compliance with the Global Investment Performance Standards except for. . ."

Discussion: When the firm claims compliance with the GIPS standards, it is indicating that all the applicable requirements of the Standards have been met on a firm-wide basis. Either all the applicable required provisions of the Standards have been met and the firm can claim compliance, or all the applicable required provisions of the Standards have *not* been met and the firm may not claim compliance with the GIPS standards.

Cross Reference: Provision 0.A.1, Provision 0.A.7, Provision 0.A.15

0.A.9 Statements referring to the calculation methodology used in a COMPOSITE presentation as being "in accordance [or compliance] with the Global Investment Performance Standards" are prohibited.

Discussion: Compliance can only be achieved by the firm when it has met all the applicable required provisions of the Standards on a firm-wide basis. Compliance with the Standards involves more than just the use of a calculation methodology. To avoid any confusion, references to the GIPS standards should not be used in the context of reporting performance or performance presentations when the firm is not in compliance with the Standards.

Cross Reference: Provision 0.A.1, Provision 0.A.7, Provision 0.A.15

0.A.10 Statements referring to the performance of a single, existing client as being "calculated in accordance with the Global Investment Performance Standards" are prohibited except when a GIPS-compliant FIRM reports the performance of an individual account to the existing client.

Discussion: The Standards do not specifically address how an investment firm must report to its existing clients the performance of their portfolios. The Standards provide an ethical framework for the calculation and presentation of the investment performance history of an investment management firm, allowing clients, prospective clients, and consultants the best opportunity to fairly evaluate the past performance of the firm.

If a firm that claims compliance with the GIPS standards decides to report to an existing client the return of their portfolio, the firm may note on the existing client's performance report that the return was calculated in accordance with the Global Investment Performance Standards (if the statement is true).

Cross Reference: Provision 0.A.1, Provision 0.A.7, Provision 0.A.15

FUNDAMENTALS OF COMPLIANCE — FIRM FUNDAMENTAL RESPONSIBILITIES REQUIREMENTS

0.A.11 FIRMS MUST make every reasonable effort to provide a compliant presentation to all prospective clients. That is, FIRMS cannot choose to whom they want to present compliant performance. (As long as a prospective client has received a compliant presentation within the previous 12 months, the FIRM has met this REQUIREMENT.)

Discussion: Once a firm claims compliance with the GIPS standards, it must make every reasonable effort to provide all prospective clients with a presentation that complies with all the applicable requirements of the Standards; the firm may not choose to whom to present performance in compliance with the Standards. It is up to the firm to determine how it defines prospective client.

This requirement does not preclude the firm from showing additional and/or supplemental information to help the prospective client interpret the performance information. Instead, this requirement ensures that once a firm represents to the investing public that it complies with the GIPS standards, it shows all prospective clients an appropriate compliant presentation.

Provided the firm has given a compliant presentation to a prospective client within the past 12 months, the firm may present other information that does not meet the requirements of the GIPS standards. Information provided by firms claiming compliance with the Standards should be fairly presented and not be misleading.

If the firm does not have an appropriate composite to present to a prospective client, the firm must disclose that it does not currently manage the specific style or strategy appropriate for the prospective client. The firm must be able to clearly demonstrate the strategies and investment products the firm currently manages and must make a list and description of all firm composites available to the prospective client. The firm is not prohibited from providing any information the prospective client specifically requests. Also, supplemental information can always be provided in addition to the firm's existing composites.

Cross Reference: Provision 0.A.12, Provision 0.A.13, Appendix A of the GIPS standards

---

0.A.12 FIRMS MUST provide a COMPOSITE list and COMPOSITE DESCRIPTION to any prospective client that makes such a request (a sample list and COMPOSITE DESCRIPTION are included in Appendix B). FIRMS MUST list "discontinued" COMPOSITES on the FIRM'S list of COMPOSITES for at least 5 years after discontinuation.

Discussion: Provision 4.A.2 requires that firms must disclose (on their composite presentations) the availability of a complete list and description of all of the firm's composites; the list must be available to prospective clients and provided upon request.

In addition to the list of the composites, the description of each composite must be included. The description, which must also be disclosed on each composite presentation (see Provision 4.A.20), is general information regarding the strategy of the composite. The description may be more abbreviated than the full (complete) composite definition, but it must include all salient features of the composite.

Firms must include "discontinued" composites on the firm's list of composites for at least five years after discontinuation.

Cross Reference: Provision 0.A.11, Provision 0.A.13, Provision 4.A.2, Provision 4.A.20, Appendix B of the GIPS standards

Application:

1. *Our firm has five terminated composites on our list and description of composites. GIPS provision 0.A.13 requires the firm to provide a compliant presentation for any composite on the list, upon request. Does that include terminated composites?*

Yes. If requested, a firm must provide a compliant presentation for a terminated composite on the list. One objective of the GIPS standards is to ensure the fair representation of a firm's investment performance track record. This includes not only currently managed strategies but also those that the firm previously maintained for at least the past five years.

0.A.13 FIRMS MUST provide a compliant presentation for any COMPOSITE listed on the FIRM'S list and a COMPOSITE DESCRIPTION to any prospective client that makes such a request.

Discussion: For any composite on the firm's list of composites, a presentation that complies with the Standards must be provided to any prospective client that makes such a request. It is up to the firm to determine how it defines prospective client. Firms should not market a composite to a prospective client who has assets to invest which are less than the composite's minimum asset level.

Cross Reference: Provision 0.A.11, Provision 0.A.12, Provision 3.B.3, Provision 4.A.2, Provision 4.A.20, Appendix A of the GIPS standards

0.A.14 When the FIRM jointly markets with other FIRMS, the FIRM claiming compliance with the GIPS standards MUST be sure that it is clearly defined and separate relative to any other FIRMS being marketed and that it is clear which FIRM is claiming compliance.

Discussion: In order to avoid confusion when jointly marketing with other firms, the firm claiming compliance must be sure that it is clearly defined relative to the other firms being marketed and that it is apparent which firm is claiming compliance.

Cross Reference: Guidance Statement on Definition of the Firm (Section 4-4), Provision 0.A.2, Provision 0.B.1, Provision 4.B.1

0.A.15 FIRMS are encouraged to comply with the RECOMMENDATIONS and MUST comply with all applicable REQUIREMENTS of the GIPS standards, including any updates, reports, guidance statements, interpretations, or clarifications published by CFA Institute and the Investment Performance Council, which will be made available via the CFA Institute website (www.cfainstitute.org) as well as the *GIPS Handbook*.

Discussion: The GIPS standards are ethical standards for investment performance presentation to ensure fair representation and full disclosure of a firm's performance. The GIPS standards consist of provisions that firms are required to follow in order to claim compliance. Firms are encouraged to adopt the recommended provisions to achieve best practice in performance presentation. Certain recommended elements in the GIPS standards may become requirements in the future.

The GIPS standards must be applied with the objectives of full disclosure and fair representation of investment performance. Meeting the objectives of full disclosure and fair representation will likely require more than compliance with the minimum requirements of the GIPS standards. If an investment firm applies the GIPS standards in a performance situation that is not addressed specifically by the Standards or is open to interpretation, disclosures other than those required by the GIPS standards may be necessary. To fully explain the performance included in a presentation, firms are encouraged to present all relevant additional information and supplemental information.

All requirements, clarifications, updated information, and guidance must be adhered to when determining a firm's claim of compliance and will be made available via the *GIPS Handbook* and the CFA Institute website (www.cfainstitute.org).

Cross Reference: Provision 0.A.1, Provision 0.A.6, Provision 0.A.8

FUNDAMENTALS OF COMPLIANCE — DEFINITION OF THE FIRM RECOMMENDATIONS

0.B.1 FIRMS are encouraged to adopt the broadest, most meaningful definition of the FIRM. The scope of this definition SHOULD include all geographical (country, regional, etc.) offices operating under the same brand name regardless of the actual name of the individual investment management company.

Discussion: Possible criteria to consider when defining the firm in the broadest, most meaningful manner should include, but are not limited to:

- All offices operating under the same brand name (e.g., XYZ Asset Management),
- Other names resulting from mergers, acquisitions, etc., trading under a different name for branding purposes,
- Financial service holding companies defined as one global firm with multiple brands, several legal entities, multiple offices, investment teams, and investment strategies,
- An investment management firm with one brand, but multiple strategies and investment teams,
- All offices trading under a globally recognizable trading name with regional/country specific additions (e.g., XYZ Asset Management Asia),
- Investment management firms in most countries must register with one or more governmental agencies or regulators. The GIPS standards recognize a regulatory registration as a possible definition of a firm for purposes of compliance, but also require firms consider the manner in which they are holding themselves out to the public when determining the firm definition.

Cross Reference: Guidance Statement on Definition of the Firm (Section 4-4), Provision 0.A.1, Provision 0.A.2, Provision 0.A.3, Provision 0.A.14, Provision 4.A.1

Application:

1. *ABC Global Asset Management has offices in the United States, the United Kingdom, and Japan. Because of different record-keeping policies, the U.S. firm was able to claim compliance with the GIPS standards in 1996, the U.K. firm was able to claim compliance with the GIPS standards in 1999, and the Japanese firm was able to claim compliance with the GIPS standards in 2002. The entire parent organization now wants to redefine the firm globally (ABC Global Asset Management) to claim compliance with the GIPS standards and re-state five years of combined history. How should they do this?*

ABC Global Asset Management would define a new firm for purposes of the GIPS standards that would include all of its global offices. Considering all of its various strategies, the newly defined global firm will then combine portfolios into composites on a global scale, rather than according to the previously defined composites based on geographic office.

FUNDAMENTALS OF COMPLIANCE — VERIFICATION RECOMMENDATIONS

0.B.2 FIRMS are encouraged to undertake the verification process, defined as the review of a FIRM'S performance measurement processes and procedures by an independent third-party verifier. A single verification report is issued in respect to the whole FIRM; verification cannot be carried out for a single COMPOSITE. The primary purpose of verification is to establish that a FIRM claiming compliance with the GIPS standards has adhered to the Standards.

Discussion: The primary purpose of verification is to establish that a firm claiming compliance with the GIPS standards has adhered to the Standards. Verification will also increase the understanding and professionalism of performance measurement teams and consistency of presentation of performance results.

The verification procedures attempt to strike a balance between ensuring the quality, accuracy, and relevance of performance presentations and minimizing the cost to firms of independent review of performance results. Firms should assess the benefits of improved internal processes and procedures, which are as significant as the marketing advantages of verification. The verification procedures were developed with the goal of encouraging broad acceptance of verification.

Verification adds value and credibility to the claim of compliance. Today, verification is strongly encouraged and is expected to become mandatory in the future. The expectation is that mandatory verification will be implemented by 2010. Leading up to 2010, all aspects of the mandatory verification debate will be evaluated, and the industry will be provided sufficient time to implement any changes.

Cross Reference: Verification (Section 3-9), Provision 0.B.3, Provision 4.B.3

0.B.3 FIRMS that have been verified are encouraged to add a disclosure to COMPOSITE presentations or advertisements stating that the FIRM has been verified. FIRMS MUST disclose the periods of verification if the COMPOSITE presentation includes results for periods that have not been subject to FIRM-wide verification. The verification disclosure language SHOULD read:

"[Insert name of FIRM] has been verified for the periods [insert dates] by [name of verifier]. A copy of the verification report is available upon request."

Cross Reference: Verification (Section 3-9), Provision 0.B.2, Provision 4.B.3

INPUT DATA – REQUIREMENTS

1.A.1 All data and information necessary to support a FIRM'S performance presentation and to perform the REQUIRED calculations MUST be captured and maintained.

Discussion: A fundamental principle of the GIPS standards is the need for firms to be able to ensure the validity of their claim of compliance if questioned by a client, potential client, verifier, or regulator. This requirement reflects that principle. Firms must be able to recalculate their performance history as well as other required information (such as composite dispersion) or validate data and information contained in their performance presentations.

The GIPS standards require that the data be captured for all periods for which performance is presented. Thus, whether a firm presents performance for 5 years, 10 years, or performance since inception, the firm must have the underlying data necessary to recreate the performance presentation of all their composites for those periods. This requirement mirrors the regulatory requirements of many countries. To meet this requirement, the firm must determine which records would suffice and maintain these records for all portfolios/composites for each period of performance presented. The firm must have established policies and procedures for capturing and maintaining the data and information used in its performance presentations.

Cross Reference: Guidance Statement on Performance Record Portability (Section 4-7), Provision 5.A.4

Application:

1. *Firm A claims compliance with the GIPS standards. It maintains hard copies of the records supporting compliance for three years and discards all records older than three years in an effort to save office space. The performance reported on all its composite presentations shows five years of history. Is the firm in compliance with the GIPS standards?*

No. A firm must maintain data necessary to support a firm's claim of compliance. Because Firm A presents 5 years of performance history, it must maintain the records to support the firm's 5-year history and all other relevant data on the firm's composite presentations. Because the Standards require firms to build a 10-year performance history, the firm must continue to maintain the records to support the firm's eventual 10-year performance history.

2. *Firm B does not have the information necessary to substantiate the required calculations that would support the firm's performance record prior to the date of a fire in its storage facility that destroyed its records and electronic back-up systems. Is the firm precluded from claiming compliance with the GIPS standards?*

The GIPS standards require firms to present, at a minimum, five years of annual investment performance that is compliant with the GIPS standards. If any year prior to the date of the fire is required to be included in the presentation to meet the initial five-year requirement, as long as a firm can recapture the information that would support its performance record for those years, the firm could claim compliance and include performance for years prior to the date of the fire in its performance presentations. For instance, Firm B could reconstruct the information necessary by obtaining the information from clients, custodians, consultants, verifiers, or any other party outside the firm that might have duplicate copies of those records. If the firm were able to collect data to support a five-year record, then it would be able to claim compliance with the GIPS standards, provided all the other requirements of the Standards are also met.

1.A.2 PORTFOLIO valuations MUST be based on MARKET VALUES (not cost basis or book values).

Discussion: The Standards require the use of market values (defined as the current price at which investors buy or sell securities at a given time) in order to best identify the fair economic value of the firm's portfolios. In cases of frequently traded securities, standardized pricing quotations must be used and must be supportable. In the case of thinly traded securities, the firm may use a reasonable method for valuation as long as the method is consistently applied. Amortization or accretion valuation methods for cash and cash-equivalent positions are permitted as long as that valuation method reasonably approximates market value. The GIPS standards also recommend that firms disclose when a change in calculation methodology or valuation source results in a material impact on the performance of a composite return.

Private equity assets have separate valuation guidelines that must be followed. Please see the Private Equity Valuation Principles in Appendix D of the GIPS standards.

Cross Reference: Guidance Statement on Calculation Methodology (Section 4-1); Provision 0.A.3, Provision 1.A.3, Provision 1.A.4, Provision 1.A.6, Provision 1.B.1, Provision 4.B.2

Application:

1. *Firm B has several portfolios invested in emerging market debt and other thinly traded securities. What is a reasonable method for valuation of these securities?*

Firm B must determine a reasonable valuation method for the thinly traded securities held in its portfolios. One example of a "reasonable method" is to seek out three separate bids from three unaffiliated brokers, average those three prices, and consider this average to be a fair and acceptable representation of the market value. The valuation method policy developed by the firm must be applied consistently over time to ensure relatively consistent asset valuations.

2. *Should we exclude local bank certificates of deposit (CDs) from total firm assets and performance calculations because they can not be priced on a market value basis (i.e., these local bank nonbrokered CDs are currently priced at cost)?*

If they are held as assets in actual, fee-paying discretionary portfolios defined within the firm, local bank CDs must be included in all appropriate calculations. The value for which the bank would redeem the CD on the valuation date, which would include principal and interest earned to date, would be the market value for the asset (a reasonable estimate of the current value of assets if they were sold on that date to a willing buyer). If the bank has a penalty for early withdrawal of funds, the penalty would not be included in the valuation, unless the funds were actually withdrawn and the penalty incurred.

1.A.3 For periods prior to 1 January 2001, PORTFOLIOS MUST be valued at least quarterly. For periods between 1 January 2001 and 1 January 2010, PORTFOLIOS MUST be valued at least monthly. For periods beginning 1 January 2010, FIRMS MUST value PORTFOLIOS on the date of all LARGE EXTERNAL CASH FLOWS.

Discussion: In order to improve the accuracy of time-weighted performance calculations, the GIPS standards have gradually increased the minimum required frequency of portfolio valuation from quarterly, to monthly, to the date of any large external cash flow in 2010. A large external cash flow, which is to be defined by the firm for each composite, is the level at which a client-initiated external flow of cash and/or securities into or out of a portfolio is likely to distort performance if the portfolio is not revalued. Firms must define the amount in terms of (1) the value of the cash/asset flow (or in terms of a percentage of portfolio or composite assets) and (2) whether it is a single flow or an aggregate of a number of flows within a stated period of time.

Private equity assets have separate valuation guidelines that must be followed. Please see the Private Equity Valuation Principles in Appendix D of the GIPS standards.

Real estate assets have additional guidelines on valuation frequency that must be followed. Please see Provisions 6.A.1 and 6.A.2 of the GIPS standards.

Cross Reference: Guidance Statement on Calculation Methodology (Section 4-1), Provision 1.A.2, Provision 1.A.4, Provision 1.A.7, Provision 1.B.3, Provision 2.A.2, Provision 2.A.6, Provision 2.B.2, Provision 2.B.3, Provision 4.A.25

Application:

1. *Firm A has been in existence since 1995. The firm has calculated its performance using quarterly valuations of portfolios. In January 2002, the firm seeks to show history since its inception that meets the requirements of the GIPS standards. Does it have to recreate its performance history because it does not meet the monthly valuation requirement?*

Assuming it has satisfied all the other required provisions, Firm A can show its history from 1995 through 2000 using its original performance calculations for its portfolios valued on a quarterly basis. However, the firm is required to use monthly valuations for periods beginning 1 January 2001. Therefore to claim compliance, Firm A must revalue its portfolios on a monthly basis and recalculate the performance for all periods on or after 1 January 2001.

1.A.4 For periods beginning 1 January 2010, FIRMS MUST value PORTFOLIOS as of the calendar month-end or the last business day of the month.

Discussion: Consistency in monthly portfolio valuation dates will result in improved comparability of data, especially when firms choose to present year-to-date composite data or monthly or quarterly data as Additional Information.

Cross Reference: Guidance Statement on Calculation Methodology (Section 4-1), Provision 1.A.2, Provision 1.A.3, Provision 1.A.7, Provision 1.B.3, Provision 2.A.6, Provision 2.B.2, Provision 4.A.25

Application:

1. *Our firm values portfolios as of the last Friday of the month. Can this methodology be continued?*

Yes, firms may value portfolios as of the last Friday of a month through 2009, with appropriate disclosure. (See Provision 4.A.25). Valuation methodologies should be applied consistently.

1.A.5 For periods beginning 1 January 2005, FIRMS MUST use TRADE DATE ACCOUNTING.

Discussion: For the purposes of the GIPS standards, trade-date accounting is defined as "recognizing the asset or liability on the date the transaction is entered into." Trade-date accounting determines the correct economic value of the portfolio assets as of the transaction date. Requiring trade-date accounting ensures there is not a significant lag between trade execution and when the trade is reflected in the performance of a portfolio. When using trade-date accounting, the change in market value will be reflected for each valuation between trade date and settlement date.

Recognizing the asset or liability within at least three days of the date the transaction is entered into (Trade Date, T + 1, T + 2, or T + 3) will satisfy the trade-date accounting requirement for purposes of the GIPS standards. In some markets for some assets, the trade date and the settlement date (defined as "recognizing the asset or liability on the date in which the exchange of cash, securities, and paperwork involved in a transaction is completed") may coincide.

Cross Reference: Guidance Statement on Calculation Methodology (Section 4-1)

Application:

1. *Firm B claims compliance with GIPS but uses settlement-date accounting. Beginning 1 January 2005, what will Firm B have to do to remain in compliance with the Standards?*

To remain in compliance with the Standards, Firm B must discontinue its practice of using settlement-date accounting and begin using trade-date accounting (Trade Date, T + 1, T + 2, or T + 3) for periods beginning 1 January 2005. However, Firm B is not required to go back and recalculate the historical performance of its composites for periods prior to 1 January 2005. As with any requirement that becomes effective for periods after a specified date, historic composite returns calculated and presented in compliance with the GIPS standards do not have to be recalculated and presented in conformance with a newly implemented provision, unless specifically stated.

When converting from settlement-date valuations to trade-date valuations, firms must be sure that the ending market value for the last settlement-date period is used as the beginning market value for the first trade-date period (in the absence of cash flows). For example, assume the following:

29 July – Client makes initial deposit of $100.
30 July – Firm buys one share of XYZ stock at $75 for settlement on 2 August, and the remaining $25 is held in cash. XYZ closes the day at $76.
31 July – XYZ closes at $76.50.
1 August – XYZ closes at $77.
2 August – XYZ closes at $78.

The market value of the portfolio for each day could be calculated as follows:

	Trade-Date Basis	Settlement-Date Basis
29 July	$100.00	$100.00
30 July	$101.00	$100.00
31 July	$101.50	$100.00
1 August	$102.00	$100.00
2 August	$103.00	$103.00

The return for the entire period is:

$$R = (103 - 100)/100 = 3\%.$$

This result is true regardless of the accounting methodology used (i.e., trade-date or settlement-date).

Assume that the firm is switching from settlement-date to trade-date valuations as of the close of business on 31 July. In order for the performance to be correct, when the two subperiods are geometrically linked, the return must equal 3 percent.

In this example, the settlement-date values are used to calculate the return for July, which produces a return of 0 percent.

In order to arrive at the correct return when the two subperiods are geometrically linked, the return for August must be calculated by using the settlement-date beginning market value and the trade-date ending market value. This produces a return of

$$R = (103 - 100)/100 = 3\%.$$

Geometrically linking the two subperiods generates the correct return of

$$R = ((1 + 0\%) \times (1 + 3\%)) - 1 = 3\%.$$

Therefore, the correct way for firms to switch from settlement-date to trade-date is to use the settlement-date beginning value and the trade-date ending value for the first month in which they use the new methodology.

2. *Mutual funds in the United States function on a T + 1 schedule. Therefore, if a bond is purchased on 31 January, it is not included in the Net Asset Value (NAV) calculation for 31 January. It is included in the NAV calculation 1 February. Does the requirement for trade-date accounting mean that firms managing mutual funds must account for the funds in their own portfolio management software systems in order to base performance on trade-date net assets as opposed to NAV's (T + 1) in order to remain compliant with the GIPS standards?*

A fund recognizing the bond purchase in the portfolio at trade date + 1 day will satisfy the requirements of the GIPS standards. For the purposes of compliance with the GIPS standards, portfolios are considered to satisfy the trade-date accounting requirement provided that transactions are recorded and recognized consistently and within normal market practice—typically, a period between trade date and up to three days after trade date (T + 3).

3. *When should we record an incoming cash flow to a portfolio: on the date we are notified the cash is incoming or the date that we actually receive the funds? In our situation, we are notified of incoming funds in order to allow us to place trades so that the incoming funds are fully invested when the cash contribution is actually received into the portfolio. We use a trade-date accounting methodology for all securities; however, we do not reflect cash flows in the portfolio until the cash is physically received (i.e., settlement date). Is this the most accurate methodology to use for reporting performance when there is an external cash flow to the portfolio?*

Either the notification date or the date of receipt is acceptable, and firms must be aware of the potential impact of this decision on performance calculation systems. The firm should establish a policy to determine which date to use and apply the policy consistently. The firm should also be aware of any accounting requirements established by regulators for a particular client type. Similarly, for cash distributions from a portfolio, the choice of which date to reflect the external cash flow is left up to the firm, but should be established in the firm's cash flow policies and procedures, and applied consistently.

4. *If a portfolio contains foreign stocks, when the stocks are settled, the foreign exchange rate will vary from the rate used at trade date, causing a foreign currency gain or loss. Should these gains and losses be included with the original stock transaction or are they just shown as a cash adjustment?*

The firm should determine a methodology for recognizing foreign exchange gains and losses when the stock transactions are settled and use it consistently. The firm must ensure that the transactions in the portfolio are accurately reflected.

1.A.6 ACCRUAL ACCOUNTING MUST be used for fixed-income securities and all other assets that accrue interest income. MARKET VALUES of fixed-income securities MUST include accrued income.

Discussion: Accrual accounting allows the recording of financial transactions as they come into existence as legally enforceable claims. When determining what market value to report for a security that pays interest income, firms must include the income that would have been received at the end of the performance period had the security actually paid interest income earned during the performance period.

Accrued interest income must be included in the beginning and ending portfolio market values when performance is calculated. Interest should be accrued for a security in the portfolio using whatever method is customary and appropriate for that security.

Some instruments already include accrued income as part of the security's market price. If income for these instruments is being accrued as part of the income recognition process, steps should be taken to ensure that the income is not double counted.

Accrued income for short-term cash/cash equivalents can be more difficult to calculate. Unlike bonds with a known coupon rate, there may not be a published interest rate for some short-term securities, such as overnight deposits. Firms must develop a methodology for accounting for short-term interest earnings and consistently apply the method selected. Firms could consider using the last actual known interest rate to accrue income for the most recent period. When the actual rate becomes known, an adjustment can then be made to allocate the actual income earned to the proper period. In this way, there is no systematic underestimation or overestimation of income, and income is also properly assigned to the period when earned. Cash-basis accounting (recording the income for short-term cash/cash equivalents as it is actually received) will tend to lag the suggested accrual method by recognizing income a month after it was earned; however, either method is acceptable. The method chosen must be used consistently.

Cross Reference: Guidance Statement on Calculation Methodology (Section 4-1); Provision 1.A.2, Provision 1.B.1, Provision 2.A.1

Application:

1. *Firm B seeks to have all of its clients' funds 100 percent invested at all times. However, because of the nature of cash flows in the buying and selling of assets, cash may be held in the accounts for a short period. The firm holds this cash in a money market account. How should Firm B account for the income generated by the assets in the money market account when calculating investment performance?*

Both the market value and interest earned on the money market account must be included in the portfolio's rate of return calculation. The firm has two options. Because the money market fund is clearly a cash substitute in this case, Firm B could recognize interest income on a cash basis. Firm B could also choose to recognize interest income on an accrual basis. Because there is no published interest rate for money market funds on which to accurately accrue the income, Firm B may use the last actual interest rate from the money market fund to accrue income for the current period, and when the actual rate for the current period becomes known, the firm can adjust returns to allocate the actual income earned to the proper period. Once Firm B chooses an accounting method, that method must be applied consistently to ensure continuity and consistency of results.

2. *Should the monthly increases in the value of zero coupon fixed-income securities be reported as interest income or capital gains and losses?*

Interest should be accrued for a security in the portfolio using whatever method is customary and appropriate for that security. Because the Standards do not require that the return on bonds be broken out between income and gain or loss, as long as the monthly change in value is reflected in the valuation of the security, the total return will be properly reflected in the portfolio.

3. *How should a firm claiming compliance with the GIPS standards treat bonds in default when calculating their performance results?*

If a bond goes into default during the accrual cycle, a firm must recognize the loss when it occurs. The performance figures must not be recalculated. The accrual of interest must be included in the calculation method up until the point of the bond's default. At that point, the calculation method would reflect the loss of accrued interest by adjusting the amount of accrued interest to zero.

When and if the bond comes out of default and there is a reasonable expectation that the bond will commence paying interest, including back interest, the firm must begin accruing for such interest payments. The firm may not allocate such payments over periods when they were originally due but not paid.

1.A.7 For periods beginning 1 January 2006, COMPOSITES MUST have consistent beginning and ending annual valuation dates. Unless the COMPOSITE is reported on a noncalendar fiscal year, the beginning and ending valuation dates MUST be at calendar year-end (or on the last business day of the year).

Discussion: Consistency in the annual beginning and ending composite valuation dates will result in improved comparability of data. Within a composite presentation, the annual reporting periods must be consistent and the portfolios in the composite must have consistent beginning and ending valuation dates corresponding to the reporting period.

Cross Reference: Guidance Statement on Calculation Methodology (Section 4-1), Provision 1.A.3, Provision 1.A.4, Provision 1.B.3, Provision 2.A.6, Provision 2.B.2, Provision 4.A.25

Application:

1. *Our firm reports performance in compliance with the Standards for years ending 30 June for our High-Yield composite; all the other composites are reported at 31 December. Will we be required to change to 31 December reporting for all of the firm's composites?*

No, the firm is not required to change the year-end valuation and reporting date from 30 June to 31 December for the High-Yield composite. Each composite at the firm may have different starting and ending valuation dates; however, the starting and ending valuation dates must correspond to the reporting dates for the composite. Within each composite's presentation, the annual periods must be consistent. The firm must consistently report data for years ending 30 June for the High-Yield composite. The firm may decide in the future to create a composite presentation for the High-Yield composite based on 31 December years; however, the firm may not mix 30 June and 31 December valuation and reporting dates in the same composite presentation of annual performance.

INPUT DATA — RECOMMENDATIONS

1.B.1 ACCRUAL ACCOUNTING SHOULD be used for dividends (as of the ex-dividend date).

Discussion: Accrual accounting determines the correct economic value of the portfolio assets and allows the recording of financial transactions as they come into existence as legally enforceable claims. It is recommended that dividends be recognized when earned (accrual basis) versus when paid (cash basis).

Cross Reference: Guidance Statement on Calculation Methodology (Section 4-1); Provision 1.A.2, Provision 1.A.6, Provision 2.A.1

1.B.2 When presenting NET-OF-FEES RETURNS, FIRMS SHOULD accrue INVESTMENT MANAGEMENT FEES.

Discussion: The net-of-fees return is defined as the gross-of-fees return reduced by the investment management fee. Investment management fees (the fees payable to the investment management firm for the ongoing management of a portfolio) are typically either asset based (percentage of assets), performance based (based on performance relative to a benchmark), or a combination of the two, but they may take different forms as well.

Accrual accounting allows the recording of financial transactions as they come into existence as legally enforceable claims. In order to reflect the most accurate net-of-fees return, fees and expenses should be accrued, when possible. Net-of-fees returns could be skewed if the calculation reflects fees as they are actually paid. It is more accurate to calculate the net-of-fees return that reflects investment management fees as they are earned.

The Standards do not require a specified methodology for calculating performance net-of-fees. The firm must develop a consistent calculation methodology that presents performance fairly, must not be misleading, and must be applied consistently.

Cross Reference: Interpretive Guidance for Fees Provisions (Section 4-6)

Application:

1. *An investment management firm manages both pooled funds and separate client accounts and charges investment management fees for its services to both. Clients may hold pooled funds as part of their separate account investments and in this case are being charged double for investment management services at both the pooled funds and separate account level. The firm deposits on a monthly basis, a "fee rebate" to client accounts holding the pooled funds. How should this "fee rebate" be treated in performance calculations?*

If an investment management firm reduces its management fee charged to clients, the recommended method is to waive the appropriate portion of the management fee so that there is neither a withdrawal nor deposit of cash (i.e., payment or refund of fees). The net-of-fees return must reflect (be reduced by) the effect of the fee minus the rebate. The net-of-fees return will be higher than if it were calculated using the full fees charged at both the pooled fund and separate account levels. The gross-of-fees return must be calculated as if the fee were not charged and the rebate not given.

2. *We want to report the net-of-fees performance numbers of a composite. Should we state the actual net-of-fees performance returns for all portfolios, which would reflect the deduction of the actual fee paid by each portfolio, or can we use a model fee?*

The net-of-fees return is defined as the gross-of-fees return reduced by the investment management fee incurred. Firms are permitted to use either the actual investment management fee incurred by each portfolio in the composite, or the highest investment management fee incurred by portfolios in the composite to reduce the gross-of-fees return to calculate the net-of-fees return.

1.B.3 Calendar month-end valuations or valuations on the last business day of the month are RECOMMENDED.

Discussion: This recommendation encourages early adoption of Provision 1.A.4. Consistency in monthly portfolio valuation dates will result in improved comparability of data, especially when firms choose to present year-to-date composite data at the end of a month or quarter.

Cross Reference: Guidance Statement on Calculation Methodology (Section 4-1); Provision 1.A.2, Provision 1.A.3, Provision 1.A.4, Provision 1.A.7, Provision 2.A.6, Provision 2.B.2, Provision 4.A.25

CALCULATION METHODOLOGY — REQUIREMENTS

2.A.1 Total return, including realized and unrealized gains and losses plus income, MUST be used.

Discussion: Total return, which is measured over a specified period, has two components: the appreciation or depreciation (capital change) of the assets in the portfolio over the specified period, and the income earned on the assets in the portfolio over the specified period. In calculating the performance of the portfolios within a composite, the GIPS standards require firms to use a total rate of return.

Cross Reference: Guidance Statement on Calculation Methodology (Section 4-1), Provision 1.A.6, Provision 1.B.1, Provision 2.A.2, Provision 2.A.4, Provision 2.A.5, Provision 2.B.1

Application:

1. *Over the past month, Client X's portfolio, which had no external cash flows, started with $1000 and ended with $1038. The capital change was $15, and the income earned was $23. What is the portfolio's total return for the month?*

Capital change:	$1015/$1000	=	1.5%
Income:	$23/$1000	=	2.3%
Total Return:	$1038/$1000	=	3.8%

2.A.2 TIME-WEIGHTED RATES OF RETURN that adjust for EXTERNAL CASH FLOWS MUST be used. Periodic returns MUST be geometrically linked. EXTERNAL CASH FLOWS MUST be treated in a consistent manner with the FIRM'S documented, COMPOSITE-specific policy. At a minimum:

a. For periods beginning 1 January 2005, FIRMS MUST use rates of return that adjust for daily-weighted EXTERNAL CASH FLOWS.

b. For periods beginning 1 January 2010, FIRMS MUST value PORTFOLIOS on the date of all LARGE EXTERNAL CASH FLOWS.

Discussion: In calculating the performance of the portfolios within a composite, the GIPS standards require firms to use a time-weighted rate of return, or an appropriate approximation, that adjusts for external cash flows. When calculating the time-weighted rate of return, interim (subperiod) returns must be geometrically linked to calculate period returns. There are separate calculation requirements for specific asset classes, such as private equity and real estate. Firms should refer to these provisions and guidance in Section 3-7 and Section 3-8.

Calculation methods that include adjustments to remove the effects of external cash flows from the performance return are called time-weighted rate-of-return (TWRR) methods. The GIPS standards require a time-weighted rate of return because external cash flows are generally client-driven and the impact of these cash flows on performance should not impact the performance attributed to the investment management firm. By removing the effects of external cash flows, a time-weighted rate of return best reflects the firm's ability to manage the portfolio's assets according to a specified strategy or objective, allowing prospective clients the best opportunity to fairly evaluate the past performance of the firm and to facilitate comparison between investment management firms.

The most accurate method of calculating a TWRR for individual portfolio performance is to determine the market value of the portfolio prior to each external cash flow, calculate a rate of return for the subperiods (each period between the cash flows) according to the following formula, and geometrically link the subperiod returns to calculate the portfolio return for the period. An external cash flow is a flow of cash or securities into or out of a portfolio (capital additions or withdrawals) that is client initiated. Dividend and interest income payments are not considered external cash flows. Dividends and interest income payments are cash flows that impact total return; they are not considered external cash flows for which an adjustment must be made in the time-weighted calculation.

3-3

The formula to calculate total return in the absence of external cash flows for a period, or the "true" time-weighted rate of return formula, is:

$$R_{TR} = \frac{(EMV - BMV)}{BMV}$$

where R_{TR} is the total return, *EMV* is the full economic market value of the portfolio at the end of the period, including all income accrued up to the end of the period, and *BMV* is the portfolio's market value at the beginning of the period, including all income accrued up to the end of the previous period.

This formula represents the growth (or decline) in the value of a portfolio, including both capital appreciation (or capital depreciation) and income, as a proportion of the beginning market value with no external cash flows over a period. The numerator in the formula reflects the income earned and the change in the portfolio's value over the period, which has been earned by the capital available to be invested. The denominator in the formula reflects the capital available to be invested to earn the change in value calculated in the numerator.

This formula calculates total return in the absence of external cash flows. Because most portfolios do experience external cash flows, which can often be unpredictable, the formula must be adjusted so that external cash flows do not skew the portfolio return. Revaluing and subsequently calculating performance for a portfolio at the time of each external cash flow removes the effects of external cash flows on the portfolio return. The Guidance Statement on the Treatment of Significant Cash Flows offers additional guidance on handling external cash flows that are so significant that the implementation of the investment strategy of the portfolio is disrupted. Firms should consider adopting the suggested methodologies in their policies and procedures.

Time-weighted total return calculation methods that adjust for external cash flows in the portfolio using the mid-point or mid-period methods, such as the Original Dietz Method, are acceptable for calculation periods prior to 1 January 2005. Because the philosophy of the GIPS standards is to present performance returns that are as accurate as practically possible, the Standards are transitioning to more precise calculation methodologies. Therefore, firms must use time-weighted total return calculations that adjust for *daily-weighted* external cash flows for calculation periods beginning 1 January 2005 at the latest; firms may use this methodology for calculation periods prior to this date. For periods beginning 1 January 2010, the Standards require that firms revalue portfolios on the date of all large external cash flows, in addition to calendar month-end or the last business day of the month. Firms may use this methodology for calculation periods prior to this date. Performance is then calculated for subperiods. The subperiods are then geometrically linked to calculate the total period total return. Each of these methodologies is described below. Once a calculation methodology is selected for a portfolio, it must be used consistently until the firm transitions to a more accurate methodology.

TWRR that adjusts for external cash flows (using mid-point or mid-period adjustment). *(Allowable for periods prior to 1 January 2005.)* Various methods approximating a TWRR are acceptable. The purpose of these methods is to produce as accurate an estimate as possible in circumstances where valuations at the time of external cash flows are not available. One example of an acceptable method is the Original Dietz Method. This method estimates when external cash flows are received into or withdrawn from a portfolio by assuming that all external cash flows occur at the midpoint of the period, thus half-weighting the net total external flow for the period when calculating the period's average capital invested (denominator).

$$R_{Dietz} = \frac{EMV - BMV - CF}{BMV + 0.5CF},$$

where BMV and EMV are defined as above and CF is the net total external cash flow for the period (contributions to the portfolio are positive flows, and withdrawals or distributions are negative flows).

TWRR that adjusts for *day-weighted* external cash flows. Calculation methods that approximate a TWRR by using a day-weighted adjustment for external cash flows that occur during the calculation period are allowed. Firms should calculate the return for each period using a denominator that reflects the weighting of external cash flows for the days they have been in the portfolio, available for investment, during the period. Examples of acceptable day-weighted methods are the Modified Dietz and Modified Internal Rate of Return (IRR) Methods. These methods are also an estimate of the true TWRR because they weight each external cash flow in the denominator by the days it is held in the portfolio.

Modified Dietz Method. The Modified Dietz Method improves upon the Original Dietz Method, which assumes that all external cash flows occur during the midpoint of the period. In an attempt to determine a more accurate return, the Modified Dietz Method weights each external cash flow in the denominator by the amount of time it is actually held in the portfolio. The formula for estimating the time-weighted rate of return using the Modified Dietz Method is:

$$R_{MDietz} = \frac{EMV - BMV - CF}{BMV + \sum_{i=1}^{n} \left(CF_i \times W_i \right)},$$

where $\sum_{i=1}^{n} \left(CF_i \times W_i \right)$ is the sum of each external cash flow, CF_i, multiplied by its weight, W_i.

The weight (W_i) is the proportion of the total number of days in the period that external cash flow, CF_i, has been held in the portfolio. The formula for W_i is

$$W_i = \frac{CD - D_i}{CD},$$

where CD is the total number of calendar days in the period and D_i is the number of calendar days since the beginning of the period in which external cash flow, CF_i, occurred.

The numerator is based on the assumption that the external cash flows occur at the end of the day. If external cash flows were assumed to occur at the beginning of the day, the numerator would be $(CD - D_i) + 1$. A firm may differentiate between beginning-of-day and end-of-day external cash flow assumptions. The key is to establish a policy and treat external cash flows consistently.

The chief advantage of the Modified Dietz Method is that it does not require portfolio valuation on the date of each external cash flow. Its chief disadvantage is that it provides a less accurate estimate of the true time-weighted rate of return than when the portfolio is valued at the time of each external cash flow. The estimate suffers most when a combination of the following conditions exists: (1) one or more large external cash flows occur; (2) external cash flows occur during periods of high market volatility — that is, the portfolio's returns are significantly nonlinear.

Modified IRR Method. The Modified IRR Method determines the modified internal rate of return for the period. In the Modified IRR approach, which has been changed to take into effect the exact timing of each external cash flow, the IRR is that value of R that satisfies the following equation:

$$EMV = \sum_{i=0}^{n} F_i \left(1 + R\right)^{W_i}.$$

The external cash flows, F_i, are also the same as with the Modified Dietz Method with one important exception: The market value at the start of the period is also treated as an external cash flow; that is, $BMV = F_0$.

The IRR is obtained by selecting values for R and solving the equation until the result equals EMV. For example, if three external cash flows (including the market value at the start of the period) have occurred, the computational formula will have three terms:

$$EMV = F_0 \left(1+R\right)^{W_0} + F_1 \left(1+R\right)^{W_1} + F_2 \left(1+R\right)^{W_2}.$$

The first term deals with the first external cash flow, F_0, which is the value of the portfolio at the beginning of the period; W_i is the proportion of the period that the external cash flow F_i was held in the portfolio. Because F_0 is in for the whole period, $W_0 = 1$. The larger the value of F_i in the term, the more it will contribute to the total, but the smaller the exponent (i.e., the value of W_i), the less the term will contribute to the sum. The usual effect is that the first term, with a large F_0 and W_0 equal to 1, will contribute far more than the other terms.

The advantages and disadvantages of the Modified IRR Method are the same as those of the Modified Dietz Method. The Modified IRR Method has the additional disadvantage of requiring an iterative process solution and is thus less desirable than the Modified Dietz Method when manual calculation is required. It is also possible to have multiple answers if there are both positive and negative external cash flows. Calculator and computer programs are available, however, for solving for the Modified IRR.

TWRR that requires portfolio revaluation for performance calculations at the time of large external cash flows. *(Allowable for any calculation period; required for periods beginning 1 January 2010.)* In order to calculate a more accurate time-weighted return, a large external cash flow must be defined by each firm for each composite to determine when the portfolios in that composite are to be revalued for performance calculations. A large external cash flow is the level at which a client-initiated external flow of cash and/or securities into or out of a portfolio may distort performance if the portfolio is not revalued. Firms must define the amount, for each composite, in terms of (1) the value of the cash/asset flow, or in terms of a percentage of portfolio or composite assets, and (2), if it is a single flow or an aggregate of a number of flows within a stated period of time.

The actual valuation of the portfolio's assets and calculation of return each time there is a large external cash flow will result in a more accurate TWRR calculation than using either the mid-point or day-weighted methods, but is less accurate than the "true" TWRR calculation methodology, which requires revaluation and calculation with every external cash flow.

The returns calculated for each subperiod are then geometrically linked according to the following formula:

$$R_{TR} = \left(\left(1+R_1\right)\times\left(1+R_2\right)...\left(1+R_n\right)\right)-1,$$

where R_{TR} is the total return for the period and R_1, R_2, . . ., R_n are the subperiod returns for Subperiods 1 through n, respectively.

This method assumes that the large external cash flow is not available for investment until the beginning of the next day. Accordingly, when the portfolio is revalued on the date of a large external cash flow, the large external cash flow is not reflected in the ending market value, but is added to the ending market value to determine the beginning market value for the next day.

The chief advantage of this method is that it calculates a better estimate than the mid-point or day-weighting methods. The major disadvantage is that it requires precise valuation of the portfolio each time there is a large external cash flow. In practice, this method requires that firms have the ability to value portfolios on a daily basis. If all securities are not accurately priced for each subperiod valuation, errors generated in the return calculation may be greater than the errors caused by using the mid-point or day-weighting approximation methods. In such cases, it is important to be able to correct for errors, such as missed security splits, mispricings, and improperly booked transactions, because day-to-day compounding will not correct for them automatically if there are external cash flows.

Because a time-weighted rate of return using *actual* valuations at the time of large external cash flows is required for periods beginning 1 January 2010, firms using less accurate approximation methods will have to change their calculation methods by that time.

Geometric Linking

If monthly composite returns are calculated, the monthly returns are linked geometrically using this formula:

$$R_{QT} = \left(\left(1+R_{MO1}\right)\times\left(1+R_{MO2}\right)\times\left(1+R_{MO3}\right)\right)-1,$$

where R_{QT} is the composite quarterly return and R_{MO1}, R_{MO2}, and R_{MO3} are the composite returns for Months 1, 2, and 3, respectively.

Similarly, to compute the annual rate of return for composite returns calculated quarterly, the formula to use is

$$R_{YR} = \left(\left(1+R_{QT1}\right)\times\left(1+R_{QT2}\right)\times\left(1+R_{QT3}\right)\times\left(1+R_{QT4}\right)\right)-1,$$

where R_{QT1}, R_{QT2}, R_{QT3}, and R_{QT4} are composite returns for Quarters 1, 2, 3, and 4, respectively. Alternatively, firms could geometrically link the twelve monthly returns to calculate the annual return.

Cross Reference: Guidance Statement on Calculation Methodology (Section 4-1), Provision 1.A.3, Provision 2.A.1, Provision 2.A.4, Provision 2.A.5, Provision 2.B.1, Provision 2.B.3. Provision 4.B.2

Application:

1. *Does the firm violate the GIPS standards by reporting money-weighted rates of return to an existing client for their portfolio?*

No, the Standards do not address client reporting, and therefore the Standards would not be violated if the firm reported money-weighted rates of return to an existing client for their portfolio. The Standards are primarily based on the concept of presenting the firm's composite performance to a prospective client rather than presenting individual portfolio returns to an existing client. Money-weighted returns may add further value in understanding the impact to the client of the timing of external cash flows, but are less useful for comparing one firm/manager to another and are therefore only required in the Standards for private equity portfolios where the investment firm controls the cash flows. The IRR (or money-weighted return) represents the performance of the specific client's portfolio holdings (i.e., influenced by the client's timing and amount of cash flows) and measures the performance of the portfolio rather than the performance of the investment manager.

2. *Given the following information, calculate the rate of return for this portfolio for January, February, March, and the first quarter of 1998, using: Dietz, Modified Dietz, and revaluing for large cash flows methodology (assume large is defined as > five percent):*

Date	Market Value (€)	External Cash Flow (€)	Market Value Post Cash Flow (€)
12/31/97	200,000		
1/31/98	208,000		
2/16/98	217,000	+40,000	257,000
2/28/98	263,000		
3/22/98	270,000	–30,000	240,000
3/31/98	245,000		

3-3

Solution: Dietz

January

$$R_{Jan} = \frac{(208{,}000 - 200{,}000)}{200{,}000} = 4.00\%$$

February

$$R_{Feb} = \frac{(263{,}000 - 208{,}000 - 40{,}000)}{(208{,}000 + (0.5 \times 40{,}000))} = 6.58\%$$

March

$$R_{Mar} = \frac{(245{,}000 - 263{,}000 - (-30{,}000))}{(263{,}000 + (0.5 \times (-30{,}000)))} = 4.84\%$$

Quarter 1

$$R_{QT1} = ((1+0.0400)\times(1+0.0658)\times(1+0.0484)) - 1 = 16.21\%$$

Solution: Modified Dietz

January

$$R_{Jan} = \frac{(208{,}000 - 200{,}000)}{200{,}000} = 4.00\%$$

February

$$W = \frac{(28-16)}{28} = 0.43 \qquad R_{Feb} = \frac{(263{,}000 - 208{,}000 - 40{,}000)}{(208{,}000 + (40{,}000 \times 0.43))} = 6.66\%$$

March

$$W = \frac{(31-22)}{31} = 0.29 \qquad R_{Mar} = \frac{(245{,}000 - 263{,}000 - (-30{,}000))}{(263{,}000 + (-30{,}000 \times 0.29))} = 4.72\%$$

Quarter 1

$$R_{QT1} = ((1+0.0400)\times(1+0.0666)\times(1+0.0472)) - 1 = 16.16\%$$

Solution: Valuation and Calculation at time of large external cash flows:

January

$$R_{Jan} = \frac{(208{,}000 - 200{,}000)}{200{,}000} = 4.00\%$$

February

$$R_{Feb1-15} = \frac{(217{,}000 - 208{,}000)}{(208{,}000)} = 4.33\%$$

$$R_{Feb16-28} = \frac{(263{,}000 - 257{,}000)}{(257{,}000)} = 2.33\%$$

$$R_{Feb1-28} = ((1+0.0433)\times(1+0.0233)) - 1 = 6.76\%$$

March

$$R_{Mar1-21} = \frac{(270{,}000 - 263{,}000)}{(263{,}000)} = 2.66\%$$

$$R_{Mar22-31} = \frac{(245{,}000 - 240{,}000)}{(240{,}000)} = 2.08\%$$

$$R_{Mar1-31} = ((1 + 0.0266) \times (1 + 0.0208)) - 1 = 4.80\%$$

Quarter 1

$$R_{QT1} = ((1 + 0.0400) \times (1 + 0.0676) \times (1 + 0.0480)) - 1 = 16.36\%$$

3. Should securities lending income be included in the investment firm's return?

The Standards provide comparability of the performance of investment managers by utilizing composites, which are based on investment strategy. Typically, securities lending is not an active part of the portfolio strategy. Therefore, unless the securities lending is a part of the strategy defined and implemented by the investment manager, for purposes of reporting performance for the Standards, securities lending income should be treated like a cash flow and should not impact performance results in order to get an accurate representation of the investment manager's ability to implement the intended strategy of the portfolio.

2.A.3 COMPOSITE returns MUST be calculated by asset weighting the individual PORTFOLIO returns using beginning-of-period values or a method that reflects both beginning-of-period values and EXTERNAL CASH FLOWS.

Discussion: A composite is an aggregation of individual portfolios representing similar investment objectives or strategies. The objective in calculating the composite's return is to use a method that will produce the same value as if the assets of all the individual portfolios in the composite are aggregated and a return is calculated for the one "master portfolio." The composite return is the asset-weighted average of the performance results of all the portfolios in the composite.

The GIPS standards are based on the principle of asset-weighted returns. For example, if a composite contains two portfolios, one of which is 10 times the size of the other, the rate of return for the larger portfolio should have more impact on the composite return than that of the smaller portfolio. The asset-weighted return method accomplishes this by weighting each portfolio's contribution to the composite rate of return by its beginning market value (as a percentage of the composite's beginning market value).

The Standards require asset weighting of the portfolio returns within a composite using beginning-of-period weightings, beginning-of-period market value plus weighted external cash flows, or by aggregating portfolio assets and external cash flows to calculate performance as a single master portfolio.

The *beginning market value–weighted method* for calculating composite returns, R_{BMV}, uses the formula

$$R_{BMV} = \frac{\sum_{i=1}^{n} (BMV_i \times R_i)}{BMV_{TOTAL}},$$

where BMV_i is the beginning market value (at the start of the period) for a portfolio, R_i is the rate of return for Portfolio i, and BMV_{TOTAL} is the total market value at the beginning of the period for all the portfolios in the composite.

The *beginning market value plus external cash flow–weighted method* represents a refinement to the beginning market value-weighted approach. Consider the case in which one of two portfolios in a composite doubles in market value as the result of a contribution on the third day of a performance period. Under the beginning market value–weighted approach, this portfolio will be weighted in the composite based solely on its beginning market value (i.e., not including the contribution). The beginning market value plus external cash flow–weighted method resolves this problem by including the effect of external cash flows in the weighting calculation as well as in the market values. The calculation of the weighting factor must be determined by the firm and used consistently. A suggested methodology is to use the same methodology as in the Modified Dietz Method:

$$W_{i,j} = \frac{\left(CD - D_{i,j}\right)}{CD},$$

where CD is the total number of calendar days in the period and $D_{i,j}$ is the number of calendar days since the beginning of the period in which external cash flow j occurred in portfolio i.

The beginning market value plus external cash flow–weighted composite return, R_{BMV+CF}, can be calculated as follows:

$$R_{BMV+CF} = \frac{\sum_{i=1}^{n}\left(\left(BMV_i + \left(\sum_{j=1}^{m} CF_{i,j} \times W_{i,j}\right)\right) \times R_i\right)}{\sum_{i=1}^{n}\left(BMV_i + \left(\sum_{j=1}^{m} CF_{i,j} \times W_{i,j}\right)\right)},$$

where $CF_{i,j}$ is external cash flow j within the period for Portfolio i (contributions to the portfolio are positive flows, and withdrawals or distributions are negative flows).

The *aggregate return* method combines all the composite assets and external cash flows to calculate performance as if the composite were one portfolio. The method is also acceptable as an asset-weighted approach.

Cross Reference: Guidance Statement on Calculation Methodology (Section 4-1), Provision 2.A.6, Provision 2.B.2

Application:

1. *Calculate the composite return using each of the three methods based on the following data:*

<u>**Portfolio 1**</u>

Date	Market Value (€)	External Cash Flow (€)	Market Value Post Cash Flow (€)
12/31/99	100,000		
1/10/00	103,000	20,000	123,000
1/22/00	130,000		
1/31/00	133,000		

Monthly Return = 11.32%

Portfolio 2

Date	Market Value ($)	External Cash Flow ($)	Market Value Post Cash Flow ($)
12/31/99	500,000		
1/10/00	512,000		
1/22/00	530,000	–70,000	460,000
1/31/00	470,000		

Monthly Return = 8.26%

Composite Return

Beginning Market Value–Weighted Method:

$$R_{BMV} = \frac{(100{,}000 \times 0.1132) + (500{,}000 \times 0.0826)}{(100{,}000 + 500{,}000)} = 8.77\%$$

Beginning Market Value plus External Cash Flow–Weighted Method:

$$W_{PORT1} = \frac{(31-10)}{31} = 0.68$$

$$W_{PORT2} = \frac{(31-22)}{31} = 0.29$$

$$R_{BMV+CF} = \frac{\left(\left(100{,}000 + (20{,}000 \times 0.68)\right) \times 0.1132\right) + \left(\left(500{,}000 + (-70{,}000 \times 0.29)\right) \times 0.0826\right)}{\left(\left(100{,}000 + (20{,}000 \times 0.68)\right) + \left(500{,}000 + (-70{,}000 \times 0.29)\right)\right)}$$

$$= 8.85\%$$

Aggregate Return Method (using Modified Dietz Method):

$$W_{Port1} = \frac{(31-10)}{31} = 0.68$$

$$W_{Port2} = \frac{(31-22)}{31} = 0.29$$

$$R_{January} = \frac{\left((133{,}000 + 470{,}000) - (100{,}000 + 500{,}000) - (20{,}000 - 70{,}000)\right)}{\left(100{,}000 + 500{,}000 + (20{,}000 \times 0.68) + (-70{,}000 \times 0.29)\right)} = 8.93\%$$

2.A.4 Returns from cash and cash equivalents held in PORTFOLIOS MUST be included in TOTAL RETURN calculations.

Discussion: Returns earned on cash and cash equivalents held in portfolios must be combined with the returns of other assets in the portfolio to calculate the total portfolio return. The investment manager's asset allocation decisions, including allocations to cash, are a component of the implementation of an investment strategy and, thus, the return earned on assets.

If the manager does not control the actual investment of cash (e.g., cash is always invested in a custodial money market fund or invested separately by the client) but the manager does control the amount of the portfolio that is allocated to cash, then the cash assets must be included in the manager's total assets and the performance of cash must be included in the total portfolio performance. The fact that the investment of cash is technically not under the manager's control will not generally affect the total portfolio results as much as the allocation of assets to cash, which is under the manager's control.

Cross Reference: Provision 0.A.3, Provision 2.A.1, Provision 2.A.2

Application:

1. *Firm A manages the portfolios of several clients and has full investment discretion over their assets. At the end of each day, the excess cash in each portfolio is swept into the custodian's money market fund. Because Firm A does not manage the money market fund, it does not include the cash portion of the portfolio in its total return performance calculation. Is this practice in compliance with the GIPS standards?*

No. Even if Firm A does not control the cash investment, it does control the amount of portfolio assets that are held in cash equivalents. Because Firm A chose to have portfolio assets "invested" in cash, Firm A is indirectly responsible for the return the cash assets earn, and that return must be included in the total return of the portfolio.

2.A.5 All returns MUST be calculated after the deduction of the actual TRADING EXPENSES incurred during the period. Estimated TRADING EXPENSES are not permitted.

Discussion: Trading expenses refer to the transaction costs incurred in the purchase or sale of securities. For purposes of the GIPS standards, both gross-of-fees and net-of-fees returns must be reduced by the trading expenses incurred in the purchase or sale of securities. These costs must be included when calculating performance because these are costs that must be paid in order to implement the investment strategy. Trading expenses can be direct, as in the case of brokerage commissions, or indirect, as in the case of a bid–ask spread. Direct trading expenses include brokerage commissions and any other regulatory fee, duty, and/or tax (e.g., stamp duty, regulatory fee, etc.) associated with an individual transaction. Custody fees should not be included in the trading expenses. Estimated trading expenses are not permitted.

Cross Reference: Interpretive Guidance for Fees Provisions (Section 4-6), Provision 2.A.1, Provision 2.A.7, Provision 4.A.6, Provision 4.A.15, Provision 4.A.16

2.A.6 For periods beginning 1 January 2006, FIRMS MUST calculate COMPOSITE returns by asset weighting the individual PORTFOLIO returns at least quarterly. For periods beginning 1 January 2010, COMPOSITE returns MUST be calculated by asset weighting the individual PORTFOLIO returns at least monthly.

Discussion: The more frequently composite returns are calculated, the more accurate the results will be. Quarterly composite calculations will be permitted for periods prior to 1 January 2010, after which time composite returns must be calculated at least monthly.

Cross Reference: Guidance Statement on Calculation Methodology (Section 4-1), Provision 1.A.3, Provision 1.A.4, Provision 1.A.7, Provision 1.B.3, Provision 2.A.3, Provision 2.B.2, Provision 3.A.3, Provision 3.A.4

2.A.7 If the actual direct TRADING EXPENSES cannot be identified and segregated from a BUNDLED FEE:

a. when calculating GROSS-OF-FEES RETURNS, returns MUST be reduced by the entire BUNDLED FEE or the portion of the BUNDLED FEE that includes the direct TRADING EXPENSES. The use of estimated TRADING EXPENSES is not permitted.

b. when calculating NET-OF-FEES RETURNS, returns MUST be reduced by the entire BUNDLED FEE or the portion of the BUNDLED FEE that includes the direct TRADING EXPENSES and the INVESTMENT MANAGEMENT FEE. The use of estimated TRADING EXPENSES is not permitted.

Discussion: A bundled fee portfolio is a portfolio with a fee structure that combines multiple fees into one, aggregated or "bundled" fee. Bundled fees can include any combination of management, transaction, custody, and other administrative fees. Provision 2.A.5 requires that performance must reflect the trading costs incurred by the portfolio during the measurement period.

The GIPS standards define gross-of-fees return as the return on assets reduced by any trading expenses incurred during the period. To meet the requirements of the GIPS standards when calculating a bundled fee portfolio's gross-of-fees return, if the firm can identify the portion of the bundled fee that includes the trading expenses, that is the only portion of the bundled fee that must be reflected in the performance calculation. If the firm is unable to determine the portion of the total bundled fee reflecting the trading expenses, the entire bundled fee must be reflected (reduce performance) when calculating the bundled fee portfolio's gross-of-fees return.

The GIPS standards define net-of-fees return as the gross-of-fees return reduced by the investment management fee. To meet the requirements of the GIPS standards when calculating a bundled fee portfolio's net-of-fees return, if the firm can identify the portion of the bundled fee that includes the investment management fee, that is the only portion of the bundled fee that must reduce the gross-of-fees return to be reflected in the net-of-fees performance calculation. If the firm is unable to determine the portion of the total bundled fee reflecting the trading expenses and the investment management fee, the entire bundled fee must be reflected (performance must be reduced by the entire bundled fee amount) when calculating the bundled fee portfolio's net-of-fees return.

Cross Reference: Interpretive Guidance for Fees Provisions (Section 4-6), Guidance Statement for Wrap Fee/Separately Managed Account (SMA) Portfolios (Section 4-13), Provision 2.A.5, Provision 4.A.13, Provision 4.A.14, Provision 4.A.15, Provision 4.A.16

CALCULATION METHODOLOGY — RECOMMENDATIONS

2.B.1 Returns SHOULD be calculated net of nonreclaimable withholding taxes on dividends, interest, and capital gains. Reclaimable withholding taxes SHOULD be accrued.

Discussion: Global investing requires recognition of the tax consequences of investing in different countries. Some countries allow certain foreign investor types to reclaim a portion of the foreign withholding taxes that are paid when transactions or payments occur. These reclaimable foreign withholding taxes are credited back to the investor at a later date. It is recommended that reclaimable foreign withholding taxes be accrued. This recommended provision is not applicable to domestic withholding taxes (used with after-tax calculations) for individuals for payment of their domestic tax liability.

Cross Reference: Provision 4.A.7, Provision 5.B.1

Application:

1. *The Standards state in Provision 5.B.1.a that gross-of-tax performance is currently recommended for the presentation of results to prospective clients, yet Provision 2.B.1 recommends that portfolio returns should be calculated net of withholding taxes on dividends, interest, and capital gains. Please clarify.*

The case for reporting international results net of foreign withholding taxes is based on the concept of reporting performance net of transaction costs. Just as a manager's performance includes his ability to negotiate transaction costs, internationally a manager's performance is based on his ability to choose the countries in which to invest based on tax consequences. Basically, a manager has control (to some degree) over transaction costs for his clients, just as a manager has control over which countries are represented in a portfolio. Country selection is part of the performance process and should include analysis of tax treaties. Specific country tax impact should be part of the performance process, just as security selection (net of transaction costs) is part of the process.

It should be noted that if a foreign client has decided to put an investment portfolio with the firm, and it is the client's actions that are incurring the taxes, the firm would justifiably report this nondomestic account's performance on the same basis as the domestic investors; that is, the return of the foreign investor's account should be gross of domestic withholding taxes, but it could be reported either way.

2.B.2 FIRMS SHOULD calculate COMPOSITE returns by asset weighting the member PORTFOLIOS at least monthly.

Discussion: The more frequently composite returns are calculated, the more accurate the results will be.

Cross Reference: Guidance Statement on Calculation Methodology (Section 4-1), Provision 1.A.3, Provision 1.A.4, Provision 1.A.7, Provision 1.B.3, Provision 2.A.3, Provision 2.A.6, Provision 3.A.3, Provision 3.A.4

2.B.3 FIRMS SHOULD value PORTFOLIOS on the date of all LARGE EXTERNAL CASH FLOWS.

Discussion: The more frequently portfolios are valued and performance subsequently calculated, the more accurate the performance calculation. This provision encourages early implementation of a more accurate time-weighted return calculation methodology.

Cross Reference: Guidance Statement on Calculation Methodology (Section 4-1), Provision 1.A.3, Provision 2.A.2

COMPOSITE CONSTRUCTION — REQUIREMENTS

3.A.1 All actual, fee-paying, discretionary PORTFOLIOS MUST be included in at least one COMPOSITE. Although non-fee-paying discretionary PORTFOLIOS may be included in a COMPOSITE (with appropriate disclosures), nondiscretionary PORTFOLIOS are not permitted to be included in a FIRM'S COMPOSITES.

Discussion: A portfolio is an individually managed pool of assets, which may be a subportfolio, account, or pooled fund. The portfolio assets are generally managed on behalf of a client for a defined strategy. An actual portfolio is a portfolio invested in real (tangible) assets and is differentiated from hypothetical, simulated, or back-tested portfolios or advisory-only (model) portfolios.

A fee-paying portfolio incurs investment management fees, which are fees paid to the investment management firm for the ongoing management of the portfolio. These fees are typically asset based (a percentage of assets), performance based (based on performance relative to a benchmark), or a combination of the two, but fees may take other forms as well. Non-fee-paying discretionary portfolios may be included in the firm's composites. If a firm chooses to include non-fee-paying discretionary portfolios in a composite, all non-fee-paying portfolios meeting the definition of that composite should be included in the composite in the interest of fair representation of performance results. The firm must present, as of the end of each annual period, the percentage of the composite's assets represented by the non-fee-paying portfolios. If the firm chooses to include non-fee-paying discretionary portfolios in one or more of its composites, the firm is not required to include all non-fee-paying discretionary portfolios in composites. Examples of non-fee-paying portfolios are portfolios consisting of the firm's own pension plan assets or portfolios managed for friends or employees that are not charged investment management fees. If a firm temporarily waives the investment management fee for a portfolio that is normally charged a fee, the portfolio is still considered a fee-paying portfolio (with a fee of zero for that period) and must be included in a composite.

If the firm includes non-fee-paying discretionary portfolios in its composites, they are subject to the same rules as fee-paying portfolios (e.g., the firm must not move the non-fee-paying portfolio into and out of a composite without documented changes in client guidelines or in the case of the redefinition of the composite).

Discretion is the ability of the firm to implement its intended strategy. If documented client-imposed restrictions significantly hinder the firm from fully implementing its intended strategy, the firm may determine that the portfolio is nondiscretionary. There are degrees of discretion and not all client-imposed restrictions will necessarily cause a portfolio to be nondiscretionary. The firm must determine if the restrictions will, or could, interfere with the implementation of the intended strategy to the extent that the portfolio is no longer representative of the strategy. Nondiscretionary portfolios must not be included in a firm's discretionary composites. Firms make the ultimate decision as to whether or not portfolio restrictions render a portfolio nondiscretionary. Firms should also document the reasons for classifying each portfolio as nondiscretionary.

Discretion should be defined at the firm level, but may be defined at the composite level or by asset class if appropriate. Once the definition of discretion has been determined, it must be applied consistently.

It is the firm's responsibility to ensure that all of its actual, fee-paying, discretionary portfolios are included in at least one composite. Accordingly, firms should review each of their portfolios (both discretionary and nondiscretionary) on a regular basis to determine whether any portfolios should be reclassified.

Nondiscretionary portfolios must not be included in the firm's composites (i.e., composites consisting of discretionary portfolios). Some firms, however, may group some or all of the firm's nondiscretionary portfolios together to simplify portfolio administration. For purposes of complying with the Standards, this is *not* a composite and must not be included on the firm's list of composites.

Firms must include a portfolio in more than one composite if that portfolio satisfies the definition of each composite and each composite must contain all portfolios that meet the composite's definition.

Cross Reference: Guidance Statement on Composite Definition (Section 4-2), Provision 0.A.3, Provision 3.A.2, Provision 3.A.3, Provision 3.A.4, Provision 3.A.5, Provision 3.A.8, Provision 3.A.9, Provision 5.A.1, Provision 5.A.7

Application:

1. *Firm B manages several portfolios according to a particular strategy; however, the firm does not ever plan to market the strategy. Do these portfolios have to be included in a composite?*

Yes, these portfolios must be included in a composite if the portfolios are actual, fee-paying, discretionary portfolios. It is important to remember that the GIPS standards are not marketing or advertising standards, nor do they differentiate between "marketed" and "nonmarketed" composites.

The requirement for firms to include all actual, fee-paying, discretionary portfolios in at least one composite ensures that a firm presents a complete picture of its entire performance record. Without this requirement, there is a potential for firms to exclude poor performing portfolios from composites. Because the intent of the Standards is to accurately and fairly represent firm performance, all actual, fee-paying, discretionary portfolios must be included in at least one of the firm's composites. Firms must maintain a list and description of all composites, whether marketed or not, and must disclose that the list is available upon request (see Provision 4.A.2).

If client-imposed restrictions on these portfolios do not allow the implementation of the firm's strategy, the firm could either classify these portfolios as nondiscretionary (and all other portfolios with the same restrictions) or could choose to classify them as discretionary and create a composite for portfolios with the defined restrictions. Firms should, where possible and appropriate, consider classifying portfolios with defined restrictions as discretionary and grouping them with portfolios with similar restrictions in a composite.

2. *Firm C manages a portfolio that recently had new investment restrictions placed on it by the client, rendering it nondiscretionary. Should the firm retroactively remove that portfolio from its composite?*

No. Firm C has the responsibility of creating its own definition of discretion and applying this definition consistently over time to all portfolios. A portfolio that changes from discretionary to nondiscretionary status because of a new client-imposed restriction may be removed from a composite on a prospective basis only; the portfolio must not be removed retroactively.

3. *Firm D seeks to establish a record for managing aggressive growth portfolios but does not yet manage client funds to that style. To create a performance history to show potential clients, the firm uses its own capital to create a portfolio that is managed to an aggressive growth style. Can the firm present this performance in a new aggressive growth composite and remain in compliance with the GIPS standards?*

Yes. Firm D could create an aggressive growth composite consisting only of the firm's seed capital. The firm must show in the composite presentation the percentage of composite assets that are non-fee-paying, which in this case, is 100 percent (see Provision 5.A.7). The composite performance record would begin with the inception of the one portfolio and, therefore, would not have any prior history. As the firm acquires portfolios that are managed to this strategy, the new portfolios' performance will be included in the composite as soon as they meet the composite inclusion criteria the firm establishes for the composite.

4. *We have a client whose assets are divided between several portfolios. The client wants to maintain the portfolios separately. Do we consider each portfolio for this one client as separate portfolios or do we combine the separate portfolios into a single portfolio?*

One of the fundamental concepts of the Standards is the creation of composites based on the strategies implemented by the firm. The Standards require that firm composites must be defined according to similar investment objectives and/or strategies. The firm must determine how to construct its composites such that the composites represent the firm's investment strategies and present performance fairly and accurately.

If the portfolios described are all managed with the same investment strategy, then placing them in one composite may be acceptable within the requirements of the Standards. The firm must determine whether or not including the portfolios together in a composite will present performance accurately and fairly and what would be meaningful and representative.

It should be noted that if the relationship is managed as one strategy, then the firm should combine the "subportfolios" into one "master" portfolio for the appropriate composite such that composite calculations, such as composite minimum, number of portfolios, and dispersion, are calculated using the "master" portfolio. If the accounts are not managed as one strategy, they would be considered individual portfolios and would each be placed in the appropriate composites. All composite calculations, such as composite minimum, dispersion, and so on, would be calculated using the individual portfolio.

5. *Is there a minimum number of accounts, or a minimum percentage of a firm's accounts, and/or a minimum amount of money that must comprise a legitimate composite?*

No, there is not a minimum number of accounts, or a minimum percentage of a firm's accounts, and/or a minimum amount of money that must comprise a composite. All actual, fee-paying discretionary portfolios must be included in at least one composite; composites are to be defined according to similar investment objectives and/or strategies.

6. *Can a firm include a single portfolio in more than one of the firm's composites?*

Yes. The Standards state that firms must include all actual, discretionary, fee-paying portfolios in at least one of the firm's composites. If the portfolio meets the defined criteria for inclusion in more than one composite, the firm must include the portfolio in all appropriate composites. For example, a firm may have a large-cap composite and a large-cap growth composite. If the firm manages a portfolio that meets the criteria for inclusion in the large-cap composite as well as the large-cap growth composite, the firm must include the portfolio in both composites.

3.A.2 COMPOSITES MUST be defined according to similar investment objectives and/or strategies. The full COMPOSITE DEFINITION MUST be made available on request.

Discussion: A composite is an aggregation of individual portfolios representing a similar investment mandate, objective, or strategy. Creating meaningful composites is critical to fair presentation, consistency, and comparability of results over time and among firms.

The important concept is that all assets of the firm to which the Standards apply are accounted for appropriately in composites. Firms make the ultimate decision about which portfolios belong in each composite.

Composite definitions, the detailed criteria that determine the allocation of portfolios to composites, must be documented in the firm's policies and procedures. In addition, the full composite definition must be made available upon request.

Defining and constructing composites is one of the first steps in implementing the GIPS standards. Composites are the primary vehicle for presenting performance to a prospective client. The Standards require that firms include *all* actual, discretionary, fee-paying portfolios in at least one composite that is managed according to a particular strategy or style. In this way, firms cannot "cherry-pick" their best performing portfolios to present to prospective clients.

The manager must determine what definition of the composite is most appropriate: either a broad, "inclusive" definition of the composite, with a potential of a wide dispersion of portfolios returns; or a more limited, narrower, "exclusive" definition with a potential of a smaller dispersion of portfolios returns. This choice will be revealed through the required disclosures of amount of assets in the composite and either percentage of the total firm assets represented by the composite or the amount of total firm assets at the end of each annual period.

The GIPS standards require firms to develop objective criteria for defining composites. The following are guiding principles that firms must consider when defining composites:

- Composites must be defined according to investment objective and/or strategy. Composites should enable clients to compare the performance of one firm to another. The firm should also consider the definition and construction of similar products found within the competitive universe. Composites must be representative of the firm's products and be consistent with the firm's marketing strategy.
- Firms must apply the criteria for defining composites consistently (e.g., the firm may not select only certain, specific portfolios (i.e., "cherry-picking") that meet the composite definition, but must include all portfolios that satisfy the criteria for inclusion).
- Firms are not permitted to include portfolios with different investment strategies or objectives in the same composite. The performance of such a composite is meaningless. In the case where there are many portfolios with unique, defining investment characteristics, the firm may create numerous single-portfolio composites.

Composite Definition Criteria

In addition to the guiding principles above, firms may choose to define their composites according to relevant criteria and must document the definition of each composite, including any criteria or constraints. It is constructive to consider a hierarchical structure of criteria for composite definition that promotes primary and secondary strategy characteristics. It is also important to understand the defining characteristics commonly found in the marketplace for investment products. Comparability of similar strategies or products is a fundamental objective of the Standards and benefits current and prospective clients when firms define strategies similarly, using clear and unambiguous terminology.

Suggested Hierarchy for Composite Definition

The following suggested hierarchy may be helpful as firms consider how to define composites. Firms are not required to define their composites according to each level of the hierarchy.

> *Investment Mandate*
> Composites based on the summary of strategy or product description. Example: large-cap global equities.
>
> *Asset Classes*
> Composites based on a broad asset class are the most basic and should be representative of the firm's products. Firms may further define the asset class by country or region. Examples: equity, fixed income, balanced, real estate, venture capital, U.S. fixed income, European equities.
>
> *Style or Strategy*
> Firms may further define a composite based on the style or strategy in order to provide investors with additional insight and allow for increased comparability. Examples: growth, value, active, indexed, asset class sector (e.g., telecommunications), etc.

Benchmarks
Firms may define composites on the basis of the portfolios' benchmark or index provided the benchmark reflects the investment objective or strategy and there are no other composites with the same characteristics. This is often the case if the benchmark also defines the investment universe. Examples: Swiss Market Index, S&P 500 Index, Lehman Aggregate Index, etc.

Risk/Return Characteristics
Portfolios with different risk characteristics (e.g., targeted tracking error, beta, volatility, information ratio, etc.) and return objectives may be grouped together into different composites. Examples: Japanese Equity Composite with a targeted excess return of 1 percent and targeted tracking error of 2 percent would be in a separate composite from a Japanese Equity Composite with a targeted excess return of 3 percent and targeted maximum volatility of 6 percent.

Constraints/Guidelines

In addition to the fundamental criteria above, firms may choose to further define their composites based on relevant client constraints or guidelines. The following are examples of constraints or guidelines that could result in materially different strategies and, therefore, justify separate composites.

Extent of the Use of Derivatives, Hedging, and/or Leverage
In general, portfolios that use derivatives, leverage and/or hedging have a unique (different) investment strategy from those portfolios that do not utilize these techniques or instruments (see Provision 4.A.5).

Treatment of Taxes
The firm should define separate composites for portfolios with specific tax treatments if the treatment of taxes hinders the firm's ability to implement a specific investment strategy as compared to similar portfolios without specific tax treatments.

Type of Client (e.g., pension fund, private client, endowment, etc.)
Client type alone must not be used as the primary criteria for defining a composite. If portfolios of different client types have materially different investment strategies and/or styles that are specific to the type of client, the firm must create separate composites representing each of the different strategies.

Instruments Used (e.g., invest only in pooled vehicles versus individual securities)
If portfolios use specific instruments the firm may define separate composites.

Size of Portfolios
Differences in portfolio size may result in meaningful, material differences in investment strategy and justify the creation of separate composites. For example, an index strategy may be implemented via sampling (i.e., holding a sample of the index securities) for smaller portfolios, while the strategy may be implemented via a full replication of the index for larger portfolios. In this case, the strategy is actually different based on the size of the portfolio.

Client Characteristics (e.g., cash flow needs, risk tolerances)
Firms may create composites based on multiple client characteristics.

Portfolio Types (e.g., segregated (separate) portfolios, pooled portfolios (mutual funds))
Pooled funds, including mutual funds and unit trusts, may be treated as separate composites or combined with other portfolios into one or more composites of the same strategy, style, or objective.

Base Currency
Base currency must not be a criteria used for composite definition unless it is specific to the investment strategy.

Additional Considerations

Multiple Asset Class Portfolios
Multi-asset or balanced portfolios are portfolios that consist of more than one asset class. Composites should be constructed according to strategic ranges of asset mixes provided in the client investment guidelines, not according to the tactical percentage of assets invested in the different asset classes. Portfolios with varying, but similar strategic asset allocations can be grouped together if they collectively have the same strategy or style. Firms often have discretion to tactically alter the asset allocation in an effort to add value. Portfolios must not be moved into or out of composites due to changes in the tactical asset allocation. Only in the case of client-documented strategic asset allocation changes should portfolios be moved into different composites.

Whenever the firm has discretion over changes from one asset class to another, the total return on the entire portfolio should be used in compiling the performance of that portfolio. If the firm does not have discretion over the asset mix, the segments of the various asset classes, with their respective cash positions, could be included in composites of like assets.

Inception Date
In general, firms are not permitted to create composites based solely on inception date. However, in very specific situations, it may be appropriate to group portfolios into composites according to inception date (e.g., venture capital composites, after-tax composites, municipal bond composites).

Firms with Multiple offices, Branches, or Investment Divisions
Firms are only permitted to define different composites for offices, branches, or investment divisions of a firm if the portfolios are managed according to investment objectives, styles or strategies that are unique to each particular office, branch, or division. Thus, the style or strategy determines the composite, not the location or group. Composite definitions cannot span multiple firms. For additional guidance regarding how the firm can be defined, please refer to the Guidance Statement on Definition of the Firm.

Dispersion of the Portfolio Returns within a Composite
While dispersion is one measure to determine how consistently the firm has implemented its strategy across the portfolios in the composite, it can only be measured on an *ex-post* basis and, therefore, should not be used as a criterion to define a composite. A dispersion figure may serve as a good indicator of whether the criteria for composite definition are suitable and whether a composite should be redefined. There is no general rule for a maximum amount of composite dispersion. The firm should contemplate the definition of a broad, "inclusive" composite with a wide dispersion of portfolio returns versus a narrow, "exclusive" composite with a more narrow dispersion measure.

Treatment of Fees
Different types of management fees should not be used as criteria for composite definition.

Cross Reference: Guidance Statement on Composite Definition (Section 4-2), Provision 3.A.1, Provision 3.A.5, Provision 4.A.20, Provision 4.A.22

Application:

1. *Firm E has a number of fee-paying client portfolios managed to a particular investment strategy. Firm E also manages assets following this same strategy for clients who do not pay fees, and wants to include these portfolios in a composite. Should Firm E create two separate composites for its fee-paying and non-fee-paying portfolios?*

In general, management fees should not be used as criteria for composite definition. Because the assets are managed in the same manner and follow the same strategy, the non-fee-paying portfolios should be included in the same composite as the fee-paying portfolios. The Standards do not, however, require that non-fee-paying portfolios be included in a composite. If Firm E chooses to include non-fee-paying portfolios in the composite, Provision 5.A.7 requires Firm E to present, as of the end of each annual period, the percentage of the composite assets represented by the non-fee-paying portfolios.

2. *If a fund invests in publicly traded equities for both limited partnerships and for separate accounts, should the manager set up different composites for each legal structure?*

A composite should include all portfolios that are managed according to the same strategy. Differences in legal structure alone would not warrant a separate composite definition. It is up to the manager to decide how results can be presented in the most meaningful way, however, and if differences in legal structure cause the implementation of the strategy of the portfolios to differ, then the manager would place limited partnerships and separate accounts in separate composites.

3.A.3 COMPOSITES MUST include new PORTFOLIOS on a timely and consistent basis after the PORTFOLIO comes under management unless specifically mandated by the client.

Discussion: It is the responsibility of the firm to set reasonable guidelines for each composite regarding the inclusion of new portfolios into the composite. Firms are encouraged to establish a policy that includes new portfolios in composites as soon as possible, preferably at the start of the next full performance measurement period.

Firms may need time to invest the assets of a new portfolio to reflect the firm's investment strategy, and the Standards thus allow firms some discretion to determine when the new portfolio should be added to the composite. Firms must establish a policy on a composite-by-composite basis and apply it consistently.

Firms may delay the inclusion of a new portfolio into a composite in the case of specific instructions from the client. For example, a client may indicate to the firm that assets will be deposited over an extended period, which may delay the full implementation of the firm's strategy until all assets are received.

Cross Reference: Guidance Statement on Composite Definition (Section 4-2), Provision 3.A.1

Application:

1. *Firm A has two composites, a global government fixed-income composite and an emerging market fixed-income composite. Do the GIPS standards require new portfolios to be included at the same time for both of these composites?*

The GIPS standards require that firms establish a policy for including new portfolios in composites and apply the policy consistently within that composite. Different strategies may result in different time frames for inclusion based on the liquidity of the assets involved. Although in most situations it is fairly easy to purchase and sell global government fixed-income securities, emerging market debt may be more illiquid and therefore may initially require a longer period of time to implement the firm's strategy. The global government fixed-income composite might have a new portfolio inclusion policy with a shorter time frame relative to the emerging market fixed-income composite.

2. *Firm B obtains a new client who will eventually invest $25 million with the firm in their Value strategy. However, assets will be transferred to the manager in $5 million increments over a period of 18 months. The firm's policy for the Value composite is to include new portfolios at the beginning of the first full month under management. How should Firm B treat this portfolio?*

Because Firm B is not receiving the entire funding at once, it must consider whether the incremental funding will affect its ability to implement the Value strategy. The timing of the client's funding might require the firm to exclude the portfolio beyond the first month under management. In this way, the client mandate could result in an exception to the composite's policy regarding new portfolios. However, if Firm B determines that the incremental investing does not affect the implementation of the style or strategy, then Firm B must include the portfolio in the Value composite in accordance with its policy.

3. A firm manages private client portfolios. Depending upon when the portfolio came under management, returns will vary because of opportunities available at the time. Can a firm establish composites based on the date a portfolio comes under firm management?

In very specific situations, it may be appropriate to group portfolios into composites according to inception date (e.g., venture capital composites, after-tax composites, municipal bond composites). Because composites should represent consistency—or lack of consistency—of a strategy over time, a composite based on inception date would, generally, not show representative results of how the strategy performs over time as market conditions change. New portfolios are added to a composite according to reasonable and consistently applied manager guidelines.

3.A.4 Terminated PORTFOLIOS MUST be included in the historical returns of the appropriate COMPOSITES up to the last full measurement period that the PORTFOLIO was under management.

Discussion: This requirement prevents survivorship bias by retaining the performance history of the portfolio while it was managed to the composite's strategy. Once a client notifies the firm of the termination, the firm generally loses its discretion over the portfolio (e.g., the firm is restricted on its management of the portfolio). In this case, the firm should include the portfolio in the composite through the last full measurement period for which the firm has discretion. If all the portfolios are removed from a composite, for any reason, the performance record of the composite comes to an end.

Cross Reference: Guidance Statement on Composite Definition (Section 4-2), Provision 3.A.1

Application:

1. Firm A has a policy of removing terminated portfolios on the first day of the month that the firm was notified of termination. If notification of a portfolio's termination is received on 25 May, when should it likely be removed from the composite?

The firm's policy should be based on removing the portfolio from the composite at the start of the performance measurement period when the firm no longer has discretion over the assets. Assuming monthly performance measurement periods, the portfolio should be included in the composite performance calculations through 30 April but should be excluded from the composite calculations for May, if the firm had discretion over the assets through the month of April and no longer had discretion over the assets after 25 May.

3.A.5 PORTFOLIOS are not permitted to be switched from one COMPOSITE to another unless documented changes in client guidelines or the redefinition of the COMPOSITE make it appropriate. The historical record of the PORTFOLIO MUST remain with the appropriate COMPOSITE.

Discussion: Firms are only permitted to move portfolios into and out of composites because of documented changes in client guidelines or in the case where the redefinition of a composite makes it appropriate. For purposes of the GIPS standards, documentation can include, but is not limited to, letters, faxes, e-mails, and/or internal memorandums documenting conversations with clients.

This requirement seeks to preclude or at least minimize the movement of portfolios into, out of and between composites. Theoretically, once a firm creates composites based on its various investment strategies, portfolios will be managed to those strategies on a long-term basis. As a result, defining composites is a critical issue when attempting to comply with the GIPS standards.

Over time, a client's investment objective may change and moving the portfolio from one composite to another may be necessary; however, the move must be based on a directive from the client that is clearly identified and documented. The history of the existing portfolio must remain with the original composite.

Firms may adopt a new investment strategy and must create a new composite to reflect the new strategy. The firm may move some of their existing portfolios into the new composite, based on directives from their clients that are clearly identified and documented. The history of the existing portfolios must remain with the original composite.

Although investment strategies can change over time, in most cases firms should not change the definition of a composite. Generally, changes in strategy result in the creation of a new composite. In some very rare cases, however, it may be appropriate to redefine a composite. If a firm determines that it is appropriate to redefine a composite, it must disclose the date and nature of the change. Changes to composites must not be applied retroactively.

Cross Reference: Guidance Statement on Composite Definition (Section 4-2), Provision 3.A.1, Provision 3.A.2, Provision 4.A.22

Application:

1. *Firm A manages a portfolio for a client who instructs the firm to change the portfolio's mandate from an intermediate duration bond portfolio to a long duration bond portfolio. Should Firm A place this portfolio in a different composite?*

Yes, documented change in the client's investment guidelines would cause the portfolio to be removed from the intermediate duration bond composite and placed into the long duration bond composite once fully invested in the new style. If the firm does not currently have a long duration bond composite, it is recommended that the firm create one. This account transfer will be treated like a terminated account when it is removed from the intermediate duration bond composite, and it will be treated like a new account to the long duration bond composite. The portfolio's prior history must remain in the intermediate duration bond composite through the last full measurement period the portfolio was managed in the intermediate duration style.

2. *For the past five years, Firm C has maintained a global equity composite. Although the firm defined the strategy to allow investments in equity securities from any geographic area, the firm tactically did not hold any Japanese equities during that time. Now, Firm C wants to redefine the composite as global equities ex-Japan. Is this possible under the GIPS standards?*

Historically, Firm C did not actually manage the assets in the global ex-Japan style. Instead it made a tactical decision not to own Japanese equity securities. It had a broadly defined investment management style for the original composite that could have included Japanese equity securities. By redefining the strategy of the composite more narrowly, the new ex-Japan composite would not accurately reflect the investment strategy of the composite historically. Redefining composites in this way does not provide an accurate history of the mandate and would not be appropriate. Firm C is accountable for the tactical decision not to own any Japanese securities. Typically, Firm C would need to have documented changes in client guidelines in order to make such a change to the strategy of the portfolios in the composite.

3. *If we currently have a composite for a particular strategy and the implementation of that strategy changes, can the performance track record continue to be associated with the new strategy?*

As most firms evolve, they refine their investment process through the use of new technologies and resources. It would seem clients would expect their firm to refine and improve the investment process.

3-4

Within the context of the Standards, a composite is an aggregation of a number of portfolios into a single group that represents a particular investment objective or strategy. The Standards require that composites must be defined according to similar investment objectives and/or strategies. If the investment objective of the portfolios in the composite remains constant as the firm refines the investment process, the firm should not create a new composite. If, however, the investment objective/strategy of the portfolios in the composite has changed, the firm should document the changes in client guidelines and create a new composite. The performance track record starts for that new composite when portfolios meeting the definition of the new composite are added to it. The firm should clearly document its decision and decision-making process in the event its decision to create or not to create a new composite is questioned by a verifier/regulator.

4. *We currently have two composites in the small cap growth universe. The guiding principles for managing the accounts are the same, but the market cap ranges differ on the low and high ends. One product runs approximately $100 million to $1 billion. The other product runs $500 million to $1.5 billion (with flexibility up to the largest stock in the Russell 2000 Growth Index).*

   We would like to expand, with client acceptance, the market cap range for all accounts in each product to encompass the full range, essentially eliminating the need for two products. How do we approach this from a composite standpoint?

When a firm decides to combine the investment strategies/objectives of two (or more) different composites, the firm would document the changes in client guidelines and create a new composite. The new composite will consist of all portfolios of the combined composites. The existing composites that the firm wishes to combine into this new composite would cease to continue. The new composite would not have historical performance results because the new composite's strategy is newly implemented. The firm would maintain and have available the performance results of the previous composites.

5. *We are changing our investment process and the personnel involved in the management of a U.K. Fund. The risk and return objectives will be lower, and the fund will be predominantly analyst run rather than portfolio manager run, as it was previously. Does this require a change in composite?*

The firm must determine if the changes in investment process and personnel will result in a change in the investment strategy of the portfolios in the composite. If the firm determines that the changes result in a different investment strategy for the portfolios, then changes to the client guidelines for the portfolios in the existing composite must be documented. If this will be a new investment strategy offered by the firm, a new composite will be started with a current composite creation date and no composite history.

6. *One of our portfolio managers is about to be promoted, and another manager will assume responsibility for the portfolios managed to the strategy. The new manager will use the same model, but will apply his own discretion. The investment guidelines for these portfolios will not change when the new manager assumes responsibility for the portfolios. Do we need to create a new composite for the new manager's investment history?*

It does not appear that the firm is changing the investment objectives and/or strategies of the portfolios. As such, the portfolios should all continue in the composite and the composite's history will continue uninterrupted when the new manager assumes investment responsibility for the portfolios. The firm must also consider if the change in personnel is a significant event that should be disclosed (see Provision 4.A.19).

7. *We have an account for an individual in one of our composites, but the client passed away and the account had to be closed and re-opened in another legal status. How do we treat this change for composite reporting purposes?*

From the perspective of the investment management firm, it does not seem that the portfolio was actually "terminated," in that the portfolio did not leave the firm and the firm never lost its discretion over the portfolio. The change in legal status of the portfolio would not be reason to stop and start the performance, especially in light of the fact that the assets never left the portfolio, the firm was never restricted in its management of the portfolio, and the strategy of the portfolio remains unchanged.

8. *One of the portfolios in our All-Cap Growth Equity composite changed objectives towards the end of the second quarter (client agreement date: 21 June) from All-Cap ($300 million and above market cap) to Mid-Cap ($1 billion to $10 billion).*

   Should the portfolio be taken out of the All-Cap composite for June, even though the portfolio's objective only changed in the last 9 days of the month? In talking to the portfolio managers involved, no changes were implemented during the short period because of the similarity of the two styles (All-Cap vs. Mid-Cap).

   Does the client objective change automatically exclude the account from being in the All-Cap composite for June?

Shifts from one composite to another should be consistent with the guidelines set forth by the specific account agreement or with documented guidelines of the firm's client. In the situation you present, if there was any latitude within the agreement as to when the change should occur, in the interest of fair representation and full disclosure, the firm should include the account in the All-Cap Growth Equity composite only through the last full measurement period that the account was managed to that strategy.

3.A.6 Convertible and other hybrid securities MUST be treated consistently across time and within COMPOSITES.

Discussion: The Standards do not address specifics of security classification. If a firm determines that convertible bonds should be treated as equity securities, then it must be consistent with its treatment of all convertible bonds. Keeping in mind the spirit and objectives of the Standards—fair representation and full disclosure—the firm should define a policy for categorizing assets and follow it consistently.

3.A.7 CARVE-OUT segments excluding cash are not permitted to be used to represent a discretionary PORTFOLIO and, as such, are not permitted to be included in COMPOSITE returns. When a single asset class is carved out of a multiple asset class PORTFOLIO and the returns are presented as part of a single asset COMPOSITE, cash MUST be allocated to the CARVE-OUT returns in a timely and consistent manner. Beginning 1 January 2010, CARVE-OUT returns are not permitted to be included in single asset class COMPOSITE returns unless the CARVE-OUT is actually managed separately with its own cash balance.

Discussion: A carve-out is a single or multiple-asset-class segment of a multiple-asset-class portfolio. For example, the Asian securities from a Euro-Pacific portfolio or the equity portion of a balanced portfolio could be considered a carve-out. Carve-outs are generally based on asset class, geographic region, or industry sector.

Carve-out returns are only a valid track record if they are representative of what would have been achieved in a portfolio dedicated to the carved-out strategy. Additionally, the Standards require that returns from cash and cash equivalents held in portfolios must be included in total return calculations. Generally, a portfolio experiences some degree of cash flow. If the allocation of cash to the segment is not captured in the carve-out segment return, the return is not representative of what would have been achieved in a portfolio dedicated to the carved-out strategy.

Because any carve-out record used as a stand-alone record for the strategy must be representative of an actual segregated portfolio managed to that strategy, the carved-out segment must be discretionary and structured materially the same as a portfolio dedicated to that strategy. Firms must establish policies and procedures for the creation, use and calculation of carve-outs, including cash allocation, and must apply them consistently.

Cross Reference: Guidance Statement on the Treatment of Carve-Outs (4-8), Guidance Statement on the Use of Supplemental Information (4-10), Provision 2.A.4, Provision 3.B.1, Provision 4.A.11, Provision 5.A.5

Application:

1. *Our firm has a balanced portfolio with a defined asset allocation of 25 percent U.S. equity, 25 percent non-U.S. equity, and 50 percent fixed income. Although each segment is managed in the same way as a stand-alone portfolio managed to the segment's strategy, we do not segregate the segments into separate portfolios with separate cash allocations. What is an acceptable method of allocating cash to the segments?*

The Standards do not require a specified cash-allocation methodology. The firm must choose a method that allocates the cash in a timely and consistent manner, document it and apply it consistently.

One suggested methodology would be to allocate cash to each segment based on the beginning-of-period valuations: identify the cash allocation percentage for each portfolio segment at the beginning of the period. For example, at the beginning of January, identify the percentage of residual cash that will be allocated to the carve-outs at month end. Or, at the beginning of the measurement period, if the market values for the segments – excluding residual cash – are 26 percent/23 percent/51 percent, residual cash in the portfolio will be allocated 26 percent to U.S. equity, 23 percent to non-U.S. Equity, and 51 percent to fixed income.

Another methodology would be to base the allocation directly upon the target strategic asset allocation: allocate residual cash in the percentages established when the portfolio was established. In the example provided above, residual cash will be allocated to rebalance the portfolio to 25 percent to U.S. equity, 25 percent non-U.S. equity, and 50 percent fixed income.

3.A.8 Composites must include only assets under management within the defined firm. Firms are not permitted to link simulated or model portfolios with actual performance.

Discussion: Simulated, back-tested, or model results must not be included in composites, as they do not represent actual assets under management.

Similarly, firms may not blend the history of two existing composites to create historical performance for a "hybrid" or model composite (e.g., combine the results of an equity composite and a fixed-income composite to form a hypothetical balanced composite). Even though the asset-class returns are based on actual assets under management, the arbitrary method of combining them historically is subject to manipulation and does not represent real-time asset allocation decisions.

Cross Reference: Guidance Statement on the Definition of the Firm (4-4), Guidance Statement on the Use of Supplemental Information (Section 4-10), Provision 0.A.1, Provision 0.A.3, Provision 0.A.4, Provision 3.A.1

Application:

1. *Firm A wants to offer a new investment management style. To demonstrate its capability to manage assets according to the new balanced strategy, Firm A creates a new balanced composite and produces three years of performance history using hypothetical assets and a back-tested asset allocation strategy. Can Firm A present this hypothetical composite history as a GIPS-compliant presentation?*

No. Composite returns must only contain actual assets under management.

2. *Will a model portfolio, compiled by an advisor who does not have discretion to invest assets in accordance with the model, qualify for a composite?*

No, as there are not any actual, fee-paying discretionary portfolios managed to the strategy. Model or advisory-only assets are not considered assets of the firm and are not included in total firm or composite assets.

3. *Our firm had a composite that lost all of its constituent portfolios for one quarter. May we continue our track record without interruption by using the benchmark return for the missing quarter of performance?*

No, firms may not link simulated performance to actual performance earned by the firm and represent the history as that of the firm. Composite returns must represent performance of only actual discretionary assets under management.

3.A.9 If a FIRM sets a minimum asset level for PORTFOLIOS to be included in a COMPOSITE, no PORTFOLIOS below that asset level can be included in that COMPOSITE. Any changes to a COMPOSITE-specific minimum asset level are not permitted to be applied retroactively.

Discussion: Firms may establish a minimum asset level for a composite to identify portfolios that are too small to be representative of the intended strategy.

Once a minimum size is established, it must be disclosed and applied consistently, and portfolios above this limit must be included in the composite. Changes to the minimum asset level should not occur frequently. If a firm makes a change to the minimum asset level for an existing composite, the firm must disclose the change to the minimum and consistently apply the new limit going forward. The firm must not go back and re-state historical performance data to include or exclude portfolios using the new minimum asset level.

Firms must disclose the minimum asset level of the composite, if one exists, in each respective composite presentation. Portfolios may fall below the minimum because of client withdrawals or depreciation in market value. Firms must determine, as part of their policies regarding minimum asset levels, which market value will be used to evaluate composite portfolios against the minimum asset level (e.g., beginning- or ending-period market value, including or excluding cash flows, etc.). If a firm establishes a minimum, it must document the policies established regarding how portfolios are treated if they fall below the minimum and must apply these policies consistently. Firms should consider establishing a threshold for the application of the minimum asset level and a minimum time period in order to minimize portfolio movement into or out of a composite. Firms should bear in mind that if all the portfolios are removed from a composite, for any reason, the performance record of the composite comes to an end.

If a portfolio is removed from a composite, the prior history of the portfolio must remain in the composite. Like all policies, once the firm establishes a policy regarding the minimum asset level it must be applied consistently. Once a portfolio is removed, the firm must determine if the portfolio meets any other composite definition and must include it in the appropriate composite(s) in a timely and consistent manner. If after a period of time, portfolios move above the minimum or new portfolios are added to the composite, the prior performance history of the composite should be shown but not linked to the ongoing composite performance results.

Cross Reference: Guidance Statement on Composite Definition (Section 4-2), Provision 3.A.1, Provision 3.B.3, Provision 4.A.3, Provision 4.A.20

Application:

1. *We have a composite of 120 accounts with a 10-year track record. We'd like to reclassify half of those accounts and move them to other composites as they no longer fit the objective of the historical composite. This is largely because of the accounts decreasing in size whereby there are not enough assets to buy all the appropriate number of securities for the style. Would we lose the historical performance record of the composite by removing so many accounts (more than half)?*

If a firm chooses to implement a minimum asset level or change a minimum asset level for an existing composite, the firm must document and disclose the change to the minimum and consistently apply the new limit going forward. The firm must not go back and re-state historical performance figures to include or exclude portfolios using the new minimum asset level.

COMPOSITE CONSTRUCTION — RECOMMENDATIONS

3.B.1 CARVE-OUT returns SHOULD not be included in single asset class COMPOSITE returns unless the CARVE-OUTS are actually managed separately with their own cash balance.

Discussion: Although the use of carve-outs with cash allocated to the segments is not recommended, it is permitted, but only through 31 December 2009. Provision 3.A.7 requires that beginning 1 January 2010, carve-out returns are not permitted to be included in single asset class composite returns unless the carve-out is actually managed separately with its own cash balance.

Cross Reference: Guidance Statement on the Treatment of Carve-Outs (Section 4-8), Guidance Statement on the Use of Supplemental Information (4-10), Provision 2.A.4, Provision 3.A.7, Provision 4.A.11, Provision 5.A.5

3.B.2 To remove the effect of a significant EXTERNAL CASH FLOW, the use of a TEMPORARY NEW ACCOUNT is RECOMMENDED (as opposed to adjusting the COMPOSITE composition to remove PORTFOLIOS with significant EXTERNAL CASH FLOWS).

Discussion: A significant external cash flow may be defined by the firm for each composite. The definition must be determined as either a specific monetary amount or a percentage of portfolio assets, and may be influenced by the characteristics of the asset class(es) within the strategy.

The firm could choose to establish a policy to create a temporary new account when a portfolio experiences a significant external cash flow. If a portfolio experiences a significant external cash inflow, the firm would create a temporary new account for the inflow of assets. The funds will remain in the temporary account until they are fully invested to reflect the manager's mandate for the portfolio. It would be expected that the time horizon for the existence of the temporary account would be in line with the firm's established policy for including new accounts in the composite. The performance of the funds in the temporary new account will not be reflected in the firm's performance until it is assimilated into the client's portfolio and the temporary new account is liquidated. The assets of the temporary new account will be reflected in total firm assets if it is in existence at the end of a reporting period.

If the portfolio experiences a significant external cash outflow, the firm would create a temporary new account for the outflow of assets. The temporary new account will be funded with the assets the manager will distribute to the client or will liquidate to meet the cash flow needs of the client. The portfolio with the remaining assets will continue in the composite and will reflect the outflow in the performance calculation. The temporary new account will not be included in any composite's performance calculation. The assets of the temporary new account will be reflected in total firm assets if it is in existence at the end of a reporting period.

Cross Reference: Guidance Statement on the Treatment of Significant Cash Flows (Section 4-9)

3.B.3 FIRMS SHOULD not market a COMPOSITE to a prospective client who has assets less than the COMPOSITE'S minimum asset level.

Discussion: When a firm establishes a minimum asset level for including portfolios in a composite, the firm is indicating that portfolios below that level are too small to be representative of that strategy. In the interest of fair representation, it would not be in the prospective client's best interest to be shown a composite that does not represent a strategy that is available to the prospective client.

Once a firm claims compliance with the GIPS standards, it must make every reasonable effort to provide all prospective clients with a presentation that complies with all the applicable requirements of the Standards; the firm may not choose to whom to present performance in compliance with the Standards. It is up to the firm and the prospective client to determine the selection of composites provided.

Cross Reference: Guidance Statement on Composite Definition (Section 4-2), Provision 3.A.9, Provision 4.A.3

DISCLOSURES — REQUIREMENTS

4.A.1 FIRMS MUST disclose the definition of "FIRM" used to determine the TOTAL FIRM ASSETS and FIRM-wide compliance.

3-5

Discussion: To claim compliance with the GIPS standards, the firm must comply with the Standards on a firm-wide basis. Accordingly, the firm must determine exactly how it will be defined for the purpose of compliance. The Standards require that a firm must be defined as an investment firm, subsidiary, or division held out to clients or potential clients as a distinct business entity.

A distinct business entity is a unit, division, department, or office that is organizationally and functionally segregated from other units, divisions, departments, or offices and retains discretion over the assets it manages and should have autonomy over the investment decision-making process.

Possible criteria that can be used to determine this include:

- being a legal entity;
- having a distinct market or client type (e.g., institutional, retail, private client, etc.);
- using a separate and distinct investment process.

Because there are often a number of closely related units or divisions within larger investment management entities, it is critical to disclose the precise definition of the firm that is presenting the performance results and would be responsible for the management of the prospective client's assets. This provision requires the firm to disclose sufficient details of the entity that is presenting investment performance such that the firm is clearly identified.

Cross Reference: Guidance Statement on the Definition of the Firm (Section 4-4), Provision 0.A.1, Provision 0.A.2, Provision 0.A.3, Provision 0.A.14, Provision 0.B.1, Provision 4.A.21, Provision 4.B.1

Application:

1. *Firm A is a multinational investment firm, with offices around the world including Japan, Australia, the United Kingdom and the United States. Although all of its offices are part of the global parent, each office is registered with the appropriate national regulatory authority and each is held out to clients and potential clients as a distinct business entity. Firm A (U.S.) claims compliance with the GIPS standards. What should the definition of the firm disclosure be?*

Sample Disclosure: "Firm A is defined as an independent management firm with offices in Japan, Australia, the United Kingdom, and the United States. Firm A (U.S.) is a subsidiary of Firm A serving U.S. clients. Firm A also has subsidiaries in the United Kingdom, Australia, and Japan."

2. *Firm B manages money for both retail and institutional clients. An autonomous group, "Firm B Institutional Investment Management," manages institutional assets. Another autonomous group, "Firm B Retail Investors," manages retail assets. How should "Firm B Institutional Investment Management" disclose its firm definition?*

Sample Disclosure: "For the purpose of complying with the GIPS standards the firm is defined as Firm B Institutional Investment Management, the institutional asset management division of Firm B."

4.A.2 FIRMS MUST disclose the availability of a complete list and description of all of the FIRM'S COMPOSITES.

Discussion: In each compliant presentation, the firm must disclose the availability of a complete list and description of the firm's composites. The actual list does not need to be included in each presentation but must be readily available upon request. On the list, the firm must include a brief description of each composite, which is general information regarding the strategy of the composite.

This requirement exists to provide prospective clients a complete picture of the firm's composites. By requesting the list, prospective clients will have a better opportunity to evaluate whether the composite presentation they have received is the most appropriate, as well as if there are any other composites that they should also request to see. The list must include the firm's current composites as well as composites that have been discontinued or terminated during the past five years.

Cross Reference: Guidance Statement on Composite Definition (Section 4-2), Provision 0.A.12, Provision 0.A.13, Appendix B of the GIPS standards

Application:

Sample Disclosure: "A complete listing and description of the firm's composites is available upon request."

4.A.3 FIRMS MUST disclose the minimum asset level, if any, below which PORTFOLIOS are not included in a COMPOSITE. FIRMS MUST also disclose any changes to the minimum asset level.

Discussion: The firm may establish a minimum asset level for a composite to identify portfolios that are too small to be representative of the intended strategy. Firms must disclose the minimum asset level of the composite, if one exists, in each respective composite presentation.

If any changes have been made to the minimum asset level of a composite, the firm must disclose the change.

Cross Reference: Guidance Statement on Composite Definition (Section 4-2), Provision 3.A.9, Provision 3.B.3

Application:

Sample Disclosure: "The minimum portfolio size for inclusion in Composite LMN is €500,000. Prior to 2002, portfolios with assets below €400,000 were not included."

4.A.4 FIRMS MUST disclose the currency used to express performance.

Discussion: The GIPS standards require that firms disclose the currency used to express performance. In cases involving currency changes because of the Euro conversion, please refer to the Guidelines in Respect of the Impact of Euro Conversion.

Application:

Sample Disclosure: "Valuations are computed and performance results are reported in Canadian dollars."

4.A.5 FIRMS MUST disclose the presence, use, and extent of leverage or derivatives (if material), including a sufficient description of the use, frequency, and characteristics of the instruments to identify risks.

Discussion: The disclosure should contain sufficient detail so that current or prospective clients can understand the pattern of returns and the risks from the leverage or derivatives positions, if their use is material to the implementation of the strategy.

Cross Reference: Provision 5.B.2

Application:

Sample Disclosures: "Portfolios in the composite may be leveraged from time-to-time to increase equity market exposure to 150 percent of the account's value."

"The strategy includes the frequent use of naked short selling, which greatly increases exposure to fluctuations in market prices."

4.A.6 FIRMS MUST clearly label returns as GROSS-OF-FEES or NET-OF-FEES.

Discussion: Under the GIPS standards, firms may present investment performance results gross and/or net of investment management fees. Currently, the GIPS standards recommend that firms present gross-of-fees performance. Firms must clearly indicate within each presentation whether returns are gross-of-fees or net-of-fees so that potential clients can properly identify the information presented.

Cross Reference: Provision 4.A.15, Provision 4.A.16, Provision 5.B.1

4.A.7 FIRMS MUST disclose relevant details of the treatment of withholding tax on dividends, interest income, and capital gains. If using indexes that are net-of-taxes, the FIRM MUST disclose the tax basis of the BENCHMARK (e.g., Luxembourg based or U.S. based) versus that of the COMPOSITE.

Discussion: Global investing requires recognition of the tax consequences of investing in different countries. Some countries allow certain foreign investor types to reclaim a portion of the withholding taxes that are paid when transactions or income payments occur. These reclaimable withholding taxes are repaid to the foreign investor at a later date. It is recommended that reclaimable foreign withholding taxes be accrued. This provision is not applicable to domestic withholding taxes for individuals for payment of their domestic tax liability (used with after-tax calculations). This provision is applicable only on the withholding tax incurred on nondomestic holdings.

Cross Reference: Provision 2.B.1, Provision 5.B.1

Application:

Sample Disclosure: "Portfolio returns are net of all foreign withholding taxes. The benchmark return is net of withholding taxes from a Luxembourg tax perspective."

4.A.8 FIRMS MUST disclose and describe any known inconsistencies in the exchange rates used among the PORTFOLIOS within a COMPOSITE and between the COMPOSITE and the BENCHMARK.

Discussion: Firms must disclose any material difference in the exchange rates used among the portfolios in the composite and between the benchmark (i.e., the firm selects the exchange rate used for the benchmark) and the composite portfolios. Differences may exist as a result of the sources used (e.g., WM/Reuters versus Bloomberg) or the time of day (e.g., 1200h versus 1600h). This disclosure allows prospective clients to identify any variance because of differences in exchange rates that may positively or negatively impact the comparison of the composite's return to that of the benchmark.

If the same exchange rate is used for all portfolios in the composite and for the composite benchmark, no disclosure is necessary. The Standards do not require a particular source for exchange rates, but the WM/Reuters Closing Spot Rates (1600h London) are generally accepted as the source for exchange rates by many firms globally as well as by many of the published indexes.

4.A.9 If the presentation conforms with local laws and regulations that differ from the GIPS REQUIREMENTS, FIRMS MUST disclose this fact and disclose the manner in which the local laws and regulations conflict with the GIPS standards.

Discussion: The GIPS standards are a voluntary set of standards that seek to promote global "best practices" of investment performance reporting. The Standards serve as a minimum, worldwide standard for investment performance measurement and presentation. If local or country-specific laws or regulations do exist, firms are required to follow the existing laws or regulations. In some instances, local laws or regulations may conflict with the requirements and recommendations set forth in the GIPS standards.

In cases where applicable local or country-specific law or regulation conflicts with the GIPS standards, the Standards require firms to comply with the local law or regulation and make full disclosure of this conflict. This disclosure will assist clients in comparing the composite returns among firms where reporting requirements may differ because of local laws or regulations.

4.A.10 For any performance presented for periods prior to 1 January 2000 that does not comply with the GIPS standards, FIRMS MUST disclose the period of noncompliance and how the presentation is not in compliance with the GIPS standards.

Discussion: The GIPS standards allow firms to link non-GIPS compliant performance to their compliant history, provided that no noncompliant performance is shown for periods beginning 1 January 2000. If the firm chooses to present noncompliant performance for periods prior to 1 January 2000, the firm must disclose which periods are not in compliance and the reasons the performance does not comply with the GIPS standards. This disclosure will allow prospective clients to make valid comparisons among performance presentations and consider the effects of noncompliance on the historical performance.

Cross Reference: Provision 5.A.1, Provision 5.A.2, Provision 5.B.3

Application:

1. *Firm A presents its performance history since its inception in 1990 and claims compliance with the GIPS standards. The performance record since 1996 adheres to requirements of the GIPS standards. However, the firm did not include accrued income in the return calculation for the period from 1990–1995. What disclosure is necessary to allow the firm to link its pre-1996 noncompliant history with the ongoing compliant history?*

Firm A must disclose on its composite presentation that the performance record from 1990–1995 is not in compliance because accrued income was not included for fixed-income instruments when calculating the composite's constituent portfolios' returns. This disclosure allows potential clients to determine whether the firm's performance results from 1990–1995 are representative and whether the results are comparable to the performance of other firms that included accrued income during the same period.

4.A.11 For periods prior to 1 January 2010, when a single asset class is carved out of a multiple asset PORTFOLIO and the returns are presented as part of a single asset COMPOSITE, FIRMS MUST disclose the policy used to allocate cash to the CARVE-OUT returns.

3-5

Discussion: The GIPS standards allow firms to carve out a single asset class from a multiple-asset portfolio and present the information as part of a single-asset composite as long as the carve-out is representative of what would have been achieved in a portfolio dedicated to the carved-out strategy and includes cash. The method of allocating the cash to a single-asset carve-out must be disclosed. Until 1 January 2010, firms are allowed to allocate cash to the carve-out. After 1 January 2010, carve-outs must not be included in single asset-class composites unless the carve-outs are actually managed separately with their own cash.

Cross Reference: Guidance Statement on Composite Definition (Section 4-2), Guidance Statement on the Treatment of Carve-Outs (4-8), Provision 2.A.4, Provision 3.A.7, Provision 3.B.1, Provision 5.A.5

Application:

1. *Firm A carves out U.K. equity performance from its Euro-Pacific equity portfolios and combines it with its U.K. equity portfolios to create a U.K. Equity composite. Before including the carve-out in the U.K. Equity composite, the firm allocates cash to the U.K. equity segment on a pro rata basis, based on the level of U.K. equities as a percentage of the total equity exposure. What disclosure is necessary?*

The U.K. equity composite returns (which includes both the carve-out segment as well as portfolios that are invested solely in U.K. equity) may be presented as a part of a GIPS compliant presentation provided the segment meets the carve-out requirements, cash is allocated to the carve-out (until 1 January 2010), and the method used to allocate the cash to the carve-out is disclosed. The firm must include in the U.K. Equity Composite all carve-outs from all portfolios meeting this definition.

Sample Disclosure: "Firm A's U.K. Equity composite includes all dedicated U.K. equity portfolios as well as the U.K. equity segment of portfolios that are managed to the firm's Euro-Pacific Equity strategy. Cash is allocated to the carve-out segment returns on a pro rata basis depending on the proportion of U.K. assets to total portfolio assets based on beginning-of-period market values."

4.A.12 FIRMS MUST disclose the FEE SCHEDULE appropriate to the presentation.

Discussion: Within each compliant presentation, the Standards require disclosure of an appropriate fee schedule showing the firm's current investment management fees or bundled fees for a particular presentation. This schedule is typically listed by asset level ranges and should be appropriate to the particular prospective client. Fee levels tend to vary from client to client depending on the portfolio size and the ability of the client to negotiate fees. This disclosure requirement is not satisfied if the firm makes reference to another document that includes the fee schedule. The fee schedule must be part of the presentation that includes the claim of compliance with the Standards.

Cross-Reference: Interpretive Guidance for Fees Provisions (Section 4-6), Provision 4.A.6

Application:

Sample Disclosure: Gross returns are presented before the deduction of management fees and are net of all transaction costs. The firm's annual fee schedule is as follows:

First €10 million	0.80%
Next €40 million	0.60%
Above €50 million	0.30%

4.A.13 If a COMPOSITE contains PORTFOLIOS with BUNDLED FEES, FIRMS MUST disclose for each annual period shown the percentage of COMPOSITE assets that is BUNDLED FEE PORTFOLIOS.

3-5

4.A.14 If a COMPOSITE contains PORTFOLIOS with BUNDLED FEES, FIRMS MUST disclose the various types of fees that are included in the BUNDLED FEE.

Discussion: A bundled fee is a fee that combines multiple fees into one "bundled" fee. Bundled fees can include any combination of management, transaction, custody, and other administrative fees. Two specific examples of bundle fees are the wrap fee and the all-in fee.

All-In Fee: Due to the universal banking system in some countries, asset management, brokerage, and custody are often part of the same company. This system allows banks to offer a variety of choices to customers regarding how the fee will be charged. Customers are offered numerous fee models in which fees may be bundled together or charged separately. All-in fees can include any combination of investment management, trading expenses, custody, and other administrative fees.

Wrap Fee: Wrap fees are specific to a particular investment product. The U.S. Securities and Exchange Commission (SEC) defines a wrap-fee account (now more commonly known as a separately managed account or SMA) as "any advisory program under which a specified fee or fees not based upon transactions in a client's account is charged for investment advisory services (which may include portfolio management or advice concerning the selection of other investment advisors) and execution of client transactions." A typical separately managed account has a contract or contracts (and fee) involving a sponsor (usually a broker or independent provider) acting as the investment advisor, an investment management firm typically as the subadvisor, other services (custody, consulting, reporting, performance, manager selection, monitoring, and execution of trades), distributor, and the client (brokerage customer). Wrap fees can be all-inclusive, asset-based fees (which may include any combination of management, transaction, custody, and other administrative fees).

Cross Reference: Guidance Statement for Wrap Fee/Separately Managed Account (SMA) Portfolios (Section 4-13), Provision 2.A.7, Provision 4.A.15, Provision 4.A.16

Application:

Sample disclosures:

Year	% of Bundled Fee Portfolios in the Composite
2003	100
2002	100
2001	100
2000	100
1999	100
1998	0
1997	0

The bundled fee includes all charges for trading costs, portfolio management, custody, and other administrative fees.

4.A.15 When presenting GROSS-OF-FEES RETURNS, FIRMS MUST disclose if any other fees are deducted in addition to the direct TRADING EXPENSES.

Discussion: In order to assist prospective clients in better understanding the fees included in the gross-of-fees return calculation, firms must disclose if other fees are deducted in addition to the trading expenses.

3-5

Cross Reference: Interpretive Guidance for Fees Provisions (Section 4-6), Provision 2.A.5, Provision 2.A.7, Provision 4.A.6, Provision 4.A.13, Provision 4.A.14, Provision 4.A.16

4.A.16 When presenting NET-OF-FEES RETURNS, FIRMS MUST disclose if any other fees are deducted in addition to the INVESTMENT MANAGEMENT FEE and direct TRADING EXPENSES.

Discussion: In order to assist prospective clients in better understanding the fees included in the net-of-fees returns, firms must disclose if other fees are deducted in addition to the investment management fee and trading expenses.

Cross Reference: Interpretive Guidance for Fees Provisions (Section 4-6), Provision 2.A.5, Provision 2.A.7, Provision 4.A.6, Provision 4.A.13, Provision 4.A.14, Provision 4.A.15

4.A.17 FIRMS MUST disclose that ADDITIONAL INFORMATION regarding policies for calculating and reporting returns is available upon request.

Discussion: In each presentation in compliance with the Standards, firms must disclose the availability of additional information regarding policies for calculating and reporting returns. The information does not need to be included in each presentation, but it must be readily available upon request.

Cross Reference: Guidance Statement on Calculation Methodology (Section 4-1), Provision 0.A.6

Application:

> *Sample Disclosure*: "Additional information regarding the firm's policies and procedures for calculating and reporting performance results is available upon request."

4.A.18 Beginning 1 January 2006, FIRMS MUST disclose the use of a subadvisor(s) and the periods a subadvisor(s) was used.

Discussion: Some firms utilize a subadvisor to manage part or all of a particular strategy. For example, if a firm specializes in managing equities, it might hire a subadvisor to manage the fixed-income portion of its balanced portfolios. The Standards require that firms must include the performance of assets assigned to a subadvisor in a composite provided the firm has the authority to allocate the assets to a subadvisor.

If a firm has discretion over the selection of the subadvisor (i.e., can hire and/or fire), the firm must claim the subadvisor's performance as part of its performance history and include the assets in the firm's total assets. Because the subadvisor has discretion over the actual investment of the assets and the firm has discretion over the selection of the subadvisor, both the firm and the subadvisor are able to claim the performance of the assets as their own. The firm is able to claim this performance because the subadvised portion of the portfolio is essentially viewed as an asset (similar to purchasing a mutual fund within the portfolio) and the firm must be held responsible for its decision to utilize a subadvisor. The firm can only include the subadvisor's performance record relevant to those assets assigned by the firm. If a firm does not have discretion over subadvisor selection, it must not include the subadvisor's performance in its performance history.

Cross Reference: Guidance Statement on Definition of the Firm (Section 4-4), Provision 0.A.4

Application:

Sample Disclosure: "A subadvisor was used to provide international equity exposure in the growth composite for the year 2006."

4.A.19 FIRMS MUST disclose all significant events that would help a prospective client interpret the performance record.

Discussion: The GIPS standards are based on the principles of fair representation and full disclosure. Meeting these objectives requires a good faith commitment on the part of the presenter to adhere to the spirit of the GIPS standards. This provision requires that firms disclose all significant events that would help explain the firm's performance record to a prospective client. Significant events are defined by the firm and should include, for example, the occurrence of a material change in personnel responsible for investment management. The primary goal of this requirement is to provide relevant information to prospective clients so that they can understand the potential impact the significant event may have on the investment strategy.

Depending on the situation, a general statement describing the significant event that has occurred may be sufficient. Other situations may require firms to disclose specific information pertaining to the significant event.

Cross Reference: Provision 0.A.5, Provision 5.A.4

Application:

1. *Firm A has an equity composite that is managed by one portfolio manager who is prominently displayed in the firm's marketing materials. This manager leaves the firm and another manager is hired to continue managing the composite according to the same strategy. What disclosures should be made?*

Each firm must determine what significant events would help a prospective client interpret the performance record. When a strategy has a single investment decision maker who leaves and is replaced with a new investment decision maker, this event qualifies as a significant event that must be disclosed. Although the investment strategy remains the same with the new manager, the firm must disclose the change in personnel responsible for the management of the equity composite. The firm must also include a statement that the manager responsible for the history of the composite is no longer with the firm and the date of the original manager's departure.

2. *Firm B acquires another firm. The amount of firm assets and assets in each of Firm B's composite increases significantly after the purchase. Should the firm make any disclosures regarding these events?*

Yes, the GIPS standards require that firms disclose any significant events within the investment management firm that would help prospective clients understand the performance record. An acquisition of a new entity would likely qualify as a significant event, as many aspects of the firm's management, operations, investment processes, and staffing may change. Prospective clients should be informed of such changes.

Sample Disclosure: "Firm B acquired Firm X on 1 June 2000. As a result, Firm B's assets as well as its research function were greatly expanded by including Firm X's resources."

4.A.20 FIRMS MUST disclose the COMPOSITE DESCRIPTION.

Discussion: The composite's description is general information regarding the strategy of the composite. A description may be more abbreviated than the composite definition but includes all salient features of the composite.

Cross Reference: Guidance Statement on Composite Definition (Section 4-2), Provision 0.A.12, Provision 3.A.2, Provision 4.A.2

Application:

> *Sample Disclosure:* "The composite includes all nontaxable balanced portfolios with an asset allocation of 30 percent S&P TSX and 70 percent Scotia Canadian Bond Index Fund, which allow up to a 10 percent deviation in asset allocation."

4.A.21 If a FIRM is redefined, the FIRM MUST disclose the date and reason for the redefinition.

Discussion: In some cases, because of corporate restructuring and merger and acquisition activities, the changes within the firm may be so significant that it is held out to the public as a new firm. The new firm must determine if there is a continuation from the prior firm or if the restructuring is so substantial that it is essentially a new firm.

Changes in investment style or personnel are not valid reasons for redefining the firm, unless the changes are such that the firm is held out to the public in a significantly different way. A simple name change is not sufficient reason to redefine the firm and restart the performance record. In some cases, a firm definition may change without the firm losing its performance history. In all cases, the underlying principles of the Standards must be considered: fair representation and full disclosure. The Standards require that changes in a firm's organization are not permitted to lead to alterations of historical composite results.

Cross Reference: Guidance Statement on Definition of the Firm (Section 4-4), Provision 0.A.1, Provision 0.A.2, Provision 0.A.3, Provision 0.A.5, Provision 0.B.1, Provision 4.A.1

Application:

> *Sample Disclosure:* "As of 1 January 2006, XYZ Firm includes both the London and Tokyo office of XYZ Company. Previously the firm included only the London office."

4.A.22 If a FIRM has redefined a COMPOSITE, the FIRM MUST disclose the date and nature of the change. Changes to COMPOSITES are not permitted to be applied retroactively.

Discussion: Although investment strategies can change over time, in most cases firms should not change the definition of a composite. Generally, changes in strategy result in the creation of a new composite. In some very rare cases, however, it may be appropriate to redefine a composite.

Cross Reference: Guidance Statement on Composite Definition (Section 4-2), Provision 3.A.1, Provision 3.A.2, Provision 3.A.5

Application:

Sample Disclosure: "As of 1 January 2006, the Large-Cap composite has been redefined to exclude carve-outs."

4.A.23 FIRMS MUST disclose any changes to the name of a COMPOSITE.

Cross Reference: Guidance Statement on Composite Definition (Section 4-2)

Application:

Sample Disclosure: "As of 1 January 2006, the S&P 500 Composite has been renamed the Large-Cap Growth Composite."

Note: The date of the change is not required to be disclosed, but in the interest of full disclosure, it is suggested that firms include this reference.

4.A.24 FIRMS MUST disclose the COMPOSITE CREATION DATE.

Discussion: Firms are required to disclose the date on which the firm first grouped portfolios to create a composite. The composite creation date is not necessarily the earliest date for which performance is reported for the composite, but is based on when the firm first grouped the individual portfolios together to form the composite. The intent of this disclosure is to enable prospective clients to determine whether the composite was created with the benefit of hindsight (i.e., whether the firm was able to evaluate its performance history prior to grouping portfolios together into a composite).

Cross Reference: Guidance Statement on Composite Definition (Section 4-2)

Application:

1. *Firm A comes into compliance with the GIPS standards on 1 January 1999 by re-stating its history since 1 January 1994 in compliance with the Standards. What is the composite creation date for Firm A's composites?*

The composite creation date depends on when the firm first grouped the portfolios together for each respective composite. If the firm is reporting a composite in compliance with the Standards for the first time in 1999 but had grouped the portfolios in the composite together in 1994, the composite creation date is 1994.

4.A.25 FIRMS MUST disclose if, prior to 1 January 2010, calendar month-end PORTFOLIO valuations or valuations on the last business day of the month are not used.

Discussion: Consistency in monthly portfolio valuation dates will result in improved comparability of data, especially when firms choose to present year-to-date composite data, or performance at the end of a month or quarter.

Cross Reference: Guidance Statement on Calculation Methodology (Section 4-1), Provision 1.A.3, Provision 1.A.4, Provision 1.B.3

Application:

Sample Disclosure: "Portfolios in the Value Composite are valued as of the last Friday of the month as well as the last business day of the year."

3-5

4.A.26 FIRMS MUST disclose which DISPERSION measure is presented.

Discussion: The GIPS standards do not mandate a specific measure or methodology to calculate composite dispersion. Instead, firms are permitted to choose a method and apply it consistently. Because firms may choose which measure to present, disclosure of the chosen method is required in the compliant presentation.

Cross Reference: Guidance Statement on Calculation Methodology (Section 4-1), Provision 5.A.1

Application:

Sample Disclosure: "Internal dispersion is calculated using the equal-weighted standard deviation of the annual returns of all portfolios that were included in the composite for the entire year."

DISCLOSURES — RECOMMENDATIONS

4.B.1 If a parent company contains multiple defined FIRMS, each FIRM within the parent company is encouraged to disclose a list of the other FIRMS contained within the parent company.

Discussion: A parent company may have two or more units, divisions, departments, or offices that are defined as separate firms within the context of the Standards. The firm's definition will reflect the specific circumstances at each firm and must reflect how the entity (firm) is held out to the public as a distinct business entity. In the interest of fair representation and full disclosure, it is recommended that each firm within the parent company disclose a list of the firms within the parent company.

Cross Reference: Guidance Statement on Definition of the Firm (Section 4-4), Provision 0.A.2, Provision 0.B.1, Provision 4.A.1

Application:

Sample Disclosure: "The Firm is the institutional division of ABC parent company. Both the private banking and retail divisions of ABC parent company claim compliance with the GIPS standards."

4.B.2 FIRMS SHOULD disclose when a change in a calculation methodology or valuation source results in a material impact on the performance of a COMPOSITE return.

Discussion: Firms have discretion over a variety of the components of the total return calculation. Although the Standards prohibit firms from changing a calculation methodology or a valuation source for the sole purpose of increasing a performance return, changes can be made when a more accurate calculation will result and the change is implemented consistently going forward. When the firm makes a change to a calculation methodology or a valuation source, if the impact on the performance return of the composite is material, the change should be disclosed.

Cross Reference: Guidance Statement on Calculation Methodology (Section 4-1)

Application:

Sample Disclosure: "Effective 1 January 2005, portfolio returns are calculated daily. Previously, portfolio returns were calculated monthly using the Dietz method."

4.B.3 FIRMS that have been verified SHOULD add a disclosure to their COMPOSITE presentation stating that the FIRM has been verified and clearly indicating the periods the verification covers if the COMPOSITE presentation includes results for periods that have not been subject to FIRM-wide verification.

Discussion: Firms are encouraged to undertake the verification process, defined as the review of a firm's performance measurement processes and procedures by an independent third-party verifier. The initial minimum period for which verification can be performed is one year of a firm's presented performance. A single verification report is issued in respect to the whole firm; verification cannot be carried out for a single composite. The primary purpose of verification is to establish that a firm claiming compliance with the GIPS standards has adhered to the Standards. The verification disclosure language should read: "(Insert name of Firm) has been verified for the periods (insert date) by (name of verifier). A copy of the verification report is available upon request."

Cross Reference: Verification (Section 3-9), Provision 0.B.2, Provision 0.B.3

PRESENTATION AND REPORTING — REQUIREMENTS

5.A.1 The following items MUST be reported for each COMPOSITE presented:

a. At least 5 years of performance (or a record for the period since FIRM or COMPOSITE inception if the FIRM or COMPOSITE has been in existence less than 5 years) that meets the REQUIREMENTS of the GIPS standards; after presenting 5 years of performance, the FIRM MUST present additional annual performance up to 10 years. (For example, after a FIRM presents 5 years of compliant history, the FIRM MUST add an additional year of performance each year so that after 5 years of claiming compliance, the FIRM presents a 10-year performance record.)

Discussion: In order to claim compliance, a firm is required to meet all applicable requirements of the GIPS standards on a firm-wide basis when creating the initial five-year track record of investment performance history. All of the firm's actual, fee-paying discretionary portfolios must be placed in appropriate composites to create the five-year record. If the firm (or composite) has been in existence less than five years, the firm must present performance since inception of the firm (or the composite).

Once a firm has its initial five years of history, the firm must continue to add annual returns that comply with the GIPS standards to each composite presentation for the next five years (at a minimum), so that after five years of claiming compliance with the Standards, the firm will have a 10-year performance record for its composites. Firms may also choose to present a composite's history for more than 10 years.

Please see the sections of the GIPS standards on Real Estate (Section 3-7), Private Equity (Section 3-8) and the Guidance Statement for Wrap-Fee/Separately Managed Accounts (SMA) Portfolios (Section 4-13) for additional information on the effective dates for these asset types.

In addition, the convergence of all Country Versions of the GIPS standards (CVGs) may have specific implications for a firm that previously claimed compliance with a CVG. If the firm previously claimed compliance with a CVG, at a minimum, the firm must continue to show the historical CVG-compliant track record up to 10 years (or since inception). Firms previously claiming compliance with a CVG are granted reciprocity to claim compliance with the GIPS standards for historical periods prior to 1 January 2006.

Cross Reference: Provision 4.A.10, Provision 5.A.2, Provision 5.B.3

Application:

1. *Firm A has been in existence since 1990. Beginning 1 January 2001, what periods of performance must Firm A present to claim compliance with the GIPS standards?*

At a minimum, Firm A must show historical performance in compliance with the GIPS standards from 1 January 1996 through 31 December 2000, which represents a five-year compliant performance record. Each year for at least five years thereafter, the firm must continue to add an annual return to its existing composites. A 10-year GIPS-compliant performance record is then available after 31 December 2005.

During this 10-year period, Firm A may create new composites and terminate others. It is possible that these new or terminated composites will not have a 10-year record at 31 December 2005.

2. *Firm B has been in existence since 1 January 1998 and has re-stated its entire performance history in compliance with the GIPS standards on 1 January 2006. What periods of performance must Firm B present to claim compliance with the Standards?*

When first claiming compliance with the Standards, Firm B must show its most recent five-year history in compliance with the Standards because the firm has been in existence more than five years. The firm could also choose to show performance since inception (i.e., an eight-year performance record, 1998 through 2005), or any period in between (i.e., a six- or seven-year performance record). Firm B must continue to build to a 10-year history, at a minimum, going forward.

3. *Firm C has been in existence since 1985 and is currently considering its options for coming into compliance with the GIPS standards. The firm determines its performance history does not satisfy one of the GIPS calculation requirements. For various reasons, the firm cannot re-state performance from the last five years in order to create a five-year compliant record as required by the GIPS standards; however, it is able to recreate the performance from the last year and show a one-year "GIPS-compliant" return. Can Firm C claim compliance with the GIPS standards?*

No. The GIPS standards require firms to present at least five years of performance (or performance since firm inception if firm is less than five years). In order to claim compliance, Firm C must build a compliant performance record going forward and should be able to claim compliance in four years.

4. *Can a firm that has only been in existence for three years claim compliance with the GIPS standards?*

Yes, firms that have been in existence less than five years may claim compliance. The firm must do so for the period since the firm's inception, which in this case would be for three years.

5. *Our firm has been compliant with the Standards since its inception. Our initial composite with our growth-equity strategy has over five years of performance history. We subsequently added a new mid-cap strategy leading to the creation of a separate mid-cap composite. This mid-cap composite does not have the five years of performance history yet. Is the 5-year building to 10-year requirement on a firm-wide basis or is it on an individual composite basis? May we show the mid-cap composite as compliant without the five years of history?*

The 5-year building to 10-year requirement is on a firm-wide basis.

The firm must include all actual, fee-paying, discretionary portfolios in composites. It is not required that every composite have an initial five-year history corresponding to the firm's first five years of existence. Composites may come and go during the firm's existence, but all appropriate portfolios within the firm must be in an appropriate composite for the 5-year building to 10-year period.

5.A.1 The following items MUST be reported for each COMPOSITE presented:

b. Annual returns for all years.

Discussion: The GIPS standards require, at a minimum, the presentation of annual investment performance. Returns can be presented based on calendar year, fiscal year, or any other consistent annual period. Firms should disclose the presentation periods.

The annual periods must be continuous (i.e., there are no gaps in performance within the annual periods). Partial-year returns may be presented provided the periods covered are clearly disclosed. Partial-year returns are not permitted to be annualized.

Cross Reference: Provision 5.B.1, Provision 5.A.3

Application:

1. *Firm B claims compliance with the GIPS standards and presents annualized performance for one-, three-, and five-year periods. Does this satisfy the presentation requirements of the GIPS standards?*

No. Although the firm may present annualized performance returns as additional information, it must present annual returns for at least five years.

2. *Provision 5.A.1.b requires the presentation of annual returns for all years. My firm was just created this year and as such, does not yet have any annual returns. Can my firm claim compliance with the Standards now or must we wait until we have at least one annual return?*

The firm may claim compliance as soon as it meets the requirements of the Standards and has performance to report. Provision 5.A.1.a requires at least five years of performance (or a record for the period since firm inception, if inception is less than five years) that is compliant with the GIPS standards. This provision is not intended to prevent a new firm from complying with the Standards until it has an entire 12 month period of performance. If the firm is less than 12 months old, it is permitted to present its performance since inception and claim compliance.

5.A.1 The following items MUST be reported for each COMPOSITE presented:

c. The number of PORTFOLIOS and amount of assets in the COMPOSITE, and either the percentage of the TOTAL FIRM ASSETS represented by the COMPOSITE or the amount of TOTAL FIRM ASSETS at the end of each annual period. If the COMPOSITE contains 5 PORTFOLIOS or less, the number of PORTFOLIOS is not REQUIRED.

Discussion: Each composite presentation must include information on the number of portfolios and the amount of assets held in the composite. The presentation must also include either the percentage of the total firm assets that the composite represents or the amount of total firm assets. These figures must be determined as of the end of each annual period that performance results are presented.

Total firm assets are defined as all assets for which the firm has investment management responsibility. This includes assets managed outside the firm by subadvisors for which the firm has the authority to assign (allocate) the assets, discretionary as well as nondiscretionary assets, and non-fee-paying assets. Total firm assets do not include assets to which the Standards can not be applied. Total firm assets include cash and cash equivalents (money market funds, certificates of deposit, etc.). Firms must be sure that assets are not double counted, as double counting assets would not fairly represent the firm's assets.

This requirement provides information to potential clients on the profile of the composite (whether it is composed of a small number of portfolios or many), the size of the composite (measured by the amount of assets it contains), and the relative size of the composite in relation to the total assets managed by the firm (can either be calculated from the data provided or derived from the presentation of the percentage of firm assets represented in the composite).

In cases where there are five portfolios or fewer in a composite and the disclosure of the exact number of portfolios could compromise client confidentiality, firms may state that the composite contains "five or fewer portfolios," or similar language, rather than the exact number of portfolios in the composite. This option allows firms to protect the identity and confidentiality of its clients.

Cross Reference: Provision 0.A.3, Provision 3.A.1

Application:

1. *Our composite presentation includes disclosure of both total firm assets and the percentage of the total firm assets represented by the composite. May we include both disclosures in the presentation?*

Yes, firms may show both disclosures in their presentations. Because only one of these disclosures is required, the firm may choose in the future to discontinue showing one of the disclosures.

5.A.1 The following items MUST be reported for each COMPOSITE presented:

d. A measure of DISPERSION of individual PORTFOLIO returns for each annual period. If the COMPOSITE contains 5 PORTFOLIOS or less for the full year, a measure of DISPERSION is not REQUIRED.

Discussion: A measure of internal composite dispersion represents the distribution of individual annual portfolio returns within the composite. It allows prospective clients to determine how consistently the firm implemented its strategy across the portfolios in the composite for the full annual period.

The GIPS standards do not mandate a specific measure or methodology to calculate composite dispersion. Instead, the firm is permitted to choose a method for each composite and apply it consistently. The firm may change the method of dispersion reported but should not use different measures from year to year and should document its reasons for changing its methodology. Measures may include, but are not limited to, high/low, interquartile range, and standard deviation (asset weighted or equal weighted). Firms are required to disclose which dispersion measure is presented.

Because the dispersion measure represents the spread of annual returns of individual portfolios within the composite for the full year, only the portfolios that have been managed for the full annual period are to be included in the dispersion calculation. If the firm reports both net- and gross-of-fees performance results in the composite presentation, the firm should disclose on which results the dispersion measure is presented.

If there are portfolios in the composite at the end of the annual reporting period that have not been in the composite for the full annual period, the firm must create a subset of the composite consisting of only those portfolios that have been managed for the full annual period to use to calculate and report the composite dispersion.

In cases where there are five portfolios or fewer in a composite for the full annual period, firms are not required to calculate a measure of dispersion and may state that the composite contains “five or fewer portfolios,” or similar language.

Standard Deviation. A widely used measure of dispersion is the standard deviation across equal-weighted portfolios, S_C. The definition is as follows:

$$S_C = \sqrt{\frac{\sum\left(R_i - MEAN\left(R_{EQUAL}\right)\right)^2}{n-1}},$$

where R_i is the return on the ith portfolio that has been in the composite for the full annual period, n is the number of portfolios in the composite for the full annual period, and $MEAN(R_{EQUAL})$ is the equal-weighted mean return of the portfolios in the composite for the full annual period, which is calculated as:

$$MEAN\left(R_{EQUAL}\right) = \frac{R_{PORT1} + R_{PORT2} + \ldots R_{PORTn}}{n},$$

where R_{PORT1} is the time-weighted return for the first portfolio in the composite for the full annual period and n is the number of portfolios in the composite for the full annual period. The use of both n and $n - 1$ in the denominator of the standard deviation calculation can be supported. Because only portfolios that have been managed for the full annual period are included in the dispersion calculation, *n* may be different from the number of portfolios shown in the presentation.

High–Low and Range. The high–low and range are the simplest and most easily understood measures of dispersion. Their key advantages are simplicity, ease of calculation, and ease of interpretation. One disadvantage of these measures is that one extreme value or outlier can skew the appearance of the data. In addition, by themselves, the high–low and the range of returns are not particularly rigorous.

Cross Reference: Provision 4.A.26

Application:

3-6

1. *Firm A has a composite that consists of 15 portfolios. Ten of the portfolios have been in the composite for the entire year. How would Firm A calculate a measure of composite dispersion?*

	Beginning Market Value ($)	Annual Return (%)
Portfolio 1	100,000	5.2
Portfolio 2	300,000	4.9
Portfolio 3	200,000	5.5
Portfolio 4	500,000	5.6
Portfolio 5	100,000	5.1
Portfolio 6	250,000	4.7
Portfolio 7	450,000	5.2
Portfolio 8	200,000	4.8
Portfolio 9	300,000	5.3
Portfolio 10	200,000	5.0
Composite Market Value	$2,600,000	
Equal-Weighted Return	5.1%	

Firm A could disclose the high–low or range of portfolio returns (i.e., high–low = 4.7% – 5.6%; range = 0.9%) or could disclose the standard deviation for each period. The standard deviation is calculated as follows:

$$S_R = \sqrt{\frac{(0.052-0.051)^2 + (0.049-0.051)^2 \ldots + (0.050-0.051)^2}{10-1}} = 0.0029$$

or 0.29%.

2. *As of 31 December 2000, Firm B has 18 portfolios in its Aggressive Growth composite, which earned 22.4 percent for the year. However, the composite lost three portfolios and gained five portfolios during the year. Which portfolios would firm B use to calculate a dispersion measure for the composite?*

Firm B would calculate a dispersion measure using only those 13 portfolios that were included in the composite for the full year.

3. *If the dispersion measure is calculated for "full-year-only" portfolios but the linked-quarter performance for the year includes portfolios that were added or removed from the composite during the year, do the two numbers really have relevance to one another?*

It is acknowledged that, by using only portfolios that have been managed for the full year to calculate annual composite dispersion, the dispersion number will not precisely correlate to the actual reported annual performance. The dispersion result will be accurate enough to provide a prospective client an idea of what the composite dispersion is for the year. The GIPS standards do not require a specific formula for calculating dispersion. A firm could present the standard deviation, the range, quartiles, or any other appropriate measure of dispersion.

5.A.2 FIRMS may link non-GIPS-compliant returns to their compliant history so long as the FIRMS meet the disclosure REQUIREMENTS for noncompliant performance and only compliant returns are presented for periods after 1 January 2000. (For example, a FIRM that has been in existence since 1995 and that wants to present its entire performance history and claim compliance beginning 1 January 2005 MUST present returns that meet the REQUIREMENTS of the GIPS standards at least from 1 January 2000 and MUST meet the disclosure REQUIREMENTS for any noncompliant history prior to 1 January 2000.)

Discussion: The GIPS standards allow firms to link non-GIPS-compliant performance to the composite's compliant history, provided that the dates of and reason for noncompliance are disclosed and no noncompliant performance is shown for periods after 1 January 2000. Performance for periods after 1 January 2000 that does not comply with the GIPS standards is not permitted to be presented as part of a GIPS-compliant presentation for any reason (except for the real estate, private equity, and wrap-fee asset categories).

Cross Reference: Provision 4.A.10, Provision 5.A.1, Provision 5.B.3

Application:

1. *Firm A has been in existence for 10 years and determines that it would like to begin to claim compliance with the GIPS standards this year. Is Firm A required to re-state its entire history in compliance with the GIPS standards in order to claim compliance?*

No. Firm A needs only to initially present the most recent five years of its performance history that adhere to the GIPS requirements in order to claim compliance (see Provision 5.A.1.a). In addition to the required performance returns, Firm A could link its history prior to 2000 without re-stating its pre-2000 performance in compliance with the GIPS standards, provided it discloses why the history prior to 2000 is not compliant.

5.A.3 Returns of PORTFOLIOS and COMPOSITES for periods of less than 1 year are not permitted to be annualized.

Discussion: The GIPS standards require that firms only present the performance of actual assets under management. When annualizing performance for periods of less than one-year, the partial-year return is "extended" in order to create an annual return. The extrapolation of the partial-year return produces a simulated return. Therefore, Provision 5.A.3 states that performance for periods of less than one year is not permitted to be annualized.

Cross Reference: Provision 5.A.1, Provision 5.B.1

Application:

1. *Firm A was established on 1 March 1998 and claims compliance with the GIPS standards. The firm presents the performance history for its balanced composite in annual increments by calendar year. From its inception through 31 December 1998, the balanced composite earned a return of 14.6 percent. Can Firm A annualize the 10-month return and present the result as the annual return for 1998?*

No. Firms are not permitted to annualize partial year returns. The firm must clearly disclose that the composite's 1998 cumulative return is for the partial period of 1 March 1998 through 31 December 1998.

3-6

5.A.4 a. Performance track records of a past FIRM or affiliation MUST be linked to or used to represent the historical record of a new FIRM or new affiliation if:

i. Substantially all the investment decision makers are employed by the new FIRM (e.g., research department, PORTFOLIO managers, and other relevant staff),
ii. The staff and decision-making process remain intact and independent within the new FIRM, and
iii. The new FIRM has records that document and support the reported performance.

b. The new FIRM MUST disclose that the performance results from the past FIRM are linked to the performance record of the new FIRM,

c. In addition to 5.A.4.a and 5.A.4.b, when one FIRM joins an existing FIRM, performance of COMPOSITES from both FIRMS MUST be linked to the ongoing returns if substantially all the assets from the past FIRM'S COMPOSITE transfer to the new FIRM.

d. If a compliant FIRM acquires or is acquired by a noncompliant FIRM, the FIRMS have 1 year to bring the noncompliant assets into compliance.

Discussion: When a manager, group of managers, or an entire firm joins a new firm, the performance track record of a past firm or affiliation must be linked to or used to represent the historical record of a new firm or new affiliation if the stated conditions are met.

The important determinant of allowable performance record portability is whether the acquiring firm continues the original strategy that defined the composite with all of its continuing factors. If the firm can meet the conditions of portability where substantially all the investment decision makers are employed by the new firm (i.e., research department, portfolio managers, and other relevant staff), which allows the decision-making process to remain intact (unchanged) in the new firm, appropriate disclosures are made and documentation is in place, then the composite performance from the old firm *must* be linked with the ongoing results of the new firm. The ongoing results may consist of accounts from the old firm that have transferred to the new firm and continue the same style/strategy, as well as accounts from the new firm that meet the definition of the composite.

Provision 5.A.4.c states that when one firm joins an existing firm and the conditions stated in 5.A.4.a and 5.A.4.b are met, performance of composites from both firms must be linked to the ongoing returns of the new firm if substantially all the assets from the past firms' composites transfer to the new firm. "Ongoing returns" means the composite strategy is continued. See the Guidance Statement on Performance Record Portability for a discussion of "surviving composites" when firms merge.

The GIPS standards recognize the difficulties that firms encounter when transferring assets from one firm to another. Similar to the idea of a grace period to facilitate the addition of new portfolios into existing composites (see Provision 3.A.3), Provision 5.A.4.d permits a one-year grace period to bring the assets of a noncompliant firm into compliance with the Standards. The assets of the noncompliant firm must meet all the requirements of the Standards as of the first full reporting period one year after the acquisition date. In the meantime, although not all assets under management are in compliance with the GIPS standards (because of the acquisition), the merged firm may continue to claim compliance with the GIPS standards with appropriate disclosure.

Cross Reference: Guidance Statement on Performance Record Portability (Section 4-7), Guidance Statement on the Use of Supplemental Information (4-10), Provision 0.A.5, Provision 1.A.1

Application:

1. *At Firm X, managers A, B, and C are part of a six-person investment management team responsible for managing Firm X's Growth and Income composite. Firm Y hires Managers A, B, and C to start a growth and income strategy at Firm Y. Can Firm Y link the performance of Managers A, B, and C while at Firm X to the ongoing performance the managers will earn at Firm Y and comply with the GIPS standards?*

The firm must determine if Managers A, B and C constitute "substantially all of the investment decision-makers" for the strategy. If the decision-making process remains intact (unchanged) in the new firm, it could be justified that substantially all of the investment decision-makers are employed by Firm Y and the rules of portability are met. If not, the historical performance from Firm X can be shown as supplemental information, provided it is clearly labeled as such.

2. *At Firm T, Manager D is responsible for Firm T's Emerging Market Composite. Although Manager D makes all the investment decisions for the portfolios in the composite, Manager D is supported by Firm T's research department and trading desk. Firm U is seeking to establish an emerging market investment strategy and hires Manager D to join Firm U. Can Firm U link the historical performance of Manager D while at Firm T to the performance of its new strategy and comply with the GIPS standards?*

The firm must determine if the decision-making process remains intact (unchanged) in Firm U. If Firm U continues the original strategy of the composite with all of its continuing factors, appropriate disclosures are made and documentation is in place, the performance must be linked.

3. *Firm X hires an entire investment team responsible for a successful emerging markets strategy in order to establish an identical investment strategy at Firm X. Some of the assets in the composite moved with the investment team and the investment process for the strategy will remain intact and independent in Firm X. Can Firm X link the performance of the investment team and comply with the GIPS standards?*

Firm X must link the historical performance to its new emerging markets composite only if Firm X has the records of the emerging markets composite sufficient to support the performance history of the emerging markets investment team. If the records are not readily available, Firm X can seek the permission of the team's previous firm to obtain copies or try to obtain them from third parties who may have retained the records such as clients, custodians, or consultants.

4. *Firm D and Firm J, each with a similar European Fixed-Income composite decide to merge. The new merged firm, Firm DJ, will combine the management expertise and resources from both firms in order to offer one European Fixed-Income strategy. To show a performance history for this collective composite, Firm DJ wants to combine the historical performance of the two similar composites. Can these historical track records be blended and shown in compliance with the GIPS standards?*

No. Firm DJ cannot combine the history of the two pre-merger composites and show it as a presentation in compliance with the GIPS standards. Firm DJ must determine whether one of the historical composites can serve as the "surviving" composite. If there was a clear survivor, the surviving composite's history would be linked to the ongoing record of Firm DJ's new European Fixed-income composite. The performance of the nonsurviving composite must be made available upon request.

If there was no clear surviving strategy, the new European Fixed-income composite would not have any performance history, as it represents a new strategy for the firm. The history of the styles at both Firm D and Firm J can be shown separately as supplemental information.

For instance, if the management of the new composite is led by the managers from Firm D and is managed in a similar manner as was previously done at Firm D, Firm DJ would choose Firm D's performance history as the surviving record, and its composite must be linked to the ongoing record of DJ's European Fixed-income composite.

If the management philosophy of the new composite represents a blending of the two previous management styles, there is not a surviving composite. The new European Fixed-income composite would not have any performance history; however, the track records of the composites at both Firm D and Firm J can and should be shown to prospective clients as supplemental information.

3-6

5. *Manager Q leaves Firm S to join Firm V. Manager Q was the sole investment decision maker for the composite, all of the assets in the composite transferred with Manager Q to Firm V, Manager Q obtained copies of the historical records supporting performance (with the permission of Firm S) and the investment process for the composite will remain intact and independent at Firm V. Because all the rules of portability apply, Firm V links Manager Q's performance history to its composite's ongoing results at Firm V. Can Firm S continue to claim the historical track record even though the manager responsible for the performance is no longer with the original firm?*

Yes. The Guidance Statement on Performance Record Portability states, "Performance is the record of the firm, not of the individual." If Firm S continues managing new portfolios according to the same style and objectives by replacing manager Q with a new manager, Firm S must use the historical performance of that composite to represent the ongoing performance achieved by the new manager. However, the firm must disclose any significant events within the firm (such as personnel changes) that would help a prospective client interpret the performance record (see Provision 4.A.19).

6. *Firm A currently claims compliance with the GIPS standards. On 31 December 2003, Firm A acquires Firm B, which does not claim compliance with the GIPS standards. Must Firm A stop claiming compliance until all of the assets acquired from Firm B are brought into compliance?*

No. Firm A can continue to claim compliance with the GIPS standards provided that it incorporates all of the acquired assets of Firm B and brings them into compliance with the Standards by 1 January 2005 (similar to the treatment of the acquisition of a new account).

5.A.5 Beginning 1 January 2006, if a COMPOSITE includes or is formed using single asset class CARVE-OUTS from multiple asset class PORTFOLIOS, the presentation MUST include the percentage of the COMPOSITE that is composed of CARVE-OUTS prospectively for each period.

Discussion: The GIPS standards permit firms to carve out a single asset class from a multiple-asset class portfolio and include the performance information in a single-asset composite return, provided the carve-out return is representative of what would have been achieved in a portfolio dedicated to the carved-out strategy and includes the cash component of the portfolio that is allocated to the single asset class.

If a firm includes carve-out returns in a single-asset-class composite, the single-asset-class composite presentation must state the percentage of the composite that is composed of carve-outs for all periods beginning 1 January 2006 or later. This disclosure provides prospective clients with the information needed to determine the amount of the total composite return that is derived from carve-outs (which are managed as part of a broader strategy).

Cross Reference: Guidance Statement on the Treatment of Carve-Outs (4-8), Provision 3.A.7, Provision 3.B.1, Provision 4.A.11

Application:

Sample Disclosure: The firm may add a column in the performance section of the composite presentation and could title it "Percent of composite that is carve outs"; or the firm could add a written disclosure providing the percentage of the composite composed of carve-outs from 1 January 2006, prospectively, for all periods.

5.A.6 The total return for the BENCHMARK (or BENCHMARKS) that reflects the investment strategy or mandate represented by the COMPOSITE MUST be presented for each annual period. If no BENCHMARK is presented, the presentation MUST explain why no BENCHMARK is disclosed. If the FIRM changes the BENCHMARK that is used for a given COMPOSITE in the performance presentation, the FIRM MUST disclose both the date and the reasons for the change. If a custom BENCHMARK or combination of multiple BENCHMARKS is used, the FIRM MUST describe the BENCHMARK creation and re-balancing process.

Discussion: Benchmarks are important tools that aid in the planning, implementation, and review of a portfolio's investment policy. They also help facilitate discussions with prospective clients regarding the relationship between risk and return. As a result, the GIPS standards require firms to provide an appropriate benchmark return in all composite presentations. The benchmark should be appropriately identified. In the instances where a benchmark is not provided, firms must explain why a benchmark is not appropriate.

When custom benchmarks are used, the firm must explain how the benchmark is created and how the benchmark is calculated. For example, if the firm combines two indices for the composite benchmark, WW index and XX index, the firm must disclose that the WWXX benchmark is based on a combination of the WW index and the XX index and is a 50 percent allocation of each index for each period, or it is rebalanced based on beginning-of-period assets, and so on.

Firms must disclose any changes to the benchmark over time. If the investment management style has not changed but the firm believes a new benchmark is a more appropriate comparative measure for the composite, the firm must explain in the composite presentation its reasons for changing the benchmark. In most cases, the firm should only change the benchmark going forward and not change historical presentations of the original benchmark. However, because benchmarks are continually evolving, if the firm deems the new benchmark to be a better representation of an investment strategy, the firm may consider changing the benchmark retroactively. The firm must disclose the date the benchmark is changed and the reason it has been retroactively applied. In addition, firms are encouraged to continue to present the old benchmark. Changes to the benchmark primarily intended to make historical performance look better by lowering the benchmark return violate the spirit of the Standards.

Application:

1. *Firm A manages an equity composite in which the investment strategy has attempted to mirror the S&P 500 Index. Firm A now wants to expand the investment strategy to include non-U.S. large-cap equities and change the benchmark to a blended index of the S&P 500 and the MSCI EAFE indexes. If Firm A discloses the date of the benchmark change, provides the reason for the change, and explains how the new index is created and rebalanced, is Firm A in compliance with the GIPS standards?*

No. In this case because the benchmark defined the strategy for the composite, a change in the benchmark results in a change to the investment strategy. A change in the strategy results in the need for Firm A to create a new composite reflecting the new strategy.

2. *Firm B has historically used the S&P 500 as the benchmark for its U.S. Equity composite. However, Firm B recently changed its benchmark retroactively to the Wilshire 5000 on the composite presentation. In the presentation, the firm provides the date of the change and explains that the Wilshire 5000 is a benchmark that better reflects the composite's investment history. However, the change was made because the lower return of the Wilshire 5000 provided a lower hurdle rate for the returns of the composite. Is this change permissible under the GIPS standards?*

No. Firm B has changed its benchmark primarily to improve its historical performance by lowering the benchmark return. Firm B has violated the GIPS standards even though it has technically met the requirements of the Standards by providing the date and reason for the change.

3. *Firm C historically used the MSCI EAFE index as the benchmark for the firm's Global ex-U.S. strategy, even though the strategy included investments in emerging markets and the benchmark did not. When the MSCI ACWI ex-U.S. index was introduced, the firm changed benchmarks because the new index included emerging markets, which more closely represented the firm's strategy. Is this permissible according to the GIPS standards?*

Yes. In this case the can firm change the benchmark to the MSCI ACWI ex-U.S. because it is more representative of the composite's investment strategy. The firm must disclose the date of the change as well as the reason for the change. If historical data is available for the new benchmark, the firm could consider changing the benchmark retroactively. The firm must disclose if the benchmark has been changed retroactively, provided the change does not violate the spirit of the Standards and the appropriate disclosures are shown.

5.A.7 If a COMPOSITE contains any non-fee-paying PORTFOLIOS, the FIRM MUST present, as of the end of each annual period, the percentage of the COMPOSITE assets represented by the non-fee-paying PORTFOLIOS.

Discussion: Non-fee-paying portfolios may be included in the firm's composites. If the firm decides to include non-fee-paying portfolios in a composite, firms are required to disclose the percentage of composite assets represented by non-fee-paying portfolios as of the end of each annual period. Examples of non-fee-paying portfolios are portfolios consisting of the firm's own pension plan assets or portfolios managed for friends or employees that are not charged investment management fees. If a firm temporarily waives the investment management fee for a portfolio that is normally charged a fee, the portfolio is still considered a fee-paying portfolio (with a fee of zero for that period) and may not be excluded from the composite because it is non-fee-paying.

Non-fee-paying portfolios are permitted but are not required to be included in a composite; however, firms may choose to include them in one or more appropriate composites. If the firm includes non-fee-paying portfolios in a composite, they are subject to the same rules as fee-paying portfolios (e.g., the firm must not move the non-fee-paying portfolio into and out of a composite without documented changes in client guidelines, and should include all other non-fee-paying portfolios meeting the definition of the composite). The decision of whether or not to include non-fee-paying portfolios in a composite may be made on a composite-by-composite basis.

If non-fee-paying portfolios are included in a composite, firms must disclose the percentage of the composite that is represented by non-fee-paying portfolios. Firms must make this disclosure for each annual period. If the composite does not contain any non-fee-paying portfolios, no disclosure is necessary.

Cross Reference: Guidance Statement on Composite Definition (4-2), Provision 3.A.1

Application:

1. *Firm A has a number of fee-paying portfolios managed to a growth investment strategy. Firm A also manages several pro-bono portfolios following this same strategy for other clients who do not pay fees on these portfolios. All of the growth portfolios are included in one composite with non-fee-paying assets composing 15 percent of the total assets of the composite as of 31 December 1999. What disclosure is required by the GIPS standards with regard to the non-fee-paying assets in the composite?*

Firm A could make the following disclosure as part of its Growth composite presentation when presenting 1999 performance data: "This composite contained 15 percent non-fee-paying portfolios 31 December 1999." Alternatively, the firm could add a column to its performance table titled, "Percent Composite Assets Composed of Non-Fee-Paying Portfolios," and list the percentage at the end of each annual period.

2. *How should incubator fund performance be presented under the GIPS standards?*

Incubator funds typically are accounts set up with firm assets to initiate a new style of asset management. As such, they are typically non-fee-paying accounts. The Standards require that only fee-paying portfolios be included in the firm's composites. However, the Standards permit firms to include non-fee-paying portfolios in its composites. If non-fee-paying portfolios are included in one of the firm's composites, the Standards require that the firm present the percentage of the composite assets represented by the non-fee-paying portfolios as of the end of each annual period.

If the fund represents an investment style or objective that is unique with respect to other management styles of the firm, it must be included in a single-portfolio composite. If at any time the firm discontinues this strategy, however, the composite would also discontinue.

PRESENTATION AND REPORTING — RECOMMENDATIONS

5.B.1 It is RECOMMENDED that FIRMS present the following items:

a. COMPOSITE returns gross of INVESTMENT MANAGEMENT FEES and ADMINISTRATIVE FEES and before taxes (except for nonreclaimable withholding taxes)

Discussion: There is a range of different types of costs and/or fees that a client incurs when maintaining an investment portfolio. In general, the three main types of fees and/or costs are investment management fees, brokerage commissions, and administrative fees. Administrative fees include custody fees and may also include accounting fees, consulting fees, legal fees, performance measurement fees, and other applicable fees. The investment firm should only be held responsible for those fees that it can control.

In some situations, the only fees that the firm controls are the investment management fee and the direct trading expenses (i.e., the direct cost of buying or selling the assets). Therefore, only the investment management fee and the direct trading expenses should affect the firm's returns. Even though custody fees are a necessary additional cost of owning a portfolio, many investment managers are not involved in the selection of the custodian or in the negotiation of the custody fees. Accordingly, custody fees should not be deducted when calculating the firm's returns.

Cross Reference: Interpretive Guidance for Fees Provisions (4-6), Provision 2.A.5, Provision 2.B.1, Provision 4.A.6, Provision 4.A.7, Provision 4.A.14, Provision 4.A.15, Provision 4.A.16

3-6

5.B.1 It is RECOMMENDED that FIRMS present the following items:

b. Cumulative returns for COMPOSITE and BENCHMARKS for all periods

Discussion: Cumulative returns for the composite and benchmark for all periods provide additional useful information to prospective clients by indicating what the total rate of return was for a defined period of performance. Cumulative returns can be provided in addition to the annual performance returns that are required under the Standards.

To calculate cumulative returns, R_{CUM}, of a composite for any period, the historic monthly, quarterly, or annual subperiod returns are geometrically linked according to the following formula:

$$R_{CUM} = \left(\left(1+R_1\right)\times\left(1+R_2\right)...\left(1+R_n\right)\right)-1,$$

where R_1 is the composite return for period 1 and R_n is the composite return for the most recent period.

Cross Reference: Guidance Statement on the Use of Supplemental Information (4-10)

Application:

1. Firm ABC has the following quarterly returns for Composite FGH:

	Q1	Q2	Q3	Q4
2000	2.3	–4.7	6.9	3.2
2001	–7.2	–2.9	5.4	–8.0

a. Calculate the cumulative returns for the following time periods for Composite FGH:

2000 = ((1.023) × (0.953) × (1.069) × (1.032) –1) = 0.076 or 7.6%
2001 = ((0.928) × (0.971) × (1.054) × (0.92) –1) = –0.126 or –12.6%

b. 18 months (from Q1 2000 through Q2 2001):

((1.023) × (0.953) × (1.069) × (1.032) × (0.928) × (.971) –1) = –0.031 or –3.1%

5.B.1 It is RECOMMENDED that FIRMS present the following items:

c. Equal-weighted mean and median returns for each COMPOSITE

Discussion: Averaging the performance of all the portfolios in a composite for a specified period, regardless of size, provides an equal-weighted composite return for that period. The equal-weighted mean return is the simple (unweighted) average of the individual portfolio returns in a composite. The simple average, together with the standard deviation, provides a measure of the manager's ability to obtain consistent returns for all portfolios regardless of size.

The GIPS standards recommend presentation of equal-weighted mean and median returns for the composite.

The formula for the equal-weighted mean composite return, R_{EQUAL}, is

$$R_{EQUAL} = \frac{R_{PORT1} + R_{PORT2} + ... R_{PORTn}}{n},$$

where R_{PORT1} is the time-weighted return for the first portfolio in the composite and n is the number of portfolios in the composite.

For a series of returns with an odd number of returns in the series, listed from low to high, the median return is the number in the middle.

For a series of returns with an even number of returns in the series, the median is the average of the two numbers in the middle of the series.

For example, the median return for a composite that has the following three annual returns, 2.3 percent, 2.7 percent, 3.9 percent, the middle number, the three-year median return, is 2.7 percent.

If the composite has the following returns for four years, 2.3 percent, 2.7 percent, 3.9 percent, 4.1 percent, the four-year median return is ((2.7% + 3.9%)/2), or 3.3 percent

Cross Reference: Guidance Statement on the Use of Supplemental Information (4-10)

5.B.1 It is RECOMMENDED that FIRMS present the following items:

d. Graphs and charts presenting specific information REQUIRED or RECOMMENDED under the GIPS standards

---

Discussion: Graphs and charts included in the presentation can convey information in a format that may be better understood by some prospective clients. Firms should carefully consider how graphs and charts are constructed and presented, such that the objectives of fair representation and full disclosure are maintained.

Cross Reference: Guidance Statement on the Use of Supplemental Information (4-10)

5.B.1 It is RECOMMENDED that FIRMS present the following items:

e. Returns for quarterly and/or shorter time periods

Discussion: In addition to annual returns, firms may choose to present returns for quarterly or shorter time periods as Additional Information.

Cross Reference: Guidance Statement on the Use of Supplemental Information (4-10), Provision 5.A.1, Provision 5.A.3

5.B.1 It is RECOMMENDED that FIRMS present the following items:

f. Annualized COMPOSITE and BENCHMARK returns for periods greater than 12 months

---

Discussion: Annualized, or average annual compound returns, represent the geometric average return achieved over the defined period of more than one year. Annualized performance is only permitted for periods of one year or more.

$$\text{Annualized Return } (\%) = ([(1 + R)^{(1/n)}] - 1) \times 100,$$

where R is the cumulative return for the period, which is the geometrically linked returns during the period, and n is the number of years in the period

For example, a portfolio's cumulative return for a five-year period is 150.0 percent. It has a five-year average annual compound return, or annualized return, of 20.11 percent:

$$((1 + 1.50)^{(1/5)}) - 1 = 0.2011 = 20.11 \text{ percent.}$$

If the 150 percent is earned over 12.5 years, its 12.5 average-annual compound return, or annualized return, is

$$((1 + 1.50)^{(1/12.5)}) - 1 = 0.0761 = 7.61 \text{ percent.}$$

Cross Reference: Guidance Statement on the Use of Supplemental Information (4-10), Provision 5.A.1, Provision 5.A.3

5.B.1 It is RECOMMENDED that FIRMS present the following items:

g. COMPOSITE-level country and sector weightings.

3-6

Discussion: Presenting composite-level country and sector weightings may be useful for prospective clients when considering the diversification of investments in the composite. Firms may present this additional information within the performance data, as a separate chart or graph, etc.

Cross Reference: Guidance Statement on the Use of Supplemental Information (4-10)

5.B.2 It is RECOMMENDED that FIRMS present relevant COMPOSITE-level risk measures, such as beta, tracking error, modified duration, information ratio, Sharpe ratio, Treynor ratio, credit ratings, value at risk (VaR), and volatility, over time of the COMPOSITE and BENCHMARK.

Discussion: Risk should be understood as being uncertain in nature and impact. The use of a variety of risk measures with an understanding of each of their shortcomings will provide valuable information, because no one statistic can consistently capture all the elements of risk for an asset class or a style of management.

Risk disclosures should facilitate comparison among investment management firms and must be appropriate to the investment strategy represented by the composite. The Standards do not specifically state which risk measures should be used, or the methodology behind a particular risk measure. Practitioners should display the risk measures they believe are appropriate.

Cross Reference: Guidance Statement on the Use of Supplemental Information (4-10), Provision 4.A.5

5.B.3 After presenting the REQUIRED 5 years of compliant historical performance, the FIRM is encouraged to bring any remaining portion of its *historical* track record into compliance with the GIPS standards. (This does not preclude the REQUIREMENT that the FIRM MUST add annual performance to its track record on an *on-going* basis to build a 10-year track record.)

Discussion: Provision 5.B.3 encourages firms to bring any noncompliant historical track record of the firm into compliance with the Standards.

Cross Reference: Provision 4.A.10, Provision 5.A.1, Provision 5.A.2

REAL ESTATE

Introduction and Scope

The GIPS standards Real Estate provisions apply where returns are primarily derived from the holding, trading, development, or management of real estate assets. Real estate includes land, buildings under development, completed buildings, and other structures or improvements held for investment purposes. The Standards apply to firms managing real estate regardless of the level of control the firm has over management of the real estate investments (see the discussion of discretion below). The provisions apply irrespective of whether a real estate investment is producing revenue and also apply to real estate investments with leverage or gearing.

Investment types not considered as real estate and therefore addressed elsewhere in the general provisions of the GIPS standards include the following:

- publicly traded real estate securities including any listed securities issued by public companies;
- commercial mortgage backed securities (CMBS);
- private debt investments, including commercial and residential loans where the expected return is solely related to contractual interest rates without any participation in the economic performance of the underlying real estate.

If a portfolio includes a mix of real estate and other investments that are not real estate, then these requirements and recommendations only apply to the real estate portion of the portfolio, and the GIPS carve-out provisions (Sec II.3.A.7.) must also be applied.

Recognizing that firms may not be able to gather historical valuations and/or records for transactions of real estate assets in order to create a five-year performance history, firms may link non-compliant performance for these assets for periods prior to 1 January 2006 to compliant performance with appropriate disclosure as to why the performance is not in compliance with the Standards.

Compliance

It is important that firms managing real estate investments understand that compliance with the GIPS standards refers to firm-wide compliance which requires adherence not just to the real estate provisions but to all the provisions of the GIPS standards.

Composite Construction

The real estate investment industry continues to debate the efforts, alternatives, and meaningful relevance of composite construction. One of the key principles of the GIPS standards is the notion of the presentation of composite performance, where a composite is defined as an aggregation of one or more portfolios representing a particular investment objective or strategy. The real estate provisions of the GIPS standards embrace the notion of composite-level reporting and require real estate investment management firms to present performance in composites defined by investment objective or strategy.

Users and recipients of performance presentations, however, frequently request property-level performance presentations, which may not be consistent with the composite construction principles of the GIPS standards. Although firms are not prohibited from presenting information according to specific requests from prospective clients, firms are required to make every reasonable effort to provide a fully compliant presentation of a composite based on investment objective or strategy.

For example, the GIPS composite construction provisions require firms to prepare composites, where the composite tracks the investment strategy that is pursued for a client or group of clients. But a real estate investment management firm may be asked to prepare a presentation consisting of only their office building investments, which requires extracting the performance of all office building investments from multiple portfolios within the firm.

If this grouping represents what would have been achieved with a strategy dedicated to office building investments, the firm may consider this a composite consisting of carve-outs and apply the GIPS carve-out provisions and guidance (see the Guidance Statement on the Treatment of Carve-Outs). If this grouping does not represent what would have been achieved with a strategy dedicated to office building investments, carving out the property-level office building investment returns from portfolios with vastly different investment objectives and strategies will likely not satisfy the composite construction requirements of the Standards. This property-level grouping should then only be presented as supplemental information to a compliant composite presentation (see the Guidance Statement on the Use of Supplemental Information).

Discretion

The GIPS standards require that all actual, fee-paying discretionary portfolios be included in at least one composite, although the definition of discretion remains with the firm. Discretion is the ability of the firm to implement its intended strategy. As stated in the Guidance Statement on Composite Definition, there are degrees of discretion and not all client-imposed restrictions will necessarily cause a portfolio to be non-discretionary. The firm must determine if the restrictions will, or could, interfere with the implementation of the intended strategy to the extent that the portfolio is no longer representative of the strategy.

The following guidelines are recommended to facilitate appropriate and consistent classification of real estate portfolios as discretionary or nondiscretionary.

Discretionary Management

Real estate portfolios are considered discretionary if the firm has sole or primary responsibility for major investment decisions. Major decisions may include portfolio strategy, investment search and selection, purchases, sales, investment structuring, financing, capital improvements, and operating budgets. Clients may not delegate complete investment discretion to firms for real estate investments, but in many cases, the consent requirements and investment constraints imposed do not inhibit the firm's investment policy or decision making to any significant extent. Therefore, the existence of client-imposed investment restrictions—such as leverage limits or required client approval of major decisions—do not preclude classification of a real estate portfolio as discretionary. Acceptance of primary responsibility by the firm and, therefore, the presence of a discretionary management relationship may be inferred if a portion of the firm's compensation is tied to performance or if the firm's success is assessed based on comparison of the firm's performance to a selected industry benchmark.

Nondiscretionary

Real estate portfolios are considered nondiscretionary if client-imposed investment limitations and restrictions hinder or prohibit application of the firm's desired investment strategy. As an example, taxable clients may prohibit or significantly limit repositioning of their portfolios through active or timely sales in order to minimize capital gains taxes. Alternatively, clients may mandate liquidation of their portfolios at a time when the firm believes pricing is not optimal. Additionally, firms may accept special assignments, such as portfolios taken over from other firms, with mandates that are not consistent with their own investment strategy.

Time-Weighted and Internal Rate of Return

The GIPS standards require the use of a time-weighted rate of return because it removes the effects of cash flows, which are generally client-driven. Therefore, a time-weighted rate of return best reflects the firm's ability to manage the assets according to a specified strategy or objective, and is the basis for the comparability of composite returns among firms on a global basis.

The one exception to the time-weighted rate of return requirement is in the case of private equity investments where an internal rate of return (IRR) is required. An IRR reflects the effects of the timing of cash flows in a portfolio and is required for private equity assets because the firm controls the cash flows into and out of the portfolio. In these situations, a time-weighted rate of return will not offer the best measure for an investor to compare returns between private equity funds because the time-weighted rate of return will not capture the critical effects of cash flow management within the control of the private equity manager.

Some view the real estate asset class comparable to private equity because of similarities in asset illiquidity, valuation frequency and reliability, and extended holding periods. As such, real estate investment management firms are recommended to present the since inception internal rate of return in addition to time-weighted rates of returns.

Separation of Income and Capital Appreciation Components

The GIPS standards for real estate investments require the presentation of component returns, specifically (1) the income return and (2) the change in capital value. Component reporting is important because of the lack of liquidity in real estate investments. If all other investment attributes are equal, higher current income is generally more desirable with real estate, because it equates to lower risk in achieving the total return. The calculation methodology for component returns must also be disclosed. Specifically, component returns are calculated separately using chain-linked (geometrically-linked) time-weighted rates of return. Although not required, some investment managers may adjust the chain-linked component returns so that the sum of the income return and the capital return is equal to the total return; the manager is required to disclose this practice.

Calculating Component Returns

The GIPS standards require that returns from cash and cash equivalents held in portfolios must be included in total return calculations. Firms must also reduce both gross-of-fees and net-of-fees returns by the trading expenses incurred. For periods beginning 1 January 2005, firms must use approximated rates of return that adjust for daily-weighted external cash flows (where external cash flows are defined as cash, securities or assets that enter or exit a portfolio). Firms must calculate and present the composite's income and capital appreciation component returns in addition to the composite's asset-weighted total return.

Income Return
The income return measures the portion of the portfolio's total return that is generated by the income from the operations of the real estate portfolio (real estate assets and cash/cash equivalents) during the period. The income return is computed as a percentage of the weighted-average capital employed during the measurement period. The GIPS standards require interest income to be accrued (see GIPS Provision 1.A.6).

Capital Return
The capital return measures the portion of the portfolio's total return that is generated from the change in the market value of the real estate portfolio (real estate assets and cash/cash equivalents) during the period. It is computed as a percentage of the weighted-average capital employed during the measurement period.

Capital Employed
The weighted-average capital employed (real estate assets and cash/cash equivalents) during the measurement period, i.e., the average capital available to be invested during the measurement period.

Disclosures

In addition to the other disclosure requirements of the GIPS standards, expanded disclosure for real estate composites is imperative because of the subjective nature of real estate valuation and the lack of consistent valuation methods around the world.

Requirements

- Income and capital appreciation component returns must be presented, in addition to total returns.
- Calculation methodology for component returns must be disclosed.

- Firm's description of discretion must be disclosed.
- Valuation methods and procedures (e.g., discounted cash flow valuation model, capitalized income approach, sales comparison approach, the valuation of debt payable in determining the value of leveraged real estate) must be disclosed.
- Range of performance returns for individual accounts in the composites must be presented.
- Source of valuation—independent appraiser versus internally prepared—for each reporting period must be disclosed.
- Frequency that real estate investments are valued by an external valuer must be disclosed.

Valuation

3-7

Market value is the most probable price that a property should bring in a competitive and open market under all conditions requisite to a fair sale, the buyer and seller each acting prudently and knowledgeably, and assuming the price is not affected by undue stimulus. Implicit in this definition are the consummation of a sale as of a specified date and the passing of title from seller to buyer under conditions whereby:

a. Buyer and seller are typically motivated;
b. Both parties are well informed or well advised, and each party is acting in what they consider their own best interests;
c. A reasonable time is allowed for exposure in the open market;
d. Payment is made in terms of cash currency or in terms of financial arrangements comparable thereto; and,
e. The price represents the normal consideration for the property sold unaffected by special or creative financing or sales concessions granted by anyone associated with the sale.

Source of Valuation

Globally, valuation procedures and methodologies are not consistent and there is acknowledgment that a range of valuation methodologies exist. However, the GIPS standards require firms implement specific valuation procedures for real estate investments.

There are two sources of property valuation:

Independent Valuation
Independent valuation is conducted by third-party appraisers, hired for a fee agreed to in advance which, in instances where the purpose of the appraisal is to estimate market value, is always noncontingent with respect to outcome. An assessment of market value must be performed by a third party who is a professionally designated, certified, or licensed valuer/appraiser who must conduct the external valuation pursuant to the valuation standards of the local governing appraisal body (or bodies). Independent valuers must be a professionally designated, certified or licensed valuer/appraiser and must be authorized by the professional or government body overseeing valuation standards in each country or state. Predominant professional organizations (for example, Appraisal Institute and Royal Institute of Chartered Surveyors) subscribe to essentially the same valuation theories, principles, and practices. Notably, valuers/appraisers must undergo formal and rigorous training and testing and must accumulate sufficient industry experience to qualify.

Internal Valuation
The second source of valuation is performed internally by the real estate investment firm. An internal valuation should consider professional industry approaches to estimating value (e.g., discounted cash flow valuation model, capitalized income approach, sales comparison approach, cost approach), and a professional review and assessment of the known economic, market, and financial variables and factors that can cause material changes in the value of real estate investments. Prudent assumptions must be employed, and the internal valuation process must be applied consistently from period to period, except where a process change would result in a more accurate estimate of market value.

The goal of the internal process is that the performance presentation is supported by investment values that are confirmed by the investment manager based on the employment of a professional valuation process that would generally mirror the process employed by the investment manager in assigning values to real estate investments throughout the acquisition and sale processes.

Frequency of Valuation of Real Estate:

Requirements:

- Real estate investments must be valued at market value at least once every 12 months. For periods beginning 1 January 2008, real estate investments must be valued at least quarterly.
- Real estate investments must be valued by an external, professionally designated, certified, or licensed commercial property valuer/appraiser at least once every 36 months.

Recommendations:

- Real estate investments should be valued at least quarterly.
- Real estate investments should be valued by an external valuer/appraiser at least once every 12 months.
- If calculating and presenting the internal rate of return, firms should use quarterly cash flows at a minimum.

Application:

1. *The GIPS standards state that the value of a real estate portfolio must be reviewed at least once every 12 months. Is this an internal review and if so, what does it entail?*

The 12-month valuation requirement for real estate can be satisfied with an internal review or external valuation. In an internal review, the valuation is determined internally, by the firm's management. The firm could determine that relying on values reported in annual reports generally satisfies the current 12-month review requirement because the issuance of the annual report should include a review of the real estate portfolio, a review of net asset value for financial and performance purposes, and review and disclosure of any factors that may result in a material change to net asset value. However, beginning 1 January 2008, real estate investments must be valued at least quarterly.

An external appraisal is not required every 12 months; the minimum requirement is at least once every 36 months. The frequency of independent external appraisals must be disclosed.

2. *Where do real estate mortgages fit within the GIPS standards?*

For the purpose of performance reporting, real estate mortgages with fixed or variable interest rates are considered fixed-income securities. Therefore, the core sections of the GIPS standards are applicable.

Participation and convertible mortgages (i.e., hybrid mortgages) are considered real estate investments. Firms should consider allocating component returns as follows:

- Basic cash interest (current receivable): allocate to income return component.
- Contingent interest (current receivable): allocate to income return component.
- Basic accrued interest (deferred): allocate to appreciation return component.
- Additional contingent interest (deferred; payable at maturity, prepayment, or sale): allocate to appreciation return component.

Therefore, if the return is currently payable from operations, allocate to the income return. All other sources of return that are deferred or realizable in the future should be allocated to the appreciation component.

3. *Should the real estate returns be presented net of leverage, after the effects associated with mortgage and similar long-term liabilities?*

Yes, real estate returns should be presented net of leverage (interest expense related to third-party debt) coupled with appropriate disclosure on the amount of leverage that is employed in producing the returns.

PRIVATE EQUITY

Introduction and Scope

Private equity has become an increasingly mainstream asset for sophisticated investors. Private equity entails investment in nonpublic companies at various stages of development and encompasses venture, buyout and mezzanine investing. Investors typically invest in private equity assets either through individual funds, usually limited partnerships with a specified investment stage and geographic focus, or via a fund-of-funds, through which commitments are made to multiple underlying funds. Some investors may also invest directly into unquoted companies, often on a co-investment basis alongside individual funds. Secondary investment—the acquisition of an interest in a private equity fund from the original investor before the end of the fund's fixed life—is also embraced within the broad definition of private equity.

When investing in private equity through funds or funds of funds, an investor makes an initial commitment of capital that is then "called" or drawn down as the investment managers of the underlying funds find investment opportunities. Capital is chiefly returned to the investor via distributions on the sale or recapitalization of individual unquoted companies by the underlying funds, although in some cases investors may also receive earnings-derived distributions.

Private equity investment vehicles typically have a limited life (i.e., they are not open-ended) and are generally illiquid. The ultimate return of the investment is not known until the fund or partnership is finally liquidated. Because of the unique characteristics of this asset class, additional performance reporting requirements are needed. The GIPS standards, which are based on the principles of fair representation and full disclosure, seek to provide prospective clients with the critical pieces of information needed to evaluate the firm's performance.

The concept of fair value used in the GIPS standards private equity provisions mirrors the fair value principles used in international accounting standards. In order for any performance-reporting requirements to be meaningful, the return calculations must be based on fair value of the underlying securities. Unlike investments in publicly traded securities where there are well-defined prices, it is difficult to find an objective valuation of private equity investments. This difficulty has led to harmonized guidelines (developed by the British Venture Capital Association (BVCA), European Venture Capital Association (EVCA), and the U.S. Private Equity Industry Guidelines Group (PEIGG)), developed in an attempt to standardize the methods used for valuing these assets. *The GIPS Private Equity Valuation Principles outline high-level guidelines for valuation, whereas the various regional guidelines provide the supporting methodology.*

Recognizing that firms may not be able to gather historical valuations and/or records for transactions of private equity assets in order to create a five-year performance history, firms may link non-compliant performance for these assets for periods prior to 1 January 2006 to compliant performance with appropriate disclosure as to why the performance is not in compliance with the Standards.

Investment Structures

Limited Partnerships (GIPS private equity provisions are applicable)
The predominant vehicle in the global private equity industry is the independent, private, fixed-life, closed-end fund, usually organized as a limited partnership. These funds typically have a fixed life of 10 years that can be extended by a pre-set number of defined periods (e.g., 2 one-year periods) upon agreement of the investors. It is termed a Closed-End Fund in that the number of investors/shares is fixed for the life of the fund and closed to new investors.

The limited partnership is a fund of pooled interests managed by a general partner who raises capital (i.e., committed capital or commitments) from outside investors (limited partners). The general partner charges an investment management fee, typically from one to three percent per annum on the total commitments raised. Most funds require at least a nominal one percent investment by the general partner. In addition, the general partner will take a profit split (known as the carried interest or simply the "carry") of usually 20 percent of profits.

The general partner will "call" the capital from its investors in tranches as needed for investment into underlying companies. These capital calls are also termed "drawdowns." Another unique feature of these types of vehicles is that any proceeds from investments must be distributed to investors; reinvestment is only acceptable if predefined terms appear in the contract between the general partner and the limited partners.

In this type of structure the cash flows are fairly easy to enumerate as the performance is calculated on the basis of the cash flows between the limited partner and the partnership. The investment management fee is typically charged on the total assets committed to the fund rather than on the value of the invested capital of the portfolio.

Direct Investments (GIPS private equity provisions are applicable)
Investments can be made in private equity assets directly, rather than via a fund or partnership. Direct investments are made both by institutions and by high-net-worth individuals. Many institutions making direct investments into unquoted companies do so on a co-investment basis alongside private equity funds in which they are limited partners, in line with a formal pre-set co-investment agreement.

Captive and Semi-Captive Funds (GIPS private equity provisions are not applicable)
The private limited partnership is not the only investment vehicle that makes private equity investments. Some vehicles are organized as captive vehicles or semi-captive vehicles. Captive refers to a fund that only invests for the interest of its owner organization. This parent may be a regular corporation, a financial corporation, insurance company, university, and so on. The salient feature is that the fund only invests its parent's capital—there are no outside investors. Corporate venture groups of technology companies are examples of this type of vehicle, although several insurance companies and investment banks also have similar vehicles.

The notable feature of this type of vehicle is that typically the vehicle is not a fixed-life investment pool—it is "evergreen" (i.e., a fund with no fixed cost basis as the parent can contribute additional capital or withdraw capital from the vehicle whenever it chooses). This lack of a fixed cost basis complicates the cash flow calculations because the cost basis fluctuates as the capital managed increases and decreases. The other problem is that a fund of this type charges no management fee to its owner and does not really have a "carried interest" profit split, although a few creative groups have compensation schemes for the investment officers that work in a similar manner to carried interest.

Another type of hybrid vehicle, called a semi-captive fund, mixes capital from both outside investors and the parent organization. These funds typically charge a management fee and carried interest to the outside investors and are usually closed-ended, as the number of investors is fixed, but a number of evergreen semi-captives also exist.

As such, captive and semi-captive structures are not comparable to private fixed-life limited partnerships on a net-of-fees basis. Therefore, the scope of the GIPS private equity provisions is in no way directed toward captive or evergreen funds within this industry. These structures must follow the general provisions of the GIPS standards.

Open-End Funds (GIPS private equity provisions are not applicable)
Another investment structure is an open-end public entity that acts much like a publicly-quoted mutual fund. The fund is a public investment vehicle traded on an exchange and priced daily. These vehicles typically operate much like a mutual fund or publicly-traded company and are not required to follow the GIPS private equity provisions, but must follow the general provisions of the GIPS standards.

3-8

Funds/Partnerships vs. Composite

Although most private equity investment vehicles are structured as limited partnerships or closed-end pooled funds, the GIPS standards are structured around the concept of composites. A composite is an aggregation of portfolios with a similar investment style or strategy. In relation to private equity, the composite is an aggregation of funds/partnerships with the same strategy and "vintage year" (year of first capital drawdown). In most cases, a composite will contain only one fund/partnership. If a firm has multiple funds/partnerships with the same vintage year and strategy, they must be combined into a single composite. A co-investment fund will most likely be placed in a separate composite from the underlying linked fund. Accordingly, firms should realize that all provisions and guidance related to composites apply to funds and partnerships. For example, when the Standards state that the cumulative annualized SI-IRR (since inception—internal rate of return) must be presented for the composite, because each composite will typically contain only one fund or partnership, this will be the same as the annualized SI-IRR for the fund or partnership. It is important to remember that the GIPS standards are primarily designed for presenting the firm's performance to prospective clients rather than reporting performance to an existing client.

It is also important for firms to realize that Provision 3.A.1 states in part that, "All actual, fee-paying, discretionary portfolios must be included in at least one composite." Firms must understand that the GIPS standards are aimed at a firm-wide level of compliance and not just selected composites/funds.

Within the private equity asset class, the GIPS concept of "carve-outs" is not applicable. A carve-out is a subset of a portfolio's assets used to create a track record that reflects a narrow segment of a broader mandate. In particular, it could be argued that a fund-of-funds composite is invested across many separate strategies. Breaking out and showing the substrategies as stand-alone composites would be misleading because a prospective investor could not solely invest in the substrategies. Furthermore, the value added of a fund-of-funds manager is to aggregate across various fund strategies. If a manager would like to separately disclose the substrategies for comparison purposes, this information must be presented as Supplemental Information (See the Guidance Statement on the Use of Supplemental Information).

Input Data

As mentioned above, performance reporting is of little value unless the underlying valuations are based on sound valuation principles. The GIPS Private Equity Valuation Principles establish a broad foundation for valuing private equity assets. These broad principles can be supplemented with more detailed valuation guidelines such as the harmonized European guidelines. One of the goals of the GIPS standards is to improve comparability among firms. The GIPS Private Equity Valuation Principles help to achieve that goal by requiring that firms use the same fundamental principles as the core of their valuation methodology. The concept of fair value used in the GIPS Private Equity Valuation Principles is the amount at which an asset could be acquired or sold in a current transaction between willing parties in which parties each acted knowledgeably, prudently, and without compulsion. Fair value does not assume an intention or ability to sell at the date of valuation but is an estimate of the likely exchange price involving subjective judgments, which must be based on reasonable estimates of the company's current and future performance.

The GIPS standards require that portfolios be valued monthly beginning 1 January 2001, and beginning 1 January 2010, portfolios will be required to be valued at the time of any large external cash flow. Because the Standards require a SI-IRR for private equity assets, however, increased frequency in valuations will not result in increased accuracy of the return calculation. The Standards only require that annual returns be presented and therefore the only valuation that is needed is at the year-end. More frequent valuations are generally required for client reporting purposes and are considered good business practice. The GIPS private equity provisions recommend quarterly valuations because this will allow firms to report performance on a more frequent basis. Firms that do not value on at least a quarterly basis can only present performance through the prior year-end.

Calculation Methodology

An internal rate of return (IRR) reflects the effects of the timing of cash flows in a portfolio. The IRR is required for private equity assets because the firm controls the cash flows into and out of the portfolio. A time-weighted rate of return (TWRR) will not offer the best measure for an investor to compare returns between private equity funds because the TWRR will not capture the critical effects of cash flow management within the control of the private equity manager. Although the GIPS private equity provisions advocate that the IRR is the most accurate measure of performance for an individual private equity manager, it may not be so at higher levels of aggregation. In the case where an investor (e.g., a limited partner) is trying to calculate the return at a wider portfolio level, including a number of private equity funds, that investor has no control over the timing of any cash flows. In this situation of a wider portfolio, a TWRR is more applicable and will provide a comparability measure at a portfolio level with other private equity portfolios as well as other asset classes. It is inappropriate to directly compare IRR and TWRR figures to each other. This clarification is provided in recognition that the main purpose for the GIPS private equity provisions is to provide comparability between private equity firms and not necessarily to standardize the performance presentation of the investors.

The IRR is the annualized implied discount rate (effective compounded rate) that equates the present value of all of the appropriate cash inflows (paid-in capital such as draw downs for net investments) associated with an investment with the sum of the present value of all the appropriate cash outflows (such as distributions) accruing from it and the present value of the unrealized residual portfolio (unliquidated holdings). For interim cumulative return measurement, any IRR depends upon the valuation of the residual assets. The subperiod IRR, r, is calculated as follows:

$$0=\sum_{i=0}^{n} CF_i \left(1+\frac{r}{c}\right)^{-(ic)},$$

where CF is the cash flow for period i, n is the total number of cash flows, i is the period of the cash flow, c is number of annual cash flow subperiods (e.g., $c = 365$ for daily cash flows), and r is the subperiod IRR. The subperiod IRR is converted to the annualized IRR, R, as follows:

$$R=(1+r)^{(1/c)}-1$$

As discussed in the section on investment structures, the predominant private equity investment vehicle is the independent private fixed-life fund. The cash flows are easily identified and enumerated as the fund has a fixed-cost basis of investment. It is reasonable to assume that because this type of fund has a fixed life, the return on investment is fairly easy to calculate. Because of the straightforward nature of the cash flows and closed-end basis of the fund, there are rarely any intractable or mathematical problems, such as multiple IRR's or unbounded solutions that often arise from complicated cash flow streams.

One of the reasons IRR is preferred is that this type of partnership generally has a fixed number of investors and a fixed commitment basis and proceeds cannot be reinvested so the cost basis of investment does not increase and decrease as it would with an evergreen or open-end fund. An open-end fund can find its investment pool increased (decreased) as investors invest (withdraw) more capital or by the addition (withdrawal) of investors.

One of the basic tenets of performance attribution is that the manager not be rewarded or penalized by decisions outside of their control. In an open-end fund as mentioned previously, the timing of cash flows in and out of the fund is totally at the discretion of the investors. As a result, a time-weighted return will (paradoxically) remove timing of the cash flows out of the performance calculation. Accordingly, open-end funds must follow the provisions of the general GIPS standards and report a time-weighted rate of return.

In a private equity independent, fixed-life fund, the decisions to raise money, take money in the form of capital calls, and distribute proceeds are totally at the discretion of the private equity fund manager. Therefore, timing is part of the investment decision process and thus the manager should be rewarded or penalized by those timing decisions—thus the need for a time-value of money measurement such as the IRR.

Firms are required to deduct carried interest, the investment management fee and any transaction expenses when calculating net-of-fees returns. As noted above, the carried interest can often have a greater impact than the actual investment management fees. In the case of investment advisors that have discretion over the selection of venture capital or private equity funds or partnerships for their clients, the investment advisor must calculate all returns net of all the fund or partnership investment management fees and carried interest. Investment advisor net-of-fees returns must, in addition, be net of all the investment advisor's fees, expenses, and carried interest.

Composite Construction

It is only appropriate to create composites that show a firm's capabilities or past performance with regard to a particular investment strategy. Firms must also separate funds with different vintage years into different composites. The following hierarchy may be helpful as firms consider how to define private equity composites:

Vintage Year
Strategy (venture, buyout, generalist, mezzanine, fund-of-funds, other private equity)
Substrategy (size of fund, stage, etc.)
Geography

Firms must remember that the GIPS standards have formal requirements in place regarding composite construction, which can be found in Section 3 of the Standards. (In order to fully understand composite construction topics one should also read the *Guidance Statement on Composite Definition*). Of most importance, "firms are required to include *all* actual, discretionary, fee-paying portfolios (funds/partnerships) in at least one composite that is managed according to a particular strategy or style." Creating meaningful composites is critical to the fair representation, consistency, and comparability of performance results over time and among firms.

Disclosures

Firms are required to disclose the vintage year of each composite. The vintage year is the year in which the private equity fund or partnership first draws down or calls capital from its investors. The disclosure of the vintage year increases comparability by allowing prospective clients to understand the time frame when the fund was initiated. In addition, firms are required to disclose the final realization date of a composite for all closed (discontinued) private equity composites. Similar to the vintage year statistic, the final realization date also aids in determining the time frame that the partnership was in existence in order to determine the appropriate comparability of one investment to another. Firms are also required to disclose the investment strategy of the composite.

Firms are required to disclose the composite's unrealized appreciation or depreciation. This disclosure helps prospective clients determine the potential for returns to change in the future based on the potential changes in the valuation of the investments within the composite. Firms must also disclose the total committed capital (or capitalization). Total committed capital is the total value of capital that investors have agreed to invest.

In addition to requiring the use of the GIPS Private Equity Valuation Principles, the Standards require the firm to disclose if it complies with any other valuation guidelines (e.g., BVCA or EVCA). The valuation methodology disclosure is important to determine the comparability of different returns and other important statistical information. If valuation methodologies are substantially different, certain investments may not be able to be compared to one another without very precise and appropriate valuation adjustments. Firms are required to document their procedures for reviewing valuations and must disclose that those procedures are available upon request.

Presentation and Reporting

Firms are required to present the annualized Since Inception IRR (SI-IRR) for private equity composites. The firm is required to present an annualized SI-IRR for each year since the vintage year. Unless disclosed, calendar year period-ends are assumed. For example, assume a composite has a vintage-year date of 1 January 1999. As shown in the table below, the firm would present the SI-IRR for 1999, the annualized SI-IRR (covering 1999 and 2000) for 2000, the annualized SI-IRR (covering 1999–2001) for 2001, and the annualized SI-IRR (covering 1999–2002) for 2002. Periods less than one year must not be annualized.

Year	Annualized Gross-of-Fees SI-IRR (%)	Annualized Net-of-Fees SI-IRR (%)
1999	–5.2	–8.2
2000	10.3	7.3
2001	29.6	25.6
2002	22.4	18.3

When presenting private equity performance, firms are required to present both gross-of-fees and net-of-fees returns. Net-of-fees returns must be net of the investment management fee, carried interest (the management firm's portion of any realized gains as well as the implied carried interest component of any unrealized gains in the portfolio), transaction expenses, and any other fees. In general, in cases where an investor is not able to negotiate the investment management and/or administrative fees, it may be most appropriate to present performance returns net of the nonnegotiable fees. In addition, if any fees are paid outside of the fund vehicle, they still must be incorporated in the net-of-fees return. Firms must disclose when fees are paid outside of the fund vehicle.

For each year presented, firms are required to report paid-in capital to date, total current invested capital, and cumulative distributions to date. The paid-in capital to date is the amount of the total committed capital that the firm has drawn down (called) from investors. The total current invested capital is the amount of the paid-in capital that is actually invested in private equity assets. The total distribution equals the total amount of capital or income that has been returned to investors. This measure gives prospective clients an understanding of the amount of initial invested capital returned to investors relative to other composites with similar vintage years and strategies.

The internal rate of return is not the only useful metric used to gauge performance. It assumes, for example, that the residual value of a composite is totally liquid, whereas in reality, the residual value is the unrealized (and often illiquid) portion of the composite. For performance calculation there are one non-cash-flow item—residual value (net of investment management fees and carried interest)—and two cash flow items—drawdowns from limited partners (also referred to as capital calls or paid-in capital) and distributions (cash and/or stock) to limited partners.

These three components can be used to calculate the internal rate of return assuming the residual value is taken as a terminal cash flow value. Only part of the return, however, is actually realized (i.e., the distributions). Accordingly, realization multiples (such as the Distributions to Paid-In Capital or DPI) provide additional information as to how much of the return has actually been realized and how much is still unrealized.

The Standards require firms to report the investment multiple (Total Value to Paid-In capital or TVPI) and the realization multiple (DPI) for each year presented. The investment multiple is calculated by dividing the residual value plus distributed capital by the paid-in capital. The investment multiple gives prospective clients information regarding the value of the composite relative to its cost basis. The realization multiple (DPI) is calculated by dividing the cumulative distributions by the paid-in capital. The DPI is a measure of how much of the return has actually been returned to investors. In the early life of an independent fixed-life fund, the DPI will be zero until distributions are made. As the fund matures, the DPI will increase. Once the DPI is greater than one, the fund has broken even. A DPI of greater than one means that the fund has generated capital gains. In addition, firms must present the ratio of Paid-In Capital to committed capital (or PIC multiple). This ratio gives prospective clients information regarding how much of the total commitments have been drawn down.

The private equity provisions also require the presentation of the Residual Value to Paid-In capital (RVPI). The RVPI is calculated as the residual value divided by paid-in capital. RVPI is a measure of how much of the return is unrealized. As a fund matures, the RVPI will increase to a peak and then decrease as the fund matures and eventually liquidates to a residual market value of zero. At that point, the entire return of the fund has been distributed.

If a benchmark is used, the private equity provisions require the presentation of a cumulative annualized SI-IRR for that benchmark that reflects the same strategy and vintage year as the composite. Firms must disclose the calculation methodology of the benchmark (e.g., monthly cash flows) and if a custom benchmark is used, how that benchmark is constructed. If no benchmark is presented, then the firm must disclose why no benchmark is appropriate. If a custom benchmark is used, then the firm must describe the benchmark creation and rebalancing process.

Application:

1. *What was the process for developing the GIPS private equity provisions and who was consulted?*

The GIPS Private Equity Subcommittee was drawn from professionals around the world with private equity experience in a range of industry roles. The provisions have circulated for public comment amongst investors, private equity firms and organizations, as well as other professionals with a private equity interest.

2. *How do the GIPS private equity valuation provisions relate to those of regional private equity organizations such as the EVCA, BVCA, PEIGG, etc.?*

The GIPS standards seek to encourage convergence of performance standards globally and find common ground in the difficult and subjective area of private equity valuations. The GIPS private equity provisions include a commitment to the fair value approach and provide guidance on a number of issues but do not seek to develop independently a full set of guidelines on valuation methodology.

3. *If my firm only manages private equity must I comply with the GIPS standards in its entirety to claim compliance?*

The claim of compliance with the GIPS standards is voluntary. However, claiming compliance requires adherence to all aspects of the Standards. Firms managing private equity assets will want to pay particular attention to provisions contained in the Fundamentals of Compliance section of the GIPS standards.

4. *Will the GIPS private equity provisions provide assurance of comparability between funds?*

The provisions should ensure consistency in the presentation of the most important performance measures. Interim valuations will remain subjective and precise comparability cannot be assured. Marking to Fair Value is, however, designed to give a much more consistent approach to valuation and thereby improve comparability.

5. *Will the GIPS Standards private equity provisions be endorsed by trade associations?*

Trade associations were consulted during the development of the private equity provisions and they are expected to support the new provisions.

6. *Do the GIPS private equity provisions override accounting requirements and standards?*

The GIPS private equity provisions are a minimum level of reporting to investors. They do not override any statutory obligation or accounting standard that may arise in any particular jurisdiction.

7. How should tax payable be treated?

In general, any taxes payable by the investors should be ignored in calculating the returns both net- and gross-of-fees. Some small withholding tax or income tax deducted prior to receipt by the fund or payable by the fund may arise and the net- and gross-of-fees cash flows should be reduced by these amounts.

8. How is fair value defined and how does this compare with accounting standards?

The concept of fair value used in the GIPS private equity provisions mirrors the fair value principles used in international accounting standards. Fair value is the amount at which an asset could be acquired or sold in a current transaction between willing parties in which parties each acted knowledgeably, prudently, and without compulsion. Fair value does not assume an intention or ability to sell at the date of valuation but is an estimate of the likely exchange price involving subjective judgments, which must be based on reasonable estimates of the company's current and future performance. In sales of private company holdings, a buyer is likely to reflect in the price any restrictions applying to the asset, including the extent to which liquidity can be achieved in any subsequent resale.

9. Can managers value investments on a cost basis and still be compliant with the fair value approach?

A general policy of holding investments at cost is not compliant with the GIPS standards. In some circumstances, cost is the best estimate of fair value, for example, where it reflects a recent arm's length transaction with no subsequent events or information affecting its validity. There may also be circumstances where a fair value estimate is not reasonably ascertainable and in these circumstances cost less a reduction for any value impairment is the only practical option.

10. Should early-stage venture investments be treated differently than more mature investments?

More mature investments with established profit, growth, and cash flow characteristics are in practice easier to benchmark against quoted market multiples for valuation purposes than are early-stage investments. In principle, early-stage investments should also be valued at fair value, although it is recognized that there will be instances where fair value cannot be estimated with any reasonable accuracy. In these instances, cost less estimated impairment needs to be used. Where early stage investments have raised material amounts of further funding on an arm's length basis, this practice does provide a market-based value.

11. Please clarify the recognition of management fees and carried interest accrual.

In constructing cash flows for calculating performance, management fees should be recognized as dated cash flows accrued at the quarterly, annual, or other periodic date when such management fees are payable. This method is in contrast to the occasional practice or treatment in which management fees are simply subtracted from the ending net asset value used in calculating performance. This latter treatment delays recognition of the management fee and thus artificially increases the rate of return calculated by an IRR calculation.

Carried interest accrual creates another problematic treatment. The net asset value used at the end of the period for which performance will be made up of largely unrealized and some realized investments yet to be distributed. The net asset value should have subtracted actual carried interest for realized investments that have not been distributed and should have fair value estimates of accrued carried interest subtracted for any investments that have yet to be realized. The intent is to provide an estimate of what the limited partner would receive if the unrealized portfolio were liquidated and distributed at the date of performance calculation.

12. Must all private equity funds be included in at least one composite?

Yes. Firms are required to include all discretionary, fee-paying portfolios (funds/partnerships) in at least one composite that is managed according to a particular strategy or style. Firms must also separate funds with different vintage years into different composites.

13. What are composites and how do they relate to private equity?

The GIPS private equity provisions follow the terminology of the broader GIPS standards in using the concept of a composite. In practice, for most private equity investment firms, secondary firms, and fund of funds, individual funds are raised from time to time with a specific investment strategy and a vintage year defined by reference to the date of the first investment drawdown of cash for either investment of fee. Thus, each fund is a composite, and the terms are interchangeable. More complex situations may arise where managed accounts exist, if these have the same mandate and vintage year, they should be aggregated.

14. How should side-by-side funds be handled?

For funds that may have an auxiliary parallel or "side-by-side" fund vehicle, that vehicle should be included in the performance calculation for the entire fund. An acid test for deciding whether to include such a vehicle in the performance calculation is:

If a parallel or side-by-side vehicle's capital is included to determine the entire fund's capitalization (so called "capital under management") then that parallel or side-by-side vehicle should be included in the performance calculations of the entire parent fund. Performance can be calculated separately for the fund vehicle as additional information but is required to be included in the calculation for the parent.

15. What disclosures at the asset level are required by GIPS private equity provisions?

None.

16. Why show both gross-of-fees and net-of-fees returns?

The gross-of-fees return is designed to show how well the invested capital performed, with the net-of-fees return reflecting the impact of management fees, performance fees (carried interest), and certain other costs. The investor needs an appreciation of both to understand the dynamics of the asset class.

17. What is a proper benchmark?

Investors in private equity are generally looking to outperform comparable quoted indices. Examples of relevant benchmarks would be a small-capitalization index (covering the same countries as the fund) for funds investing in comparably sized companies or a quoted technology index for those investing in venture funds. The index chosen will need to be a total return index (e.g., including dividends reinvested). The preferred calculation methodology involves notionally investing/divesting the fund cash flows into/out of the appropriate index and using the index cash flows to calculate an IRR.

In addition, many private equity associations and some specialist performance measurement firms provide data on median-and top-quartile performance for different classes of private equity. These returns for the same vintage year can be useful benchmarks. Although benchmarks are quite individual, the best benchmark for the composite should reflect the overall composite strategy, not necessarily individual clients' benchmark preferences.

18. Which fees are not deducted from the gross-of-fees and net-of-fees returns?

All fees associated with making, managing, and divesting an asset (defined as transaction expenses in the GIPS glossary) must be deducted from the gross-of-fees return. management fees, carried interest and transaction expenses must be deducted from the net-of-fees return. In line with the general GIPS provisions, fees relating to the expenses incurred in running the fund itself, defined as administrative fees, and including custody fees and fund legal and accounting fees, do not have to be deducted in calculating the gross- or net-of-fees returns.

VERIFICATION

Firms that claim compliance with the GIPS standards are responsible for their claim of compliance, and for maintaining that compliance. Once a firm claims compliance with the Standards, it may voluntarily hire an independent third party to verify its claim of compliance. This third-party verification will increase the level of confidence in the firm's claim of compliance.

The primary purpose of verification is to provide assurance that a firm claiming compliance with the GIPS standards has adhered to the Standards on a firm-wide basis. Verification is performed with respect to an entire firm, not on specific composites. Verification tests:

- whether the investment firm has complied with all the composite construction requirements of the GIPS standards on a firm-wide basis;
- whether the firm's processes and procedures are designed to calculate and present performance results in compliance with the GIPS standards.

Any independent third party can perform the verification. A firm cannot perform its own verification.

Verification adds value and credibility to the claim of compliance. Today, verification is strongly encouraged and is expected to become mandatory in the future. The expectation is that mandatory verification will be implemented by 2010. Leading up to 2010, all aspects of the mandatory verification debate will be evaluated and the industry will be provided sufficient time to implement any changes.

Cross Reference: GIPS Verification (Section 2-3), Guidance Statement on Verification (Section 5-7), Provision 0.B.2, Provision 0.B.3, Provision 4.B.3

GIPS ADVERTISING GUIDELINES

PURPOSE OF THE GIPS ADVERTISING GUIDELINES

The Global Investment Performance Standards provide the investment community with a set of ethical standards for firms to follow when presenting their performance results to potential clients. The Standards serve to provide greater uniformity and comparability among investment managers without regard to geographical location and to facilitate a dialog between firms and their prospective clients about the critical issues of how the firm achieved historical performance results and determines future investment strategies.

The GIPS Advertising Guidelines attempt to serve as industry global best practice for the advertisement of performance results. The GIPS Advertising Guidelines do not replace the GIPS standards nor do they absolve firms from presenting performance presentations that adhere to the requirements of the full GIPS standards. The guidelines only apply to firms that already satisfy all the requirements of the Standards on a firm-wide basis and claim compliance with the Standards. Firms that claim compliance can choose to advertise that claim using the GIPS Advertising Guidelines.

The guidelines are mandatory for firms that include a claim of compliance with the GIPS Advertising Guidelines in their advertisements. The guidelines are voluntary for firms that do not include a claim of compliance in their advertisements. All firms are encouraged to abide by these ethical guidelines.

3-10 The claim of compliance is a firm-wide commitment to fair representation and full disclosure. Although it is not required for firms to include the claim of compliance in any or all of their advertisements, firms claiming compliance with the Standards should ensure that all marketing materials, whether or not they contain the claim of compliance, are not misleading, and adhere to the objectives of fair representation and full disclosure.

Firms that do not comply with the GIPS standards and firms that choose not to advertise their claim of compliance should carefully consider any reference to the Standards in an advertisement or presentation of performance. Referencing the GIPS standards in an advertisement or presentation of performance in a context other than the claim of compliance could be confusing to the public and should be avoided to eliminate the possibility of any misrepresentation or perceived misrepresentation.

Definition of Advertisement

For the purposes of these guidelines, an advertisement includes any materials that are distributed to or designed for use in newspapers, magazines, firm brochures, letters, media, or any other written or electronic material addressed to more than one prospective client. Any written material (other than one-on-one presentations and individual client reporting) distributed to maintain existing clients or solicit new clients for an advisor is considered an advertisement.

Once a firm claims compliance with the GIPS standards, Provision 0.A.11 requires that it make every reasonable effort to provide all prospective clients with a full, complete presentation that complies with all the applicable requirements of the Standards (not the advertising provisions). The firm may not choose to whom they will provide a compliant performance presentation. This requirement ensures that once a firm represents to the investing public that it complies with the GIPS standards, it shows all prospective clients an appropriate, full and complete compliant presentation.

Relationship of GIPS Advertising Guidelines to Regulatory Requirements

The GIPS Advertising Guidelines are guidelines that promote an ethical framework for advertisements. They do not change the scope of the activities of local regulatory bodies regarding the regulation of advertisements. Firms advertising performance results must also adhere to all applicable regulatory rules and requirements governing advertisements. Firms are encouraged to seek legal or regulatory counsel because it is likely that additional disclosures are required. In cases where applicable law or regulation conflicts with the GIPS Advertising Guidelines, the guidelines require firms to comply with the law or regulation. Firms must disclose any conflicts between laws/regulations and the GIPS Advertising Guidelines.

The calculation and advertisement of pooled unitized products, such as mutual funds and open-ended investment companies, are regulated in most markets. These advertising guidelines are not intended to replace the regulations when a firm is advertising performance solely for a pooled unitized product. However, should a GIPS-compliant firm choose to advertise performance results, the firm must apply all applicable laws and regulations as well as the GIPS Advertising Guidelines in order to include a claim of compliance with the GIPS standards.

ADVERTISING GUIDELINES — REQUIREMENTS

All advertisements that include a claim of compliance with the GIPS Advertising Guidelines MUST include the following:

1. A description of the FIRM.

Discussion: A description of the firm should include general information regarding the firm claiming compliance with the GIPS standards. A description may be more abbreviated than the firm definition but includes all salient features of the firm. See Provision 0.A.2 for additional guidance on the definition of the firm.

Cross Reference: Provision 0.A.2

Application:

Samples:

Sample 2 Asset Management Company is an independent investment management firm established in 1997. Sample 5 Asset Management Company manages a variety of equity, fixed-income, and balanced assets for primarily Swiss and European clients.

Sample 3 Realty Management Firm (the "Firm"), a subsidiary of ABC Capital, Inc., is a registered investment adviser under the Investment Advisors Act of 1940. The Firm exercises complete discretion over the selection, capitalization, asset management, and disposition of investments in wholly-owned properties and joint ventures.

Sample 4 Investments is the institutional asset management division of Sample 4 Plc and is a registered investment advisory firm specializing in qualitative, growth-oriented investment management.

All advertisements that include a claim of compliance with the GIPS Advertising Guidelines MUST include the following:

2. How an interested party can obtain a presentation that complies with the REQUIREMENTS of GIPS standards and/or a list and description of all FIRM COMPOSITES.

Discussion: An advertisement is considered any written material distributed to maintain existing clients or solicit new clients for the firm. In order for potential new clients to know how to obtain more information about the firm and its products, contact information must be included in the firm's advertisements so that a potential client (interested party) can obtain the complete composite presentation and/or the list and description of the firm's composites.

Cross Reference: Provision 0.A.12, Provision 0.A.13

Application:

Sample: To receive a complete list and description of Sample 4 Investments' composites and/or a presentation that adheres to the GIPS standards, contact Jean Paul at +12 (034) 5678910, or write Sample 4 Investments, One Plain Street, Resultland 12KJ4, or jpaul@sample4inv.com.re.

All advertisements that include a claim of compliance with the GIPS Advertising Guidelines MUST include the following:

3. The GIPS Advertising Guidelines compliance statement:

[Insert name of firm] claims compliance with the Global Investment Performance Standards (GIPS®).

3-10

Discussion: The advertising guidelines only apply to firms that already satisfy all the requirements of the Standards on a firm-wide basis and claim compliance with the Standards. Firms that claim compliance can choose to advertise that claim using the GIPS Advertising Guidelines. The guidelines are mandatory for firms that include the claim of compliance with the GIPS Advertising Guidelines in their advertisements.

Application:

Sample: Sample Four Investments claims compliance with the Global Investment Performance Standards (GIPS®)

All advertisements that include a claim of compliance with the GIPS Advertising Guidelines and that present performance results MUST also include the following information (the relevant information MUST be taken/derived from a presentation that adheres to the REQUIREMENTS of the GIPS standards):

4. A description of the strategy of the COMPOSITE being advertised.

Discussion: Composite definitions can be lengthy and, because of the brevity of an advertisement, it is not essential that the full (complete) composite definition be disclosed. Instead, the description of the strategy should include brief information regarding the composite's definition. A description may be more abbreviated than the composite definition but includes all salient features of the composite.

Cross Reference: Provision 4.A.20

Application:

Samples:

The Global Equity Growth Composite strategy focuses on earnings, growth of earnings, and key valuation metrics.

The Small-Cap Growth Composite includes all institutional portfolios invested in U.S. equities with strong earnings and growth characteristics and small capitalizations.

The Large-Cap Growth Composite includes all institutional portfolios invested in U.S. equities with strong earnings and growth characteristics and large capitalizations.

The High-Yield Fixed-Income Composite includes all institutional portfolios invested in high-yield debt securities.

The GARP Equity Composite includes all institutional portfolios invested in growth stocks that are reasonably priced and valued "cheap" compared with their peers.

The Small/Mid-Cap Growth Composite includes all institutional portfolios invested in U.S. equities with strong earnings and growth characteristics.

All advertisements that include a claim of compliance with the GIPS Advertising Guidelines and that present performance results MUST also include the following information (the relevant information MUST be taken/derived from a presentation that adheres to the REQUIREMENTS of the GIPS standards):

5. Period-to-date COMPOSITE performance results in addition to either:

a. 1-, 3-, and 5-year cumulative annualized composite returns with the end-of-period date clearly identified (or annualized period since COMPOSITE inception if inception is greater than 1 and less than 5 years). Periods of less than 1 year are not permitted to be annualized. The annualized returns MUST be calculated through the same period of time as presented in the corresponding compliant presentation; or

b. 5 years of annual COMPOSITE returns with the end-of-period date clearly identified (or since COMPOSITE inception if inception is less than 5 years). The annual returns MUST be calculated through the same period of time as presented in the corresponding compliant presentation.

3-10

Discussion: Firms advertising performance results must also adhere to all applicable regulatory rules and requirements governing advertisements. Firms are first required to present period-to-date composite performance results. The firm may present period-to-date performance either through a specified date, through the most recent month end, or through the most recent quarter end, given a reasonable amount of time after the end of the period-to-date for the calculation of performance.

In addition to the period-to-date composite performance, firms must choose to present performance in accordance with one of the methods as described in 5.a OR 5.b above.

5.a requires presentation of annualized, or average annual compound returns, representing the geometric average return achieved over the defined period of more than one year. Annualized performance is only permitted for periods of one year or more.

$$\text{Annualized Return (\%)} = ([(1 + R)^{(1/n)}] - 1) \times 100,$$

where R is the cumulative return for the period, which is the geometrically linked returns during the period, and n is the number of years in the period.

For example, a portfolio's cumulative return for a five-year period is 150 percent. It has a five-year average annual compound return, or annualized return, of 20.11 percent. $((1 + 1.50)^{(1/5)}) - 1 = 0.2011$ = 20.11 percent. If the 150 percent is earned over 12.5 years, its 12.5 average-annual compound return, or annualized return, is $((1+1.50)^{(1/12.5)}) - 1 = 0.0761$ = 7.61 percent.

If the composite has more than a year of history but does not have a five-year performance history, the firm must present the since inception cumulative annualized return (average annual compound return) in addition to the most recent one-year return. If appropriate the firm should also present the three-year annualized return.

5.b, as described above, requires the firm to present the annual returns for the most recent five years (or annual returns since inception if the composite has been in existence less than five years). The annual returns must be the same as those presented in the corresponding compliant presentation.

In addition, firms could choose to present annualized, annual, and/or cumulative returns in the same advertisement. Firms should ensure consistency of time periods as described in the provision above. The Guidance Statement on the Use of Supplemental Information provides additional guidance.

Cross Reference: Guidance Statement on the Use of Supplemental Information, Provision 5.A.1, Provision 5.B.1

Application:

Samples:

3-10

Sample reflecting Provision 5.a (one-year, three-year, and five-year annualized returns) for a corresponding compliant presentation with annual periods ending 31 Dec:

Sample 4 Investments: Global Equity Growth Composite Performance

	Ending 31 Mar 04	Ending 31 Dec 03		
Results shown in US$ before fees*	Period to Date (3 months)	1 Year	3 Year Annualized Return	5 Year Annualized Return
Global Equity Growth	–3.84%	–19.05%	–14.98%	0.42%
MSCI World Index	–4.94%	–19.54%	–16.37%	–1.76%

*Gross-of-Fees

Sample reflecting Provision 5.b (5 years of annual returns) for a corresponding compliant presentation with annual periods ending 31 Dec:

Sample 4 Investments: Global Equity Growth Composite Performance

Results are shown in US$ before fees*	31 Dec 2003	31 Dec 2002	31 Dec 2001	31 Dec 2000	31 Dec 1999
Global Equity Growth Composite	–19.05%	–17.05%	–8.47%	31.97%	25.87%
MSCI World Index	–19.54%	–16.52%	–12.92%	25.34%	24.80%

*Gross-of-Fees

Sample reflecting Provision 5.a (one-year, three-year, and five-year annualized returns) for a corresponding compliant presentation with annual periods ending 31 March and used in advertisements prior to availability of 30 June data:

Sample 4 Investments: Global Equity Growth Composite Performance

Ending 31 March 2005

Results are shown in HK$ and are net-of-fees	1 Year	3 Year Annualized Return	5 Year Annualized Return
Global Equity Growth Composite	24.1%	-6.3%	2.7%
ACC Consulting Firm's Universe of Global Equity Growth Managers	17.9%	-0.3%	-0.9%

All advertisements that include a claim of compliance with the GIPS Advertising Guidelines and that present performance results MUST also include the following information (the relevant information MUST be taken/derived from a presentation that adheres to the REQUIREMENTS of the GIPS standards):

> **6. Whether performance is shown gross and/or net of INVESTMENT MANAGEMENT FEES.**

Discussion: Firms advertising performance results must also adhere to all applicable regulatory rules and requirements governing advertisements. The GIPS standards require that all performance must be calculated after the deduction of actual trading expenses and permit firms to present investment performance results gross and/or net of investment management fees. Currently, the GIPS standards recommend that firms present gross-of-fees performance. Firms must clearly indicate within each presentation whether returns are gross-of-fees or net-of-fees so that potential clients can better understand the information presented.

Cross Reference: Provision 1.B.2, Provision 2.A.5, Provision 2.A.7, Provision 4.A.6, Provision 5.B.1

Application:

Samples: "Results shown net-of- fees"; or, "Gross-of-Fees Returns"; or similar language

All advertisements that include a claim of compliance with the GIPS Advertising Guidelines and that present performance results MUST also include the following information (the relevant information MUST be taken/derived from a presentation that adheres to the REQUIREMENTS of the GIPS standards):

> **7. The BENCHMARK TOTAL RETURN for the same periods for which the COMPOSITE return is presented and a description of that BENCHMARK. (The appropriate COMPOSITE BENCHMARK return is the same BENCHMARK TOTAL RETURN as presented in the corresponding GIPS-compliant presentation.) If no BENCHMARK is presented, the advertisement MUST disclose why no BENCHMARK is presented.**

Discussion: Benchmarks are important tools that aid in the planning, implementation and review of a portfolio's investment policy. They also help facilitate discussions with prospective clients regarding the relationship between risk and return. As a result, the GIPS standards require firms to provide an appropriate benchmark return in all composite presentations. In the instances where a benchmark is not provided, firms must explain why a benchmark is not appropriate.

The benchmark must be appropriately identified. The description should include all salient features of the benchmark, and could be as brief as the name of the benchmark for a readily-recognized index.

Application:

Samples: "The benchmark presented is the S & P 500"; or, "MSCI World Index"; or, "The benchmark presented is the 30% S&P TSX; 70% Scotia Canadian Bond Index Fund rebalanced monthly."

All advertisements that include a claim of compliance with the GIPS Advertising Guidelines and that present performance results MUST also include the following information (the relevant information MUST be taken/derived from a presentation that adheres to the REQUIREMENTS of the GIPS standards):

8. The currency used to express returns.

Discussion: The GIPS standards require that firms disclose the currency used to express performance. In cases involving currency changes because of the Euro conversion, please refer to the Guidelines in Respect of the Impact of Euro Conversion.

Cross Reference: Provision 4.A.4

Application:

Samples: "Valuations are computed and performance results are reported in Canadian dollars."; or, "Performance results are expressed in Euros"; or, "Performance returns are presented in Sterling."

3-10

All advertisements that include a claim of compliance with the GIPS Advertising Guidelines and that present performance results MUST also include the following information (the relevant information MUST be taken/derived from a presentation that adheres to the REQUIREMENTS of the GIPS standards):

9. The description of the use and extent of leverage and derivatives if leverage or derivatives are used as an active part of the investment strategy (i.e., not merely for efficient PORTFOLIO management) of the COMPOSITE. Where leverage/derivatives do not have a material effect on returns, no disclosure is REQUIRED.

Discussion: The disclosure should contain sufficient detail so that current or prospective clients can understand the pattern of returns and the risks from the leverage or derivatives positions, if their use is material to the implementation of the strategy.

Cross Reference: Provision 4.A.5

Application:

Samples: "Portfolios in the composite may be leveraged to increase exposure to 150% of the account's value"; or "The strategy includes the use of naked short selling, which greatly increases exposure to fluctuations in market prices."

All advertisements that include a claim of compliance with the GIPS Advertising Guidelines and that present performance results MUST also include the following information (the relevant information MUST be taken/derived from a presentation that adheres to the REQUIREMENTS of the GIPS standards):

> **10. When presenting non-compliant performance information for periods prior to 1 January 2000 in an advertisement, FIRMS MUST disclose the period(s) and which specific information is not compliant as well as provide the reason(s) the information is not in compliance with the GIPS standards.**

Discussion: The GIPS standards allow firms to link non-GIPS-compliant performance to their compliant history, provided that no noncompliant performance is shown for periods beginning 1 January 2000. If the firm chooses to present noncompliant performance for periods prior to 1 January 2000, the firm must disclose which periods are not in compliance and the reasons the performance does not comply with the GIPS standards. This disclosure will allow prospective clients to make valid comparisons among performance presentations and consider the effects of noncompliance on the historical performance.

Cross Reference: Provision 4.A.10

Application:

1. *Firm A presents its performance history since its inception in 1990 and claims compliance with the GIPS standards. The performance record since 1996 adheres to requirements of the GIPS standards. However, the firm did not include accrued income in the return calculation for the period from 1990–1995. What disclosure is necessary to allow the firm to link its pre-1996 noncompliant history with the ongoing compliant history?*

Sample disclosure: "Performance results prior to 1 January 1996 are not in compliance with the GIPS standards as the firm did not include accrued income for fixed-income instruments when calculating the composite's constituent portfolios' returns."

Firm A must disclose in its advertisement that the performance record from 1990–1995 is not in compliance because accrued income was not included for fixed-income instruments when calculating the composite's constituent portfolios' returns. This disclosure allows potential clients to determine whether the firm's performance results from 1990–1995 are representative and whether the results are comparable to the performance of other firms that included accrued income during the same period.

2. *Firm B presents its performance history since its inception in 1996 and claims compliance with the GIPS standards. However, the firm did not include all portfolios in composites for the period prior to 2000. What disclosure is necessary?*

Sample disclosure: "Performance results prior to 1 January 2000 are not in compliance with the GIPS standards as the firm did not include all portfolios in composites on a firm-wide basis."

Revised Effective Date: 1 January 2006
Adoption Date: 4 March 2004
Effective Date: 1 June 2004
Retroactive Application: Not Required
Public Comment Period: Aug – Nov 2002

GUIDANCE STATEMENT ON CALCULATION METHODOLOGY (REVISED)

Introduction

Achieving comparability among investment management firms' performance presentations requires as much uniformity as possible in the methodology used to calculate portfolio and composite returns. The uniformity of the return calculation methodology is dependent on accurate and consistent input data, a critical component to effective compliance with the GIPS® standards. Although the GIPS standards allow flexibility in return calculation, the return must be calculated using a methodology that incorporates the time-weighted rate of return concept for all assets (except Private Equity assets). For information on calculating performance for these assets, see the separate Private Equity Provisions and Guidance.

The Standards require a time-weighted rate of return because it removes the effects of cash flows, which are generally client-driven. Therefore, a time-weighted rate of return best reflects the firm's ability to manage the assets according to a specified strategy or objective, and is the basis for the comparability of composite returns among firms on a global basis.

In this Guidance Statement, the term "return" is used rather than the more common term "performance" to emphasize the distinction between return and risk and to encourage the view of performance as a combination of risk and return. Risk measures are valuable tools for assessing the abilities of asset managers; however, this Guidance Statement focuses only on the return calculation.

Money- or dollar-weighted returns may add further value in understanding the impact to the client of the timing of external cash flows, but are less useful for return comparison and are therefore not covered by this Guidance Statement.

Guiding Principles

Valuation Principles — The following are guiding principles that firms must use when determining portfolio values as the basis for the return calculation:

- Portfolio valuations must be based on market values (not cost basis or book values).
- For periods prior to 1 January 2001, portfolios must be valued at least quarterly. For periods between 1 January 2001 and 1 January 2010, portfolios must be valued at least monthly. For periods beginning 1 January 2010, firms must value portfolios on the date of all large external cash flows.
- For periods beginning 1 January 2010, firms must value portfolios as of calendar month-end or the last business day of the month.
- Firms must use trade-date accounting for periods beginning 1 January 2005. (Note: for purposes of the Standards, trade-date accounting recognizes the transaction on

the date of the purchase or sale. Recognizing the asset or liability within at least 3 days of the date the transaction is entered into satisfies this requirement.)

- Accrual accounting must be used for fixed income securities and all other assets that accrue interest income. Market values of fixed-income securities must include accrued income.
- Accrual accounting should be used for dividends (as of the ex-dividend date).

Calculation Principles — The following are guiding principles that firms must use when calculating **portfolio** returns:

- Firms must calculate all returns after the deduction of the actual trading expenses incurred during the period. Estimated trading expenses are not permitted.
- Firms must calculate time-weighted total returns, including income as well as realized and unrealized gains and losses.
- The calculation method chosen must represent returns fairly, must not be misleading, and must be applied consistently.
- Firms must use time-weighted rates of return that adjust for external cash flows. External cash flows are defined as cash, securities, or assets that enter or exit a portfolio (capital additions or withdrawals) and are generally client-driven. Income earned on a portfolio's assets is not considered an external cash flow.
- The chosen calculation methodology must adjust for daily-weighted external cash flows for periods beginning 1 January 2005, at the latest. An example of this methodology is the Modified Dietz method.
- For periods beginning 1 January 2010, at the latest, firms must calculate performance for interim periods between all large external cash flows and geometrically link performance to calculate period returns. (Note: as such, at 1 January 2010, or before if appropriate, each firm must define, prospectively, on a composite-specific basis, what constitutes a large external cash flow.) For information on calculating a "true" time-weighted return see below.
- External cash flows must be treated in a consistent manner with the firm's documented, composite-specific policy.
- Firms must calculate portfolio returns at least on a monthly basis. For periods prior to 2001, firms may calculate portfolio returns on a quarterly basis.
- Periodic returns must be geometrically linked.

4-1

Calculation Principles — The following are guiding principles that firms must use when calculating **composite** returns:

- Composite returns must be calculated by asset weighting the individual portfolio returns using beginning-of-period values or a method that reflects both beginning-of-period values and external cash flows.
- The aggregate return method, which combines all the composite assets and cash flows to calculate composite performance as if the composite were one portfolio, is acceptable as an asset-weighted approach.
- For periods prior to 1 January 2010, firms must calculate composite returns by asset weighting the individual portfolio returns at least quarterly. For periods beginning 1 January 2010, composite returns must be calculated by asset weighting the individual portfolio returns at least monthly.
- Periodic returns must be geometrically linked.

Cash Flow Principles — The following are guiding principles that firms must consider when defining their Cash Flow policies:

- An **external cash flow** is a flow of cash, securities, or assets that enter or exit a portfolio, which are generally client driven. When calculating approximated rates of return, where the calculation methodology requires an adjustment for the daily-weighting of cash flows, the formula reflects a weight for each external cash flow. The cash flow weight is determined by the amount of time the cash flow is held in the portfolio.

- When calculating a more accurate time-weighted return, a **large external cash flow** must be defined by each firm for each composite to determine when the portfolios in that composite are to be revalued for performance calculations. It is the level at which a client-initiated external flow of cash and or securities into or out of a portfolio may distort performance if the portfolio is not revalued. Firms must define the amount in terms of the value of the cash/asset flow, or in terms of a percentage of portfolio or composite assets.
- The large external cash flow (described above) determines when a portfolio is to be revalued for performance calculations. This is differentiated from a **significant cash flow**, which occurs in situations where cash flows disrupt the implementation of the investment strategy. Please see the Guidance Statement on the Treatment of Significant Cash Flows, which details the procedures and criteria that firms must adhere to and offers additional options for dealing with the impact of significant cash flows on portfolios.

Time-Weighted Rate of Return

Valuing the portfolio and calculating interim returns each time there is an external cash flow ought to result in the most accurate method to calculate the time-weighted rates of return, referred to as the "true" Time-Weighted Rate of Return Method.

A formula for calculating a true time-weighted portfolio return whenever cash flows occur is:

$$R_i = \frac{\left(EMV_i - BMV_i\right)}{BMV_i},$$

4-1

where EMV_i is the market value of the portfolio at the end of sub-period i, excluding any cash flows in the period, but including accrued income for the period. BMV_i is the market value at the end of the previous sub-period (i.e., the beginning of the current sub-period), plus any cash flows at the end of the previous sub-period, where an inflow is positive and an outflow is negative, and including accrued income up to the end of the previous period. The cash inflow is included in the BMV (previous period EMV + positive cash inflow) of the sub-period when the cash inflow is available for investment at the start of the sub-period; a cash outflow is reflected in the BMV (previous period EMV + negative cash outflow) of the sub-period when the cash outflow is no longer available for investment at the start of the sub-period.

The sub-period returns are then geometrically linked to calculate the period's return according to the following formula:

$$R_{TR} = \left(\left(1+R_1\right)\times\left(1+R_2\right)...\left(1+R_n\right)\right)-1,$$

where R_{TR} is the period's total return and R_1, $R_{2...}$ R_n are the sub-period returns for sub-period 1 through n respectively.

Approximation of Time-Weighted Rate of Return

As mentioned in the Introduction, the GIPS standards require firms to calculate returns using a methodology that incorporates the time-weighted rate of return concept (except for Private Equity assets). The Standards allow flexibility in choosing the calculation methodology, which means that firms may use alternative formulas, provided the calculation method chosen represents returns fairly, is not misleading, and is applied consistently.

Calculating a true time-weighted rate of return is not an easy task and may be cost intensive. For these reasons, firms may use an approximation method to calculate the total return of the individual portfolios for the periods and sub-periods. The most common approximation methods combine specific rate of return methodologies (such as the original Dietz method, the Modified Dietz method, the original Internal Rate of Return (IRR) method, and the Modified IRR method) for sub-periods and incorporate the time-weighted rate of return concept by geometrically linking the sub-period returns.

Just as the GIPS standards transition to more frequent valuations, the Standards also transition to more precise calculation methodologies. Therefore, the GIPS standards require firms to calculate approximated time-weighted rates of return that adjust for daily-weighted cash flows by 1 January 2005 (e.g., Modified Dietz method) and will require the calculation of a more accurate time-weighted rate of return with valuations occurring at each large external cash flow as well as calendar month-end or the last business day of the month for periods beginning 1 January 2010.

This Guidance Statement does not contain details on the different formulas for calculating approximate time-weighted rates of return.

Composite Return Calculation

Provision 2.A.3 requires that composite returns must be calculated by asset weighting the individual portfolio returns using beginning-of-period values or a method that reflects both beginning-of-period values and external cash flows.

The intention is to show a composite return that reflects the overall return of the set of the portfolios included in the composite.

To calculate composite returns, firms may use alternative formulas so long as the calculation method chosen represents returns fairly, is not misleading, and is applied consistently.

According to the *Beginning Market Value-Weighted Method* the composite return, R_{BMV}, can be calculated using the formula:

$$R_{BMV} = \frac{\sum_{i=1}^{n}\left(BMV_i \times R_i\right)}{BMV_{TOTAL}},$$

where BMV_i is the beginning market value (at the start of the period) for a portfolio, R_i is the rate of return for Portfolio i, and BMV_{TOTAL} is the total market value at the beginning of the period for all the portfolios in the composite.

The *Beginning Market Value Plus Cash Flow-Weighted Method* represents a refinement to the asset-weighted approach. Consider the case in which one of two portfolios in a composite doubles in market value as the result of a contribution on the third day of a performance period. Under the asset-weighted approach, this portfolio will be weighted in the composite based solely on its beginning market value (i.e., not including the contribution). The beginning market value and cash flow-weighted method resolves this problem by including the effect of cash flows in the weighting calculation as well as in the market values. Assuming that cash flows occur at the end of the day, the weighting factor for each cash flow is calculated as:

$$W_{i,j} = \frac{\left(CD - D_{i,j}\right)}{CD},$$

where CD is the total number of calendar days in the period and $D_{i,j}$ is the number of calendar days since the beginning of the period in which cash flow j occurred in portfolio i.

The beginning market value plus cash flow-weighted composite return, R_{BMV+CF}, can be calculated as follows:

$$R_{BMV+CF} = \frac{\sum_{i=1}^{n}\left\{\left(BMV_i + \left(\sum_{j=1}^{m} CF_{i,j} \times W_{i,j}\right)\right) \times R_i\right\}}{\sum_{i=1}^{n}\left(BMV_i + \left(\sum_{j=1}^{m} CF_{i,j} \times W_{i,j}\right)\right)},$$

where $CF_{i,j}$ is the cash flow j within the period for portfolio i (contributions to the portfolio are positive flows, and withdrawals or distributions are negative flows) and R_i is the return for portfolio i.

The *Aggregate Return Method* combines all the composite assets and cash flows before any calculations occur to calculate returns as if the composite were one portfolio. The method is also acceptable as an asset-weighted approach.

Geometric Linking of the Periodic Composite Returns

To calculate the composite return over more than one (sub-)period, the composite return over the total period is calculated by geometrically linking the individual composite sub-period returns using the following formula:

$$R_{CT} = \left(\left(1+R_{C1}\right)\times\left(1+R_{C2}\right)\ldots\left(1+R_{Cn}\right)\right)-1,$$

where R_{CT} is the composite return over the total period and R_{C1}, R_{C2}, and R_{Cn} are the individual composite returns for the sub-periods 1, 2, and *n*, respectively.

Additional Considerations

Changes To The Methodology — Where appropriate, in the interest of fair representation and full disclosure, firms should disclose when a change in a calculation methodology or valuation source results in a material impact on the composite return.

Third-Party Performance Measurement — Firms may use portfolio returns calculated by a third-party performance measurer as long as the methodology adheres to the requirements of the GIPS standards.

Different Valuation And/Or Calculation Method — Firms are permitted to include portfolios with different valuation and/or calculation methodologies within the same composite (as long as the methodologies adhere to the requirements of the GIPS standards). Firms must be consistent in the methodology used for a portfolio (e.g., firms cannot change the methodology for a portfolio from month-to-month).

4-1

Month End Valuations — Firms must be consistent in defining the (monthly) valuation period. The valuation period must end on the same day as the reporting period. In other words, firms must value the portfolio/composite on the last day of the reporting period (or the nearest business day). Aggregating portfolios with different ending valuation dates in the same composite is not permitted after 1 January 2006.

Trading Expenses — Returns must be calculated after the deduction of all trading expenses. Trading expenses are the costs of buying or selling a security, and include brokerage commissions and any other regulatory fee, duty, etc. associated with an individual transaction.

Trade-Date Accounting — Firms must use trade-date accounting for periods beginning 1 January 2005. Trade-date accounting recognizes an asset or liability on the date the transaction is entered into. Recognizing the asset or liability within at least 3 days of the date the transaction is entered into satisfies the trade-date accounting requirement. As a result, the account will recognize any change between the price of the transaction and the current market value.

Taxes — Firms must disclose relevant details of the treatment of withholding tax on dividends, interest income, and capital gains. Returns should be calculated net of non-reclaimable withholding taxes on dividends, interest, and capital gains. Reclaimable withholding taxes should be accrued.

Grossing-Up Or Netting-Down Of Investment Management Fees — Firms are allowed to include portfolios with different grossing-up methodologies within the same composite. Firms must be consistent in the methodology used for a portfolio (e.g., firms cannot change the methodology for a portfolio from month-to-month). Please see the guidance on Fees for the GIPS standards.

Large Cash Flows — The firm must have an established policy on defining and adjusting for large cash flows and apply this policy consistently. Actual valuation at the time of any large external cash flow is required for periods beginning 1 January 2010.

Disclosures — Firms must disclose that additional information regarding policies for calculating and reporting returns is available upon request. Generally, the firm's policies and procedures on calculating and reporting returns could serve as the basis for this information.

Effective Date

This Guidance Statement was originally effective 1 June 2004 and was revised to reflect the changes to the GIPS standards effective as of 1 January 2006.

Firms are encouraged, but not required, to apply this guidance prior to the original Effective Date of 1 June 2004; however, the original guidance must be applied to all presentations that include performance for periods on and after that date.

The revisions made to this guidance (effective 1 January 2006) must be applied to all presentations that include performance for periods after 31 December 2005.

Key GIPS Provisions Specifically Applicable to Calculation Methodology

1.A.2 Portfolio valuations must be based on market values (not cost basis or book values).

1.A.3 For periods prior to 1 January 2001, portfolios must be valued at least quarterly. For periods between 1 January 2001 and 1 January 2010, portfolios must be valued at least monthly. For periods beginning 1 January 2010, firms must value portfolios on the date of all large external cash flows.

1.A.4 For periods beginning 1 January 2010, firms must value portfolios as of the calendar month-end or the last business day of the month.

1.A.5 For periods beginning 1 January 2005, firms must use trade date accounting.

1.A.6 Accrual accounting must be used for fixed-income securities and all other assets that accrue interest income. Market values of fixed-income securities must include accrued income.

1.A.7 For periods beginning 1 January 2006, composites must have consistent beginning and ending annual valuation dates. Unless the composite is reported on a noncalendar fiscal year, the beginning and ending valuation dates must be at calendar year-end (or on the last business day of the year).

2.A Calculation Methodology — Requirements

2.A.1 Total return, including realized and unrealized gains and losses plus income, must be used.

2.A.2 Time-weighted rates of return that adjust for external cash flows must be used. Periodic returns must be geometrically linked. External cash flows must be treated in a consistent manner with the firm's documented, composite-specific policy. At a minimum:

a. For periods beginning 1 January 2005, firms must use approximated rates of return that adjust for daily-weighted external cash flows.

b. For periods beginning 1 January 2010, firms must value portfolios on the date of all large external cash flows.

2.A.3 Composite returns must be calculated by asset weighting the individual portfolio returns using beginning-of-period values or a method that reflects both beginning-of-period values and external cash flows.

2.A.4 Returns from cash and cash equivalents held in portfolios must be included in total return calculations.

2.A.5 All returns must be calculated after the deduction of the actual trading expenses incurred during the period. Estimated trading expenses are not permitted.

2.A.6 For periods beginning 1 January 2006, firms must calculate composite returns by asset weighting the individual portfolio returns at least quarterly. For periods

4-1

beginning 1 January 2010, composite returns must be calculated by asset weighting the individual portfolio returns at least monthly.

2.A.7 If the actual direct trading expenses cannot be identified and segregated from a bundled fee:

a. when calculating gross-of-fees returns, returns must be reduced by the entire bundled fee or the portion of the bundled fee that includes the direct trading expenses. The use of estimated trading expenses is not permitted.

b. when calculating net-of-fees returns, returns must be reduced by the entire bundled fee or the portion of the bundled fee that includes the direct trading expenses and the investment management fee. The use of estimated trading expenses is not permitted.

2.B Calculation Methodology — Recommendations

2.B.1 Returns should be calculated net of nonreclaimable withholding taxes on dividends, interest, and capital gains. Reclaimable withholding taxes should be accrued.

2.B.2 Firms should calculate composite returns by asset weighting the member portfolios at least monthly.

2.B.3 Firms should value portfolios on the date of all large external cash flows.

Applications:

1. Does the firm violate the GIPS standards by reporting money-weighted rates of return to an existing client for their portfolio (which contains no private equity assets)?

4-1

No, the Standards would not be violated if the firm reported money-weighted rates of return to an existing client for their portfolio. The Standards are primarily based on the concept of presenting the firm's composite performance to a prospective client rather than presenting individual portfolio returns to an existing client. The IRR (or money-weighted return) represents the performance of the specific client's fund holdings (i.e., influenced by the client's timing and amount of cash flows) and measures the performance of the fund rather than the performance of the fund manager. Money-weighted returns may add further value in understanding the impact to the client of the timing of external cash flows, but are less useful for comparison purposes.

IRRs are only required in the GIPS standards when calculating performance for private equity assets where the investment firm controls the cash flows.

2. The GIPS standards currently state that firms are required to use trade-date accounting as of 1 January 2005. How should trade date be defined?

For the purposes of the GIPS standards, trade-date accounting is defined as "recognizing the asset or liability within at least 3 days of the date the transaction is entered into." Settlement-date accounting is defined as "recognizing the asset or liability on the date in which the exchange of cash, securities, and paperwork involved in a transaction is completed."

When using settlement-date accounting, any movement in value between the trade date or booking date and the settlement date will not have an impact on performance return until settlement date; whereas for trade-date accounting, the change in market value will be reflected for each valuation between trade date and settlement date. If the trade and settlement dates straddle a performance measurement period-end date, then performance return comparisons between portfolios that use settlement-date accounting and those that use trade-date accounting may not be valid. The same problem occurs when comparing settlement-date portfolios and benchmarks.

The principle behind requiring trade-date accounting is to ensure there is not a significant lag between trade execution and reflecting the trade in the performance of a portfolio. For the purposes of compliance with the GIPS standards, portfolios are considered to satisfy the trade-date accounting requirement provided that transactions are recorded and recognized consistently and within normal market practice—typically, a period between trade date and up to three days after trade date (T+3). After 1 January 2005, all firms must recognize transactions on trade date as defined herein.

3. Given the following information, calculate the rate of return for this portfolio for January, February, March, and the first quarter of 2000, using a true time-weighted rate of return:

Solution:

Date	Market Value (€)	Cash Flow (€)	Market Value Post Cash Flow (€)
12/31/99	500,000		
1/31/00	509,000		
2/19/00	513,000	+50,000	563,000
2/28/00	575,000		
3/12/00	585,000	–20,000	565,000
3/31/00	570,000		

January

$$R = \frac{(509{,}000 - 500{,}000)}{500{,}000} = 1.80\%$$

February

1/31/00 – 2/19/00 $\quad R = \frac{(513{,}000 - 509{,}000)}{509{,}000} = 0.79\%$

2/19/00 – 2/28/00 $\quad R = \frac{(575{,}000 - 563{,}000)}{563{,}000} = 2.13\%$

1/31/00 – 2/28/00 $\quad R_{FEB} = ((1+0.008)\times(1+0.021)) - 1 = 2.92\%$

March

2/28/00 – 3/12/00 $\quad R = \frac{(585{,}000 - 575{,}000)}{575{,}000} = 1.74\%$

3/12/00 – 3/31/00 $\quad R = \frac{(570{,}000 - 565{,}000)}{565{,}000} = 0.88\%$

2/28/00 – 3/31/00 $\quad R_{Mar} = ((1+0.017)\times(1+0.009)) - 1 = 2.62\%$

Quarter 1

$$R_{QT1} = ((1+0.018)\times(1+0.029)\times(1+0.026)) - 1 = 7.48\%$$

4-1

Revised Effective Date: 1 January 2006
Adoption Date: 13 March 2002
Effective Date: 1 April 2002
Retroactive Application: Required
Public Comment Period: Sep – Dec 2001

GUIDANCE STATEMENT ON COMPOSITE DEFINITION (REVISED)

Introduction

Three of the most fundamental issues that a firm must consider when becoming compliant with the GIPS® standards are the definition of the firm, the firm's definition of discretion, and the firm's composite definition principles and guidelines. The definition of the firm is the foundation for firm-wide compliance and creates defined boundaries whereby total firm assets can be determined. The firm's definition of discretion establishes criteria to judge which portfolios should be in a composite to accurately reflect the application of the firm's investment strategy. Once the firm and discretion have been defined, composites can be constructed based on the strategies implemented by the firm. Firms are reminded that, under the GIPS standards, they must comply with all applicable laws and regulations.

A composite is an aggregation of individual portfolios representing a similar investment mandate, objective or strategy and is the primary vehicle for presenting performance to prospective clients. The firm must include all actual, fee-paying, discretionary portfolios in at least one composite. In this way, firms cannot "cherry-pick" their best performing portfolios to present to prospective clients. Non-fee-paying portfolios may be included in the firm's composites; however, firms are required to disclose the percentage of composite assets represented by non-fee-paying portfolios as of the end of each annual period. If the firm includes non-fee-paying portfolios in its composites, they are subject to the same rules as fee-paying portfolios (e.g., the firm must not move the non-fee-paying portfolio into and out of a composite without documented changes in client guidelines or the redefinition of the composite make it appropriate). Firms are permitted to include a portfolio in more than one composite, provided it satisfies the definition of each composite.

4-2

Before defining composites, the firm must establish reasonable criteria that support the fundamental principle of fair representation. A variety of criteria must be analyzed to identify whether portfolios are similar and should be grouped together into a composite.

Guiding Principles

The GIPS standards encourage firms to develop objective criteria for defining composites. The following are Guiding Principles that firms must consider when defining composites:

- Composites must be defined according to similar investment objectives and/or strategies. Composites should enable clients to compare the performance of one firm to another. The firm should also consider the definition and construction of similar products found within the competitive universe. Composites must be representative of the firm's products and be consistent with the firm's marketing strategy.
- Firms must apply the criteria for defining composites consistently (e.g., the firm may not select only certain, specific portfolios (i.e., "cherry-picking") that meet the composite definition, but must include all portfolios that satisfy the criteria for inclusion).
- Firms are not permitted to include portfolios with different investment strategies or objectives in the same composite. The performance of such a composite is meaningless. In the case where there are many portfolios with unique, defining

investment characteristics, it may be necessary for the firm to create numerous single-portfolio composites.
- Portfolios must not be moved into and out of composites except in the case of documented, client-driven changes in investment objectives or guidelines or in the case of the redefinition of the composite. The historical record of the portfolio must remain with the appropriate composite.

Discretion

Discretion is the ability of the firm to implement its intended strategy. If documented client-imposed restrictions significantly hinder the firm from fully implementing its intended strategy the firm may determine that the portfolio is non-discretionary. Non-discretionary portfolios must not be included in a firm's discretionary composites. There are degrees of discretion and not all client-imposed restrictions will necessarily cause a portfolio to be non-discretionary. The firm must determine if the restrictions will, or could, interfere with the implementation of the intended strategy to the extent that the portfolio is no longer representative of the strategy. For example, if a client requests that the firm not purchase any tobacco stocks in their portfolio, the firm should first consider if this restriction will hinder the implementation of the intended strategy. If so, the firm could either classify this portfolio as non-discretionary (and all other portfolios with this restriction) or could choose to classify it as discretionary and create a composite for portfolios with tobacco restrictions. Firms should, where possible, consider classifying these portfolios as discretionary and grouping them with portfolios with similar restrictions in a separate composite.

Firms must document, in writing, their policies and procedures used in establishing and maintaining compliance with all the applicable requirements of the GIPS standards. As such, each firm must document its definition of discretion and must apply the definition consistently. Ideally, discretion is defined at the firm level, but may be defined at the composite level or by asset class. Firms should also document the reasons for classifying a portfolio as non-discretionary. It is the firm's responsibility to ensure that all of its actual, fee-paying discretionary portfolios are included in at least one composite. Accordingly, firms should review each of their portfolios (both discretionary and non-discretionary) on a regular basis to determine whether any portfolios should be re-classified. According to the GIPS verification procedures, available in the GIPS standards at Section III. Verification, a verifier must determine if the firm's definition of discretion is appropriate and has been applied consistently over time.

Examples of client-imposed restrictions that may cause a portfolio to be classified as non-discretionary include, but are not limited to:

- Restricting trading activities due to conditional client approval,
- Restricting asset allocation (i.e., firm cannot alter asset allocation established by client),
- Tax considerations (e.g., low-cost basis stocks, etc.),
- Limiting the sale of certain securities (e.g., sentimental holdings),
- Restricting the purchase of certain securities or types of securities (e.g., firm cannot buy tobacco stocks, firm cannot buy futures, firm cannot buy securities below a specific quality, etc.),
- Cash flow requirements (e.g., the client requires large cash distributions on a regular basis), or
- Legal restrictions.

Few of these restrictions are reason to *automatically* classify a portfolio as non-discretionary, as the firm must determine if the restriction will significantly hinder the implementation of the intended strategy. In addition, the outsourcing of performance measurement or record keeping by a third-party does not negate the firm's responsibility related to compliance and is not a sufficient reason to classify assets as non-discretionary.

In the case of client-restricted securities (e.g., low-cost basis stocks, held to maturity securities, etc.), the firm may choose to classify the restricted portion of the portfolio as non-discretionary (also commonly referred to as "un-managed" or "un-supervised") and keep the remaining discretionary portion of the portfolio in the composite, provided the remaining portion is representative of the composite's strategy. When considering if a portion of a portfolio should be classified as non-discretionary, firms should consider if the asset(s) affect the management of the portfolio's investment strategy. All calculation and composite construction requirements would apply to the remaining discretionary portion of the portfolio.

Non-discretionary portfolios are not permitted to be included in the firm's composites (i.e., composites consisting of discretionary portfolios). Some firms, however, may group some or all of the firm's non-discretionary portfolios together to simplify composite administration. According to the Standards, this is not a composite and must not be included on the firm's list of composites.

Minimum Asset Level

The GIPS standards contain two provisions that refer to a minimum asset level. GIPS provision 3.A.9 provides that if the firm sets a minimum asset level for portfolios to be included in a composite, no portfolios below that asset level can be included in that composite. GIPS provision 4.A.3 provides that a firm must disclose the minimum asset level, if any, below which portfolios are not included in a composite. Firms may establish a minimum asset level for a composite to identify portfolios that are too small to be representative of the intended strategy. Firms should not market a composite to a prospective client who has assets to invest which are less than the composite's minimum asset level. Firms must disclose the minimum asset level of the composite, if one exists, in each respective composite presentation and must consistently apply the minimum. Firms must document and disclose changes to the minimum asset level and must not retroactively apply the new limit. Portfolios below the minimum are not necessarily non-discretionary; however, asset level can affect discretion.

4-2

Portfolios may fall below the minimum due to client withdrawals or depreciation in market value. Firms must determine, as part of their policies regarding minimum asset levels, which market value will be used to evaluate composite portfolios against the minimum asset level (e.g., beginning market value, ending market value, beginning market value plus cash flows, etc.). If a firm establishes a minimum, it must document its policies regarding how portfolios will be treated if they fall below the minimum and must apply these policies consistently. Firms should consider establishing a threshold for the application of the minimum asset level and a minimum time period in order to minimize portfolio movement into or out of a composite. For example, the firm establishes a range of +/-5% of the minimum asset level when determining when to remove a portfolio from the composite and/or the firm establishes that a portfolio must remain above/below the minimum for at least two periods prior to removal/addition. If a portfolio is removed from a composite, the prior history of the portfolio must remain in the composite. Like all policies, once the firm establishes a policy regarding the minimum asset level it must be applied consistently. Once a portfolio is removed, the firm must determine if the portfolio meets any other composite definition and must include it in the appropriate composite(s) in a timely and consistent manner.

Firms should bear in mind that if all the portfolios in a composite fall below the minimum level and, according to the firm's policies, are removed from the composite, the performance record of the composite would come to an end. If after a period of time, portfolios move above the minimum or new portfolios are added to the composite, the prior performance history of the composite should be shown but not linked to the on-going composite performance results.

Composite Creation Date

Firms must disclose the creation date of the composite, which is the date when the firm first groups the portfolios to create a composite. This is not necessarily the earliest date for which performance is reported for the composite (i.e., composite inception date).

Composite Definition

Creating meaningful composites is critical to fair presentation, consistency, and comparability of results over time and among firms. A composite's definition must include detailed criteria that determine the allocation of portfolios to composites and must be made available upon request. Firms must document principles and polices related to composite definition.

While investment strategies can change over time, in most cases firms should not change the definition of a composite. Generally, changes in strategy result in the creation of a new composite. In some very rare cases, however, it may be appropriate to redefine a composite. If a firm determines that it is appropriate to redefine a composite, it must disclose the date and nature of the change. Changes to composites must not be applied retroactively. It is required that firms disclose any changes to the name of a composite. Discontinued composites must continue to be listed on the firm's list of composites for five years after discontinuation. When requested, firms must provide a compliant presentation for any composite on the firm's list of composites.

Firms are only permitted to move portfolios into and out of composites due to documented changes in client guidelines or in the case where the re-definition of a composite make it appropriate. For purposes of the GIPS standards, documentation can include, but is not limited to, letters, faxes, emails, and/or internal memorandums documenting conversations with clients. The historical record of the portfolio must remain with the appropriate composite.

Composite Definition Criteria

In addition to the Guiding Principles above, firms may choose to define their composites according to relevant criteria and must document the definition of each composite, including any criteria or constraints. It is constructive to consider a hierarchical structure of criteria for composite definition that promotes primary and secondary strategy characteristics. It is also important to understand the defining characteristics commonly found in the marketplace for investment products. Comparability of similar strategies or products is a fundamental objective of the Standards and benefits current and prospective clients when firms define strategies similarly, using clear and unambiguous terminology.

4-2

Suggested Hierarchy for Composite Definition

The following suggested hierarchy may be helpful as firms consider how to define composites. Firms are not required to define their composites according to each level of the hierarchy.

Investment Mandate
Composites based on the summary of strategy or product description.
Example: "Large-Cap Global Equities"

Asset Classes
Composites based on a broad asset class are the most basic and should be representative of the firm's products. Firms may further define the asset class by country or region.
Example: Equity, fixed income, balanced, real estate, venture capital, U.S. fixed income, European equities, etc.

Style or Strategy
Firms may further define a composite based on the style or strategy in order to provide investors with additional insight and allow for increased comparability.
Example: Growth, value, active, indexed, asset class sector (e.g., telecommunications), etc.

Benchmarks
Firms may define composites on the basis of the portfolios' benchmark or index provided the benchmark reflects the investment objective or strategy and there are no other composites with the same characteristics. This is often the case if the benchmark also defines the investment universe.
Example: Swiss Market Index, S&P 500, Lehman Aggregate, etc.

Risk/Return Characteristics
Portfolios with different risk characteristics (e.g., targeted tracking error, beta, volatility, information ratio, etc.) and return objectives may be grouped together into different composites.
Example: Japanese Equity Composite with a targeted excess return of 1% and targeted tracking error of 2% would be in a separate composite from a Japanese Equity Composite with a targeted excess return of 3% and targeted maximum volatility of 6%.

Constraints/Guidelines

In addition to the fundamental criteria above, firms may choose to further define their composites based on relevant client constraints or guidelines. The following are example of constraints or guidelines that could result in materially different strategies and, therefore, justify separate composites.

Extent of the Use of Derivatives, Hedging and/or Leverage
In general, portfolios that use derivatives, leverage and/or hedging have a unique investment strategy from those portfolios that do not utilize these techniques or instruments. Accordingly, firms must consider whether portfolios that use leverage, derivatives, and/or hedging should be included in separate composites from portfolios that are restricted from using such instruments or strategies.

Treatment of Taxes
The firm should define separate composites for portfolios with specific tax treatments if the treatment of taxes hinders the firm's ability to implement a specific investment strategy as compared to similar portfolios without specific tax treatments. For example, the different tax situations of corporate or insurance clients and private clients may require different investment strategies in terms of emphasizing growth versus yield or dividend versus interest income. If so, firms are required to define separate composites appropriate to the different strategies.

4-2

Type of Client (e.g., pension fund, private client, endowment, etc.)
Client type alone must not be used as the primary criteria for defining a composite. In some cases, the client type determines the investment strategy because of characteristics that are unique to the client type. If portfolios of different client types have materially different investment strategies and/or styles that are specific to the type of client, the firm must create separate composites representing each of the different strategies.

Instruments Used (e.g., invest only in pooled vehicles versus individual securities)
If portfolios use specific instruments the firm may define separate composites.

Size of Portfolios
Differences in portfolio size may result in meaningful, material differences in investment strategy and justify the creation of separate composites. For example, an index strategy may be implemented via sampling (i.e., holding a sample of the index securities) for smaller portfolios, while the strategy may be implemented via a full replication of the index for larger portfolios. In this case, the strategy is actually different based on the size of portfolio.

Client Characteristics (e.g., cash flow needs, risk tolerances)
Firms may create composites based on multiple client characteristics. For example, a firm may choose to create a composite composed of growth equity, taxable clients that allow leverage and have a targeted tracking error of 4%.

Portfolio Types (e.g. segregated (separate) portfolios, pooled portfolios (mutual funds))
Pooled funds, including mutual funds and unit trusts, may be treated as separate composites or combined with other portfolios into one or more composites of the same strategy, style, or objective.

Base Currency
Base currency must not be a criteria used for composite definition unless it is specific to the investment strategy.

Additional Considerations

- **Multiple Asset Class Portfolios**
  Multi-asset or balanced portfolios are portfolios that consist of more than one asset class. Composites should be constructed according to strategic ranges of asset mixes provided in the client investment guidelines, not according to the tactical percentage of assets invested in the different asset classes. Portfolios with varying, but similar strategic asset allocations can be grouped together if they collectively have the same strategy or style. Firms often have discretion to tactically alter the asset allocation in an effort to add value. Portfolios must not be moved into or out of composites due to changes in the tactical asset allocation. Only in the case of client-documented strategic asset allocation changes can portfolios be moved into different composites.

- **Inception Date**
  In general, firms are not permitted to create composites based solely on inception date. However, in very specific situations, it may be appropriate to group portfolios into composites according to inception date (e.g., venture capital composites, after-tax composites, municipal bond composites).

- **Firms with multiple offices, branches, or investment divisions**
  Firms are only permitted to define different composites for offices, branches, or investment divisions of a firm if the portfolios are managed according to investment objectives, styles or strategies that are unique to each particular office, branch, or division. Thus, it is the style or strategy that determines the composite, not the location or group. Composite definition cannot span multiple firms. For additional guidance regarding how the firm can be defined, please refer to the Guidance Statement on Definition of the Firm.

- **Dispersion of the portfolio returns within a composite**
  While dispersion is one measure to determine how consistently the firms has implemented its strategy across the portfolios in the composite, it can only be measured on an ex-post basis and, therefore, must not be used as a criterion to define a composite. A dispersion figure may serve as a good indicator of whether the criteria for composite definition are suitable and whether or not to redefine the composite. There is no general rule for a maximum amount of composite dispersion. The firm should contemplate the definition of a broad, "inclusive" composite with a wide dispersion of portfolio returns versus a narrow, "exclusive" composite with a more narrow dispersion measure.

- **Treatment of Fees**
  Different types of management fees should not be used as criteria for composite definition.

Effective Date

This Guidance Statement was originally effective 1 April 2002 and was revised to reflect the changes to the GIPS standards effective as of 1 January 2006. Firms are required to apply this revised guidance to all periods.

Key GIPS Provisions Specifically Applicable to Composite Definition

3.A.1 All actual, fee-paying, discretionary portfolios must be included in at least one composite. Although non-fee-paying discretionary portfolios may be included in a composite (with appropriate disclosures), nondiscretionary portfolios are not permitted to be included in a firm's composites.

3.A.2 Composites must be defined according to similar investment objectives and/or strategies. The full composite definition must be made available on request.

3.A.3 Composites must include new portfolios on a timely and consistent basis after the portfolio comes under management unless specifically mandated by the client.

3.A.4 Terminated portfolios must be included in the historical returns of the appropriate composites up to the last full measurement period that the portfolio was under management.

3.A.5 Portfolios are not permitted to be switched from one composite to another unless documented changes in client guidelines or the redefinition of the composite make it appropriate. The historical record of the portfolio must remain with the appropriate composite,

3.A.9 If a firm sets a minimum asset level for portfolios to be included in a composite, no portfolios below that asset level can be included in that composite. Any changes to a composite-specific minimum asset level are not permitted to be applied retroactively.

3.B.3 Firms should not market a composite to a prospective client who has assets less than the composite's minimum asset level.

4.A.2 Firms must disclose the availability of a complete list and description of all of the firm's composites.

4.A.3 Firms must disclose the minimum asset level, if any, below which portfolios are not included in a composite. Firms must also disclose any changes to the minimum asset level.

4.A.22 If a firm has redefined a composite, the firm must disclose the date and nature of the change. Changes to composites are not permitted to be applied retroactively.

4.A.23 Firms must disclose any changes to the name of a composite.

4.A.24 Firms must disclose the composite creation date.

Applications:

4-2

1. *Firm A has a client that has multiple accounts (e.g., personal trust and a personal investment account) and manages these accounts as one "master" portfolio. For purposes of the Standards, can Firm A treat these accounts as one portfolio and include them in an appropriate composite?*

If multiple portfolios are managed as one "master" portfolio, the firm can treat this "master" portfolio as any other portfolio and include it in an appropriate composite. Firms must treat this as one portfolio for purposes of calculating the dispersion measure and the number of portfolios within the composite. Firms must consider if account restrictions, such as tax considerations, of any of the individual portfolios affect the overall asset allocation process or the implementation of the firm's strategy for the "master" portfolio. Firm must be careful not to double count assets (e.g., counting both the "master" portfolio and underlying portfolio assets) when calculating composite and total firm assets.

2. *If we currently have a composite for a particular strategy, and the strategy changes, can the performance track record continue to be associated with the new strategy? The change in question is the addition of resources to the investment process. To be precise, we have added a fundamental portfolio manager to a strategy that was previously run using a quantitative (models) process. The new portfolio manager is an additional layer added on top to further refine the stock picks. The quant models will still be used as before.*

As most firms evolve, they modify their investment process through the use of new technologies and resources. It would seem clients would expect their firm to refine and improve the investment process.

A composite is an aggregation of a number of portfolios into a single group that represents a particular investment objective or strategy. The Standards require that composites must be defined according to similar investment objectives and/or strategies. In the situation you present, if the investment objective of the portfolios in the composite remains constant as the firm modifies its investment process, the firm should not create a new composite. If, however, the investment objective/strategy of the portfolios in the composite has changed, the firm should create a new composite, and the performance track record starts for that new composite when portfolios meeting the definition of the new composite are added to it. The firm should clearly document its decision and decision-making process in the event the creation of a new composite is questioned by a verifier/regulator.

3. *We are starting an investment strategy but currently do not have any clients. As such, we would like to start the strategy with a proprietary portfolio. However, once we receive a client account managed in this strategy (which may happen up to 2-3 years later) we will close the proprietary portfolio.*

   Can we create a composite and continue to use the historical performance of the proprietary portfolio by simply adding any subsequent client accounts we receive to the composite? The composite would contain the historical performance of the proprietary portfolio but would continue on with only the new client portfolios, just as a normal composite would.

Yes, the situation you describe is appropriate. Performance of a proprietary portfolio (also known as a seed or incubator fund) may be included in a composite if the fund is composed of actual assets under management. As with any other terminated account, the performance history of the proprietary portfolio will remain in the composite up to the last full measurement period that the proprietary portfolio was under management. As other portfolios managed to the same strategy are added to the composite, the historical performance of the composite will continue to include the proprietary portfolio's performance.

4. *If a fund invests in publicly traded equities for both limited partnerships and for separately managed accounts, should the manager set up different composites for each legal structure?*

A composite should include all portfolios that are managed according to the same strategy. Differences in legal structure alone would not warrant separate composite definitions. However, it is up to the firm to decide how results can presented in the most meaningful way, and if differences in legal structure cause the results of portfolios to differ, then the manager would split limited partnerships and separately managed accounts into separate composites.

5. *Can a firm include a single portfolio in more than one of the firm's composites?*

4-2

Yes. The Standards state that firms must include all discretionary fee-paying portfolios in at least one of the firm's composites. Portfolios must be included in each composite for which it meets the prescribed criteria for inclusion. For example, a firm may have an all-cap equity composite and a large-cap equity composite. If the firm manages a portfolio that meets the criteria for inclusion in the all-cap equity composite as well as the large-cap equity composite, the firm must include the portfolio in both composites.

6. *Why should each discretionary fee-paying portfolio be included in at least one composite? If a portfolio represents a style we never plan to market in the future, why should we have to include it in a composite?*

The Standards are ethical guidelines for firms to follow when presenting their performance results. The Standards are based on the principles of fair representation and full disclosure. They are not marketing guidelines.

The requirement for firms to include all fee-paying discretionary portfolios in at least one composite ensures that firms record an accurate picture of the firm's complete performance record. Without this requirement, there is a potential for firms to exclude poor performing portfolios from the appropriate composites. Portfolios that might otherwise belong in the composite could be grouped with "unmarketed" portfolios. Because the intent of the Standards is to accurately and fairly represent firm performance, all fee-paying discretionary portfolios must be included in at least one of the firm's composites.

Firms are also required to disclose that a complete list of the firm's composites is available on each compliant presentation. Potential clients can review descriptions of all composites to determine if any similarities exist. Prospective clients can also request to see additional information on the firm's historical performance record through other composites on the list. These requirements exist to provide prospective clients with a complete picture of the firm's investment performance achieved on all accounts under the firm's discretion.

Adoption Date: 28 June 2005
Revised Effective Date: 1 January 2006
~~*Original Effective Date: AIMR-PPS 1 January 2005*~~
~~*Italian IPPS 1 January 2002*~~
Retroactive Application: Not Required

GUIDANCE STATEMENT FOR COUNTRY-SPECIFIC TAXATION ISSUES

Introduction

The purpose of the GIPS standards is to ensure accurate and consistent reporting of investment performance in a fair, comparable format that provides full disclosure. The GIPS standards create an ethical framework whereby investment performance results are calculated and presented according to fundamental principles based on the principles of fair representation and full disclosure.

The GIPS standards do not address every aspect of performance measurement, valuation, attribution, or coverage of all asset classes. However, the IPC anticipates that the GIPS standards will evolve over time to include additional aspects of investment performance, which include developing some basic principles to broadly address the effects of taxation on investment performance.

Background

4-3

Historically, the IPC endorsed two Country Version of GIPS that included additions relating to taxation issues — the AIMR-PPS standards and Italian Performance Presentation Standards (IPPS). The AIMR-PPS standards include a section related to the calculation and presentation of after-tax performance results. The IPPS standards include a section related to grossing up performance for Italian withholding taxes.

Topic

The IPC has questioned whether or not it would be possible to entirely eliminate the need for County Versions of GIPS (CVG) and has determined to approach the subject by creating a guidance statement that initially incorporates the two country-specific sets of guidance relating after tax performance reporting in a Guidance Statement under the GIPS standards. This initial approach will allow to eliminate the CVGs in the US and Italy.

Future Development

Beyond this initial guidance statement, the IPC is also considering developing some basic principles to broadly address the effects of taxation on investment performance. These tax-related provisions and/or guidance for the GIPS standards will be applicable to all firms that claim compliance with the GIPS standards and choose to present pre-tax or after-tax composite returns, regardless of the firm's domicile.

Because tax regulation is extremely divergent from country to country, the IPC presumes that these provisions and guidance will only consist of some basic, worldwide accepted principles with the topic of comparability of performance results among managers from different countries. At the same time the IPC acknowledges that some countries have a longer history in after-tax performance presentation and therefore have developed detailed provisions and/or guidance relating to the topic. Based on the principles of GIPS, the IPC fosters the notion of worldwide best practice and will aim to adjust and include these pre-tax or after-tax performance presentation provisions in a global framework.

Attachments:

I. United States After-Tax Guidance (Applicability, GIPS Requirements and Recommendations); pages 3-7
II. Italian "Grossing-up" Taxation Guidance (Explanation, GIPS Requirements and Recommendations); page 8
Appendix A. Additional Guidance on United States After-Tax Calculation and Presentation; pages 9-48
Appendix B.Assogestioni formula for calculating the gross-of-tax value of the shares of an Italian open-end fund; pages 49-53

I. GIPS United States After-Tax Guidance

Effective Date: 1 January 2005
Retroactive: No

Applicability

Firms that previously claimed compliance with the AIMR-PPS standards and chose to present their composite performance results after the effect of taxes were required to comply with the modified after-tax provisions and guidance as of 1 January 2005. They were developed giving consideration to U.S. tax codes and regulations.

As of 1 January 2005, if a firm:

(1) Previously claimed compliance with the AIMR-PPS standards, and/or claims compliance with the GIPS standards; and
(2) chooses to present after-tax performance results to a client subject to U.S. taxation (except when reporting to an existing client the performance of his portfolio),

the firm must abide by the GIPS Country-Specific Taxation Issues Guidance requirements outlined below.[1]

The GIPS Country-Specific Taxation Issues Guidance supplements all of the required and recommended elements of the GIPS standards. They were developed giving consideration to U.S. tax codes and regulations available in 2002.

The effective date of the GIPS Country-Specific Taxation Issues Guidance is 1 January 2005. Until that time, firms are strongly encouraged to follow these provisions but may still calculate and report their after-tax performance according to the previous AIMR-PPS after-tax provisions (1994 provisions).

When reporting after-tax performance to an existing client, firms that are compliant with the GIPS Country-Specific Taxation Issues Guidance may choose to include a claim that the existing client's portfolio return was calculated "in accordance" with the after-tax calculation methodology of the GIPS Country Specific Taxation Issues Guidance — provided the return satisfies the minimum requirements of the Standards. Firms that choose to include such a claim must include the following statement alongside it:

> "The after-tax returns shown are subject to the limitations of the specific calculation methodology applied. Since the client's actual circumstances and tax rates determined after the fact may differ from the anticipated tax rates used in this process, the reported returns may not equal the actual after-tax returns for specific clients."

[1] *The calculation and presentation of after-tax mutual fund performance is regulated in the US by the SEC — this guidance is not intended to replace those requirements when a firm is advertising after-tax performance solely for a mutual fund.*

Requirements

A.1 Calculation Methodology

A.1.a. Firms must utilize a realized basis "pre-liquidation" calculation methodology, namely a methodology equivalent to the After-Tax Modified Dietz Method, the After-Tax Modified BAI (Linked Internal Rate of Return) Method or the After-Tax Daily Valuation Method.

Modified Dietz Method for Calculating "Pre-Liquidation" After-Tax Return

$$\text{"Pre-Liquidation" After-Tax Return} = \frac{(\text{End Value} - \text{Start Value} - \text{Sum of Portfolio Flows} - \text{Realized Taxes})}{(\text{Start Value} + \text{Sum of Day-Weighted Portfolio Flows})}$$

Modified BAI (Linked Internal Rate of Return) for Calculating "Pre-Liquidation" After-Tax Return

The "Pre-Liquidation" After Tax Return is the value of R that satisfies the following equation:

$$\text{End Value} - \text{Realized Taxes} = [F_i \, (1 + R)^{W_i}]$$

Daily Valuation Method for Calculating "Pre-Liquidation" After-Tax Return

$$\text{"Pre-Liquidation" After-Tax Return} = \frac{(\text{End-of-Day Market Value} - \text{Start-of-Day Market Value} - \text{Realized Taxes})}{\text{Start-of-Day Market Value}}$$

A.1.b. The tax liability or benefit must be recognized in the same period that the taxable event occurs. Managers who use daily valuation methods may account for taxes either on the day when a taxable event occurs or at the end of the month.

A.1.c. Taxes calculated on income must be recognized on an accrual basis.

A.1.d. Taxes calculated on income and realized capital gains or losses must be taken into account regardless of whether taxes are paid from assets outside the account or from the account assets.

A.1.e After-tax returns must consistently utilize over time and within each composite either the "anticipated tax rates" or the maximum federal (or federal/state/local/city) tax rate(s) applicable to each client.

A.1.f. Firms must utilize the tax rates in effect for the period to which the after-tax return calculation is applicable.

A.1.g. The before-tax returns for composites that hold tax-exempt securities must be presented without "grossing-up" tax-exempt income.

A.1.h. Each portfolio in the composite must be given full credit for net realized losses, as it is assumed these losses will be offset by gains at a later date or from other assets.

A.2. Composite Construction

A.2. All fee-paying discretionary portfolios **that are managed on a tax-aware basis** (i.e., taking into account the client's tax profile when conducting security buy and sell decisions) must be included in at least one of the firm's after-tax composites.

A.3. Disclosures — Firms must disclose the following:

a. If applicable, the name of the before-tax composite from which the portfolios that comprise the after-tax composite were drawn.
b. The after-tax composite as a percentage of the taxable portfolios that are included the before-tax composite (from which the portfolios that comprise the after-tax composite were drawn).
c. The accounting convention used for the treatment of realized capital gains (e.g. highest cost, lowest cost, FIFO, LIFO, specific identification, etc.).
d. A disclosure to read, "The after-tax returns shown are subject to the limitations of the specific calculation methodology applied. Since the client's actual circum-

stances and tax rates determined after the fact may differ from the anticipated tax rates used in this process, the reported returns may not equal the actual after-tax returns for specific clients."

e. The tax rate methodology ("anticipated tax rates" or maximum federal (or federal/state/local/city) tax rates) utilized for the composite and the benchmark.

A.4. Presentation and Reporting

A.4.a. All before-tax input data, calculation, composite construction, disclosure and presentation requirements as prescribed in the GIPS standards must be followed for each after-tax composite (i.e., for each after-tax composite, the firm must create a presentation that includes both the required before-tax and after-tax performance returns and disclosures).

A.4.b. If the after-tax composite is drawn from a before-tax composite that includes taxable and tax-exempt portfolios, firms must report both the after-tax composite presentation and the presentation of the before-tax composite (from which the after-tax composite was drawn).

A.4.c. After-tax returns must be reported on at least an annual basis for the composite. The effective date of the GIPS Country-Specific Taxation Issues Guidance is 1 January 2005; therefore, after 2004, firms must present additional annual performance so that by 31 December 2014, at the latest, firms that choose to present after-tax results will have the required 10-year track record that complies with the GIPS Country-Specific Taxation Issues Guidance.

A.4.d. Firms must report a measure of the dispersion of individual component portfolio returns around the aggregate composite return on an after-tax basis (and a before-tax basis) for each annual period that after-tax returns are presented. The measure of dispersion must be calculated using the same method for both the after-tax and before-tax performance returns.

A.4.e. Firms must report the percentage of unrealized capital gains as compared to total after-tax composite assets as of the end of each reporting period.

A.4.f. Firms must report the dollar-weighted "anticipated tax rate" on ordinary income for each composite or the maximum federal tax rate on interest and dividend income of the portfolios in the composite.

A.4.g. Firms must not link "non-compliant" after-tax performance results to performance that meets the requirements of the GIPS Country-Specific Taxation Issues Guidance, except to present it as information supplemental to a compliant after-tax composite presentation.

Recommendations

B.1. Calculation Methodology

B.1.a. It is recommended that after-tax performance be calculated based on each client's "anticipated tax rates" for interest, dividends, short- and long-term capital gains, etc. However, if the "anticipated tax rates" are unknown, use of the maximum federal (or federal/state/local/city) tax rate for the specific investor category is permissible.

B.1.b. Additional non-discretionary supplementary return information may be provided for those withdrawals that are client directed and are beyond the control of the manager that force the realization of non-discretionary capital gains.

B.1.c. If after-tax returns are reported for benchmarks, adjustments should be made for the actual or approximate Net Realized Gains incurred during the period. When an approximation is used, a description of the method and the assumptions should be disclosed.

B.1.d. The accrued interest should include the amortization of premiums and the accretion of discounts on all bonds if required by the client's tax situation. Firms should take into account the tax consequences of such items as the original issue discount (OID), the market discount and the de minimus rules.

B.1.e. Whether using the "anticipated tax rates" or the maximum federal tax rate, firms are encouraged to apply tax rates to at least the first decimal place (e.g., 38.6%).

B.2. Composite Construction

B.2.a. In addition to investment objective or style, portfolios may be grouped into composites based on client type, tax rate, and/or vintage year (or similar proxy to associate portfolios with similar unrealized capital gains).

B.3 Disclosures

B.3.a. If employing a calculation methodology other than "pre-liquidation," firms may provide these returns as Supplemental Information. Firms must provide a disclosure with an appropriate list of key assumptions used in calculating the supplemental returns.

B.3.b. If realized losses are greater than realized gains during the period, firms are recommended to disclose the percentage benefit of tax-loss harvesting for the composite.

B.3.c. Firms should disclose their policies relating to the amortization of premiums and accretion of discounts.

B.4. Presentation and Reporting

Firms are recommended to present the following:

a. Firms that present returns in accordance with the previous after-tax provisions (1994 provisions) may continue to present those returns for periods prior to 1 January 2005. These results may also be linked to the after-tax performance calculated under the restated after-tax provisions, provided all after-tax performance shown after 1 January 2005 adheres to the restated after-tax provisions.
b. Any Supplemental Information the firm deems valuable.
c. Annual after-tax benchmark returns.

II. GIPS Italian "Grossing-up" Taxation Guidance

Effective Date: March 2002
Retroactive: No

In view of the specific features of Italian tax legislation, this document has been developed to provide guidance that managers must comply with if they intend to present performance of composites including Italian open-end funds grossed-up for Italian withholding tax.

Funds governed by Italian law are subject to a full-settlement withholding tax of 12.5% that is applied to the difference between the value of the fund's investments at the beginning and end of the year. In the case of corporate investors this withholding tax is reclaimable. Moreover, taxation has an impact on the calculation of the net share price introducing a money weighted bias.

Firms which claim compliance with the GIPS standards and present the performance of composites including funds governed by Italian law that have been grossed up must comply with the GIPS Country-Specific Taxation Issues Guidance described below.

6.A.1 ***Grossing-up of performance.*** *Firms which present the performance of composites including grossed-up portfolios (portfolios whose gross performances have been calculated based on net official performances) must use a grossing-up formula consistent with the tax regime in force in the reference period and must show the effects that the tax regime has* *on the net performance and how the formula applied takes them into account. If the grossing-up formula is not widely adopted and accepted, the firm must give a detailed description of the analytical model on which it is based and specify the hypotheses adopted and its manner of working;*

6.A.2 ***Construction of composites.*** *No composite may contain portfolios whose performance depends on different tax regimes unless the various performances are suitably grossed up. If the grossing-up formula used is based on specific hypotheses regarding the effects of the tax regime on the way the portfolio is managed, they must be described. Portfolios managed on the basis of different hypotheses regarding the effects of the tax regime may not belong to the same composite;*

6.A.3. ***Grossed-up performances as supplementary information.*** *Firms which present the performance of composites including grossed-up portfolios must present net performance of grossed-up portfolios as well;*

6.B.1. ***Grossing-up of Italian open-end funds.*** *It is recommended that portfolios made of Italian open-end funds be grossed up using the widely adopted and accepted Assogestioni formula, which is shown in Appendix B.*

APPENDIX A. ADDITIONAL GUIDANCE ON UNITED STATES AFTER-TAX CALCULATION AND PRESENTATION

The purpose of the following Interpretive Guidance is to provide insight on the requirements and recommendations of the AIMR-PPS standards and to ensure continuity for those firms dependent on this Guidance. All references to AIMR-PPS are simply to preserve historical compliance documentation and do not conflict with GIPS standards compliance.

4-3

A. Applicability and Scope of the AIMR-PPS After-Tax Provisions

The after-tax provisions are voluntary, as investment management firms that follow the AIMR-PPS standards are not required to present after-tax composite performance results. Under the current after-tax rules (1994 rules), firms are only required to follow the after-tax provisions outlined in the AIMR-PPS standards when including the claim of compliance on an after-tax composite presentation. In other words, if a firm chooses to present after-tax performance results that do not include the claim of compliance, the AIMR-PPS standards are not explicitly clear and do not mandate that firms follow the after-tax provisions in those situations.

However, after 1 January 2005, firms that claim compliance with the AIMR-PPS standards and choose to report after-tax performance results (except when reporting an existing client's portfolio performance) must comply with all of the after-tax requirements. This volunteerism is consistent with the overall AIMR-PPS standards and the hope is that firms will embrace the after-tax provisions with the expectation that they will be increasing the credibility of the information that they are providing to clients and prospects.

The after-tax provisions apply to firms that claim compliance with the AIMR-PPS standards and choose to present their performance results after the effect of taxes. These after-tax provisions (Section II.9. of the AIMR-PPS standards) supplement all of the required and recommended elements of the AIMR-PPS standards (outlined in Section II of the AIMR-PPS standards). Firms that comply with the AIMR-PPS standards are also reminded that compliance requires adherence to all applicable laws and regulations.

The after-tax provisions were developed giving consideration to U.S. tax codes and regulations available in 2002. The AIMR-PPS Implementation Committee recognizes that firms who manage assets on a tax-aware basis for clients subject to Canadian tax regulation may not be able to apply the after-tax requirements as specified.

Therefore, to avoid potential conflicts between the after-tax provisions and Canadian tax codes and regulations, firms managing these "Canadian taxable portfolios" are exempt from the requirements of the after-tax provisions. They are encouraged to adopt the after-tax requirements whenever possible. Meanwhile, the Implementation Committee is working to develop specific guidance that considers Canadian tax codes.

B. Effective Date of Provisions and Historical After-Tax Performance Record

The effective date of the "restated after-tax provisions" is 1 January 2005. Until the restated provisions become effective, firms should begin to commit resources and design performance software to incorporate these future changes to the after-tax provisions. Firms are strongly encouraged to implement the restated after-tax provisions prior to their effective date. Firms may choose to retroactively apply these restated after-tax provisions on or before their effective date of 2005 in order to develop a longer historical track record.

On 1 January 2005, firms may but are not required to produce a 10-year history of compliant after-tax returns, as required by the AIMR-PPS standards for before-tax composites. Instead, from 1 January 2005, going forward, firms that choose to show after-tax results must build a cumulative year-to-year compliant after-tax track record so that by 31 December 2014, at the latest, firms that choose to present after-tax results will have the 10-year record required under the AIMR-PPS standards. To facilitate the transition from the previous after-tax provisions to the restated after-tax provisions, firms who chose to present their after-tax results in compliance with the AIMR-PPS standards and calculated after-tax returns according to the previous after-tax provisions (1994 provisions) may continue to present their compliant historical after-tax performance results (under the previous provisions) alongside their ongoing after-tax performance results (under the restated provisions) for periods up to the end of 2004. However, performance for periods after 1 January 2005 must be calculated and presented according to the restated after-tax provisions. Further, the performance results under the previous provisions (1994 provisions) up to the end of 2004 may also be linked with the results under the restated provisions beginning in (or before) 2005.

Firms must not link "non-compliant" after-tax performance results to performance that meets the requirements of the AIMR-PPS standards (either the 1994 after-tax provisions or the restated after-tax provisions), except to present it as information supplemental to a compliant after-tax composite presentation.

C. Calculation Methodology

i. Definitions of After-Tax Return

The AIMR-PPS provisions require that all returns, including after-tax returns, be time-weighted returns. This enables the evaluation of a manager's performance over time and permits the comparison of different managers who have different patterns of portfolio inflows and outflows during the measurement period.

The before-tax return measures the rate of change in value, with appropriate adjustment for any portfolio inflows and outflows. The after-tax return subtracts a measure of net taxes incurred during the period from the before-tax return. Taxes might not be paid in the period when they are incurred. There are a number of methods for computing an after-tax return, and they differ primarily in the way they measure taxes incurred during the measurement period.

The two principal methods of computing after-tax returns on portfolio accounts are known as the "Pre-Liquidation" (or "Realized Basis") and the "mark-to-liquidation" methods. A third method, the "post-liquidation" approach, is also sometimes used in the context of mutual fund reporting, although it does not generalize well to other settings. It is a special case of the "mark-to-liquidation" approach.

The "pre-liquidation" method has two aspects. First, it calculates the before tax return on a portfolio using the total market value at the beginning and at the end of the measurement period, as well as information on any intervening inflows or outflows from the portfolio. Second, it subtracts any taxes that the taxpayer must pay when he files his tax return for the measurement period. These taxes would include taxes on dividends and interest income, as well as taxes on net capital gains realized from security sales. The "pre-liquidation" method does not include any charge for taxes that may be incurred in the future, even if those taxes are ultimately attributable to changes in security prices during the measurement period. In particular, there is no accounting for the future capital gains taxes that may be due on capital gains that Accrue, but are not realized, during the measurement period. By ignoring such future taxes, the "pre-liquidation" method may understate the total tax burden on security returns during the measurement period.

4-3

The "mark-to-liquidation" method uses a different approach. It computes the after-tax value of the portfolio at the beginning of the measurement period, net of taxes, under the hypothetical assumption that all securities in the portfolio are liquidated. It also computes the end-of-period value of the portfolio, once again net of taxes, in this case assuming that all securities are liquidated at the end of the measurement period. Any portfolio inflows or outflows are valued on a net-of-tax basis. If cash is contributed, the after-tax value of the portfolio inflow equals its before-tax value. If appreciated securities are contributed to the account, however, the after-tax value of the portfolio inflow equals the value of these securities net of any capital gains tax that would be due if the securities were sold. The "mark-to-liquidation" after-tax return equals the change in the after-tax liquidation value of the portfolio, plus the net after-tax value of the portfolio inflows or outflows to the account, as a percentage of the start-of-period net-of-tax liquidation value. Although the "mark-to-liquidation" method would appear to be more conservative by taking into account all capital gain taxes (i.e., all Unrealized Gains are taxed), even on unrealized profits, it may be distorted by using a smaller denominator since the amount assumed to be invested in later periods is only the original cost, not the full amount of assets under management.

The so-called "post-liquidation" return that is discussed in the mutual fund context is a special case of the "mark-to-liquidation" return. It corresponds to the "mark-to-liquidation" return for a single measurement period, in which the portfolio is created with cash at the beginning of the period. The "mark-to-liquidation" starting value of the portfolio is therefore equal to the before-tax value in this case. The "post-liquidation" approach also assumes that the portfolio is completely liquidated at the end of the measurement period, and that any taxes due at that point are paid. The end-of-period portfolio value for the "post-liquidation" return is therefore the same as that in the "mark-to-liquidation" return. The difficulties with the "post-liquidation" return are (1) it cannot be linked for multiple periods because doing so would create duplicate taxation of the same events, and (2) it cannot sensibly be applied in situations in which the portfolio is created with securities rather than cash. Applying it in this case will overstate the tax burden on returns during the measurement period. Some of the Tax Liability that will be associated with liquidating the portfolio at the end of the measurement period will be attributable to Unrealized Capital Gains that were included in the value of the securities at the beginning of the measurement period.

The AIMR-PPS after-tax provisions require that after-tax returns be reported on a "pre-liquidation" basis. The "pre-liquidation" approach captures the fact that taxes deferred to the future have a smaller present discounted value than taxes paid today. The "mark-to-liquidation" method makes no distinction between managers who do, and who do not, realize capital gains as they Accrue, despite the fact that a manager who defers realization will typically generate a higher after-tax return for taxable investors. It is possible, however, that "mark-to-liquidation" or "post-liquidation" returns may also be needed as supplemental information, for example to satisfy local regulations or to provide useful portfolio information for taxable clients.

Taxable clients may also be interested in the after-tax internal rate of return generated by investment managers. Internal rate of return measures can be generated either under the assumptions used to calculate "pre-liquidation" returns, or under the assumptions that lead to "mark-to-liquidation" returns. Single-period internal rate of return measures calculated using the "mark-to-liquidation" methodology, and using the "pre-liquidation" methodology, can be compounded over time to compute a cumulative internal rate of return. Such compounding would not be feasible with returns calculated using the "post-liquidation" methodology.

4-3

To provide more specific guidance on the calculation of after-tax returns, the formulae below describe the calculation of "pre-liquidation" and "mark-to-liquidation" returns. In these expressions, "taxes" refers to "net taxes" — they can be either positive or negative. Negative taxes would be associated with situations in which capital losses exceeded capital gains, and the value of the tax reduction associated with the net capital loss was also larger than the Tax Liability for dividends and interest income. Similarly, portfolio flows can be either positive or negative. These flows may consist of cash or of securities. Finally, the terms "capital gains tax rate" and "income tax rate" should be interpreted as a series of tax rates depending on the length of holding period and/or the type of security providing the income.

Pre-Liquidation Methods

Modified Dietz Method for Calculating "Pre-Liquidation" After-Tax Return

$$\text{“Pre-Liquidation” After-Tax Return} = \frac{(\text{End Value} - \text{Start Value} - \text{Sum of Portfolio Flows} - \text{Realized Taxes})}{(\text{Start Value} + \text{Sum of Day-Weighted Portfolio Flows})}$$

This expression is equivalent to:

$$\text{“Pre-Liquidation” After-Tax Return} = \text{Before-Tax Return} - \frac{\text{Realized Taxes}}{(\text{Start Value} + \text{Sum of Day-Weighted Portfolio Flows})}$$

In this expression, Realized Taxes = (Realized Gains) * (Capital Gains Tax Rate) + (Taxable Interest and Dividend Income) * (Income Tax Rate). Realized taxes are an expense, but the formulae assume that cash is not withdrawn from the portfolio in order to pay the taxes. For this reason, taxes are not included in the portfolio flow adjustment in the denominator.

Modified BAI (Linked Internal Rate of Return) for Calculating "Pre-Liquidation" After-Tax Return

The "Pre-Liquidation" After Tax Return is the value of R that satisfies the following equation:

$$\text{End Value} - \text{Realized Taxes} = [F_i (1 + R)^{W_i}]$$

Where the portfolio flows, F_i, are the same as those used in the Modified Dietz Method with one important exception: the market value at the start of the period is also treated as a cash flow, that is, Start Value = F_0. The weight, W_i, is the proportion of the total number of days in the period that cash flow F_i has been held in (or out of) the portfolio. The formula for W_i is

$$W_i = \frac{CD - D_i}{CD}$$

where CD is the total number of calendar days in the period and D_i is the number of calendar days since the beginning of the period in which cash flow F_i occurred.

Daily Valuation Method for Calculating "Pre-Liquidation" After-Tax Return

With the daily valuation method, it is possible to simplify by accounting for net portfolio flows at the end of the day.

$$\text{"Pre-Liquidation" After Tax Return} = \frac{(\text{End-of-Day Value} - \text{Start-of-Day Value} - \text{Realized Taxes})}{\text{Start-of-Day Value}}$$

Mark-To-Liquidation Methods (as supplemental information only)

The "mark-to-liquidation" returns are calculated very similarly, but substitutes "Liquidation Value" for "Value", where

Liquidation Value = Market Value – (Unrealized Gain) * (Capital Gains Tax Rate)

Modified Dietz Method for Calculating "Mark-To-Liquidation" After-Tax Return

$$\text{"Mark-to-Liquidation" After-Tax Return} = \frac{(\text{End-of-Period Liquidation Value} - \text{Start-of-Period Liquidation Value} - \text{Sum of Liquidation Value of Net Flows} - \text{Realized Taxes})}{(\text{Start-of-Period Liquidation Value} + \text{Sum of Day-Weighted Portfolio Flows at Liquidation Value})}$$

Daily Valuation Method for Calculating "Mark-To-Liquidation" After-Tax Return

$$\text{"Marked-to-Liquidation" After Tax Return} = \frac{(\text{End-of-Day Liquidation Value} - \text{Start-of-Day Liquidation Value} - \text{Realized Taxes})}{\text{Start-of-Day Liquidation Value}}$$

EXAMPLE 1

The methodology for calculating after-tax returns is illustrated by this example, which assumes the measurement period is one month and that the distribution of gains and income is made on the 10th day.

Starting Market Value	$10.00
Starting Cost Basis (long-term holding period)	5.00
Realized Long-term Capital Gains Distributions	1.75
Realized Short-term Gains and Income Distributions	0.75
Change in Market Value	0.50
Ending Market Value	10.50
Ending Cost Basis (long-term holding period)	5.00
Maximum Federal Tax Rate on Long-term Gains	20.0%
Maximum Federal Tax Rate on Dividends and Short-term Gains	39.6%

4-3

Before-tax Return	36.0%
After-tax "Pre-liquidation" Return	28.2%
After-tax "Mark-to-liquidation" Return	30.7%

In this example, since the distributions are made on the 10th day of a 30-day month, the market value needs to be adjusted, and the weighting factor in the denominator is 20/30 = 0.667. The before-tax return is 3/[10 – (1.75 + 0.75) * 0.667] = 36.0%. (If the distributions had been reinvested at month end, there would have been no cash flows during the period and the before-tax return would have been (1.75 + 0.75 + 0.5)/10 = 3/10 = 30.0%.)

The "pre-liquidation" after-tax return subtracts the taxes that are associated with capital gain realizations and income. The realized taxes amount to (0.20 * 1.75) + (0.396 * 0.75) = 0.647. The "pre-liquidation" return is (3.00 – 0.647)/(10.00 – 1.667) = 28.2%.

For the "mark-to-liquidation" after-tax return, the liquidation values at the start and end of period are needed. The unrealized taxes at the start are 0.2 * (10 – 5) = 1.0 and the starting liquidation value is 9.0. The unrealized taxes at the end are 0.2 * (10.5 – 5) = 1.1 and the ending liquidation value is 9.4. The change in liquidation value is 0.4. The "mark-to-liquidation" after-tax return is (1.75 + 0.75 + 0.4 – 0.647)/(9 – 1.667) = 30.7%.

---

ii. "Anticipated Tax Rates"

4-3

The AIMR-PPS after-tax provisions are based on the client's "Anticipated Tax Rate(s)" for interest, dividends and short- and long-term capital gains or losses. The "Anticipated Tax Rates" should be the tax rates that an investment manager expects a taxable client to face on returns generated during the prospective reporting period for each applicable asset class ("Anticipated Tax Rates" = federal tax rate + [state tax rate * (1 – federal tax rate)] + [local tax rate * (1 – federal tax rate)]). These tax rates should include the impact of applicable state and local income taxes for each portfolio. The "Anticipated Tax Rates" should be determined at the beginning of the reporting period as they should be the tax rates that guide the investment manager in the decision-making process throughout the period. Since actual client circumstances and tax rates may differ from those anticipated at the beginning of the year, the "Anticipated Tax Rates" are not necessarily equal to the client's actual tax rate. The "Anticipated Tax Rates" (including those for state and local levels) should be readily known from client specific investment policy guidelines, and therefore easily applied in determining after-tax returns. Obviously, these "Anticipated Tax Rates" should also have had a significant impact on the investment strategy that was utilized in managing the portfolio to maximize tax efficiency. However, if the "Anticipated Tax Rates" are not known, which may be the case in situations such as wrap accounts, use of the Maximum Federal Tax Rate for the specific investor category is permissible (or federal/state/local/city tax rates). Use of the "Anticipated Tax Rates" allow firms to use the same after-tax returns when reporting to individual clients and constructing composites.

It may be necessary to consult with a qualified accountant to calculate the "Anticipated Tax Rates." Also, care should be taken in combining the various tax rates. Since state and local income taxes are typically deductible in the process of calculating federal taxes, the total Anticipated Tax Rate is slightly lower than that implied by simply summing the federal, state, and local tax rates. Moreover, applying the combined "Anticipated Tax Rates" is most appropriate for fixed income accounts, especially when accounts in the composite are subject to less than the Maximum Federal Tax Rate, as taxable bonds may be purchased by portfolio managers to achieve optimal after-tax returns for such investors.

The following table shows the "Anticipated Tax Rates" (including the adjustment for the deductibility of state income taxes) on various asset components of a portfolio in the year

2000 for an individual that is subject to tax rates of 39.6% on federal income and short-term capital gains, 20.0% on federal long-term capital gains and 9.0% on all state income, with state income tax being deductible for federal purposes. The total Tax Liability or Benefit for the portfolio would simply be the sum of the individual Tax Liability or Benefits for each of the respective asset classes shown.

ASSET CLASS	ANTICIPATED TAX RATE	EXPLANATION
Taxable Income and Dividends	45.0%	39.6% + (9.0% * (1 – 39.6%)) = 45.0%
Short-term capital gains	45.0%	39.6% + (9.0% * (1 – 39.6%)) = 45.0%
Long-term capital gains	25.4%	20.0% + (9.0% * (1 – 39.6%)) = 25.4%
Treasuries	39.6%	Taxed at federal level only
State deductible municipals	0.0%	No federal or state taxes incurred
State non-deductible municipals	5.4%	Taxed at state level only; deductible from federal 9.0% * (1 – 39.6%) = 5.4%

The next two examples (Example 2 and Example 3) demonstrate acceptable methods for calculating a Dollar-Weighted Anticipated Tax Rate for the composite. Example 2 dollar-weights the individual portfolio Anticipated Tax Rates to determine a monthly tax rate while Example 3 dollar-weights the monthly composite Anticipated Tax Rates to determine an annual tax rate.

EXAMPLE 2

Example 2 provides a detailed calculation of a composite Anticipated Tax Rate for a specified reporting period.

Tax Rates for After-Tax Return Reporting for Tax-Efficient Balanced Composite
January 20XX

Portfolio	Client State	Tax Rates Federal	State	Local	Anticipated	Beginning of Period Assets	% Assets	Contribution
ABC	Michigan	35.0%	4.4%	1.0%	38.9%	$ 2,013,970	18.1%	7.0%
DEF	Iowa	38.6%	9.0%	0.0%	44.1%	$ 2,500,334	22.5%	9.9%
GHI	Illinois	30.0%	3.0%	0.0%	32.1%	$ 1,516,973	13.7%	4.4%
JKL	California	38.6%	9.3%	0.0%	44.3%	$ 2,967,458	26.7%	11.8%
MNO	New York	38.6%	6.9%	2.0%	44.8%	$ 2,111,325	19.0%	8.5%
Total						$ 11,110,060	100.0%	
Dollar-Weighted Anticipated Tax Rate:								41.7%

iii. Retroactive Tax Changes

Incorporating retroactive changes in tax rates for calculation purposes will depend on what rates the portfolio manager believes are in effect at the time portfolio decisions are made. Typically, if Anticipated Tax Rates are used, retroactive tax changes should not be reflected in the return calculation. However, if the firm uses the Maximum Federal Tax Rates, retroactive tax changes should be reflected in the return calculation.

EXAMPLE 3

Calculation of Annual Tax Rate
With change in the Federal Tax Rate Effective 1 June

Month	Composite Anticipated Tax Rate	Assets	Contribution
Jan	41.7%	$ 11,110,060	3.0%
Feb	41.6%	$ 11,329,786	3.1%
Mar	41.8%	$ 11,739,064	3.2%
Apr	41.7%	$ 11,254,069	3.1%
May	41.5%	$ 11,361,798	3.1%
Jun	39.6%	$ 11,467,425	3.0%
Jul	39.7%	$ 14,500,467	3.7%
Aug	38.5%	$ 14,579,342	3.7%
Sep	39.7%	$ 13,900,678	3.6%
Oct	39.8%	$ 14,263,007	3.7%
Nov	39.4%	$ 14,006,392	3.6%
Dec	39.6%	$ 14,139,672	3.6%
Total		$ 153,651,760	
Dollar-weighted Anticipated Tax Rate:			40.3%

D. After-Tax Composites

According to the before-tax provisions of the AIMR-PPS standards, all fee-paying discretionary portfolios must be included in at least one of the firm's composites. Similarly, firms that choose to present their performance results after the effect of taxes must include all fee-paying discretionary portfolios **that are managed on a tax-aware basis** (taking into account the client's tax profile when conducting security buy and sell decisions) in at least one of the firm's after-tax composites.

4-3

For the purposes of the AIMR-PPS standards, an after-tax composite is conceptually a subset of portfolios from a before-tax composite that is created to represent a specific tax-efficient investment mandate. Due to the unique circumstances surrounding taxable accounts, it may be necessary to separate the portfolios within a before-tax composite (that represents a broad investment mandate) into several smaller after-tax composites in order to accommodate clients' different tax structures and risk tolerances. In the same way, a before-tax composite may already be constructed to take into account the different tax-related issues and cannot be further separated; therefore, the before-tax and after-tax composite will consist of the same member portfolios. (See **Example 4** for graphical representation of the relationships that can exist between before-tax and after-tax composites.)

EXAMPLE 4 – Relationships Between Before-Tax and After-Tax Composites

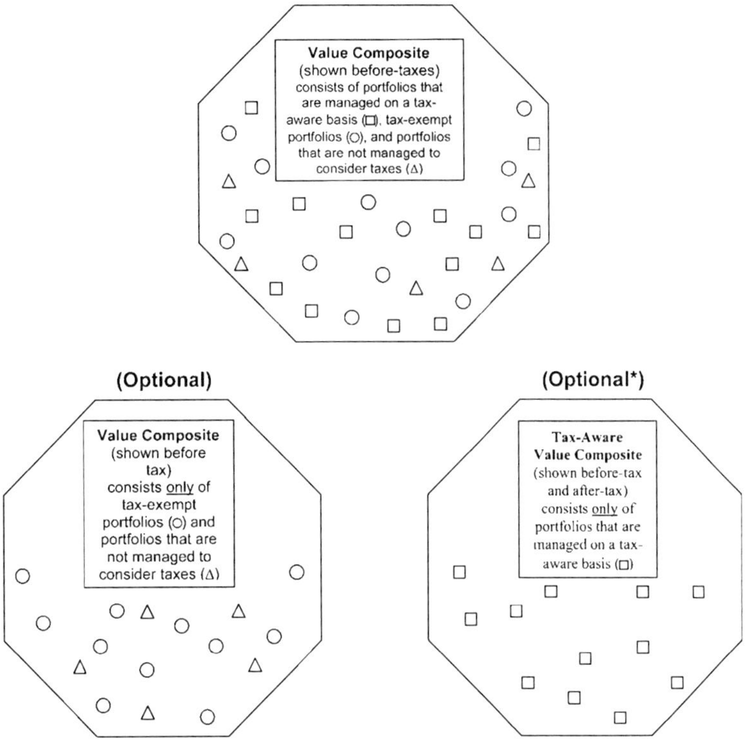

* If a firm that manages portfolios on a tax-aware basis chooses to create an after-tax composite and show after-tax results, the firm must include all of the portfolios that are in the after-tax composite also in a before-tax composite.

All firms must follow the Guidance Statement on Composite Definition, which outlines several guiding principles and interpretive guidance for defining discretion and determining the construction of composites (www.aimr.org/standards).

Since nuclear decommissioning trusts, corporate funds, post retirement medical trusts, property and casualty insurance company investment portfolios, and portfolios for high net worth individuals have differing objectives with respect to funding liabilities as well as different tax rates, they are likely also to require different investment strategies in terms of emphasizing tax-exempt versus taxable income and/or income versus long-term capital appreciation. Therefore, depending on the applicable circumstances, firms are encouraged to construct separate composites appropriate to the different strategies. In addition, even when after-tax performance is adjusted for Non-Discretionary Capital Gains, multiple composites may be necessary within the same strategy to accommodate clients' different tax structures and risk tolerances. The unique circumstances of taxable accounts, therefore, necessitate careful construction of composites. In addition to the fundamental composite definition criteria (e.g., investment mandate, asset class, style or strategy, risk/return characteristics), firms should consider the following tax-related criteria when defining after-tax composites:

- the tax rate(s),
- the client class or type (individual, property & casualty, corporate, nuclear decommissioning, etc.),
- the inception dates of the portfolios in the composite (a composite should include portfolios with similar starting dates so that Realized and Unrealized Capital Gains are somewhat similar),
- the separation of portfolios that have substantial net Unrealized Capital Gains from those that have limited net Unrealized Gains, and
- the state of domicile or residence.

The methodology for calculating after-tax composites is the same as for before-tax returns; namely, calculating the asset-weighted return for the portfolios that comprise the composite within each period and then calculating the time-weighted rate of return by geometrically linking returns over time.

i. Applications Demonstrating Relationships Between Before- and After-Tax Composites

The following applications provide examples of the concepts and principles underlying the relationships between before and after-tax composites and demonstrate potential ways to deal with each situation. (Some of the examples below represent only possible solutions to the issues presented based on the information provided. Other solutions may also be possible.)

APPLICATION 1: Tax Aware and Non-Tax Aware Portfolios Combined in One Composite Historically

Firm XYZ has claimed compliance with the AIMR-PPS standards since its inception in 1995. Firm XYZ has managed its large-cap value strategy since that date and has annual before-tax returns for the Large-Cap Value Composite from 1994 through 2002.

Regarding after-tax composite returns, Firm XYZ has been asked to present them on occasion, but it has chosen never to comply with the AIMR-PPS after-tax provisions. In 2003, Firm XYZ reviewed the modifications to the after-tax provisions of the AIMR-PPS standards and interpretive guidance and determined it would need to calculate and present after-tax performance results according to the AIMR-PPS standards after 2005 in order to maintain compliance.

Instead of waiting until 2005 to implement the changes, the firm took the original Large-Cap Value Composite (which consisted of both portfolios that are managed on a tax aware basis and tax exempt portfolios) and in 2003 created three Tax-Aware Large-Cap Value Composites according to the after-tax guidance to reflect different tax-related criteria. From 2003, going forward, the firm decided to maintain the original Large-Cap Value Composite as well as the three Tax-Aware Large-Cap Value Composites. See **Example 1.A** for a schematic representation.

4-3

Example 1.A

Example 1.A

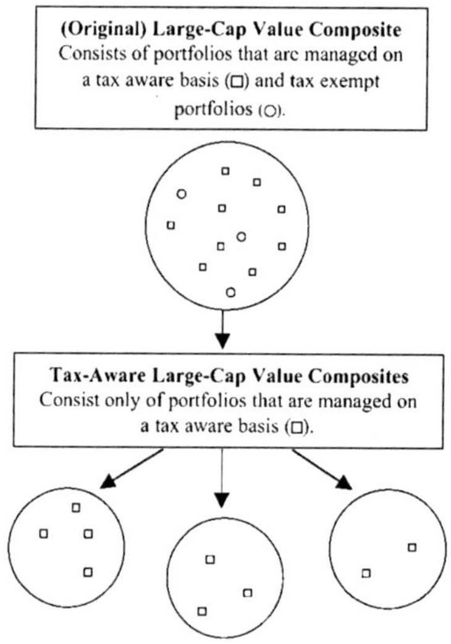

Two years later, in 2005, Firm XYZ receives a request from a prospective client to see their Tax-Aware Large-Cap Value Composite. **Example 1.B** demonstrates a sample presentation of one Tax-Aware Large-Cap Value Composite with the accompanying original Large-Cap Value Composite presentation.

Example 1.B

Tax-Aware Large-Cap Value Composite Presentation*

	2003	2004
After-Tax Return	X.XX%	X.XX%
Before-Tax Return	X.XX%	X.XX%
...		
...		

Large-Cap Value Composite Presentation*

	1995	1996	1997	1998	1999	2000	2001	2002	2003	2004
Before-Tax Return	X.XX%	X.XX%	X.XX%	X.XX%	X.XX%	X.XX%	X.XX%	X.XX%	X.XX%	X.XX%
...										

Not a complete presentation.

Application 2: Only Tax-Aware Portfolios Included in the Composite Historically

Firm ABC has claimed compliance with the AIMR-PPS standards since its inception in 1996. Firm ABC has managed its core equity strategy for taxable clients since that date and has annual before-tax returns for its Core Equity Composite from 1996 through 2002. In the past, it was not able to satisfy the requirements of the AIMR-PPS standards for reporting after-tax composite returns.

In 2003, Firm ABC decides to implement the newly modified after-tax provisions of the AIMR-PPS standards. They determine their composites are created according to the after-tax guidance and have the infrastructure in place to present after-tax composite results from 2003 going forward to 2005. See **Examples 2.A** and **2.B** for graphical representations of Firm ABC's Core Equity Composite and a sample presentation.

Example 2.A

Example 2.A

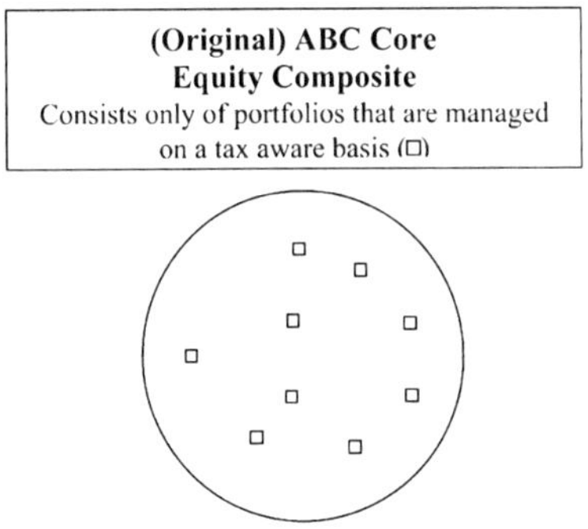

Since Firm ABC's Core Equity Composite consists of only portfolios that are managed on a tax-aware basis, there is not generally a need to create a new "after-tax" composite. However, the firm may determine to change the name of the composite to more appropriately reflect the tax awareness of the mandate.

Example 2.B

ABC Tax-Aware Core Equity Composite Presentation*

	1996	1997	1998	1999	2000	2001	2002	2003	2004	2005
After-Tax Return								X.XX%	X.XX%	X.XX%
Before-Tax Return	X.XX%	X.XX%	X.XX%	X.XX%	X.XX%	X.XX%	X.XX%	X.XX%	X.XX%	X.XX%
...										

Note: No accompanying composite report is required, since the historical before-tax returns are captured in this composite's presentation.

Not a complete presentation.

E. Disclosures

i. Tax-Loss Harvesting

One method that is commonly used to improve after-tax returns is the process of "Tax-Loss Harvesting." It involves intentionally harvesting a loss in a portfolio — i.e., purposely selling a security and incurring a loss that is used to offset a gain (either within the same portfolio or elsewhere). In most cases, if the sum of the losses is greater than the total amount of gains for the tax year, the residual amount of the loss can be carried forward to the next tax year. Most managers attempt to harvest losses at the end of the tax year, but some specialize in continually harvesting losses throughout the year.

The benefits of "Tax-Loss Harvesting" can be substantial, especially during significant market corrections, and may result in the need for additional disclosure to explain the impact of harvesting. Specifically, firms are recommended to disclose the percentage benefit of Tax-Loss Harvesting for the composite if realized losses are greater than realized gains during the period (see example 5).

4-3

EXAMPLE 5

Recommended Disclosure — Percentage Benefit Received For Tax-Loss Harvesting For the Year 2000

	Accounts	Assets ($'s)
Beginning Market Value:	5	$ 25,000,000
Contributions/Withdrawals:	10	50,000,000
Ending Market Value:	15	68,250,000
Total Short-Term Losses Realized		11,250,000
Total Short-Term Gains Realized		10,000
Total Long-Term Losses Realized		1,000,000
Total Long-Term Gains Realized		357,500
Net Short-Term Losses/Gains × 42.6%*		4,788,240
Net Long-Term Losses/Gains × 23.0%*		147,775
Benefit of Tax-Loss Harvesting:		$ 4,936,015
% Benefit:		10.59%

Tax-Loss Harvesting (taking losses purposely to offset current or future capital gains by this or other portfolios) plays a meaningful role to enhance after-tax returns. This strategy is most beneficial in periods of higher than normal market volatility and declining markets. When this occurs and there is significant growth of new accounts to the composite results may be achieved that may not be representative of future after-tax returns. The percentage benefit (dollar benefit of Tax-Loss Harvesting/((beginning market value + ending market value)/2)) for the year 2000 was 10.59%.

*Anticipated Tax Rates for the composite were 42.6% for ordinary income/short-term capital gains/losses and 23.0% for long-term capital gains/losses. This assumes a federal tax rate of 39.6% and a 5.0% state tax rate.

F. Presentation and Reporting

Additional information may be required to analyze a manager's ability to add value on an after-tax basis. When both before-tax and after-tax returns are provided, investors can analyze both the investment performance, as well as the impact of taxes.

Professionals evaluating taxable managers should realize that after-tax performance analysis is both a science and an art. The "scientific" aspects are manifested in the discrete requirements and details, while the "artisan" aspects recognize that cash flows, substantial Unrealized Capital Gains, and composite definitions can have a significant impact on after-tax results. Thus, firms should be very careful and thoughtful in determining the parameters and assumptions for composites. Also, evaluators are encouraged to consider supplemental information to gain an appreciation for a manager's ability to add value on an after-tax basis.

Another area requiring careful evaluation of after-tax performance is the dispersion or variability of returns of accounts in a composite. For taxable accounts, a taxable manager may act in the best interests of clients to achieve superior after-tax returns, but beneficial actions may lead to a greater level of dispersion than an evaluator would feel comfortable with if applying standards appropriate for tax-exempt account composites. This would be especially true when the manager, who inherits a portfolio with a large Unrealized Capital Gain position, immediately sells security positions to conform to a model portfolio which would create an excessive tax burden. Even after taking careful steps, practitioners must realize the dispersion of returns is likely to be much greater for taxable accounts than for tax-exempt accounts.

The specified requirements must be followed in order to state compliance with the AIMR-PPS standards. However, the specific format of the attached sample presentation is not required. It serves as one example of a presentation that meets the requirements of the AIMR-PPS standards. Managers are encouraged to provide the additional information listed as recommendations to fully satisfy the needs of current clients and prospects.

i. Sample AIMR-PPS Compliant Presentation for an After-Tax Composite XYZ U.S. Equities After-Tax Composite

	2004	2005	2006	2007	2008
Required: (if compliant with AIMR-PPS standards and showing after-tax performance)					
After-Tax Total Return (%)	21.99	31.03	25.02	22.02	-6.17
After-Tax Composite Dispersion (%)	3.1	5.1	3.7	3.2	2.4
Before-Tax Total Return (%)	24.31	34.02	27.33	24.03	-8.44
Before-Tax Benchmark Total Return (%)	22.95	33.35	28.58	21.04	-9.01
Before-Tax Composite Dispersion (%)	2.9	3.3	2.6	1.8	1.5
% of Unrealized Capital Gains to Composite Assets	9	25	37	43	19
% of Taxable Portfolios Included in Both the U.S. Equities After-Tax & Before-Tax Composites	75	78	81	79	82
Dollar-Weighted Anticipated Tax Rate	44.2	44.3	44.5	44.1	43.9
Number of Portfolios	26	32	38	45	48
Total Assets at End of Period (US $millions)	165	235	344	445	420
Percentage of Firm Assets	33	36	39	43	37
Total Firm Assets (US $millions)	500	653	882	1,035	1,135
Recommended:					
After-Tax Return Adjusted for Non-Discretionary Capital Gains (%)	21.99	31.07	25.25	24.12	-5.99
After-Tax Benchmark Return (%)	21.78	32.05	27.78	20.21	-9.37
Percentage Benefit from Tax Loss Harvesting	0.00	0.00	0.00	0.00	3.51

XYZ Investment Firm has prepared and presented this report in compliance with the Performance Presentation Standards of the Association for Investment Management and Research (AIMR-PPS®), the U.S. and Canadian version of the Global Investment Performance Standards (GIPS®). AIMR has not been involved with the preparation or review of this report.

Notes:

1. XYZ Investment Firm is a global portfolio investment manager that invests in U.S. and Non-U.S. Equities and Fixed Income securities. XYZ Investment Firm is defined as an independent investment management firm that is not affiliated with any parent organization.
2. Results for the full historical period are time weighted.
3. The "XYZ U.S. Equities After-Tax Composite" was drawn directly from the "XYZ U.S. Equities Composite" (before-tax).
4. Valuations are computed and returns are based on US Dollars.
5. The dispersion of annual before-tax and after-tax returns is measured by the range between the highest- and lowest- performing portfolios in the composite.
6. Performance results are presented before management and custodial fees but after all trading commissions.
7. A management fee schedule for this product is as follows:

$500,000-$2,500,000	0.65%
$2,500,000-$5,000,000	0.45%
$5,000,000 — and above	0.30%

8. The composite was created in September 2003.
9. After-tax returns are computed using "Anticipated Tax Rates."
10. The benchmark is the Vanguard U.S. 500 Stock Index Fund. After-tax performance on the benchmark is computed using a 37.6%* tax rate on net short-term realized capital gains and dividend income. From May 2005-December 2008, a 20.0% tax rate on net long-term capital gains is used. Prior to May 2005, a 28.0% tax rate on net long-term realized capital gains is used.
11. The after-tax returns shown are subject to the limitations of the specific calculation methodology applied and are not to be used for tax reporting purposes. Since the client's actual circumstances and tax rates determined after the fact may differ from the anticipated tax rates used in this process, the reported returns may not equal the actual after-tax returns for specific clients.
12. Highest cost is the accounting convention used for treatment of realized capital gains.
13. A complete list of firm composites and performance results is available upon request.

* 37.6% is the proposed maximum federal tax rate for 2004

ii. Presenting Net-of-Fees After-Tax Returns (Expensing Investment Management Fees)

It is important to note that while a separate account and a mutual fund can have the same before-tax return, tax rates, amount of capital gains and level of income generated during the period, a different net-of-fees after-tax return can be calculated for the two types of accounts. This is a result of the fact that the mutual fund can offset income by the investment management fee paid on the portfolio whereas the separate account cannot offset any income. If portfolios within a composite are able to offset some or all of the income earned by the amount of the investment management fee paid (as is the case with some pooled funds or mutual funds), firms are encouraged to disclose this practice to prospective clients.

EXAMPLE 6

	Mutual Fund	Separate Account
Before-tax Gross-of-Fees Return:	10.00	10.00
Investment Management Fees	1.00	1.00
Net-of-Fees Return	9.00	9.00
Taxes:		
Short-term Capital Gains	1.00	1.00
Tax at 38.6% (rate for 2002)	-0.39	-0.39
Long-term Capital Gains	1.00	1.00
Tax at 20.0% (rate for 2002)	-0.20	-0.20
Dividends (ordinary income)	2.00	2.00
Offset of Expenses	1.00	0.00
Taxable Dividends	1.00	2.00
Tax at 38.6% (rate for 2002)	-0.39	-0.77
Total Tax	-0.97	-1.36
Net-of-Fees After-Tax Return	8.03%	7.64%

G. Treatment of Non-Discretionary Capital Gains

The equations used to calculate the pre-liquidation after-tax return assumes that all capital gain realizations were at the discretion of the manager. When returns are combined into a composite, it may be necessary to make an adjustment to the return for those capital gains taxes that were incurred because of client-initiated withdrawals. This will allow comparability among managers.

This equation can be modified to include an adjustment term that removes the effect of client-initiated gain realizations. The adjustment term credits the manager for taxes that were not at his discretion. By reducing the tax payments, the adjustment factor should always have the effect of raising the measured after-tax return.

One way to adjust the after-tax return for client-initiated withdrawals would be to add back the capital gains Tax Liability associated with the precise set of asset sales that were used to satisfy the client's withdrawal. This approach to measuring after-tax returns, however, would create perverse incentives for managers. They would have an incentive to liquidate highly appreciated assets whenever clients requested withdrawals. By lowering the stock of Unrealized Gains in the client's portfolio, such sales would tend to raise the manager's subsequent after-tax return performance by reducing future capital gain realizations.

To avoid such opportunities for gaming the performance results, the recommended adjustment term does not depend on the actual ratio of realized gains to assets sold, but rather on the ratio of total portfolio Unrealized Gains to the entire value of the portfolio. This "gain ratio" is defined below. It equals the sum of realized gains (during the measurement period) and Unrealized Gains (at the end of the measurement period), divided by the sum of net client withdrawals (during the measurement period) and total portfolio value (at the end of the measurement period).

$$\text{Gain Ratio} = \frac{(\text{Realized Gains} + \text{End-of-Period Unrealized Gains})}{(\text{Net Client Withdrawals} + \text{Ending Asset Value})}.$$

The adjustment factor equals the capital gains tax that would be due if the manager responded to the client's withdrawal request by proportionately liquidating all securities in the portfolio. This Tax Liability depends on the capital gains tax rate, the amount of the client-initiated withdrawal, and the gain ratio. It can be written as:

$$\text{Adjustment Factor} = \text{Capital Gains Tax Rate} * \text{Net Client Withdrawal} * \text{Gain Ratio}.$$

The net client withdrawal in the adjustment factor equation is defined as the net withdrawal after subtracting both taxable and tax-free income, as well as any other positive

4-3

cash inflows actually received during the measurement period. The income measures used to define the net withdrawal should be measured on an "as-paid" basis which excludes Accruals or income not remaining in the portfolio since those amounts would not be available to meet client cash withdrawals.

The adjustment factor can be combined with the foregoing measure of after-tax returns to construct a modified after-tax return that reflects only the tax effects that were within the manager's control. The Adjusted After-Tax Return equation below shows this after-tax performance measure:

$$\text{Adjusted After-Tax Return} = \frac{(\text{End Value} - \text{Start Value} - \text{Sum of Net Cash Flows} - \text{Taxes} + \text{Adjustment Factor})}{(\text{Start Value} + \text{Sum of Day-Weighted Cash Flows})}.$$

This equation does not describe the client's results after the payment of actual taxes. Those results would depend on the precise assets that the manager sold to meet the client's withdrawal.

Investment managers should always act in accordance with the best interests of their clients. The procedure for calculating after-tax returns outlined in the Adjusted After-Tax Return equation (above) does not offer managers any benefit from selling positions with meaningful gains when such selling may prove detrimental to the client's tax burden. Since the adjustment factor depends on the capital gains taxes that would be generated by selling a fractional component of the entire portfolio, and not on the actual capital gains taxes associated with the assets actually sold.

H. After-Tax Benchmarks

There are currently no after-tax benchmarks for evaluating the after-tax performance of a portfolio. Some practitioners have devised customized ways to present such comparisons, but there is substantial variation both in the methods used and in the details of implementation. AIMR encourages the industry to conduct more research in developing after-tax benchmarks and to disclose the methods that are used to construct these benchmarks.

At the outset, one must recognize that benchmarks for after-tax reporting need to strike a balance between simplicity and flexibility for application in a wide range of contexts. True after-tax performance depends on the investor's sequence of investment flows. After-tax returns depend on when the cost basis was established and how the cash flows evolve. Two portfolios that have precisely the same current holdings will have different after-tax returns if they were initiated at different points in time and if they had different cost bases or cash flows. It is therefore impossible to envision a precise after-tax benchmark return each period that is applicable to all portfolios, even if they are managed the same. This is an important conceptual issue, since before-tax benchmarks are not subject to adjustments for tax basis and cash flows.

This customization to the investor is what sets after-tax performance evaluation apart from before-tax evaluation. Like before-tax performance evaluation, the evaluator begins with a benchmark that is appropriate for the manager being evaluated. This means that the benchmark should reflect the investment approach, or style, of the manager. For example, customized blends of commonly available style indexes make reasonably good benchmarks for most equity managers. Similarly, bond manager benchmarks should capture the quality and duration of the portfolio, sector allocations and the use of derivatives. Once an appropriate before-tax benchmark is established for the manager, the job of incorporating taxes and client effects into the benchmark can begin. In other words, a good after-tax benchmark will have all of the properties of a good before-tax benchmark, plus one more important property: it will reflect the tax status and actions of the client.

There are two broad approaches to constructing after-tax benchmarks. The first tries to develop and report an after-tax version of standard benchmark indices. Such after-tax returns would be easy to use, since practitioners could simply look them up in a table. Using such indices requires strong (and, for some taxable clients, potentially inappropriate) assumptions about the investor's returns and cash flows. The second approach, which involves the development of a "Shadow Portfolio," abandons the goal of a single benchmark return that can fit all situations. Instead, it develops a benchmark return that is tailored to the manager's style and the individual investor's cash flows and cost basis and tax rates. This approach allows for more complex modeling of the investor's returns and flows. However, it is probably not useful for a composite because of the difficulty in creating a Shadow Portfolio covering multiple client portfolios at once. These two approaches to benchmark computation can be complementary, and in many cases both approaches will be useful.

i. After-Tax Return Indices

The first conceptual approach to benchmarking is to publish an after-tax version of standard benchmark indexes, for example those currently published by Standard and Poor's. Using historical data on capital gains, dividends, and the weights of different securities in various indices, it is possible to simulate the evolving after-tax value of an indexed portfolio and hence its returns. In such a simulation, taxes would be withdrawn, and dividends re-invested, each month. Published tables following such an approach would presumably assume a single initial investment left to appreciate over time from different starting dates. If tables of such benchmark returns were used to evaluate performance, it would be necessary to aggregate across styles and over different sets of returns for a given measurement period. These returns would correspond to portfolio investments at different historical dates, and the styles would represent the style blend the manager is implementing. In this way, the benchmark calculation would reflect the manager's approach, or style, and the historical cash flow experience of an investor's specific portfolio. In addition, after-tax performance measures of this type would need to be adjusted for non-discretionary cash flows both into, and out of, the portfolio.

The principal attractions of this approach are that it relies on published, standardized data for computing benchmark returns, and that several portfolio managers who are benchmarked to the same index can be easily compared. The difficulties with this approach are the multiplicity of tables that might be needed to compute the appropriate benchmarks (one would need tables for different tax rates, and for different dates of portfolio inception), the complexity of the calculations that underlie the benchmark returns (and the associated difficulty of "checking" these calculations for individual practitioners), and the need to continually maintain historical data on stock prices and returns. Again, all of these complexities are in addition to those confronted in before-tax calculations.

The guidelines for after-tax returns for actual benchmarks of securities are the same as presented for separate account composites.

ii. Shadow Benchmark Portfolios

The second approach to computing after-tax benchmark returns uses "Shadow Portfolios" to estimate what an investor would have achieved, after taxes, if he had invested passively in his benchmark index. Shadow portfolios begin by identifying the appropriate before-tax benchmark, i.e. "the index". This approach then computes the after-tax returns on the index by replicating the investor's cash flows, cost basis, and tax rate. This "benchmark portfolio" approach could be implemented by tracking a simulated paper portfolio that corresponds to the index. Calculating the return on the Shadow Portfolio requires information and assumptions on several aspects of the portfolio. With respect to accounting data, these include information on the beginning of period market value and cost basis for the portfolio, the tax rates applicable to income from the portfolio, as well as portfolio cash flows. For the benchmark portfolio, one needs to know the capital gain realization rate, the portfolio's income receipts, and the total return.

Choosing a Shadow Portfolio that is a real mutual fund may be problematic if the fund incurs fees and tracking deviations from the index. In general, taxes incurred by a mutual fund are affected both by the actions of the investors, through deposits and withdrawals, and by the actions of the portfolio manager, through turnover and stock selection.

The rationale for creating a customized Shadow Portfolio rather than using a mutual fund benchmark is that customized portfolios can today generally be created on demand. Such Shadow Portfolios could be created as a custom mutual fund, or constructed as blends of exchange traded securities, that offer the returns on the benchmark portfolio. In such cases, the returns on these securities could be adjusted for taxes and these returns could be used for the benchmark return.

The appeal of the Shadow Portfolio approach is that the investor obtains a measurement of his actual after-tax performance that closely approximates what he would have achieved after taxes in a passive benchmarked index. Procedures for computing Shadow Portfolio returns could be standardized so results can be replicated by others with access to the relevant data on cash flows and tax rates. AIMR expects the use of the Shadow Portfolio approach to take time and effort by the industry, but believes that the effort is worth it.

One downside to the Shadow Portfolio approach is that it requires relatively complex computations and assumptions. Another is that investors who are benchmarked to the same index can have different after-tax benchmark returns for a given period. This could create some confusion among clients and managers.

When evaluators develop their own customized measures of benchmark returns, many different assumptions are needed, and these assumptions can affect the ultimate returns. AIMR suggests that in computing after-tax returns on a benchmark portfolio, the capital gain realization rate (as defined above) for the benchmark portfolio should be used to determine capital gains tax liabilities. Although the capital gain realization rate is not always available for broad market indices, it is currently reported for mutual funds. It is possible to approximate the gain realization rate for benchmark portfolios using the gain realization rate for equity index mutual funds that track the same benchmark.

iii. Potential Uses of Marked-to-Liquidation Return Benchmarks

4-3

When the separate income and capital gain information necessary to calculate an after-tax benchmark return is not available, the alternative approach of computing the marked-to-liquidation return may provide comparative information that is useful for taxable fixed income clients. This method assumes that both the portfolio and the index are fully taxed on both their Realized and Unrealized Capital Gains. If this method is used, its inaccuracies must be disclosed.

I. Supplemental Return Calculation Methodologies

As with measures of tax efficiency, there are a number of ways of measuring the after-tax return of a portfolio. Some of these, such as the pre-liquidation and marked-to-liquidation measures, have been considered and compared in the foregoing discussion. There are other approaches as well.

To develop a general approach for comparing different approaches to calculating after-tax returns, it is helpful to recognize that rates of return measures are all based on measures of changes in portfolio value. This change in value, for the special case in which there are no cash flows, is defined as:

$$\text{Change in Value} = \frac{(V(t_1) - (V(t_0))}{V(t_0)}.$$

Where $V(t_0)$ and $V(t_1)$ are the beginning-of-period and end-of-period values of the portfolio, respectively. There are three ways to measure each of these values: the current market value on a pre-liquidation basis, the current market value net of the Tax Liability associated with Unrealized Gains (marked-to-liquidation), and the "true economic value" (TEV) that is defined as the pre-liquidation value of the portfolio less the Contingent Tax Liability (CTL). This is similar to the subtraction of the entire Unrealized Gain/Loss from market value in the marked-to-liquidation method. The CTL is the present value of future tax payments embodied in the current Unrealized Gain/Loss. Several authors have commented on methodologies to calculate the CTL, but there is not as of yet one accepted methodology, hence the partial-liquidation method is presented as supplemental information. Unlike the marked-to-liquidation method which subtracts only from ending market value, the partial liquidation method views all market values, both beginning and end, as net of the CTL. This in essence acknowledges the free leverage that is employed by deferring taxes. The pre- and marked-to-liquidation methods are summarized and the "True Economic Value" method is detailed below.

Pre-liquidation method

Omitting the contingent tax liability, the value of V_m is the current market value of the portfolio. This value overstates true value if there are Unrealized Capital Gains in the portfolio. At such time as a security is sold for a gain and taxes withdrawn, V_m will be reduced.

Marked-to-liquidation method

At the other extreme, if the portfolio were to be liquidated immediately and the simplifying assumption was made that all gains, long- and short-term, are taxed at the tax rate t_g, then the marked-to-liquidation value would be $V_l = V_m - t_g(V_m - V_c)$. This liquidation value would be used as the ending wealth measure in the return calculation. In the case of an investor with no desire to liquidate, the liquidation value understates true value.

"True Economic Value" Method

Both of the foregoing definitions fall short because in general they over-simplify the Tax Liability. In general the "true" economic value (TEV) of the portfolio — a market value net of the contingent tax liability (CTL) — will depend on many factors, including the investment horizon, the final disposition of the assets, future tax rates, future returns, and the rate at which capital gains are expected to be realized. It can be useful to think of the TEV (V_f) as a simple weighted average of the two extremes, V_l and V_m, i.e., $V_l = (f * V_l) + ((1 - f) * V_m)$. The weighting factor in this expression, f, is between zero and one (see article "Measuring and Evaluating Portfolio Performance After Taxes", *Journal of Portfolio Management*, vol. 24 no. 2, (Winter 1998) by David Stein, PhD for further justification). Substituting for V_l using the expression from the marked-to-liquidation case allows one to restate the true economic value as if it were a partial-liquidation value with the partial liquidation measured by f t_g, when there are no cash flows, as

$$V_l = V_m - (f * t_g (V_m - V_c)).$$

It is possible for a firm to compute the TEV value, V_f, in this simplified form, as long as it discloses the choice of weighting factor f that is being used. This represents an approximation to what one would obtain from a calculation of the CTL. This framework is submitted as a temporary substitute and crosscheck for an accepted CTL calculation methodology. In general, either the manager or the investor might choose f.

For example, a simple choice of f = 0.5 splits the difference between, the two extremes V_l and V_m. Note that f = 0 corresponds to the pre-liquidation value, and f = 1 corresponds to the marked-to-liquidation value of the portfolio. Using a simple present value model, it can be shown that this corresponds to a choice, using one of the contemplated CTL calculation methodologies, of a horizon at 20 years, a 10% rate of realization of capital gains, a 10% market return environment, and liquidation at the horizon. Other methodologies would encompass the use of different assumptions.

The typical range of f is between 0.4 and 0.9. The value of f is higher than 0.8 when the gain realization rate is above 60%, or when the horizon is less than about 5 years. In general, with a high rate of gain realization: use a high f; with a long horizon: use a low f; with a high return expectation on the market: use a low f. Different methodologies for calculating the CTL will result in different ranges of the partial-liquidation function, f. Most would produce a varying f value over time.

J. Comparison of After-Tax Return Measures

Different results can be calculated when there is a large imbedded Unrealized Capital Gains position, which requires different calculation approaches. What are the pros and cons of the pre-liquidation, marked-to-liquidation and partial-liquidation approaches? Note that they are all straightforward to compute, given AIMR-PPS after-tax computations. The partial-liquidation return requires a more complex explanation and the requirement to specify a factor f. However, it adds to the understanding of after-tax performance.

The following table compares the after-tax performance of three managers using the three different after-tax return measures — the pre-, marked-to-, and partial-liquidation returns. The initial portfolio is the same in each case: an initial market value of $100.00, with a cost-basis of $50.00. Each manager achieves the same 10.00% before-tax return over one year with no dividends, and the capital gains tax rate is 20.00%. Manager 1 liquidates the initial portfolio and re-invests the proceeds for one year, manager 2 holds the initial portfolio unchanged for one year, and manager 3 realizes $10.00 of losses.

Numbers in bold are inputs to the calculation, while other numbers are calculated.

	Manager 1	Manager 2	Manager 3
Initial market value	**100.00**	**100.00**	**100.00**
Initial cost basis	**50.00**	**50.00**	**50.00**
Initial liquidation value	90.00	90.00	90.00
Initial CTL value[a]	95.70	95.70	95.70
Investor taxes	**-10.00**	**0.00**	**2.00**
Expected flows	10.00	0.00	-2.00
Final market value	110.00	110.00	110.00
Final cost basis	100.00	50.00	40.00
Final liquidation value	108.00	98.00	96.00
Final CTL value[a]	109.14	104.84	103.98
Pre-liquidation return	0.00%	10.00%	12.00%
Marked-to-liquidation return	8.89%	8.89%	8.89%
Partial-liquidation return	3.59%	9.55%	10.74%

[a]The CTL value here is calculated as a weighted average of the liquidation and market values, with the weight on liquidation value being 0.43, and the weight on the market value being 0.57.

4-3

Since the returns of all three final portfolios are the same, most would agree that manager 3 has the best after-tax return, followed by manager 2 and then by manager 1. Let us compare how the three after-tax return measures assess the managers.

The pre-liquidation return puts the managers in the right order. By realizing the capital gain, manager 1 has eliminated the before-tax return of 10.00%; this is the high cost of turnover for this taxable portfolio. Manager 2 has preserved the before-tax return, while manager 3 has added value through tax management. However, returns based on pre-liquidation value penalize manager 1 too heavily — although he has realized gains of $10.00, he has increased the cost basis of the portfolio, and future liquidations will be less costly. Similarly, too much credit has been given to manager 3 who has reduced the cost basis of the final portfolio and has made future turnover more costly.

The marked-to-liquidation return suggests that all three managers have performed equally well. It assumes that the tax penalty on realized gains is the same as that on Unrealized Gains, and it gives no credit to a manager who accelerates the realization of losses and defers capital gains.

The partial-liquidation return recognizes the realized Tax Liability (or credit) as well as the future Tax Liability on Unrealized Gains.

Comparing partial-liquidation returns to pre-liquidation returns for each manager, Manager 1 has a higher partial-liquidation return (3.59%) than pre-liquidation return (0.00%), reflecting the higher cost basis of the final portfolio. Similarly, manager 3 has a lower partial-liquidation return than pre-liquidation return, because the Unrealized Capital Gain is higher in the final portfolio.

K. Measures of Tax Efficiency

The tax burden on a taxable investor's returns depends both on the investor's characteristics and the choices made by the investment manager. The investor's marginal tax rates on both ordinary income and on realized capital gains, as well as specific features of the investor's tax situation such as the presence of loss-carry forwards or the applicability of the alternative minimum tax, affect the tax burden. The manager's decisions about whether to invest in securities that generate dividends and interest or capital gains, and when to realize Accrued capital gains, also affect the investor's tax burden. Because managers do affect the tax burdens faced by their clients, there is substantial demand for quantitative measures that describe the manager's contribution to the investor's tax burden.

The heterogeneity of investors makes it difficult to develop a measure that would apply in all circumstances and to all investors, but there are many statistical measures that are currently used to summarize tax-related aspects of investment performance. These measures are often described as measuring a portfolio's "tax efficiency." This is a difficult term, because in discussions of efficiency (for example in thermodynamics) one usually thinks of measuring the performance of something relative to an idealized benchmark. In the absence of an after-tax benchmark portfolio return, however, it is hard to judge whether a manager has done well, or done badly, with respect to tax management.

This point can be illustrated with a simple example. Consider a portfolio with substantial Unrealized Losses on individual securities, with a before-tax return of 10.00% during the measurement period. Assume that the manager realizes no gains, and that none of the underlying securities pays a dividend, so that the investor does not face any Tax Liability associated with the 10.00% before-tax return. Does this mean that the manager was extremely tax efficient? Not necessarily, since it might have been possible to realize losses that would have reduced the investor's tax burden on other investments. This example underscores the difficulty of judging the quality of tax management simply from information on measured returns.

There are many different approaches to measuring the "tax efficiency" of a portfolio. The most attractive ones are based on comparisons of the before-tax and after-tax returns on a portfolio, although even those measures are not ideal. There are a number of other measures, that are based on summary statistics about the portfolio or the manager's behavior, that are less informative about tax management issues.

i. Tax Efficiency Measures Based on After-Tax and Before-tax Returns

The most informative measures of how managers are affecting their client's after-tax returns are based on comparison of the before-tax and after-tax returns. Such comparisons can be based on the tax rates facing a hypothetical taxable investor — for many purposes an investor facing the highest federal marginal tax rates might be used. The difference between the before-tax return (R_{bt}) and the after-tax return (R_{at}) is one measure that provides some insight on how the manager's actions affect investor Tax Liability. This difference is likely to be most informative when it is used to compare the actions of managers with similar investment mandates, for example with respect to style or sector allocation.

One simple summary statistic is just the tax burden on the portfolio, which is defined as the difference in before-tax and after-tax returns:

$$\text{Tax Burden} = R_{bt} - R_{at}.$$

Returns in this case are measured in percentage points, i.e. as 8 percent. This difference embodies all of the information on how taxes affect returns, but for some presentation purposes it may be less attractive than other measures. The difference will tend to be larger, for example, during periods of high returns, even though the tax management of a portfolio may be independent of the level of returns.

A second summary measure that partially moves toward avoiding this problem is the relative wealth ratio. This is defined as:

$$\text{Relative Wealth Measure}_1 = \left[\frac{(1+R_{at})}{(1+R_{bt})} - 1 \right] * 1000 \cdot$$

This measure shows the amount of after-tax wealth that an investor who invested one dollar at the beginning of the period would have at period-end, relative to the before-tax wealth at the end of the period. When returns are measured in decimal percentage terms, for example with $R = 0.10$, then $1 + R$ describes the end-of-period wealth that an investor will have, per dollar of initial wealth invested. The relative wealth measure is the calculation of two such relative wealth measures, re-scaled by subtracting unity to make it easier to present. The measure can be rewritten as:

$$\text{Relative Wealth Measure}_2 = \left[\frac{(R_{at} - R_{bt})}{(1+R_{bt})} \right] * 1000 \cdot$$

Notice that the Relative Wealth Measure_2 depends on the tax burden measure as outlined above, i.e. on the difference between before-tax and after-tax returns.

One appealing feature of the relative wealth measure is that by scaling the difference between pre- and after-tax returns by a factor that depends on the portfolio's before-tax return, it makes it easier to compare the tax burden on portfolios with different before-tax returns. As defined in the Relative Wealth Measure_1 or Relative Wealth Measure_2, however, this calculation will often be negative in periods with positive before-tax returns, since the after-tax return is likely to fall below the before-tax return. Additionally, the relative wealth measure is an accurate calculation for tax efficiency when using the "post liquidation" method, as adopted by the SEC for mutual fund after-tax reporting.

Both the tax burden and the relative wealth measure are more useful statistics of tax burdens than the "capture ratio", which is defined as:

4-3

$$\text{Capture Ratio} = \frac{R_{at}}{R_{bt}} \cdot$$

The logic of the capture ratio is that it describes the after-tax return received by the investor, as a fraction of the before-tax return. However, when the before-tax return is negative, this measure is poorly defined. While the capture ratio may work well in rising markets, it is less versatile than either the tax burden or the relative wealth measure.

Neither the tax burden nor the relative wealth measure provides a completely satisfactory calculation of the degree to which a manager has managed a portfolio to achieve the best possible after-tax returns. Neither takes account of the potential losses that the manager might have realized, or of the investment options that the manager might have pursued but did not. These are difficult problems to surmount, however, and these measures do offer some insight on a manager's tax performance.

To illustrate the use of these measures, consider the following two examples:

Concept	Example 1	Example 2
Before-Tax Return	+ 25.0%	– 10.0%
After-Tax Return	+ 21.0%	– 8.0%
Tax Burden	– 4.0%	+ 2.0%
Relative Wealth Measure	– 32.0	+ 22.0
Capture Ratio	84.0%	80.0%

Note that the capture ratio reflects quite different information in the two cases. When both before-tax and after-tax returns are positive, a lower value of the capture ratio reflects a poorer performance on the part of the manager. When both values are negative, however, a lower value is beneficial to the investor, since it indicates that he has not shared in as much of the loss on an after-tax basis as on a before-tax basis.

ii. Tax Efficiency Measures That Are Not Return-Based

There are many other measures that are sometimes suggested as indicators of tax efficiency. None is completely satisfactory, and AIMR does not suggest that any of these measures be used to gauge the quality of tax management for taxable clients. Nevertheless, it is useful to catalogue these measures and to note their potential drawbacks.

The "turnover ratio" is often cited as an indicator of a manager's attention to tax management issues. This ratio is calculated by dividing the lesser of purchases or sales by the average value of portfolio assets during the period. The turnover ratio suffers from several drawbacks, including the lack of information on whether sales were designed to realize losses that could actually improve the portfolio's after-tax return. It also makes no attempt to control for factors in the marketplace that might induce higher or lower levels of turnover, such as the level of corporate control transactions. There are many variants of the turnover rate, with different modifications, but all suffer from the absence of a link between turnover and investor after-tax returns.

Many measures of tax efficiency focus on the manager's realization of capital gains. The "Capital Gain Realization Rate" is a more attractive measure of tax efficiency than turnover is, since it focuses on the extent to which asset sales result in taxable capital gains. The capital gain realization rate (CGRR) is defined as total gains realized during a measurement period, divided by the potential gains that could have been realized during the period. It is only well defined in cases where the underlying portfolio has potential realizable gains. A related concept, the capital loss realization rate (CLRR), can be defined for cases in which a portfolio has Net Unrealized Losses rather than Gains.

Potential gains in a given measurement period are the average of two terms: (1) the amount of outstanding gains (or losses) at the start of the period and (2) the sum of realized net gains during the period and the amount of outstanding gains (or losses) at the end of the period. When this sum is positive, the capital gain realization rate (CGRR) is defined as:

$$\text{CGRR} = \frac{\text{Net Realized Gains During Measurement Period}}{\left[\dfrac{\text{(Amount of Unrealized Gains / Losses at Start of Period + Net Realized Gains During Period + Amount of Unrealized Gains / Losses at End of Period)}}{2}\right]}.$$

To illustrate the use of this ratio, consider a case in which a portfolio is worth \$10,000 at the beginning of the measurement period, with a purchase basis of \$7,500. During the measurement period, the assets appreciate in value, so that they are worth \$12,000 just before the period-end, at which point the manager sells \$2,000 worth of securities and generates a capital gain of \$1,000. The proceeds from the sale are re-invested in assets with a basis of \$2,000, so the end-of-period basis is \$8,500. In this case, the Net Realized Gain is \$1,000, the start-of-period amount of Unrealized Gains is \$2,500, the end-of-period amount of Unrealized Gains is \$3,500, and the capital gain realization ratio is:

$$\text{CGRR} = \left[\frac{\$1{,}000}{\dfrac{(\$2{,}500 + \$1{,}000 + \$3{,}500)}{2}}\right] = 0.286 \text{ or } 28.6\%.$$

The manager chose to realize 28.6% of the portfolio's Unrealized Gains during the measurement period.

The capital gain realization rate is only a useful concept in situations when the portfolio being analyzed has potential Unrealized Capital Gains. This will be the case whenever the denominator (i.e. the sum of net gains realized during the period and the amount of Unrealized Gains at the beginning and end of the period) is greater than zero. (In the unlikely case of this sum being precisely equal to zero, the capital gain realization rate would involve a division by zero, and therefore would be undefined.) It is possible for the

4-3

capital gain realization rate to be negative, since a manager might realize losses even when a portfolio has Net Unrealized Capital Gains. This is an artifact of heterogeneity in the returns on different securities. Even when a portfolio has Net Unrealized Gains, there can be some securities with Unrealized Losses, and vice versa.

When the potential gain realization for a portfolio takes a negative value, then rather than computing the capital gain realization rate, it is appropriate to compute the capital loss realization rate (CLRR). This ratio is defined in the same way as the CGRR above. If the manager realizes net losses during the period, and the portfolio has Net Unrealized Losses, then the CLRR will be positive. A negative value of the CLRR will indicate that the manager has realized gains on a portfolio with Net Unrealized Losses.

The capital gain realization rate and the capital loss realization rate provide some information on the extent to which manager actions are affecting the tax burden on taxable clients. In most cases, higher values of the CGRR will translate into higher tax burdens, and lower after-tax returns, for taxable investors. This pattern is reversed when using the capital loss realization rate: higher values of the CLRR indicate that the manager has realized a larger fraction of the losses on a portfolio with net losses, and that will usually be associated with lower taxes and higher after-tax returns for taxable investors. These simple statements may not apply in all cases, and the manager must be aware of that possibility. For example, a taxable investor might have tax loss carry-forwards that postpone the utilization of tax losses realized during the current period. The capital gain realization rate is preferable to turnover as an indicator of how a manager's actions affect investors' tax burdens, since a manager could have high turnover either as a result of loss harvesting or as a result of trading stocks with Accrued gains.

Three variants of the capital gain realization rate are sometimes used in practice. One divides capital gain realizations during the measurement period by the amount of portfolio assets. This is less informative than the gain realization rate, since it takes no account of the amount of gains or losses in the portfolio that might have been realized. A second variant known as the "Capital Gains Ratio" divides capital gains realized during the measurement period by the maximum amount of capital gains that could have been realized. This ratio also becomes uninformative when the portfolio has Unrealized Losses rather than Unrealized Gains. It is also based on comparing actual experience with a "liquidation based" measure of the portfolio's return, even though the portfolio management problem is explicitly an ongoing, multi-period problem. Finally, there is a "Modified Capital Gains Ratio" that is defined as:

4-3

$$\text{Modified Capital Gains Ratio} = \frac{1 + \dfrac{(\text{Net Realized Gains})}{\text{Total Asset Value}}}{1 + \dfrac{(\text{Net Realized Gains} + \text{Unrealized Gains})}{\text{Total Asset Value}}}.$$

This ratio has many of the same drawbacks as the Capital Gains Ratio, since it is in effect comparing actual realizations with a liquidation scenario.

Yet another tax efficiency measure based on capital gain realizations is sometimes known as the "accountant's ratio". It equals the ratio of short-term capital gains realized during the measurement period to total capital gains realized during the period. The logic behind this measure is that if a manager is realizing many short-term gains, the manager may not be considering the tax consequences of trading decisions. While there may be some information in this measure, it does not consider the broader question of the level of capital gain realizations. It therefore provides only a partial perspective on the portfolio manager's sensitivity to tax management issues.

A final measure of tax efficiency is the "Capital Gains Tax Efficiency Measure". This measure calibrates the capital gains taxes paid on the portfolio on a scale that ranges from the lowest amount of taxes that might have been paid, if all losses had been realized but gains had been deferred, to the highest amount of potential taxes, if all gains had been realized. To identify these two polar cases, define:

$$\text{Maximal Capital Gains Taxes} = \text{Capital Gains Taxes on All Unrealized Gains at Beginning of Period} + \text{Short-Term Capital Gains Taxes on All Gains Accruing During the Period.}$$

The first term in this expression, capital gains taxes on unrealized beginning-of-period gains, would include both short-term and long-term gains if the beginning-of-period portfolio included assets with both types of gains. The second term would be calculated assuming that all gains accruing during the period were realized while they were short-term. These gains might be calculated on an aggregate basis for the portfolio, for example as the end-of-period market value of the portfolio, less the initial market value plus the sum of within-period cash flows, investment income, and realized gains. They could also be calculated, when record-keeping permits, by summing the gains on only those positions with accrued gains within the period. The second approach would provide a more accurate measure of maximal potential taxes, since it would not allow any offsetting of Unrealized Gains and Losses. If the two components of the "maximal capital gains tax" are greater than or equal to zero, the capital gains tax measure should also be greater than or equal to zero.

A parallel calculation can be done to assess the minimal potential capital gains taxes on a portfolio:

$$\text{Minimal Capital Gains Taxes} = \text{Deduction for Realizing All Unrealized Capital Losses at Beginning of Period} + \text{Deduction for Short-Term Capital Loss on All Losses Accruing During the Period.}$$

Each of the deductions in the Minimal Capital Gains Tax equation should be negative or zero, so the minimal capital gains tax defined by this equation is less than or equal to zero.

The capital gains tax efficiency measure compares actual capital gains taxes with the maximal and minimal taxes. Actual taxes are defined as the short-term capital gains tax rate times any net short-term realized gains, plus the long-term capital gains tax rate times any net long-term realized gains. If a manager realizes net short-term losses or net long-term losses, it is possible for the actual capital gains tax liability to be negative. The capital gains tax efficiency measure is defined as:

$$\text{Capital Gains Tax Efficiency Measure} = \frac{(\text{Maximal Capital Gains Taxes} - \text{Actual Taxes})}{(\text{Maximal Capital Gains Taxes} - \text{Minimal Capital Gains Taxes})}.$$

Since minimal capital gains taxes are less than or equal to zero, the denominator of this expression is a positive number at least as great as maximal capital gains taxes. This ratio indicates how much of the difference between the maximal and the minimal capital gains Tax Liability was actually incurred as a result of the manager's trading decisions.

L. Model Request-For-Proposal Questions

The following model request-for-proposal (RFP) questions may be used by consultants, plan sponsors, and others in soliciting after-tax investment results as well as by investment managers responding to such requests. Requesters may choose to use some or all of these questions.

1. Please provide the criteria employed to formulate after-tax composites.
2. Please provide the methodology for calculating after-tax returns or the source of the information for the benchmark. In addition, list all assumptions necessary to calculate the after-tax returns for the benchmark.
3. If employing a calculation methodology other than "pre-liquidation" as supplemental information, please provide a list of all assumptions.
4. Please include all taxable account composites for this particular investment strategy. Be sure to include relevant notes that distinguish the composites from one another.

4-3

M. Challenges

i. Systems and Software Issues

After-tax performance reporting and composite construction requires enhancements to the firm's systems and accounting software.

To accurately compute after-tax returns firms must take into consideration the tax implications in the next section "Accounting Issues." The following accounting information is needed: acquisition dates of securities, cost basis of securities, the amount of distributable income, short- and long-term capital gains calculated for tax purposes.

Accounting systems are generally designed to serve a particular segment of the industry. For example, a mutual fund system provides net asset values (NAVs), taxable income and capital gains distributions. An insurance system emphasizes amortization and accretion of fixed income securities and provides regulatory reports. An investment management company selects an accounting system to satisfy their high priority needs. Unfortunately, tax-lot accounting is not always a functional option of a firm's software. Since accounting is the heart of the daily operation, the costs of changing an accounting system include software, implementation and training, a lengthy conversion time, and reworked links to other systems such as trading, compliance, analytical, reporting, and performance.

Since a firm may use different tax elections for different clients, a performance system should be flexible enough to calculate after-tax returns based on various combinations of the tax requirements. Many current performance systems are not cost-of-transaction based. Certain systems that do incorporate tax-lot accounting may need to be enhanced to include acquisition dates, tax elections based on different security types, transaction based calculations, and calculations to take into account for the impact of taxes or tax credits.

ii. Accounting Issues

4-3

The items noted below are intended to assist firms in evaluating the tax implications associated with certain securities and securities transactions. The recognition and classification of ordinary income or realized gains and losses is determined by applicable tax regulations. Providing a comprehensive list of considerations would not be practical, and the discussion items listed below are not intended to supersede any regulations particular to specific situations or the environment in which a firm may operate. Firms should consult a qualified certified public accountant or a consultant with performance reporting and tax expertise in situations where the regulations require additional analysis or interpretation.

Interest and dividend income must be included in a portfolio's market value in the same manner for both before-tax and after-tax performance reporting. The amount of income and realized gains or losses should be determined based on the tax rules applicable to the client. One exception is that the AIMR-PPS standards recommend that dividend income be recorded on the ex-dividend date, which would generally be required for tax purposes. (Note: The AIMR-PPS standards state for periods beginning 1 January 2005, Accrual accounting must be used for dividends as of the ex-dividend date).

Interest income must be accounted for on an Accrual basis and should take into consideration adjustments to cost basis through Amortization and accretion. The cost basis of fixed income securities purchased at a price other than par value should be adjusted for Amortization and accretion as required by the applicable tax code when calculating after-tax returns.

Amortization of premiums on taxable bonds is elective. (Code Sec. 171) If elected, Amortization should be calculated using the yield-to maturity method for bonds issued after 27 September 1985. For tax-exempt bonds, Amortization of premiums is required. Usually, no deduction is allowed for tax purposes, but the tax basis of the bonds is still reduced. Special rules apply to debt securities that are callable or convertible. The effect of Amortization is a decrease in the security's tax basis with a corresponding increase in unrealized appreciation or a decrease to unrealized depreciation and a reduction to current income.

The rules relating to accretion of discounts are segregated between original issue discount ("OID") and market discount. OID is the excess of the stated redemption price at maturity over its issue price. The amount of OID recognized and the required methodology for accretion are determined based on the type of security and the date of issuance. In general, many securities will fall under the following requirements:

- Tax-exempt securities issued subsequent to 27 September 1985 use the yield to maturity method when calculating OID accretion.
- Taxable securities issued after 1 July 1982 accrete OID using the constant interest method.
- Special rules apply to non-government short-term obligations.

A debt instrument with a fixed maturity of greater than one year at the time of issuance and purchased in the secondary market after 30 April 1993, at less than par could include market discount. The amount of market discount is determined after taking into consideration any OID at the time of acquisition. Additional considerations are required for taxable securities issued on or prior to 30 April 1993. An investor can elect to accrete market discount using a ratable or constant interest method (Code Sec. 1276(b) (1), (2)). Market discount may be accreted currently or deferred until the disposition of the related security. If the election is made to defer accretion of market discount, the impact is a recharacterization of capital gain to ordinary income upon disposition. No adjustment is made if the security is sold at a loss. Current accretion of OID and market discount will result in higher interest income with a corresponding increase to the cost basis of the security.

OID and market discount are considered to be zero, and therefore would not require accretion, if such amounts were deemed to be de minimus. A de minimus discount is defined as an amount less than one quarter of one percent of the stated redemption price at maturity, multiplied by the number of complete years to maturity. Special rules apply to certain securities that are subject to accelerated principal collection (i.e. REMICs and CMOs). The de minimus rule is not applicable to OID for tax-exempt securities.

The tax implications of interest income earned from ("tax-exempt") municipal securities and U.S. government obligations must be taken into consideration when computing after-tax returns. In general, interest income from direct obligations of the U.S. Government is not subject to state income tax. In most instances, interest income from non-AMT "tax-exempt" municipal securities is tax-free at the federal level as well as in the issuing state but subject to applicable income tax in all other states. In some circumstances, interest income on "tax-exempt" municipal bonds classified as alternative minimum tax (AMT) bonds may be subject to state and federal income taxes. However, capital gains on both "tax-exempt" municipal bonds and U.S. Government obligations are subject to federal taxes as well as applicable state income taxes, regardless of the state of issuance.

There are several classifications of special situation securities, such as "taxable" municipal bonds, "triple tax-free" bonds issued by some agencies, protectorates, or other instrumentalities of the U.S. Government. Investors should consult qualified tax counsel for additional guidance if there is any uncertainty regarding the tax status of these securities.

The Dividend-Received Deduction may impact dividend income earned from domestic corporations. Since dividends have already been taxed at least once (as income to the issuing corporation), a C corporation may deduct 70% of the dividends received or Accrued from domestic corporations. (Code Sec. 243(a)(1)) The deduction is 80% for dividends received or Accrued from a 20% (or more) owned corporation. (Code Sec. 243(c)(2)) Finally, members of an affiliated group (as specially defined) that file separate returns may deduct 100% of the dividends received from other group members if certain requirements are met. (Code Sec. 243(a)(3), (b))

Dividends from registered investment companies ("RICs") — mutual fund dividends — are eligible for the dividends-received deduction but only to the extent of the amounts the RIC received from domestic corporations that it would have been allowed to treat as dividends in computing its own dividends-received deduction if it had been a regular corporation.

4-3

(Code Sec. 243(d)(2), Code Sec. 854(b)(4)) Dividends from otherwise qualifying stock, which has been held for less than 45 days, may not be eligible for the deduction.

Dividends received on certain public utility preferred stock are eligible for the dividends-received deduction, but the deduction is reduced if the utility was entitled to a dividends-paid deduction on those dividends. (Code Sec. 244(a))

Investment management firms should have the option to include the effect of foreign tax credits, as they can have a material effect on the calculation of after-tax returns. In the return calculation, the dividend should be reduced by the applicable tax rate and then increased by the amount of the tax credit.

Security dispositions will generally result in realized gains and losses that are taxed at differing rates depending on the amount of time such security was owned. Currently, holding periods of more than one year are considered long-term while those of one-year or less are considered short-term. (Code Sec. 1222(1), (2), (3), (4)) Holding periods are determined based on the trade date of investment transactions. They are computed in terms of calendar months, not days, and begin on the day after the acquisition and ends on the day of disposition. Various tax rules can impact the timing of when a gain or loss is recognized and the characterization of the gain or loss as long or short term.

Special rules apply to gains and losses incurred from certain transactions that involve a foreign currency. "Section 988" transactions require analysis of the gain or loss that is related to a fluctuation in exchange rates. Foreign currency gains and losses attributable to section 988 transactions are treated as ordinary income for tax purposes. Realized gains and losses from the sale of equity securities are not subject to the rules, however, complex rules are applicable when determining the nature of gains and losses associated with the sale of any debt security denominated in a foreign currency.

A short sale occurs when an investor borrows a stock (or other property) from a lender and simultaneously sells the security to a third party. At a later date, the investor provides a similar security necessary to "cover" the original transaction and closes the short position. A short sale results in a capital gain or loss only if the property used to close the sale is a capital asset, i.e. a hedging transaction results in ordinary income or loss.

4-3

Provisions enacted by the Taxpayer Relief Act of 1997 around "constructive sales", have, for the most part eliminated the tax deferral benefits of short sales. Prior to the Act, certain hedging strategies such as short sales against the box, forward contracts, and notional principal contracts could be used to lock in gains on appreciated financial positions without immediate recognition of income. Subject to certain exceptions, a constructive sale of an appreciated financial position will require the taxpayer to recognize a gain as if the position were sold at its fair market value as of the date of the constructive sale and immediately repurchased.

Certain financial instruments which are traded and priced daily, e.g. regulated futures contracts (RFC's), certain foreign currency contracts, non-equity options and dealer equity options, are referred to as section 1256 contracts and are subject to two specific rules:

- The mark-to-market rule which treats that instrument as sold on the last day of a taxpayer's taxable year, and
- The 60-40 rule treats 60 percent of any capital gain or loss from such deemed sale or an actual sale as long term and 40 percent as short-term, regardless of how long the instrument has been held.

Then, when the section 1256 contract is actually terminated, it will also result in a taxable gain or loss. However, if delivery of the underlying property is taken, the tax basis of the property received is decreased or increased by the gains or losses already recognized. These instruments may also be subject to the straddle rules outlined in section 1256.

The tax treatment of nonlisted (primarily equity) purchased options, e.g. puts and calls, depends largely upon the holding period:

- If a put or call is sold or lapses, any gain or loss is long-term or short-term depending on the holding period of the option.
- If a call option is exercised, its cost is added to the taxpayer's basis of the securities purchased.
- If a put option is exercised, its cost reduces the amount of the proceeds received upon sale of the underlying securities.
- If, however, the put is acquired at a time when the underlying stock has been held for one year or less, then any gain upon termination of the put is short-term, and the holding period of the underlying stock may be forfeited through the date of termination of the put.
- Purchased options may be subject to the straddle rules.

The tax treatment of nonlisted (primarily equity) written options, e.g. puts and calls, is parallel to purchased options and depends largely upon the holding period:

- If a put or call is closed out or lapses, any gain or loss is short-term.
- If a call is exercised, the premium received is added to the sale proceeds and capital gain or loss is calculated based on the holding period of the stock.
- If a put is exercised, the premium received decreases the basis in the stock acquired. The holding period of the stock begins on the date of its purchase, not the date the put was written.
- Written options may be subject to the straddle rules.

Tax straddles are defined as offsetting positions for which the fair values are expected to fluctuate inversely to each other. An offsetting position results whenever holding one or more other positions has substantially diminished the risk of loss attributable to holding another position. Complex tax rules (Code Sec. 1092) must be considered when determining if any realized losses should be deferred and the resultant characterization of realized gains and losses between short and long term.

A wash sale loss is any loss sustained upon a sale (or other disposition) of stock or securities where within a period beginning 30 days before the date of the disposition and ending 30 days after that date (a total of 61 days), the taxpayer has acquired (or has entered into a contract or option to acquire) substantially identical stock or securities (Code Sec. 1091). Such losses are deferred for tax purposes and increase the cost basis of the security that was purchased. Similarly, losses recognized from short sales are not allowed if identical securities are sold within the 61-day period referred to previously. Wash sales apply to all classes of taxpayers (individuals, corporations, etc.) except securities dealers where losses may be regularly sustained in the normal course of business. Finally, an acquisition by gift, bequest, inheritance, or tax-free exchange that is made within the 61-day period does not bring the wash sale rule into play.

The calculation of before-tax and after-tax performance depends largely on the tax treatment of income and gains or losses, as well as complex rules around Amortization and accretion requirements. As previously noted, the definitions and regulations associated with the items discussed above include general summaries of complex tax regulations. Qualified tax counsel should always be consulted regarding the treatment of specific transactions as they relate to the calculation of after-tax performance.

N. Glossary of Terms

Amortization/Accrual Basis — the recognition of transactions ratably over the period to which they apply, without regard to the receipt or payment of related cash. For example, Amortization is applicable to the premium paid versus par on the purchase of a bond and accrual is applicable to the discount versus par on the purchase of a bond and also to the interest payments received on a bond.

Anticipated Tax Rates — the tax rates that an investment manager expects a taxable client to incur on returns generated during the prospective reporting period for each applicable asset class. These tax rates should include the impact of applicable state and local income taxes and should be determined at the beginning of the reporting period.

Dollar-Weighted Anticipated Tax Rate — the money-weighted average of the monthly composite Anticipated Tax Rates for a given period.

Maximum Federal Tax Rate — the highest income tax rate in effect for the applicable client according to the Federal tax code for a given measurement period.

Net Realized Gains — the net amount of realized gains and realized losses. References to net realized gains should be interpreted to mean the net amount of realized capital gains/losses.

Non-Discretionary Capital Gains — those realized capital gains/losses incurred as a result of a client-directed transaction.

Realized Basis Pre-Liquidation Return — the after-tax return that reflects the net Tax Liability or Benefit associated with the accrued taxable income and net realized gains that occurred during the measurement period (without considering the tax implications of unrealized gains).

Shadow Portfolio — a portfolio that replicates the cash flows and structure (e.g., cost basis, and tax rate(s)) of the respective index being used as a benchmark.

Tax Liability or Benefit — those taxes or benefits incurred in a given period resulting from the recognition of income and realized capital gains/losses, without regard to when (or if) the taxes will be paid. Also referred to as the tax burden or realized taxes.

Tax-Loss Harvesting — the process of intentionally realizing capital losses in order to offset realized capital gains in the portfolio in which the transaction took place or in another client portfolio.

Unrealized Capital Gains — the difference between market value and cost of securities owned, at a given point in time. If market value exceeds cost, the net amount will be positive (unrealized gains). If cost exceeds market value, the net amount will be negative (unrealized losses). References to unrealized capital gains should be interpreted to mean the net amount of unrealized capital gains/losses.

APPENDIX B. ASSOGESTIONI FORMULA FOR CALCULATING THE GROSS-OF-TAX VALUE OF THE SHARES OF AN ITALIAN OPEN-END FUND

This appendix contains a description of the Assogestioni formula for calculating the gross value of the shares of an Italian open-end fund, which makes it possible to gross up the net value of shares in order to eliminate the effects of Italian taxation.

1. Introduction

As regards the method of taxing open-end funds, it is worth noting that, apart from Italy, most countries do not tax the operating results of open-end funds directly but require the related income to be included in individual taxpayers' income tax returns. Other things being equal, this difference in the tax treatment of fund revenues influences the mechanisms for determining the net value of shares and hence the measures of performance based on that value. For this reason it is desirable to establish a method for grossing up the net values of the shares of Italian funds, so as to eliminate the effects of taxation on the performance of Italian open-end funds. Funds set up under Italian law are subject to a withholding tax of 12.5% on the difference between the initial and final values of the investments made during the year.[2] Each funds tax liability is calculated daily and an equivalent amount set aside in a tax provision until payment is made the following year. Fund shares are consequently quoted net of taxation.

The gross share price of an Italian open-end fund is defined as the price at which the shares would be quoted if all the effects of the taxation of the income the fund receives gross were eliminated.[3] This appendix contains a description of the formula used to obtain the gross share price and a series of notes on when and how it can be applied.

2. Option 1 - The Assogestioni formula

Consider the case of a generic Italian open-end fund that calculates its share value every day. Let N_i be the net share price and χ_i the number of shares outstanding on day *i*. In addition, let T_i be the tax liability accrued. It should be noted that T_i is the amount that is set aside for tax purposes but which is still part of the fund's assets and therefore still available to the manager until the day set for settlement. The variable ST_i is defined as the sum of the tax liabilities accrued but not yet settled at the end of day i.[4] Let P_i be the amount per share of any income distributed on day *i*. Lastly, let L_i be the gross share price of the fund at time *i*.

It can be shown that:

$$L_i = L_{i-1} \frac{x_i \left(N_i + P_i\right) + ST_{i-1} + T_i}{x_i N_{i-1} + ST_{i-1}} \qquad (1)$$

2.1 The tax lever effect

If the fund receives only income subject to full-settlement withholding tax $\tau = 12.5\%$, it can be shown that:

$$T_i = \frac{\tau}{1-\tau} x_i \left(N_i - N_{i-1}\right). \qquad (2)$$

Putting $g_i = \frac{L_i}{L_{i-1}} - 1$ gives:

$$N_i = \underbrace{N_{i-1}\left(1+g_i\right)}_{\text{management eff.}} - \underbrace{N_{i-1} g_i \tau}_{\text{direct tax eff.}} + \underbrace{\frac{g_i ST_{i-1}\left(1-\tau\right)}{x_i}}_{\text{indirect tax eff.}} \qquad (3)$$

which expressed in terms of the rate of change, $\frac{N_i}{N_{i-1}} = 1 + \pi_i$, becomes:

$$\pi_i = g_i - g_i \tau + g_i \frac{ST_{i-1}\left(l-\tau\right)}{N_{i-1} x_i} \qquad (4)$$

Equation (3) shows that the net share price on day *i* is the previous day's net share price revalued at the gross rate of growth N_{i-1} $(1 + g_i)$ minus the direct effect of taxation on the operating result,

$N_{i-1} g_i \tau$, plus $\frac{g_i ST_{i-1}(1-\tau)}{x_i}$, which can be interpreted as the indirect effect of taxation produced by the tax liability accrued but still to be settled on day $i-1$. The indirect tax

[2]The tax base is the increase in a fund's net assets, i.e. the sum of all the positive and negative changes that occur during the year (taxation of the net operating result). If the operating result is negative, the loss can be carried forward as a tax loss for four years.

[3]Italian funds receive certain categories of income net of full-settlement tax. The grossing-up of such tax is forbidden by Recommendation 2.B.1.

[4]$ST_{i+1} = ST_i + T_{i+1} - TL_{i+1}$ where TL_{i+1} denotes the tax liability settled at the end of day $i + 1$.

4-3

effect is the result of the management of the tax liability/claim in the period preceding its settlement. The term ST_{i-1} in equation (1) corrects the indirect tax effects on the basis of the assumption that the manager manages a quantity of available assets given by the sum of the fund's net assets and the tax liability accrued but not yet settled.[5]

3. Option 2 - Modified Assogestioni formula

However, the Assogestioni formula can be modified and applied where the manager manages only the fund's net assets and invests the additional resources consisting of any outstanding tax liability in a liquidity account.[6] In this case in fact it is sufficient to put ST_{i-1} = 0 in (1), giving, if $P_i = 0$:

$$\frac{L'_i}{L'_{i-1}} = \frac{N_i}{N_{i-1}}\left(1+\frac{T_i}{x_i N_i}\right), \qquad (5)$$

in other words, on the assumption that the manager manages only the fund's net assets (whether these are larger or smaller than the assets effectively available), the gross performance is equal to the net performance corrected for a tax factor equal to the direct effect of the full-settlement tax on the fund's net assets. If the fund receives only income subject to the full-settlement tax τ, it can be shown that:

$$g'_i = \frac{L'_i}{L'_{i-1}} - 1 = \frac{1}{1-\tau}\left(\frac{N_i}{N_{i-1}} - 1\right) = \frac{1}{1-\tau}\pi_i \cong 1.143\pi_i \qquad (6)$$

Since the Assogestioni formula gives a gross share price that depends on the assumptions made regarding the way in which the funds concerned invest their tax liability/claim, **the manager defines its composites on the basis of a criterion of homogeneousness in this respect and calculates the gross share prices using the appropriate formula (with or without the *ST* term). Full information must be provided on this process.**

4. Examples

4-3

Some examples are given below of the application of the Assogestioni formula to a real fund, with a comparison of the results obtained with the various admissible assumptions (with or without the *ST* term) and a summary of the effects on the gross share prices.

i	N_i	χ_i	ST_i	T_i	$\frac{ST_{i-1}}{N_{i-1}\chi_i}$	L_i	L'_i	π_i	g_i	g'_i
0	15.354	107,238,499	104,910,713			15.354	15.354			
1	14.638	107,520,608	93,910,207	–11,000,506	0.064	14.585	14.536	–4.66%	-5.01%	-5.33%
2	13.981	108,167,138	83,766,409	–10,143,798	0.059	13.878	13.790	–4.49%	–4.84%	-5.13%
3	13.434	108,762,321	75,259,129	–8,507,280	0.055	13.290	13.173	-3.91%	–4.24%	–4.47%
4	13.697	108,593,174	79,336,650	4,077,522	0.052	13.573	13.468	1.96%	2.13%	2.24%
5	14.137	106,372,795	86,031,584	6,694,934	0.054	14.046	13.963	3.21%	3.48%	3.67%
6	14.190	706,689,691	86,837,669	806,086	0.057	14.103	14.023	0.37%	0.41%	0.43%
7	14.128	106,408,433	85,899,764	–937,906	0.058	14.036	13.953	–0.44%	–0.47%	–0.50%
8	14.440	107,151,308	90,671,107	4,771,344	0.057	14.371	14.305	2.21%	2.39%	2.52%
9	14.848	107,840,436	96,955,615	6,284,508	0.058	14.810	14.767	2.83%	3.05%	3.23%
10	15.198	108,345,644	102,370,059	5,414,444	0.060	15.186	15.164	2.36%	2.54%	2.69%

[5]If the fund is in credit, the available assets are equal to the difference between the net assets and the tax claim accrued.
[6]If the fund has a tax credit, the manager borrows a corresponding amount.

More generally, it can be shown that the following inequalities hold:

	$\frac{ST_{i-1}}{N_{i-1}x_i} \in (-1,0)$	$\frac{ST_{i-1}}{N_{i-1}x_i} \in \left(0, \frac{\tau}{(1-\tau)}\right)$	$\frac{ST_{i-1}}{N_{i-1}x_i} > \frac{\tau}{(1-\tau)}$
$\pi > 0$	$0 < \pi < g' < g$	$0 < \pi < g < g'$	$0 < g < \pi < g'$
$\pi < 0$	$g < g' < \pi < 0$	$g' < g < \pi < 0$	$g' < \pi < g < 0$

Where the net performance of the fund is positive and there is an unsettled tax liability and the manager is assumed to invest these resources in the same way as the fund's net assets, the performance of the gross share price g is better or worse than that of the net share price π depending on the relative size of the direct tax effect (measured by the relationship $\frac{\tau}{(1-\tau)} \cong 0.143$) with respect to the size of the indirect tax effect (measured by the relationship $\frac{ST_{i-1}}{N_{i-1}x_i}$).

If the direct effect prevails over the indirect effect (the first two columns), the performance of the gross share price g is better than that of the net share price π.[7] Conversely, if as a result of large redemptions,[8] the indirect effect prevails over the direct effect (the last column on the right), the performance of the net share price is better than that of the gross share price owing to the preponderance of the tax lever effect. The other cells of the table complete the various possible combinations of net performance, tax position (debit or credit), and ways of managing the tax component (g and g') and provide an overall picture of the relationships between the different quantities.

The example that follows presents the case of the fund referred to above that acquires a tax credit

($ST < 0$) following a period in which the overall performance was negative:

i	N_i	χ_i	ST_i	T_i	$\frac{ST_{i-1}}{N_{i-1}\chi_i}$	L_i	L'_i	π_i	g_i	g'_i
202	12.249	83,928,658	-47,252,978	–1,686,879	–0.044	11.720	11.808	–1.13	-1.35%	-1.29%
203	12.096	83,618,163	–49,079,242	–1,826,265	–0.046	11.544	11.639	–1.25	-1.50%	-1.43%
204	12.484	83,454,179	–44,452,499	4,626,743	–0.049	11.989	12.066	3.21	3.85%	3.67%
205	12.582	82,936,752	–43,287,143	1,165,356	–0.043	12.102	12.174	0.79	0.94%	0.90%
206	12.736	82,813,152	–41,466,486	1,820,658	–0.042	12.278	12.345	1.22	1.46%	1.40%
207	12.952	82,657,123	–38,914,844	2,551,642	–0.039	12.526	12.584	1.70	2.02%	1.94%
208	12.772	82,679,756	–41,045,077	–2,130,233	–0.036	12.319	12.384	–1.39	-1.65%	-1.59%
209	12.700	82,742,838	–41,898,670	–853,593	–0.039	12.237	12.304	–0.56	-0.67%	-0.64%
210	12.950	82,735,638	–38,936,391	2,962,279	–0.040	12.524	12.581	1.97	2.34%	2.25%
211	12.888	82,719,496	–39,670,805	–734,414	–0.036	12.452	12.512	–0.48	-0.57%	-0.55%
212	12.958	82,698,102	–38,848,916	821,889	–0.037	12.533	12.590	0.54	0.64%	0.62%

[7]In this case the net share price "suffers" from the tax levied more than it benefits from the effects of the investment of the unsettled tax liability.

[8]A sudden reduction in the number of shares χ_i may push the ratio $\frac{\tau}{(1-\tau)}$ above the level given by $\frac{ST_{i-1}}{N_{i-1}x_i}$.

The last example shows the results of a simulation of the effects of a sudden withdrawal of resources on the net and gross measures of performance. The simulation was carried out keeping the data on gross share prices shown in the previous tables unchanged and imposing a rapid fall in the number of shares. From day 210 the ratio $\frac{ST_{i-1}}{N_{i-1}x_i}$ is equal to more than 1, so that the indirect tax effect prevails over the direct tax effect and the movements in the net share price are approximately twice as large as those in the gross share price.

i	N_i	χ_i	ST_i	T_i	$\frac{ST_{i-1}}{N_{i-1}\chi_i}$	L_i	L'_i	π_i	g_i	g'_i
202	99.058	127,788,962	-11,414,402	-20,696,753	0.001	98.922	98.909	-1.13%	-1.29%	-1.29%
203	97.822	131,465,585	-34,629,595	-23,215,193	-0.001	97.510	97.499	-1.25%	-1.43%	-1.43%
204	100.951	131,694,530	24,246,418	58,876,013	-0.003	101.085	101.063	3.2%	3.67%	3.66%
205	101.746	132,274,844	39,255,347	15,008,930	0.002	101.992	101.972	0.79%	0.90%	0.90%
206	102.994	133,652,299	63,099,414	23,844,067	0.003	103.419	103.403	1.23%	1.40%	1.40%
207	104.749	133,757,018	96,631,506	33,532,092	0.005	105.423	105.416	1.70%	1.94%	1.95%
208	103.283	134,313,433	68,500,346	-28,131,160	0.007	103.749	103.730	-1.40%	-1.59%	-1.60%
209	102.698	140,972,585	56,715,084	-11,785,262	0.005	103.080	103.058	-0.57%	-0.64%	-0.65%
210	106.921	507,455	57,021,225	306,141	1.088	105.400	107.901	4.11%	2.25%	4.70%
211	105.868	504,734	56,945,292	-78,933	1.057	104.823	106.687	-0.98%	-0.55%	-1.13%
212	107.049	509,382	57,031,254	85,962	1.056	105.473	108.047	1.12%	0.62%	1.28%

4-3

Revised Effective Date: 1 January 2006
Adoption Date: 13 March 2002
Effective Date: 1 April 2002
Retroactive Application: see "Effective Date" section
Public Comment Period: Sep – Dec 2001

GUIDANCE STATEMENT ON DEFINITION OF THE FIRM (REVISED)

Introduction

Three of the most fundamental issues that a firm must consider when becoming compliant with the GIPS® standards are the definition of the firm, the firm's definition of discretion, and the firm's composite definition principles and guidelines. The definition of the firm is the foundation for firm-wide compliance and creates defined boundaries whereby total firm assets can be determined. The firm's definition of discretion establishes criteria to judge which portfolios should be in a composite to accurately reflect the application of the firm's investment strategy. Once the firm and discretion have been defined, composites can be constructed based on the strategies implemented by the firm.

The GIPS standards must be applied on a firm-wide basis. As the first step in complying with the Standards, the firm must be defined fairly and appropriately. Compliance with the GIPS standards relies on a clear and consistent definition of the firm. The Standards require that the definition of the firm be disclosed on the composite presentations, and the verification principles require that verifiers determine if the firm is, and has been, appropriately defined.

In addition, the definition of the firm delineates the universe of "all" portfolios that must be included in total firm assets under management. Fundamental to the Standards is the premise that all actual, fee-paying discretionary portfolios must be included in at least one composite.

As merger and acquisition activity can affect the definition of the firm, the Guidance Statement on Performance Record Portability should also be considered.

Guiding Principles

When defining the firm, it is important to consider the following:

- How the firm holds itself out to the public.
- The firm definition must be appropriate, rational and fair.
- Firms are encouraged to adopt the broadest, most meaningful definition of the firm.
- Firms must not use the definition of the firm as a substitute for defining composites (e.g., defining the firm too narrowly, as to only encompass one product).

Defining the Firm

The Standards require that firms must be defined as an investment firm, subsidiary, or division held out to clients or potential clients as a distinct business entity.

A distinct business entity is a unit, division, department, or office that is organizationally and functionally segregated from other units, divisions, departments, or offices and retains discretion over the assets it manages and should have autonomy over the investment decision-making process.

Possible criteria that can be used to determine this include:

- being a legal entity,
- having a distinct market or client type (e.g., institutional, retail, private client, etc.), or
- using a separate and distinct investment process.

As previously stated, firms are encouraged to adopt the broadest, most meaningful definition of the firm and consider how it is held out to the public. The scope of this definition should include all geographic (country, regional, etc.) offices operating under the same brand name regardless of the actual name of the individual investment management company. These include, but are not limited to:

- All offices operating under the same brand name (e.g., XYZ Asset Management),
- Other names resulting from mergers, acquisitions, etc., trading under a different name for branding purposes,
- Financial service holding companies defined as one global firm with multiple brands, several legal entities, multiple offices, investment teams, and investment strategies,
- An investment management firm with one brand, but multiple strategies and investment teams,
- All offices trading under a globally recognizable trading name with regional/country specific additions (e.g., XYZ Asset Management Asia),
- Investment management firms in most countries must register with one or more governmental agencies or regulators. The GIPS standards recognize a regulatory registration as a possible definition of a firm for purposes of compliance, but also require firms consider the manner in which they are holding themselves out to the public when determining the firm definition.

Additional Considerations

In addition to the Guiding Principles listed above, firms should consider the following when defining the firm:

- The Standards require that when the firm jointly markets with other firms, the firm claiming compliance with the GIPS standards must be sure that it is clearly defined and separate relative to any other firms being marketed and that it is clear which firm is claiming compliance.
- The Standards recommend that if a parent company contains multiple defined firms, each firm within the parent company is encouraged to disclose a list of the other firms contained within the parent company.
- The use of a third party (e.g., custodian, broker/dealer, etc.) to perform record keeping or performance measurement is not a valid reason for excluding assets from the definition of the firm.
- Systems incompatibilities cannot be used as a reason for excluding assets from the definition of the firm (i.e., a firm cannot make the claim of compliance for only those assets that are measured and monitored on compatible systems).

Inception of the Firm/Redefinition of the Firm

In some cases, due to corporate restructuring and merger and acquisition activities, the changes within the firm may be so significant that it is held out to the public as a new firm. The new firm must determine if there is a continuation from the prior firm or if the restructuring is so substantial that it is essentially a new firm.

Changes in investment style or personnel are not valid reasons for redefining the firm, unless the changes are such that the firm is held out to the public in a significantly different way. A simple name change is not sufficient reason to redefine the firm and restart the performance record. In some cases, a firm definition may change without the firm losing its performance history. Please refer to the Guidance Statement on Performance Record Portability for related guidance. In all cases, the underlying principles of the Standards must be considered: fair representation and full disclosure. If a firm is redefined, Provision 4.A.21 requires that the firm disclose the date and reason for the redefinition. The Standards require that changes in a firm's organization are not permitted to lead to alteration of historical composite results.

Total Firm Assets

The definition of the firm also determines the boundaries for determining total firm assets. This includes all assets for which a firm has investment management responsibility and includes assets managed outside the firm (e.g., by subadvisors) for which the firm has discretionary authority. The Standards state that total firm assets must be the aggregate of the market value of all discretionary and non-discretionary assets under management within the defined firm. This includes both fee-paying and non-fee-paying assets.

Assets to which the Standards cannot be applied are not to be considered by firms when claiming compliance and are not to be included in total firm assets. Such assets include investment vehicles that are based on cost or book values rather than market values.

Subadvisors

Some firms utilize a subadvisor to manage part or all of a particular strategy. For example, if a firm specializes in managing equities, it might hire a subadvisor to manage the fixed income portion of its balanced portfolios. The Standards require that firms must include the performance of assets assigned to a subadvisor in a composite provided the firm has the authority to allocate the assets to a subadvisor.

If a firm has discretion over the selection of the subadvisor (i.e., can hire and/or fire), the firm must claim the subadvisor's performance as part of its performance history and include the assets in the firm's total assets. Because the subadvisor has discretion over the actual investment of the assets and the firm has discretion over the selection of the subadvisor, both the firm and the subadvisor are able to claim the performance of the assets as their own. The firm is able to claim this performance because the sub-advised portion of the portfolio is essentially viewed as an asset (similar to purchasing a mutual fund within the portfolio) and the firm must be held responsible for its decision to utilize a subadvisor. The firm can only include the subadvisor's performance record relevant to those assets assigned by the firm. If a firm does not have discretion over subadvisor selection, it must not include the subadvisor's performance in its performance history.

The Standards require that beginning 1 January 2006, firms must disclose the use of a subadvisor(s) and the periods a subadvisor(s) was used.

Effective Date

This Guidance Statement was originally effective 1 April 2002 and was revised to reflect the changes to the GIPS standards effective as of 1 January 2006.

Firms claiming compliance prior to 1 January 2006 were required to retroactively apply the original guidance for all periods prior to 31 December 2005; however, the revisions to this guidance (effective 1 January 2006) are not required to be retroactively applied. Firms have until 1 January 2006 to redefine themselves as necessary to comply with this Guidance Statement.

All firms coming into compliance on or after 1 January 2006 must apply this revised guidance to all periods.

Key GIPS Provisions Specifically Applicable to Definition of the Firm:

0.A Definition of the Firm — Requirements

0.A.1 The GIPS standards must be applied on a firm-wide basis.

0.A.2 Firms must be defined as an investment firm, subsidiary, or division held out to clients or potential clients as a distinct business entity.

0.A.3 Total firm assets must be the aggregate of the market value of all discretionary and nondiscretionary assets under management within the defined firm. This includes both fee-paying and non-fee-paying assets.

0.A.4 Firms must include the performance of assets assigned to a subadvisor in a composite provided the firm has discretion over the selection of the subadvisor.

0.A.5 Changes in a firm's organization are not permitted to lead to alteration of historical composite results.

0.B Definition of the Firm — Recommendations

0.B.1 Firms are encouraged to adopt the broadest, most meaningful definition of the firm. The scope of this definition should include all geographical (country, regional, etc.) offices operating under the same brand name regardless of the actual name of the individual investment management company.

0.A Document Policies and Procedures — Requirements

0.A.6 Firms must document, in writing, their policies and procedures used in establishing and maintaining compliance with all the applicable requirements of the GIPS standards.

Applications:

1. *An investment management firm uses a subadvisor to manage a portion of the assets for a strategy that the firm manages. Should the assets managed by the subadvisor be excluded from the composite performance?*

If the firm has discretion over the selection of the subadvisor, then the assets managed by a subadvisor on behalf of the firm must be included in the firm's composite performance and total firm assets. Once the assets are given to a subadvisor to manage, the firm will not have control over exactly how those assets are invested by the subadvisor. Nevertheless, the firm chose to invest the assets by placing them with a subadvisor and has the discretion to hire or fire the subadvisor.

The firm can only include the subadvisor's performance record relevant to those assets assigned by the firm.

2. *According to this Guidance Statement, "Assets to which the Standards cannot be applied are not to be considered by firms when claiming compliance and are not to be included in total firm assets. Such assets include investment vehicles that are based on cost or book values rather than market values." Does this mean that cash substitutes, such as CDs and money market funds held in portfolios, are not to be considered by firms when claiming compliance and are not to be included in total firm assets?*

Money market funds, CDs and other cash substitutes ARE to be considered by firms when claiming compliance and are to be included in total firm assets. A market value for these assets can be determined.

3. *Previously, our firm was a department within a larger organization. Recently, the department was able to complete a buy-out, and we are now an independent investment advisor. What must the firm do in order to continue the claim of compliance?*

A firm's definition reflects how it holds itself out to the public. As the department was previously within the larger organization, if the department claimed compliance as a separate firm without the parent organization being included in that firm definition, there may not need to be any changes. The department may have been and may continue to be a distinct business entity held out to the public as such. It may be necessary for the department to disclose any significant events that would help prospective clients interpret the performance record.

However, if the department and parent organization were historically combined in the same firm definition for purposes of claiming compliance, the definition of the firm has changed with the buy-out and the claim of compliance with the Standards must be reevaluated.

4. An investment management firm has a Euro-zone fixed income composite that contains the following three portfolios:

a. a fund that is invested in European bonds with net assets of 20,

b. a fund that is invested in bonds of one country of the Euro-zone with net assets of 30, and

c. a private portfolio invested entirety in the 2 above mentioned funds. Net assets of this portfolio are 10.

How should GIPS 5.A.1.c be interpreted?

- *Is it correct to say that the number of portfolios of the composite described above is 3?*
- *Is it correct to say that the amount of assets in the composite is 20+30+10=60?*
- *Is it correct to say that the total firm's assets is 50 or that the total firm's assets is 60 (in the case this firm only owns that one composite)?*

The question is that of eliminating double counting assets. Is it correct to say that showing the above composite's asset level of 60 is not misleading to the reader? (The firm will also disclose what % the composite represents of the firm's assets, therefore showing 110% of firm's assets means that some assets are counted more than once. For example, because the management of the private portfolio above is not geared towards choosing the securities in the portfolio, but rather geared towards realizing the proper asset allocation between both funds.)

The GIPS standards are based on the principles of fair representation and full disclosure. Double counting assets would not fairly represent the firm's assets. The composite would have 3 portfolios and have net assets of 50. If there are no other assets within the firm, then total firm assets would be 50.

Adoption Date: 5 Dec 2001

GUIDELINES IN RESPECT OF THE IMPACT OF EURO CONVERSION

Preamble

The guidelines below refer only to the "in" currencies and will in due course extend to other currencies, if/when they convert to Euro.

These guidelines should be observed by all persons responsible for managing investment funds, whether segregated client funds or mutual funds (e.g., UCITS, SICAVs, unit trusts, OEICs and similar pooled investment or savings products) or providers of performance measurement services or indices.

Continuity of investment performance can be achieved for clients and funds within any domestic markets, but it is more difficult to prepare acceptable historical data for cross-border marketing. Two worked examples are attached in appendix, which should help to clarify the issues.

The Euro exists as an actual currency since 1 January 1999. At that time, eleven currencies and the ECU converted to the Euro (see worked example A). Other currencies are expected to convert to the Euro in the future (see worked examples A and B). For each currency, ECD (Euro Conversion Date) will designate the date of the conversion to the Euro, which may be 1 January 1999 or later.

Overriding Principles

1. For an individual client, the conversion to Euro should not have any effect on historical performance data or accounting information. The historical facts for that client have not changed.
2. The Euro does not exist as an actual currency until 1 January 1999. Therefore it is impossible to create any valid historical information in Euro, whether of funds, individual securities, indices or exchange rates.
3. Historical performances which were validly comparable before ECD should remain comparable afterwards. Such comparisons should preserve rank ordering among fund returns.
4. Fund performances which were not validly comparable before ECD cannot become retrospectively comparable by virtue of the creation of / conversion to the Euro.

Presentation of Historical Data

5. For a number of purposes (not restricted to performance measurement) it will be desirable to present time series which cover periods before and after ECD. The data after ECD may be presented in Euro but a major issue is how to present the data prior to ECD. In all cases, the presentations must show the original currency of the historical data.
6. Total return data for periods prior to ECD can be geometrically linked with post-ECD returns, but the original currency of the historical data must be disclosed. Although time series of total returns in different member currencies may converge prior to ECD, the individual histories must be kept separate, in accordance with overriding principle number 4.

7. Nominal amounts such as price, value, net asset value, dividends or earnings pose a particular difficulty. For convenience, it is likely that an individual client will wish to see historical values converted to Euro at the fixed conversion rate for his individual local currency. Otherwise any time series would have a discontinuity at ECD. However, due to overriding principle number 2, the history so converted must not be described as being in Euro. The correct form of words would be:

"French Francs (or Greek Drachma) converted to Euro at the fixed conversion rate"

or use the International Organisation for Standardisation (ISO) endorsed currency abbreviations, eg:

<<FRF(EUR)>>, or <<GRD(EUR)>>

8. Computer systems used for investment accounting and/or performance measurement may store the historical data in whichever way is practical for the particular application. However, it will always be necessary to keep track of the original currency of any data, even if it is converted at the ECD Euro conversion rate to make subsequent analysis easier. Otherwise it will be too easy to breach overriding principle number 4.

9. Many index providers and quantitative analysts are already calculating and presenting data in "synthetic Euro" terms, covering periods before 1 January 1999. It is extremely important that such data is referred to as being in "synthetic Euro," as there is otherwise a risk of breaching principle number 2.

Composites and Peer Groups or Mutual Fund Categories

10. Comparing or aggregating fund performance requires special attention if the original input data is expressed in different currencies. After having checked that the funds have maintained similar investment objectives during the period under review, it is necessary (see appendix) to convert total return data prior to ECD into one single pre-ECD currency, using the historical exchange rate, before converting to euro at the fixed conversion rate for local investor's convenience. The presentations must disclose the original currencies and the single pre-ECD currency used for conversion.

11. As a result of the creation of the Euro, as well as other currencies joining the Euro subsequently, it is likely that individual benchmarks and objectives will have changed or will change for many funds. As a result, both composites (used by investment managers for performance presentation) and peer groups or mutual fund categories (used by external providers of performance measurement data) will have changed or will change. In addressing such changes, overriding principles numbers 3 and 4 must always be taken into account.

12. The providers and users of performance comparisons will have to accept that ECD will create a discontinuity in many cases. Performance providers must check that funds have maintained similar investment objectives during the period under review before aggregating funds or combining composites, peer groups or mutual fund categories. The general principles of composite construction, as laid out in GIPS (Global Investment Performance standards) should be applied throughout.

Mutual Fund Mergers

13. The practice of "merging" mutual funds will continue and could well increase following ECD, particularly as new investment universes or new asset classes and/or mutual fund categories are created. If more than one currency is involved, the same principles should be applied with regard to the use of historical track records for merged funds.

Consultants and Commentators

It would be most helpful if consultants, the financial and investment media and other commentators on the performance of funds could take into account the principles in this note when providing information and/or requesting information from fund managers.

First issue by Dugald Eadie (11 January 1999)
EFFAS Permanent Commission on Performance Measurement

Update by Alain Ernewein (10 November 2000)
European Investment Performance Committee

APPENDIX: PERFORMANCE MEASUREMENT AND THE EURO

Worked Example A: Currencies converting to the Euro on 1 January 1999

Funds 1 and 2 have maintained similar investment objectives, tracking the same index. Fund 1 is valued in French franc (FRF), Fund 2 in Irish punt (IEP). The example shows that if performance data is converted in euro without care, Fund 1 may appear superior to Fund 2 despite reality being the opposite.

A 1. Fixed conversion rates would allow conversion of historic prices in euros :

	29/12/95	31/12/96	31/12/97	30/12/98	30/12/99	31/12/00
Fund 1						
Unit Price (FRF)	100	105	110	117	123	135
Unit Price (EUR)				17.84	18.75	20.58
Recast Unit Price ('euro')	15.24	16.01	16.77	17.84	18.75	20.58
Fund 2						
Unit Price (IEP)	100	98	104	110	117	130
Unit Price (EUR)				139.67	148.56	165.07
Recast Unit Price ('euro')	126.97	124.43	132.05	139.67	148.56	165.07

A 2. In creating a 'euro' track record, achieved returns appear to remain unchanged.

Our 'recast euro' returns (incorrectly) indicate that Fund 1 **outperforms** Fund 2 :

	1996	1997	1998	1999	2000	Ann'sed
Fund 1 (Recast euro)	+5.0%	+4.8%	+6.4%	+5.1%	+9.8%	**+6.2%**
Fund 2 (Recast euro)	–2.0%	+6.1%	+5.8%	+6.4%	+11.1%	**+5.4%**

A 3. But prior to EMU, currencies fluctuated relative to each other :

	29/12/95	1996	1997	1998	1999	2000	Ann'sed
Exchange Rate (IEP/FRF)	7.84900	8.80400	8.56550	8.32896	8.32896	8.32896	
Currency Return (IEP/FRF)		+12.2%	–2.7%	–2.8%	0.0%	0.0%	**+1.2%**

A 4. So we cannot compare 'recast euro' track records in currencies that used to be different.

The solution is to distinguish between the linked currencies FRF(EUR) and IEP(EUR),

	1996	1997	1998	1999	2000	Ann'sed
for a French investor						
Fund 1 FRF(EUR)	+5.0%	+4.8%	+6.4%	+5.1%	+9.8%	**+6.2%**
Fund 2 FRF(EUR)	+9.9%	+3.2%	+2.8%	+6.4%	+11.1%	**+6.6%**
for an Irish investor						
Fund 1 IEP(EUR)	–6.4%	+7.7%	+9.4%	+5.1%	+9.8%	**+4.9%**
Fund 2 IEP(EUR)	–2.0%	+6.1%	+5.8%	+6.4%	+11.1%	**+5.4%**

4-5

When calculated in FRF, IEP (or in DEM or USD), performance figures **are** different ; but in any case, Fund 1 **under performs** Fund 2. Performance figures can be converted from one currency to another using historical exchange rates.

Worked Example B: Currencies converting to the Euro later than 1 January 1999

The first historical example is the Greek Drachma (GRD) that converts to the Euro on 1 January 2001. The following guidelines will extend to other currencies if/when they convert to Euro.

B 1. Historical data

	31/12/97	**31/12/98**	**31/12/99**	**31/12/00**	**31/12/01**	**31/12/02**
Fund Unit price (GRD)	100,000	105,000	110,000	117,000	123,000	135,000
Exchange/conversion rates						
Fixed conversion rate				— 1 euro = 340.750 GRD —		
Historical exch. Rate EUR/ GRD	N/A	326.738	329.926	——— 340.750 ———		

	1998	**1999**	**2000**	**2001**	**2002**	**Ann'sed**
% change GRD/EUR	N/A	–0.97%	–3.18%	0%	0%	N/A
% change GRD/FRF	–6.11%		——— same as GRD/EUR ———			**2.1%**
% change GRD/IEP	–3.44%					**–1.5%**

B 2. Presenting the fund performance

i. to a Greek investor

GRD(EUR) may be used for local investor's convenience, but not for cross-boarder purpose:

	31/12/97	**31/12/98**	**31/12/99**	**31/12/00**	**31/12/01**	**31/12/02**
Fund						
Unit price (GRD)	100,000	105,000	110,000	117,000	123,000	135,000
Unit price (EUR)					360.97	396.18

	1998	**1999**	**2000**	**2001**	**2002**	**Ann'sed**
for a Greek investor						
Fund performance GRD(EUR)	+5.0%	+4.8%	+6.4%	+5.1%	+9.8%	**+6.2**

ii. to a Euro-11 based investor

Use the Euro currency, but remember that Euro does not exist as an actual currency before 1 January 1999. Before 1 January 1999, choose (and specify) one of the eleven pre-euro currencies:

	1998	**1999**	**2000**	**2001**	**2002**	**Ann'sed**
for a Euro based investor						
Fund performance EUR	N/A	+3.7%	+3.0%	+5.1%	+9.8%	N/A
for a French investor						
Fund performance FRF(EUR)	**–1.4%**	+3.7%	+3.0%	+5.1%	+9.8%	**+4.0%**
for an Irish investor						
Fund performance IEP(EUR)	**+1.4%**	+3.7%	+3.0%	+5.1%	+9.8%	**+4.6%**

4-5

Adoption Date: 1 December 2003
Revised Effective Date: 1 January 2006
Effective Date: 1 January 2005
Retroactive Application: No
Public Comment Period: Dec 2001 – Jun 2002

INTERPRETIVE GUIDANCE FOR FEES PROVISIONS

The purpose of the GIPS standards is to create performance presentations that allow for greater comparability of returns and increase the transparency of information provided to investors. While it is impossible to develop standards that cover every situation, GIPS provide a general framework that can be applied to many different circumstances. It is important to remember the underlying principles of the GIPS standards: fair representation and full disclosure.

In the global investment industry, fees are charged in many different ways and a variety of terms are used. In order to promote comparability, it is important that firms around the world treat fees consistently and in a comparable manner. The terms that are used can confuse the matter considerably. In some parts of the world the Net-Of-Fees Return is the starting point and Investment Management Fees are added back to arrive at the Gross-Of-Fees Return. In other places the opposite is true and fees are deducted from the Gross-Of-Fees Return to arrive at the Net-Of-Fees Return. In some regions the terms fee, duty, cost, charge, and expense have different meanings, while in other regions these terms are interchangeable. This highlights the need for common definitions, which are included in the GIPS standards Glossary.

There is a range of different types of costs and/or fees that a client incurs when maintaining an investment portfolio. In general, there are three main types of fees and/or costs: Investment Management Fees, brokerage commissions, and Administrative Fees. Administrative Fees include Custody Fees and may also include accounting fees, consulting fees, legal fees, performance measurement fees, and other applicable fees. In some situations, the only fees that the firm controls are the Investment Management Fee and the Trading Expenses (i.e., the direct cost of buying or selling the assets). Therefore, only the Investment Management Fee and the Trading Expenses should impact the firm's returns. Even though Custody Fees are a necessary additional cost of owning a portfolio, many investment managers are not involved in the selection of the custodian or in the negotiation of the Custody Fees. Accordingly, in order to promote comparability, Custody Fees should not be reflected in (i.e., reduce) the firm's returns.

4-6

The GIPS standards are based on the concept of presenting composite performance to a prospective client rather than presenting individual portfolio returns to an existing client. Firms should, however, consider if existing clients will benefit from the presentation of their individual portfolio returns after the reduction of all fees associated with owning an investment portfolio (i.e., including Administrative Fees). This Client Return (the Net-Of-Fees Return reduced by all Administrative Fees) may be useful to prospective and existing clients to fully understand the actual return that has been earned and the total amount of fees incurred. These Administrative Fees, however, are typically outside the control of the investment management firm and, as such, should not reduce the firm's Gross-Of-Fees or Net-Of-Fees Returns.

The Gross-Of-Fees Return is defined to be the return on assets reduced by any Trading Expenses. It should also be reduced by non-reclaimable withholding taxes incurred during the period. Because the Gross-Of-Fees Return includes only the return on assets and the associated cost of buying and selling those assets, it is the best measure of the firm's investment management ability and can be thought of as the "investment return". In addition, because fees are sometimes negotiable, presenting Gross-Of-Fees Returns shows the firm's expertise in managing assets without the impact of the firm's or client's negotiating skills. Accordingly, firms are recommended to present Gross-Of-Fees Returns. A prospective client, however, must also consider the effect of fees on performance. **As a prospective client evaluates and compares investment firms, the most universal point of comparison is the Gross-Of-Fees Return less the Investment Management Fee that the prospective client expects to pay.** Consequently, firms are required to disclose in each composite presentation the Fee Schedule that is appropriate to the presentation.

The Fee Schedule should be current and relevant to the composite and presentation. While a current Fee Schedule may not assist a prospective client interpret historical performance, it is the most relevant. Firms should also disclose additional information related to the firm's fees (e.g., if performance-based fees are available, if other fees are charged by a subadvisor or through a fund-of-funds structure).

The Net-Of-Fees Return is defined to be the Gross-Of-Fees Return reduced by the Investment Management Fees incurred. It is important to recognize that the Net-Of-Fees Return consists of two distinct components: the Gross-Of-Fees Return and the impact of the Investment Management Fee (see Fees Example Scenario A). Firms are also encouraged to present Net-Of-Fees Returns. In order to reflect the most accurate Net-Of-Fees Return, fees and expenses should be accrued, when possible.

The GIPS standards require that returns must be calculated after the deduction of actual Trading Expenses. Trading Expenses can be:

- Direct: as in the case of brokerage commissions and any other regulatory fee, duty, and/or tax (e.g., stamp duty, SEC fee, etc.) associated with an individual transaction, or
- Indirect: such as a bid/ask spread.

For purposes of the GIPS standards, firms must include (i.e., reduce) both Gross-Of-Fees and Net-Of-Fees Returns by the Trading Expenses incurred in the purchase or sale of securities. These costs must be included because they must be incurred in order to implement the investment strategy. Estimated Trading Expenses are not permitted.

In some cases (particularly when initially compiling a 'compliant' track record), the actual fees charged to each discretionary portfolio under management are not available. Firms that wish to show Net-Of-Fees performance results are permitted to use the highest Investment Management Fee incurred by portfolios in the composite to reduce Gross-Of-Fees performance.

However, it is not permissible to use the highest Investment Management Fee to add to the Net-Of-Fees Return in order to obtain a Gross-Of-Fees Return. Adding back the highest fee would result in overstating the Gross-Of-Fees Return. When adjusting from Net-Of-Fees to Gross-Of-Fees performance, firms must use either the actual fees or the weighted-average fee for the composite.

Many custodial banks charge part of the Custody Fee based on the number and type of transactions. These fees, even though they are charged on a per transaction basis, are still part of the Custody Fee and should not be included in the Trading expenses.

Bundled Fees

In some cases, firms combine several fees together to create a Bundled Fee. A Bundled Fee can include any combination of fees including Trading Expenses, Investment Management Fees, Custody Fees, or any other related fees. A Bundled Fee can be specific to a client, as is the case with "all-in" fees, or can be specific to a particular product, as is the case with "wrap" fees. Some Bundled Fees can be segregated into the various underlying components (e.g., the firm can "un-bundle" the fee and identify each segment that comprises the Bundled Fee – see Fees Example Scenario C). In other cases, only portions of the Bundled Fee can be segregated (e.g., Investment Management Fee segment can be identified and separated, but the Custody and Trading Expenses cannot – see Fees Example Scenario D). If a firm includes a portfolio with a Bundled Fee in a composite, it must disclose that the composite contains portfolios with Bundled Fees. Firms are required to disclose the various types of fees that are included in the Bundled Fee.

In cases where the Trading Expenses cannot be identified and segregated from a Bundled Fee, either the entire Bundled Fee, or the portion of the Bundled Fee containing the Trading Expenses, must be included in (i.e., reduce) the Gross-Of-Fees and Net-Of-Fees Returns (see Fees Examples Scenarios B and D). In these cases, Custody and other Administrative Fees might be included in the Gross-Of-Fees and Net-Of-Fees Returns. Firms may also find that the Gross-Of-Fees Return is equal to the Net-Of-Fees Return. In order to assist prospective clients in better understanding the fees included in the Gross-Of-Fees Return calculation, firms must disclose if other fees are included in the Bundled Fee in addition to the Trading Expenses. When presenting Net-Of-Fees Returns, firms must disclose if other fees are included in addition to the Investment Management Fee and Trading Expenses.

Some investment product returns are typically calculated net of other fees (e.g., Custody and other Administrative Fees). In order for these portfolios to be treated consistently with regards to the definitions of Gross-Of-Fees and Net-Of-Fees in the Standards, firms are allowed to add back all fees and expenses (e.g., Investment Management, Custody, transfer agent, share registration, marketing, and regulatory fees) except for Trading Expenses. When calculating Net-Of-Fees Returns, firms are allowed to add back all fees and expenses except for Trading Expenses and the Investment Management Fee, provided that the firm can identify all these fees. Estimated fees are not permitted.

Subadvisor, Pooled Funds and Fund-of-Funds

In some situations, firms may invest a portion of a larger portfolio in a pooled fund, utilize a subadvisor, or create a fund-of-funds structure whereby additional fees are charged by the underlying fund or paid to the subadvisor. In these situations, it is most appropriate to present the return net of all fees (e.g., including Administrative Fees) since all investors must pay these fees. However, Net-Of-Fees performance must be net of Transaction Expenses and Investment Management Fees and these fees (including the underlying fees) must not be added back to calculate Net-Of-Fees performance.

In all cases, the firm must disclose in each composite presentation the current Fee Schedule appropriate to the particular composite.

Fees Examples

4-6

For the purpose of these examples, the Trading Expenses are stated as a percentage of the beginning market value. In practice, Trading Expenses are typically accounted for in the book value of securities and are, therefore, reflected in the return on assets. These examples are presented to illustrate the concepts presented in the fee provisions and assume deduction at the beginning of the period. Actual return calculations may differ based on when the fee is deducted from the portfolio and the value used as a basis for the calculation (e.g., beginning period assets, ending period assets, weighted average period assets, etc.).

Scenario A:		**Description:**
Return on Assets	8.00%	Scenario A represents a typical
Trading Expenses	0.20%	fee structure where each fee
Investment Management Fee	1.00%	can be clearly identified.
Administrative Fees (including Custody)	0.50%	

Scenario B: Bundled Fee 1		**Description:**
Return on Assets	8.00%	Scenario B illustrates a Bundled Fee
Bundled Fee: Trading, Investment Management, and Administrative Fees (including Custody).	1.70%	structure where the Bundled Fee cannot be separated.

Scenario C: Bundled Fee 2		**Description:**
Return on Assets	8.00%	Scenario C illustrates a Bundled Fee structure where the Bundled Fee can be separated.
Bundled Fee: Trading, Investment Management, and Administrative Fees included and can be separated as follows:	1.70%	
Trading Expenses	0.20%	
Investment Management Fee	1.00%	
Administrative Fee	0.50%	

Scenario D: Bundled Fee 3		**Description:**
Return on Assets	8.00%	Scenario D illustrates a Bundled Fee structure where only the Investment Management Fee can be separated from the Bundled Fee.
Bundled Fee: Trading, Investment Management, and Administrative Fees (including Custody) included and can be separated as follows:	1.70%	
Investment Management Fee	1.00%	
Trading Expenses and Administrative Fee	0.70%	

Scenario E: Bundled Fee 4		**Description:**
Return on Assets	8.00%	Scenario E illustrates a Bundled Fee structure where only the Trading Expenses can be separated from the Bundled Fee.
Bundled Fee: Trading, Investment Management, and Administrative Fees (including Custody) included and can be separated as follows:	1.70%	
Trading Expenses	0.20%	
Investment Management and Administrative Fee	1.50%	

	Scenarios				
	A	**B**	**C**	**D**	**E**
Return on Assets	8.00%	8.00%	8.00%	8.00%	8.00%
— Trading Expenses	0.20%	1.70%	0.20%	0.70%	0.20%
Gross-Of-Fees Return	**7.80%**	**6.30%**	**7.80%**	**7.30%**	**7.80%**
— Investment Management Fee	1.00%	n/a	1.00%	1.00%	1.50%
Net-Of-Fees Return	**6.80%**	**6.30%**	**6.80%**	**6.30%**	**6.30%**
— Administrative Fee	0.50%	n/a	0.50%	n/a	n/a
Client Return*	6.30%	6.30%	6.30%	6.30%	6.30%

***The Client Return is not required by the GIPS standards and is presented here as additional information that may be helpful for existing clients.**

4-6

Revised Effective Date: 1 January 2006
Adoption Date: 18 May 2001
Effective Date: 18 May 2001
Retroactive Application: Not Required
Public Comment Period: Sep – Dec 2000

GUIDANCE STATEMENT ON PERFORMANCE RECORD PORTABILITY (REVISED)

Introduction

In the current global market for merger, acquisition, and consolidation of investment management firms, past performance records are increasingly valuable assets for their owners. But historical records are the result of many factors (e.g., people, process, discipline, and strategy) that may not be easily transferred to a new entity and still warrant having the same label as the old entity. The applicability and integrity of the performance record is only as good as the ongoing integrity of the strategy and all the contributing factors. Portability of performance records is a very important area that should be clarified within the Global Investment Performance Standards (GIPS®). In addition, because the legal issues and requirements surrounding portability can be particularly complex, firms are reminded that under the GIPS standards they must comply with all applicable laws and regulations regarding portability before applying this Guidance Statement.

Performance is the record of the firm, not of the individual.

Changes in a firm's organization are not permitted to lead to alteration of historical composite results. Therefore, composites must include all accounts managed by a member of a firm, even if the individual responsible for the past results is no longer with the firm. Composites must not include portfolios managed by members of the firm before they joined the firm, unless Provision 5.A.4 (provided below) is met. If the Provision is met, performance track records must be used by the manager, or group of managers, to represent the historical record of a new affiliation or a newly formed entity. Using the performance data from a prior firm or affiliation as supplemental information is permitted as long as the past record is identified clearly as such and is not linked to the results of the new affiliation. If the provisions for portability are met, then it is possible for multiple firms to claim the same performance history as their own.

Provision 0.A.2 of the GIPS standards provides how a firm is to be defined within the context of the Standards. "Firm" mergers can happen within an affiliated group and this Guidance Statement will apply to such situations. As Provision II.5.A.4. (d) of the GIPS standards reads, "If a compliant firm acquires or is acquired by a noncompliant firm, the firms have 1 year to bring the noncompliant assets into compliance." However, the important determinant of allowable performance record portability is not a firm's former compliance with the GIPS standards but whether the acquiring firm continues the original strategy that defined the composite with all of its continuing factors.

Performance data from a prior firm may be used, with the proper disclosures, as supplemental information. If the conditions of Provision 5.A.4 (listed below) are not met, this supplemental information must not be linked to the ongoing performance of the new firm. The key issue is the linking of prior performance results to the ongoing performance record at the new affiliation.

When a manager, group of managers, or an entire firm joins a new firm, Provision 5.A.4 requires:

a. Performance track records of a past firm or affiliation must be linked to or used to represent the historical record of a new firm or new affiliation if:
   i. Substantially all the investment decision-makers are employed by the new firm (i.e., research department, portfolio managers, and other relevant staff),
   ii. The staff and decision-making process remain intact and independent within the new firm, and
   iii. The new firm has records that document and support the reported performance.

b. The new firm must disclose that the performance results from the past firm are linked to the performance record of the new firm,

c. In addition to 5.A.4.(a) and 5.A.4.(b), when one firm joins an existing firm, performance of composites from both firms must be linked to the ongoing returns if substantially all the assets from the past firm's composite transfer to the new firm.

d. If a compliant firm acquires or is acquired by a noncompliant firm, the firms have one year to bring the noncompliant assets into compliance.

If all of the above requirements are not met, the past performance record of the former firm or manager or group of managers from the former firm cannot be linked to the ongoing performance record at the new firm. However, the past performance record may be presented as supplemental information when relevant.

In the case where two firms join and two composites are to be merged, the new firm must first determine if there is a "surviving" composite. A "surviving" composite is the composite that represents the continuity of investment strategy, process, and personnel. In order to be a "surviving" composite, the staff and decision-making process of the composite must remain intact and independent at the new firm.

If the firm identifies a "surviving" composite, its performance history can be presented and linked to the ongoing performance of the merged composite. It is recommended that the performance of the "non-surviving" composite be made available as supplemental information upon request. For example, as a result of a merger, two composites ("C" and "D") are combined in a merged composite "CD." If the firm is able to satisfy all the rules of portability and determines that composite "C" is the "surviving" composite, then the performance history from composite "C" may be linked to the on-going record of composite "CD." Although the assets from composite "D" are included in composite "CD," the performance history of composite "D" are not linked to the ongoing record of composite "CD" but should be made available upon request.

If the firm determines that neither composite maintains all the elements of continuity, then there has not been a merger of composites and neither historic performance record can be linked to the ongoing composite performance record, but it is recommended that both of the "non-surviving" composites be presented as supplemental information. For example, if the staff of two firms are combined into one and the investment decision-making process is shared (and thus changed), the historical performance records of both of the non-surviving composites should be presented as supplemental information and must not be linked to the ongoing results of the new composite.

If the presenting firm is a "manager of managers" and is hired by its clients because of the presenting firm's manager selection skills and the firm maintains discretion of the underlying assets (has the control to hire or fire the subadvisor), the firm must include those assets in the total firm assets and present the performance of the underlying assets in the presenting firm's composites. Similarly, if the presenting firm replaces one subadvisor with another, the presenting firm must include within the same composite the performance of the assets assigned to the new firm going forward and leave the results from the former firm unchanged. Provision 4.A.18 requires that beginning 1 January 2006, firms must disclose the use of a subadvisor(s) and the periods a subadvisor(s) was used.

If the presenting firm does not have discretion of the underlying assets managed by the subadvisor, then the performance record of the underlying assets must not be included in the presenting firm's performance composites.

Firms must keep in mind that this Guidance Statement falls under the over-riding principles of the GIPS standards: fair representation and full disclosure. Provision 4.A.19 requires that firms must disclose all significant events that would help a prospective client interpret the performance record. As such, events that impact the firm's operations and/or investment process (for example, change in ownership, merger or acquisition, departure of key investment professional, etc.) must be disclosed.

Effective Date

This Guidance Statement was originally effective 18 May 2001 and was revised to reflect the GIPS standards effective as of 1 January 2006.

Firms are encouraged, but not required, to apply this guidance prior to the original Effective Date of 18 May 2001; however, the original guidance must be applied to all presentations that include performance for periods on and after that date.

The revisions made to this guidance (effective 1 January 2006) must be applied to all presentations that include performance for periods after 31 December 2005.

Applications:

1. *If Firm A acquires Firm B and all of the portability requirements are met, is Firm A required to present Firm B's historical performance, or can Firm A choose to not present Firm B's historical performance?*

The GIPS standards are based on the fundamental principles of fair representation and full disclosure. If all of the portability requirements are satisfied and Firm B is included in the definition of Firm A, Firm A must use Firm B's historical performance. If Firm A were permitted to exclude Firm B's historical performance, it would be cherry-picking which is against the spirit of fair representation of the GIPS standards.

2. *The Guidance Statement on Performance Record Portability states "Performance track records of a past firm or affiliation must be linked to or used to represent the historical record of a new firm or new affiliation if," certain conditions are met. What does performance track record refer to in this instance? Can a firm create the composite history based on the portfolios that transfer to the new firm if the history is representative of the old composite?*

The concept of portability revolves around the ability to bring a track record from one firm to another. It would not be representative to recreate a record with only selected portfolios. The performance track record refers to the entire composite from the old firm. In addition to meeting all the elements of the Guidance Statement, in order for a firm to be able to link the composite from the old firm to the on-going performance of the new firm, the entire composite performance history, including all portfolios, must be used. The firm must have all the records needed to substantiate that performance history.

3. *Manager A previously worked for Firm X that was not compliant with the GIPS standards. Manager A left Firm X and was hired by Firm Z. Firm Z and Manager A are satisfied that the situation meets all the rules of portability. Can Manager A's performance history at Firm X become compliant or can it not be used because it is non-compliant?*

To clarify, the performance history can never become "compliant." Compliance with the Standards can only be achieved on a firm-wide basis.

If the manager (or management team) satisfies all the requirements of the Guidance Statement on Performance Record Portability (including bringing all the supporting documentation and records to Firm Z), then Firm Z can use the records to construct a composite history that can be used. As provided in the Guidance Statement on Performance Record Portability, the important determinant of allowable performance record portability is not a firm's former compliance with the GIPS standards but whether the acquiring firm continues the original strategy that defined the composite with all of its continuing factors.

Most cases will not meet all of the portability requirements, in which case the past performance record of the manager cannot be linked to the ongoing performance record of the firm. The past performance record of the manager can be presented as supplemental information when relevant.

Please note one of the rules of portability requires that the staff and decision-making process remain intact and independent at the new firm. If the investment process is somehow changed, or if the investment staff changes, the historical records of the new manager can only be presented as supplemental information and cannot be linked to the ongoing record of the firm.

Revised Effective Date: 1 January 2006
Adoption Date: 4 March 2004
Effective Date: 1 June 2004
Retroactive Application: Not required
Public Comment Period: Aug - Nov 2002

GUIDANCE STATEMENT ON THE TREATMENT OF CARVE-OUTS (REVISED)

Introduction

A carve-out is defined as a single or multiple asset class segment of a multiple asset class portfolio. It is used to create a track record for a narrower mandate from a portfolio managed to a broader mandate. For example, the Asian securities from a Euro-Pacific portfolio or the equity portion of a balanced portfolio could be considered a carve-out. Carve-outs are generally based on asset class, geographic region, or industry sector.

Inherent Problems

Carve-outs have several problems associated with them. Because they represent only a portion of a broader, more diversified strategy, carve-out returns are only a valid track record if they are representative of what would have been achieved in a portfolio dedicated to the carved-out strategy. The use of carve-outs gives the impression that the firm has experience managing portfolios dedicated to a particular strategy, when this may not be the case. For example, a carve-out of the U.K. equities in a global equity portfolio that holds only two U.K. equities is not representative of a diversified U.K.-only portfolio.

A second problem occurs if cash is not accounted for separately and, therefore, must be allocated to the carved-out segment. If the carve-out is not accounted for separately, then the calculation of the return is potentially less accurate. The Standards require that returns from cash and cash equivalents held in the portfolio must be included in the total return. Unless the carved-out portion is accounted for as a separate portfolio there will be no cash associated with the returns. For periods prior to 1 January 2010, cash must be allocated to the returns in a timely manner using a consistent, objective methodology.

Beginning 1 January 2010, if the firm intends to carve-out an asset class, sector, industry, size range (e.g., large cap) or style type (e.g., value), each carved-out segment must have either its own cash balance or be accounted for separately, with its own associated cash position.

4-8

The rationale behind the inclusion of cash at all times in total returns is based on the principle of fair representation—a composite that includes portfolios without any cash would not be representative to the typical prospective client who hires the firm on a fully discretionary basis where cash allocation and management would be implicit. It would be misleading to present returns without cash, since this does not fairly represent how a separate portfolio would be managed.

Guiding Principles

Firms must remember the fundamental principles of the Standards, fair representation and full disclosure, and must avoid presenting misleading information. Any carve-out used as a track record must be representative of an actual segregated portfolio managed to that strategy. The carved-out segment must be discretionary and structured materially the same as a portfolio dedicated to that strategy and have a risk profile that is substantially similar. For example, the equity segment of a balanced portfolio may be structured differently than a separately managed equity portfolio because additional risks taken in the equity segment may be offset by lower risk taken in the fixed income segment. The firm must determine if the carved out segment is representative of a separately managed portfolio dedicated to the same strategy.

Firms must establish a policy for the creation, use, and calculation of carve-outs and apply the policy consistently. The calculation methodology used to calculate and allocate the return achieved on cash should be determined by the firm, documented, and applied consistently.

The GIPS standards state, "Beginning 1 January 2010, carve-out returns are not permitted to be included in single asset class composite returns unless the carve-out is actually managed separately with its own cash balance." Accordingly, it is necessary to clarify what is permissible prior to 1 January 2010 and after the provision becomes effective 1 January 2010.

The following guiding principles must be met when a firm considers creating a carve-out:

Prior to 1 January 2010

- The carve-out should be managed separately (i.e., the segment should be managed as if it were a separate portfolio, rather than a segment of a larger portfolio).
- The carve-out must be representative of a stand-alone portfolio managed to the same strategy.
- If a firm creates a carve-out of a particular strategy, then all similar portfolio segments managed to that strategy must also be carved-out and included in the composite (e.g., if the equity segment of a balanced portfolio is carved-out and included in an equity composite, then all similar equity segments of the firm's portfolios must be carved-out and included in the equity composite, provided the conditions outlined in this Guidance Statement are met).
- If a firm chooses to carve-out a portion of a portfolio, they are not compelled to carve-out other parts of the portfolio.
- When presenting net-of-fees performance of composites containing carve-outs, fees must be deducted from the carved-out returns. The fees must be representative of the fees charged for a separately managed portfolio for the asset class carved-out considering the fee schedule for the composite containing the carve-outs.
- The carve-out should have its cash accounted for separately. If the segment does not have its own cash, cash must be allocated to the segment on a consistent basis. Acceptable allocation methods include:
    1. *Beginning of Period Allocation.* Identify the cash allocation percentage for each portfolio segment at the beginning of the period. For example, at the beginning of January, identify the percentage of residual cash that will be allocated to the carve-outs at month end.
    2. *Strategic Asset Allocation.* Base the allocation directly upon the target strategic asset allocation. For example, if the portfolio is targeted to have 40% in equities and 60% in bonds, then the allocation will relate to the *actual* amounts invested.

4-8

If the portfolio had a target allocation of 40%, but at the beginning of the period only held 35% in equities, then the cash return would constitute the difference (5%). Firms must determine which method to use, document it, and apply consistently

As of 1 January 2010

- The carve-out must be managed separately (i.e., the segment must be managed as if it were a separate portfolio, rather than a segment of a larger portfolio).
- The carve-out must be representative of a stand-alone portfolio managed to the same strategy.
- If a firm creates a carve-out of a particular strategy, then all similar portfolio segments managed to that strategy must also be carved-out and included in the composite (e.g., if the equity segment of a balanced portfolio is carved-out and included in an equity composite, then all similar equity segments of the firm's

portfolios must be carved-out and included in the equity composite, provided the conditions above are met).

- If a firm chooses to carve-out a portion of a portfolio, they are not compelled to carve-out other parts of the portfolio.
- When presenting net-of-fees performance of composites containing carve-outs, fees must be deducted from the carved-out returns. The fees must be representative of the fees charged for a separately managed portfolio for the asset class carved out considering the fee schedule for the composite containing the carve-outs.
- The carve-out must have its own cash. Possible methods for properly accounting for the cash positions include:
    1. Separate portfolios: cash and securities are actually segregated into a separate portfolio at the custodian.
    2. Multiple cash accounts: each segment's cash is accounted for separately (e.g., equity cash account, fixed-income cash account, etc.).
    3. Sub-portfolios: each segment of a portfolio is accounted for as if it were a separate portfolio.

Performance Record for Discontinued Carve-outs

When a firm, which has created carve-outs using cash allocation methods for periods prior to 1 January 2010, does not choose to apply any method for accounting for the cash position to the carve-outs and thus discontinues the carve-outs for periods after 1 January 2010, then the firm must meet all of the following conditions:

- The past performance record of the carve-outs using cash allocation methods must be left unchanged within the same composites in which the carve-outs were included,
- In the composite presentation, the firm must disclose the historical inclusion of carve-outs and the period of inclusion, and
- If the firm has a composite consisting of only carve-outs using cash allocation methods and does not apply any method for accounting for the cash position to any of the carve-outs in the composite for periods after 1 January 2010, the composite is discontinued but must continue to be listed on the firm's list of composites for five years after discontinuation.

Acceptable Uses

Effective 1 January 2010, carve-outs must be managed separately with their own cash (i.e., allocation of cash will no longer be allowed as of 1 January 2010). This change will not be retroactive, so the history of existing carve-outs must not change. Carve-out track records that are representative of the composite strategy may be used like any other portfolio provided that the carve-out is accounted for separately with its own cash. Firms are not permitted to combine different carve-outs or composites to create a new, simulated strategy composite for purposes of compliance with the GIPS standards. For example, a firm may not combine an equity carve-out and a fixed income carve-out to create a simulated balanced composite. Although comprised of actual returns, this type of composite is hypothetical because it does not reflect real asset allocation decisions and therefore is viewed as model or simulated results under the GIPS standards. This information can be presented as supplemental information only but must not be linked to actual returns.

Disclosures

According to Provision 4.A.11, when a single asset class is carved-out of a multiple-asset portfolio and the returns are presented as part of a single-asset composite, firms must disclose the cash allocation method that was used for periods prior to 1 January 2010. It is recommended that firms disclose any change in the cash allocation methods.

In addition, Provision 5.A.5 requires that beginning 1 January 2006, if a composite includes or is formed using single asset class carve-outs from multiple asset class portfolios, the presentation must include the percentage of the composite that is composed of carve-outs prospectively for each period.

Effective Date

This Guidance Statement was originally effective 1 June 2004 and was revised to reflect the changes to the GIPS standards effective as of 1 January 2006.

Firms are encouraged, but not required, to apply this guidance prior to the original Effective Date of 1 June 2004; however, the original guidance must be applied to all presentations that include performance for periods on and after that date.

The revisions made to this guidance (effective 1 January 2006) must be applied to all presentations that include performance for periods after 31 December 2005.

Key GIPS Provisions Specifically Applicable to Carve-Outs

3.A.7 Carve-out segments excluding cash are not permitted to be used to represent a discretionary portfolio and, as such, are not permitted to be included in composite returns. When a single asset class is carved out of a multiple asset class portfolio and the returns are presented as part of a single asset composite, cash must be allocated to the carve-out returns in a timely and consistent manner. Beginning 1 January 2010 carve-out returns are not permitted to be included in single asset class composite returns unless the carve-out is actually managed separately with its own cash balance.

3.B.1 Carve-out returns should not be included in single asset class composite returns unless the carve-outs are actually managed separately with their own cash balance.

4.A.11 For periods prior to 1 January 2010, when a single asset class is carved out of a multiple asset portfolio and the returns are presented as part of a single asset composite, firms must disclose the policy used to allocate cash to the carve-out returns.

5.A.5 Beginning 1 January 2006, if a composite includes or is formed using single asset class carve-outs from multiple asset class portfolios, the presentation must include the percentage of the composite that is composed of carve-outs prospectively for each period.

Application:

1. *Firm B manages balanced portfolios and would like to carve-out the equities to create an equity composite. Firm B charges 0.75% for its fixed income strategy, 1.50% for its equity strategy, and 1.00% for its balanced strategy. How should the investment management fee be allocated to the equity carve-out for presenting a net-of-fees return?*

Firms must allocate fees to each segment that are appropriate to the asset class. In this case, the firm must use the 1.50% that it charges for equity management.

4-8

Revised Effective Date: 1 January 2006
Adoption Date: 13 March 2002
Effective Date: 30 June 2002
Retroactive Application: see "Effective Date" section
Public Comment Period: Jul – Oct 2001

GUIDANCE STATEMENT ON THE TREATMENT OF SIGNIFICANT CASH FLOWS (REVISED)

Introduction

Dealing with large external cash flows in a portfolio is a common struggle for most investment managers. These large flows, of cash and/or securities, can make a significant impact on investment strategy implementation and, thus, on a portfolio's and composite's performance. Accordingly, this Guidance Statement clarifies the issues related to the treatment of significant cash flows under the Global Investment Performance Standards (GIPS®).

Background

GIPS Provision II.3.A.3 requires that composites must include new portfolios on a timely and consistent basis after the portfolio comes under management unless specifically mandated by the client (e.g., a client mandates a schedule of initial cash flows over several time periods and can prolong the length of time needed to implement the strategy). GIPS Provision 3.A.4 states that terminated portfolios must be included in the historical returns of the appropriate composites up to the last full measurement period that the portfolio was under management.

The GIPS standards were developed with the understanding that new portfolios may require a period of time (a "grace period") for a firm to fully implement the intended investment management strategy. During the grace period, the portfolio is not required to be included in a composite. The necessary length of this grace period may vary from composite to composite, depending on a number of factors that impact the implementation of an investment strategy. It is also reasonable that when cash flows to a portfolio are significantly large, the same process applies that governs the introduction of a new portfolio into a composite.

External Cash Flow Definition

For the purposes of the GIPS standards, an External Cash Flow is defined as "cash, securities or assets that enter or exit a portfolio," *(i.e., capital additions or withdrawals that are generally client initiated)*. Transfers of assets between asset classes within a portfolio or manager initiated flows must not be used to move portfolios out of composites on a temporary basis. The "cash flow" may be defined by the firm as a single flow or an aggregate of a number of flows within a stated period of time.

In cases of multiple cash flows over an extended period of time, firms should refer to the Discretion section of the Guidance Statement on Composite Definition and consider whether the portfolio should be classified as non-discretionary.

For a discussion of the distinction between external/large external cash flows and Significant Cash Flows, please see the Guidance Statement on Calculation Methodology.

Significant Cash Flows

Firms that wish to remove portfolios from composites in cases of Significant Cash Flows must define what is meant by "significant" on a composite-by-composite basis. The definition may be influenced by the characteristics of the asset class(es) within the strategy, such as market liquidity, market volatility, and/or by the trading capabilities of the investment manager. (For instance, a Significant Cash Flow may be considered 10% of a portfolio's market value for an Emerging Market Fixed-Income composite but may be in excess of 50% of a portfolio's market value for a more liquid composite, such as European Equities.) In theory, the determination of significance should primarily be based on the liquidity of the asset class and the investment strategy employed. Because of the dynamic nature of global markets and the inherent subjectivity involved, it is impractical to establish absolute levels of significance for each asset class. Theoretically, cash flows that are relatively small on a composite level, but relatively large on a portfolio level, can potentially distort the portfolio's performance and skew the measure of composite dispersion. The measure of significance must be determined as either a specific monetary amount (e.g., €50,000,000) or a percentage of portfolio assets (based on the most recent valuation).

Grace Periods for the Treatment of Significant Cash Flows

Each composite should have a portfolio inclusion policy for new portfolios and an exclusion policy for terminated portfolios. It is the responsibility of the firm to set reasonable guidelines for each composite regarding the inclusion/exclusion of portfolios in the composite. Firms are encouraged to establish a policy that includes new portfolios in composites as soon as possible, preferably at the start of the next full performance measurement period. Firms are also encouraged to establish a policy that includes terminated portfolios through the last full measurement period the portfolio is under management. Similarly, these policies should be replicated for the purpose of addressing significant cash flows in composites.

Grace period policies, as well as definitions and policies concerning Significant Cash Flows, must be established and documented for each composite by the firm *before* they are implemented (preferably at the time each composite is created) and firms must not retroactively apply these policies to restate performance. Once implemented, the firm must consistently apply these policies (i.e., if a cash flow in a portfolio occurs that meets the definition of significant for that composite, the portfolio must be removed according to the guidelines). Firms must not reconsider whether a portfolio should be removed from a composite on an ex-post basis (after the fact) when it can be determined whether the cash flow has helped or hurt performance. It should be noted that the removal of a portfolio due to a Significant Cash Flow will not affect the specific portfolio's performance history. The definitions and policies for Significant Cash Flows and Grace Periods for new or cash flow-impacted portfolios can be amended, but the changes must not be applied retroactively. It is expected that the removal of portfolios due to Significant Cash Flows will be an infrequent occurrence, particularly in composites that are invested in the larger, most liquid asset classes.

Firms are recommended to periodically review their policies regarding Significant Cash Flows, especially if firms find that they are frequently removing portfolios due to Significant Cash Flows. Firms are encouraged to establish Significant Cash Flow policies and definitions for all of their composites, but are not required to do so.

Temporary Removal of Entire Portfolios with Significant Cash Flows

If a firm wishes to make use of the option to remove portfolios when Significant Cash Flows occur, then it *must* disclose the following items **in each composite presentation**:

1. how the firm defines a "Significant Cash Flow" for that composite,
2. the grace period for the composite,
3. if the definitions, policies, or grace periods for handling Significant Cash Flows have been redefined, firms must disclose the date and nature of the change, and
4. that additional information regarding the treatment of Significant Cash Flows is available upon request, which must include:
   a. the number of portfolios removed during a given period,
   b. the number of times portfolios were removed during a given period, and

c. the amount of composite assets represented by the portfolios affected by the application of these policies.

It is important to note that if all of a composite's portfolios were removed during one or more periods due to Significant Cash Flows, there would be a break in the composite performance record. Firms that have composites with only a few portfolios should strongly consider either defining the measure of significance at a very high level or possibly determining that a Significant Cash Flows policy is not appropriate for that composite. If a composite loses all of its member portfolios (whether that is due to Significant Cash Flows, portfolio termination, or some other reason), the performance record stops. If portfolios are later added to that composite, the two periods cannot be linked.

It is also important to note that removing a portfolio due to a Significant Cash Flow removes the portfolio when transaction costs are expected to be high. The intent of this Guidance Statement is not to allow firms to "hide" transaction costs, but rather to remove the potentially more disruptive effects that occur as a result of a Significant Cash Flow.

Documentation

Firms must document each time a portfolio moves into or out of a composite due to a significant cash flow. Documentation must be part of the firm's record keeping process and, at a minimum, must include:

1. the date of the cash flow; the date the firm removes the portfolio from the composite, and the date the firm returns the portfolio to the composite,
2. depending upon the firm's definition of significant cash flow: the amount of the cash flow or the amount of the cash flow as a percentage of the most recent portfolio market value, and
3. if the cash flow is moving into or out of the portfolio.

Documentation will allow third-parties to easily determine whether firms have followed their grace period policy and definition of Significant Cash Flow.

Firms must document their definitions and policies regarding Significant Cash Flows, including the definition of the Grace Period and measure of Significance. Firms must also document any changes that are made to the definitions or policies.

Temporary New Accounts

The use of Temporary New Accounts remains the most direct method for dealing with Significant Cash Flows. Under this methodology, when Significant Cash Flows occur in a portfolio, the firm may treat these cash flows as temporary "new" accounts. For example, if a Significant Cash Flow is withdrawn from a portfolio at the end of the month, the firm would move the necessary cash and/or securities into a Temporary New Account for liquidation and/or distribution to the client. Temporary New Accounts are not required to be included in any composite. The portfolio would reflect the withdrawal of funds and/or securities as a cash outflow of the portfolio, and the performance would be calculated to include this cash outflow at the date of transfer to the temporary account. The Temporary New Account would receive the funds and/or securities as a cash inflow. The assets would remain in this account until the funds are distributed. The same principles would hold true with a cash inflow. In this example, the funds would remain in the temporary account until all funds in the Temporary New Account are invested in line with the manager's standard policy for the mandate and then be transferred to the main portfolio.

Firms that are currently able to use a Temporary New Account methodology are encouraged to continue to do so. Although technology at the present time does not readily allow for the use of this method, the GIPS standards recommend the use of Temporary New Accounts to remove the effects of significant external cash flows. The removal of portfolios due to significant cash flows may no longer be permitted at some point in the future. The firm's policy for the use of Temporary New Accounts must be defined and consistently applied in the same manner as the policy for the temporary exclusion of an account from a composite.

Effective Date

This Guidance Statement was originally effective 30 June 2002 and was revised to reflect the changes to the GIPS standards effective as of 1 January 2006.

Firms must not apply these guidelines prior to the implementation date of the firm's Significant Cash Flow policy as described above and must not be used to retroactively restate performance. Firms currently coming into compliance must not apply this guidance to composite performance for periods prior to 30 June 2002.

The revisions made to this guidance (effective 1 January 2006) must be applied to all presentations that include performance for periods after 31 December 2005.

Key GIPS Provisions Specifically Related to Significant Cash Flows

3.A.3 Composite must include new portfolios on a timely and consistent basis after the portfolio comes under management unless specifically mandated by the client.

3.A.4 Terminated portfolios must be included in the historical returns of the appropriate composites up to the last full measurement period that the portfolio was under management.

3.B.2 To remove the effect of a significant external cash flow, the use of a temporary new account is recommended (as opposed to adjusting the composite composition to remove portfolios with significant external cash flows).

Revised Effective Date: 1 January 2006
Adoption Date: 1 October 2003
Effective Date: 1 January 2004
Retroactive Application: Not Required
Public Comment Period: Aug – Nov 2002

GUIDANCE STATEMENT ON THE USE OF SUPPLEMENTAL INFORMATION (REVISED)

Introduction

In preparing performance reports, firms must keep in mind the spirit and objectives of the Standards: fair representation and full disclosure. Meeting the intent of the Standards may necessitate including information in the performance reports beyond the required and recommended provisions of the Standards to adequately cover the firm's specific situations. Firms that claim compliance with the Standards are encouraged to present all relevant information, beyond that required and recommended in the Standards, to fully explain their performance.

What Is Supplemental Information?

Supplemental Information is defined as any performance-related information included as part of a compliant performance presentation that supplements or enhances the required and/or recommended disclosure and presentation provisions of the GIPS standards. Supplemental Information should provide users of the composite presentation with the proper context in which to better understand the performance results. Because Supplemental Information could have the potential to be misleading in relation to the firm's claim of compliance, this Guidance Statement defines and addresses the proper use of Supplemental Information.

What Is *Not* Supplemental Information?

- *Additional Information* that is required or recommended under the GIPS standards is not considered "Supplemental Information" for the purposes of compliance. Additional Information is not required to be labeled/identified as supplemental or separate from the required compliant information.
- *Non-Performance Related Information* is also omitted from this Guidance Statement and is not required to be labeled/identified as supplemental or separate from the required compliant information. Non-performance information includes, but is not limited to, general information regarding the firm, a description of the investment strategy, or details about the investment process.
- *Misleading Information.* Firms that claim compliance with the GIPS standards must not present information that may mislead or deceive. For example, the following two items are misleading and unrepresentative; therefore, compliant firms are prohibited from presenting this information (unless specifically requested from the firm by a prospective or current client in a one-on-one presentation):
    1. Model, hypothetical, backtested, or simulated results *linked* to actual performance results.
    2. Non-portable performance from a prior firm *linked* to current ongoing performance results.

4-10

This is not an exhaustive list and is only provided to show examples of potentially misleading information.

Guiding Principles

If a firm chooses to show Supplemental Information, it is important to consider the following guiding principles:

- Supplemental Information must satisfy the spirit and principles of the GIPS standards: i.e., fair representation and full disclosure.
- Supplemental Information must *not* contradict or conflict with the information provided in the compliant composite presentation.
- Supplemental Information must be clearly labeled and identified as supplemental to a particular composite presentation.

This Guidance Statement does *not* prohibit firms from preparing and presenting information according to specific requests from prospective clients. However, firms are required to provide a fully compliant presentation prior to or accompanying any Supplemental Information.

Examples of Supplemental Information

Supplemental information must relate directly to the compliant presentation. Examples of supplemental information include, but are not limited to:

- Carve out returns that exclude cash
- Non-portable returns
- Model, hypothetical, backtested, or simulated returns
- Representative account information, such as:
    1. Portfolio-level country weightings
    2. Portfolio-level sector weightings
    3. Portfolio-level risk measures
- Attribution
- Composite or portfolio-level specific holdings
- Peer group comparisons
- Risk-adjusted performance

Location of Supplemental Information

Supplemental information must be clearly labeled and identified as supplemental to a particular composite presentation. The presentation and location of Supplemental Information in relation to the GIPS required or recommended data depends on the type of Supplemental Information and its potential to mislead prospective clients.

There are certain situations that allow for the presentation of both compliant and Supplemental Information on the same page; however, firms should consider that there are also many situations that call for the separation of compliant and Supplemental Information. When in doubt, firms are encouraged to place the compliant and Supplemental Information on separate pages.

Firms must provide a fully compliant presentation prior to or accompanying any supplemental information. Firms must identify all Supplemental Information to a specific compliant presentation, for example:

- place Supplemental Information on the same or back of the page as the compliant data — if appropriate, or
- include a statement indicating that the Supplemental Information supplements the XYZ Composite presentation (as provided on pg. 11 *or* provided on 15 March 200X).

This Guidance Statement does *not* restrict firms from providing any specific information requested by prospective clients or their agents.

Supplemental Information — Verification

Supplemental Information is not subject to verification under the GIPS standards. It is the ultimate responsibility of the firm claiming compliance to ensure that it abides by the ethical principles and spirit of the GIPS standards each time it presents performance results.

Effective Date

This Guidance Statement was originally effective 1 January 2004 and was revised to reflect the changes to the GIPS standards effective as of 1 January 2006.

Firms are encouraged, but not required, to apply this guidance prior to the original Effective Date of 1 January 2004; however, the original guidance must be applied to all presentations that include performance for periods on and after that date.

The revisions made to this guidance (effective 1 January 2006) must be applied to all presentations that include performance for periods after 31 December 2005.

Applications:

1. Can supplemental information be presented on the same page as the compliant presentation?

Yes. Supplemental information can be presented on the same page as long as it satisfies the guiding principles of the Supplemental Information Guidance Statement (i.e., is not misleading, does not contradict or conflict with the required compliant information, is clearly labeled, and references the appropriate composite presentation that it supplements).

2. Firm A has a marketing brochure that describes the firm, staff, and investment process. One of the pages contains the compliant presentation for a specific composite. Do all the other pages of the brochure need to be labeled as supplemental information?

No. Supplemental Information is defined as any performance-related information included as part of a compliant performance presentation that supplements or enhances the required and/or recommended disclosure and presentation provisions of the GIPS standards. Supplemental information does not include general information regarding the firm or the investment strategy or process.

3. XYZ firm created a presentation booklet that primarily highlights performance information that is considered supplemental. The booklet shows an appropriate compliant presentation in the back of the book as an appendix. Is it acceptable for the supplemental information to precede the compliant presentation?

Yes, provided the supplemental information:

a. is not misleading,
b. does not contradict or conflict with the compliant information, and
c. is clearly labeled as supplemental.

The firm must include a statement indicating that the Supplemental Information supplements the compliant composite presentation.

4. Are there any limits to what can be shown as supplemental information?

The definition and guiding principles of this *Guidance Statement on the Use of Supplemental Information* are very specific about the types of information that should and should not be shown in conjunction to a fully-compliant GIPS composite presentation. When in doubt, firms should always turn their focus to the first guiding principle of the *Guidance Statement*, which is also the fundamental objective of the Standards: to ensure fair representation and full disclosure of performance results. By continually using this principle to guide the calculation and presentation of performance, firms are sure to satisfy the spirit and provisions of the GIPS standards.

Specifically, firms that claim compliance with the GIPS standards must not present information that may mislead or deceive. For example, the following two items are misleading and unrepresentative; therefore, compliant firms are prohibited from presenting this information (unless specifically requested from the firm by a prospective or current client in a one-on-one presentation):

1. Model, hypothetical, backtested, or simulated results linked to actual performance results
2. Non-portable performance from a prior firm linked to current ongoing performance results

This is not an exhaustive list and is only provided to show examples of potentially misleading information.

Revised Effective Date: 1 January 2006
Adoption Date: 13 March 2002
Effective Date: 13 March 2002
Retroactive Application: Not Required
Public Comment Period: May – Jul 2001

GUIDANCE STATEMENT FOR VERIFICATION (REVISED)

Introduction

This Guidance Statement supplements the verification procedures outlined in Section III of the Global Investment Performance Standards (GIPS®) and attempts to provide additional guidance to both verifiers as well as investment management firms seeking verification engagements.

Verifier Qualification Requirements

When an investment management firm undertakes verification of its claim of compliance with the GIPS standards, the verification must be performed by a "verifier" with appropriate professional abilities and practical experience and who is independent of the investment management firm. Verifiers generally comprise auditing, consulting, and other firms that have a high degree of knowledge regarding the investment management industry. Verifiers must consider currently accepted standards of practice within their industry (if applicable) when verifying an investment management firm's compliance with the GIPS standards.

Verifiers must be knowledgeable about the Standards and also have a practical level of expertise regarding investment management practices, including performance calculation procedures and business processes; however, the Standards do not contain specific qualification requirements to effectively verify compliance with the GIPS standards. The verifier must be "independent of the investment management firm," which means that generally neither the verifier nor the investment management firm should have a direct conflict of interest. Other consultancy or audit engagements do not necessarily constitute a direct conflict of interest. Verification firms should be cognizant of their role as advisors or performance measurers in the pre-verification stage and ensure that potential conflicts are managed, while investment management firms must satisfy themselves that the verifiers they employ manage the conflicts appropriately. Investment management firms must retain the ultimate responsibility for the decisions made. Please see the Guidance Statement on Verifier Independence for additional guidance.

A verifier is selected and appointed by the investment management firm. In the selection process, the investment management firm should give full consideration to the considerations described above and select a candidate who is fully qualified, independent and able to perform a thorough and credible verification.

Investment Management Firm — Verifier Relationship

Verifiers must maintain fairness and independence at all times when determining facts and procedures relevant to a firm's claim of compliance as well as in expressing opinions. Prior to expressing an opinion, the verifier must obtain from the management of the firm a confirmation of the claim of compliance and of other specific representations made to the verifier during verification. Typically such confirmation will include the following representations:

- the firm is in compliance with the GIPS standards on a firm-wide basis;
- the firm's management bears all responsibility for the creation of the investment performance report;

- the investment performance reports are a fair and honest representation of the firm's investment performance;
- the documented procedures that the firm used to establish and maintain compliance throughout the entire period of the verification have been followed;
- the firm has provided the verifier with all necessary documents to be able to perform verification;
- the time period the verifiers are asked to report on; and
- that no significant events that would materially influence performance results have occurred up to the date when the verifier expresses an opinion.

Using the Work of Other Verifiers

The Standards state, at Section III.A.6, that a principal verifier may accept the work of a local or previous verifier as part of the basis for the principal verifier's opinion. For example, when a firm engaged in global asset management services undertakes verification for its claim of compliance on a worldwide basis, including local offices/branches, the principal verifier may use verification results already performed for a local office/branch by a local verifier. Similarly, when another verifier has already verified a part of the firm's historical performance record, the current verifier may accept the work of the previous verifier.

A principal verifier's opinion may state that it has relied upon other named verifiers' opinions in arriving at its overall opinion. If the opinion refers to other verifiers, the principal verifier cannot be held responsible for the opinion of the other verifiers. Should the investment management firm wish that responsibility to reside with the principal verifier, it should be included in the contract between the firm and the principal verifier. In such circumstances the principal verifier should undertake the due diligence it deems necessary to satisfy its own requirements.

Verification Report

The report must confirm the verifier's opinion on the following, as provided in Section III.A.4:

1. the firm has complied with all the composite construction requirements of the GIPS Standards on a firm-wide basis, and
2. the firm's processes and procedures are designed to calculate and present performance results in compliance with the GIPS standards.

Without such a report from the verifier, the firm cannot state that is claim of compliance with the GIPS standards has been verified.

The Standards do not specify any particular format for the verification report issued by verifiers, but a report generally includes the following information in addition to the verifier's opinion:

- the report title;
- the report date;
- the report addressee;
- the definition of the firm for which the verification has been performed;
- the period(s) for which the verification has been performed;
- the responsibility of the firm's management for the claim of compliance and that of the verifier;
- a statement to the effect that verification has been performed in accordance with the GIPS standards;
- any other details that should be mentioned; and
- the signature or official seal of the verifier.

If the verifier concludes that the firm is not in compliance with the GIPS standards or that the records of the firm cannot support a complete verification, the verifier must issue a statement to the firm clarifying why a verification report was not possible, as provided in Section III.A.5 of the Standards.

Detailed Examinations of Investment Performance Presentations

It should be noted that the purpose and scope of GIPS verification is to confirm that the firm has complied with all the composite construction requirements of the Standards on a firm-wide basis and the firm's performance measurement processes and procedures are designed to calculate and present performance results in compliance with the Standards on a firm-wide basis, and are not to be seen as an attempt to confirm the appropriateness of specific performance results presented.

An investment management firm may choose to have a more detailed and specifically-focused examination (or performance audit) of a specific composite presentation in addition to the verification provided in the Standards. A performance examination may be conducted at the discretion of the firm only in addition to the verification set forth in the Standards. Therefore, even if an investment management firm undertakes a performance examination, the firm cannot make a claim of verification unless the entire firm has been verified in accordance with the GIPS standards and has received a verification report from a verifier. A Guidance Statement for Performance Examinations is being developed to provide additional guidance on this subject.

When an investment management firm undertakes a performance examination of a specific composite in addition to the verification set forth in the Standards, the verifier naturally has to perform additional procedures to determine the appropriateness of the relevant composite performance presentation.

Effective Date

This Guidance Statement was originally effective 13 March 2002 and was revised to reflect the changes to the GIPS standards effective as of 1 January 2006.

Verification and investment management firms are encouraged, but not required, to apply this guidance prior to the original Effective Date of 13 March 2002; however, the original guidance must be applied to all presentations that include performance for periods on and after that date.

The revisions made to this guidance (effective 1 January 2006) must be applied to all presentations that include performance for periods after 31 December 2005.

Applications:

1. *Is verification of a firm's claim of compliance required?*

No. The GIPS standards currently recommend that firms have a verification performed by an independent third party. Verification is a firm-wide test of a firm's compliance with certain requirements of the GIPS standards.

It should be noted that the GIPS standards state the following: Verification is strongly encouraged and is expected to become mandatory at a future date. The issue of mandatory verification will be re-evaluated by 2010 and the industry will be provided sufficient time to implement any change.

2. *Can a verification be performed on a composite or on an individual account or fund within a composite?*

No, only a firm may be verified. A verification report is issued for a firm, not for a composite, fund or account. The Standards provide that a detailed performance examination can be performed on an individual composite either after or in conjunction with a firm-wide verification.

3. *A firm's management has decided to omit measures of dispersion from composite presentations due to the complexity of the calculations and the firm's verifiers have agreed to sign a verification report with an "except for" paragraph. The verifiers contend that as long as the presentations disclose why this data is omitted, that the composites are presented in compliance with the GIPS standards. Is this correct?*

No. Provision 5.A.1.d requires that a composite's performance presentation include a measure of dispersion of individual portfolio returns for each annual period presented. Only when the composite contains five or fewer portfolios for the full year is a measure of dispersion not required to be presented. Firms may not omit required information from a "GIPS compliant" presentation and remain "in compliance." Firms must be in compliance on a firm-wide basis and meet all the requirements of the Standards to claim compliance. Firms cannot state they are in compliance "except for" certain provisions. If a firm does not include all relevant required disclosures, as well as relevant presentation and reporting requirements in a composite presentation, the firm may not claim compliance with the GIPS standards and a verifier cannot issue a verification report.

4. *Our firm has been in compliance with the GIPS standards since 2000. We obtained a verification from an independent verifier which covered the periods from 1995 through 31 December 2002. At what point does our verification "expire"?*

It would be misleading for a firm to state that a verification has been performed without specifying the appropriate time period covered by the verification. If your firm makes reference to the verification in the disclosures to a composite presentation, unless all time periods presented have been verified, you must disclose which periods have been verified.

While a verification does not expire after a certain period of time, a firm should consider whether references to a verification that covers periods more than 24 months ago have the potential to be misleading.

5. *What requirements must a verifier meet in order to be able to perform a GIPS verification?*

Any third-party that is knowledgeable about the Standards, investment performance measurement, portfolio accounting, and investment management and is independent from the investment management firm may perform a verification; independent and knowledgeable are the key words. The Guidance Statement on Verifier Independence discusses in more detail the notion of independence. While firms are encouraged to conduct a "self-check" of their compliance, perhaps by their internal audit department, this would not constitute a verification: an investment management firm's internal audit department is not independent from the investment management firm.

Adoption Date:	**31 October 2005**
Effective Date:	**1 January 2006**
Retroactive Application:	**Not Required**
Public Comment Period:	**Oct 2004 - Feb 2005**

GUIDANCE STATEMENT ON VERIFIER INDEPENDENCE

Introduction

The GIPS standards define verification as the review of an investment management firm's performance measurement processes and procedures by an independent third-party "verifier," where the phrase "independent third-party" generally means that neither the verification firm (or verifier) nor the investment management firm (also known as a verification client) has a direct conflict of interest. A direct conflict of interest exists when an independence issue between the investment management firm and the verification firm cannot be managed effectively, i.e., the conflict is not "cured." The purpose of this Guidance Statement is to guide investment management firms and their (potential) verification firms in the process of determining if independence issues exist between them.

A verification firm is selected and appointed by the investment management firm; the investment management firm must retain the ultimate responsibility for the decisions made. The GIPS standards do not contain specific qualification requirements for a verifier, other than the verifier must be an independent third party. The self-regulatory nature of the GIPS standards necessitates a strong commitment to ethical integrity on the part of the investment management firm as well as the verification firm. Verification provides substantial benefit not only to the investment management firm whose policies and processes are verified, but also to the prospective investor relying on the performance information presented by the investment management firm.

This Guidance Statement serves as minimum guidance. It is not intended to replace or supersede any applicable independence guidance for a verification firm that is subject to its existing professional independence guidance. If any conflicts exist between this guidance and the verification firm's professional independence guidance, verification firms must follow their professional independence guidance and disclose the conflict to the investment management firm (verification client).

Defining Independent

Defining the term "independent" is not a simple process. Crucial to the verification process is the assumption by all interested parties that the verifier (for purposes of this document, used interchangeably with verification firm or verification unit (of a larger/parent firm)), performs its service in an unbiased manner and is not verifying its own work.

When considering a verification engagement, the investment management firm and the verification firm must determine any known independence issues existing between the two organizations. Both the investment management firm and the verification firm should create their own policies and procedures that address independence. As part of its evaluation process, each firm should consider policies and procedures used by the other organization to address independence. For example, if an investment management firm is contemplating hiring a verification firm which offers additional products and services that the investment management firm could or does utilize, the investment management firm must understand how the verification unit achieves independence within the parent organization as well as with the investment management firm. A verifier must disclose to the investment management firm the services known to the verifier that other units of the verification firm may be providing to the investment management firm. During the process of determining if any independence issues exist, both the investment management firm and the verification firm should be cognizant of actual (existing in fact) as well as perceived (potentially viewed as) independence issues. Each organization's self-examination of independence should always keep in mind the following question: If a prospective client of the investment management firm places reliance on the verification firm's report, could the prospective client's perception of the value of the verification report potentially be changed if the prospective client knew about other existing relationships between the investment management firm and the verification firm?

For verifiers that provide services in addition to verification services, it may prove difficult for the verification unit to identify other services (especially highly sensitive or confidential services) provided to the investment management firm by other units of the verification firm without input/notification from the investment management firm. However, the investment management firm itself may be aware of services being provided by other units of the verification firm to the investment management firm. The investment management firm must then be responsible for deciding whether a service provided by the verification firm – ***but unknown to its verification unit*** – results in an independence issue.

Potential independence issues must be disclosed by the verification firm and the investment management firm to each other. Additionally, because disclosure alone does not "cure" the independence issue, the firms must then determine if the identified independence issues can be managed such that independence is achieved. It may be helpful for both the verification firm and the investment management firm to consider independence as a continuum. At one extreme of the continuum is a verification firm with no relationships with the investment management firm. At the other extreme is a verification firm with existing relationships with the investment management firm, such that if the investment management firm's verification were performed by the verification firm, the independence issue could not be appropriately managed and independence not achieved. The investment management firm and the verification firm must determine where their relationship is on this continuum and if it is appropriate to proceed with the verification engagement.

The firms should document their conclusions. If the appointment of the verification firm by the investment management firm continues beyond the initial verification, the firms should reassess independence prior to each verification engagement.

Guiding Principles

- The verification firm and its employees must be independent from its verification clients;
- The verification firm must consider any independence guidance for their profession, if applicable;
- To the best of their ability, the verification firm and the verification client (investment management firm) must consider their entire relationship when analyzing potential independence issues;
- The verification firm has an obligation to discuss with the verification client their analysis of potential independence issues and how they will be managed;
- The verification firm and the verification client must reach a conclusion regarding the verification firm's independence;
- Determining independence is the responsibility of both the verification client and the verification firm; however, the verification client (investment management firm) must retain the ultimate responsibility for the decisions made; and,
- Verifiers must not:
  - step into a management role,
  - undertake any management function or a decision-making role relative to the implementation of and compliance with the GIPS standards, or
  - be in a position to verify their own work.

Assessment of Verifier Independence

In addition to verification services, verification firms may provide additional services and products to its verification clients. The verification firm must be cognizant of its role as advisor on issues relating to compliance with the GIPS standards, which may include being a performance measurer to the verification client prior to the verification. Potential independence issues should be mitigated; existing independence issues must be "cured." Because each situation is unique, the following are suggested considerations. While not definitive, these considerations are provided to assist verification firms to more precisely define the types of services and products that may result in a potential independence issue.

1. What services/products that a verification firm might provide to a verification client should be considered when determining their status with regard to independence?
2. Are there other issues a verification firm should consider when determining their status with regard to independence?

1. What services/products that a verification firm might provide to a verification client should be considered when determining their status with regard to independence?

A verification firm can provide consulting to a verification client, including both GIPS- and non-GIPS-related services. However, when the verification unit of the verification firm provides GIPS-related services, members of the verification unit must not step into a management role or undertake any management function. Further, the verification unit must not perform (or have performed in the past) any services which would result in their reporting on their own work product and decisions or calling their own work into question during the verification. While certain tasks may be outsourced to external service providers, responsibility for the fair representation and full disclosure of a performance presentation that adheres to the GIPS standards remains with the investment management firm.

Examples of services that, if performed by the verifier, may not create an independence issue include:

- Participating as an advisor to the compliance project management team;
- Participating in the identification of issues that hinder an investment management firm's compliance;
- Educating investment management firm personnel about the GIPS standards and the compliance process;
- Providing advice on compliance issues as they arise as long as the advice does not include making decisions on these issues for the investment management firm;
- Providing generic samples of client presentations;
- Providing compliance checklists;
- Providing formulas and calculation examples;
- Providing training on performance-related topics; and
- Reviewing results of performance-system conversion testing.

Examples of services that, if performed by the verifier, create or may create an independence issue include:

- Functioning as a member of the investment management firm's compliance project management team, with responsibility for performing management tasks (e.g., compositing portfolios, defining policies, etc.);
- Acting as the project manager for the investment management firm's compliance project management team, with management decision authority;
- Making decisions about compliance issues for the investment management firm. (The verifier should only offer suggestions and present options which the investment management firm may consider when making their decisions.);
- Creating source data for the calculation of performance returns;
- Providing templates for performance calculation, if the verification client does not assume full responsibility for the calculation methodology;
- Assigning accounts to composites;

- Collating or creating the underlying data required to calculate account-level returns;
- Calculating account-level returns;
- Calculating composite-level returns;
- Preparing compliant presentations;
- Establishing policies and procedures; and
- Functioning as a data warehouse for the performance data on behalf of the investment management firm. The verifier can maintain data duplicated for its own purposes but this data must not serve as the investment management firm's primary data source.

2. Are there other issues a verifier should consider when determining their status with regard to independence?

Other issues that are not directly related to verification services or GIPS compliance may impact a verifier's independence. For example, activities where the verification firm serves as an advocate for the verification client may impair independence. A verifier should consider their personal and financial relationships with their clients and consider whether they are, in fact, independent or could be influenced by such relationships. Mere disclosure of a personal or financial relationship does not "cure" the independence issue.

Effective Date

Verification and investment management firms must follow the principles discussed herein for all verification engagements commencing after 1 January 2006.

Applications:

1. *How much time and effort must the verification firm expend in order to identify all other services provided to a verification client?*

Both the verifier and the verification client need to expend such time as is reasonable for them to, independently and jointly, satisfy themselves that none of the **known** relationships between the two organizations will impair the independence of the verifier. This is a continuing joint obligation and does not just apply on the first appointment of the verifier.

From a practical point of view, the inclusion of the word "**known**" is an essential qualifier, as both the verifier and verification client may have a business relationship which is confidential to all but a selected few. For example, a verification firm may serve in an advisory role in a corporate acquisition/sale, which would not be disclosed under any circumstances to the employees involved with the verification appointment of either the investment firm or the verification firm.

2. *As defined in the Guidance Statement on Verifier Independence, what are "management functions?"*

In the context of this Guidance Statement, "management functions" are tasks and responsibilities that are directly related to the GIPS-compliance process. Management functions include, but are not limited to:

- Identifying all portfolios of the firm;
- Assigning accounts to composites;
- Determining firm definition;
- Determining discretion definition and/or status;
- Creating composite criteria;
- Establishing policies and procedures;
- Calculating account- and composite-level returns; and
- Preparing compliant composite presentations.

3. *Is there a formal process for reporting conflicts of interest?*

No, there is no formal process for reporting conflicts of interest. If a verifier determines that a conflict of interest prevents them from accepting a verification engagement or continuing to provide verification services to a client, the verification firm should inform the client immediately of such conflict. The verifier and the client should also discuss if a newly discovered conflict extends to historic periods, which may require that any previously issued verification reports be recalled, (i.e., the investment firm must cease making any claims of verification for the period the conflict existed). If, in the future, the investment management firm is verified for that period by an independent third-party, the investment management firm may again claim that it was verified for that period.

4. *If the verification firm provides a spreadsheet template to a verification client to help in the calculation of asset-weighted standard deviations for inclusion in a composite presentation, does that create an independence issue?*

Merely providing a spreadsheet template to a verification client that includes calculation examples does not automatically create an independence issue, as long as the client assumes full responsibility for the calculation methodology.

5. *Can a verification firm participate in the process of selecting a new performance measurement system for a verification client?*

Yes, as long as the verification firm's assistance is limited to making recommendations and suggestions, with the final decision being made solely by the verification client. The verification firm must not receive any monetary or non-monetary compensation from the systems providers for their review or recommendation.

6. *Can a verification firm participate in the process of implementing a new performance measurement system for a verification client?*

Yes, a verification firm may participate in the process of implementing a new performance measurement system for a verification client, but the verification firm must be careful to not undertake management functions. The verifier must **not** have final responsibility for data conversion and reconciliation functions.

7. *In addition to performing a firm-wide verification, our verifier also performs a Performance Examination on one composite. The Performance Examination report will include a compliant presentation for the one examined composite. Can the verifier produce the compliant presentation for this composite?*

The verifier may not assume the responsibility for creating or producing a composite presentation for the investment management firm. The investment management firm must first provide a compliant presentation to the verifier. Once the Performance Examination is completed (based on the composite presentation provided by the investment management firm), the verifier may reformat/redesign the data from the compliant presentation in a separate document to be provided to the investment firm as part of its Performance Examination Report. Simply performing word processing and duplication functions does not impact the verifier's independence.

8. *Our investment management firm has used the same verification firm for the last five years. We recently discovered that an employee of the verification firm is related to a portfolio manager our firm hired this year. Will our firm be able to continue to use the verification firm for our annual verification next year?*

Both firms must take measures to ensure that the verification firm's employee maintains independence if that employee is used for the investment management firm's verification. If the employee is not a member of the verification unit, there may not be an issue. However, if the employee is in charge of the verification project for the investment management firm and, for example, is the spouse of the recently-hired investment manager, the independence issues must be evaluated.

Adoption Date: 10 August 2005
Effective Date: 1 January 2006
Retroactive Application: Not Required
Public Comment Period: Oct - Dec 2004

GUIDANCE STATEMENT FOR WRAP FEE/SEPARATELY MANAGED ACCOUNT (SMA) PORTFOLIOS

8.A. Wrap Fee/SMA Performance Presentation and Reporting — Requirements

The following are additional requirements for firms to follow when presenting wrap fee/SMA performance to prospective wrap fee/SMA sponsors or wrap fee/SMA client prospects ("wrap fee/SMA prospect") and existing wrap fee/SMA sponsors or existing wrap fee/SMA clients ("wrap fee/SMA client") in compliance with the GIPS standards ("Standards").

8.A.1. For all wrap fee/SMA composite presentations that include periods prior to the composite containing an actual wrap fee/SMA portfolio, the firm must disclose, for each period presented, that the composite does not contain actual wrap fee/SMA portfolios (i.e., that 0% or none of the composite portfolios/assets are wrap fee/SMA portfolios).

8.A.2. The firm must include the performance record of actual wrap fee/SMA portfolios in appropriate composites in accordance with the firm's established portfolio inclusion policies. Once established, these composites (containing actual wrap fee/SMA portfolios) must be used in the firm's presentation to wrap fee/SMA prospects.

8.A.3. When firms present performance to a wrap fee/SMA prospect, the composite presented must include the performance of all appropriate, actual wrap fee/SMA portfolios, if any, managed with similar investment objectives and/or strategies, regardless of the wrap fee/SMA sponsor (resulting in a "style-defined composite").

8.A.4. When firms present performance to a wrap fee/SMA prospect, performance must be shown net of the entire wrap fee.

8.A.5. When firms present composite performance to an existing wrap fee/SMA sponsor, which includes only that sponsor's wrap fee/SMA portfolios (resulting in a "sponsor-specific composite"):

- Firms must disclose the name of the wrap fee/SMA sponsor represented by the sponsor-specific composite; and
- If the sponsor-specific composite presentation is intended for the purpose of generating wrap-fee business and does not include performance net of the entire wrap fee, the presentation must disclose that the named sponsor-specific presentation is only for the use of the named wrap fee/SMA sponsor.

Introduction

The purpose of the GIPS standards is to create performance presentations that allow for greater comparability of returns and increase the transparency of information provided to prospective clients. While it is impossible to develop standards that cover every situation, the GIPS standards provide a general framework that can be applied to many different circumstances. It is important to remember the underlying principles of the Standards: fair representation and full disclosure.

In order to provide prospective clients with a variety of investment options, investment management firms offer different types of investment products/services as well as fee structures. One of these structures offers clients the ability to "bundle" one or more fees incurred during the management of a portfolio (i.e., bundled fees). Bundled fees can include any combination of management, trading, custody, and other administrative fees. Two specific examples of bundled fees are the Wrap Fee and the All-In Fee (see Appendix B for definitions of these terms). Wrap fee/SMA[1] portfolios are unique and significantly different from traditional brokerage or investment management relationships and, as a result, additional guidance is necessary for firms managing wrap fee/SMA portfolios on how to apply the GIPS standards.

Application of the GIPS standards to Wrap Fee/SMA Portfolios

A number of complex issues relating to achieving fair representation and full disclosure exist for a wrap fee/SMA investment manager to calculate, maintain, and present performance results in compliance with the GIPS standards. These issues result in several challenges, which include:

- A single fee is charged by a "sponsor" for several combined services (e.g., advisory, trading, custody, and other services).
    - The investment management firm typically has no involvement in or knowledge of the total fee that is charged by the wrap fee/SMA sponsor to individual wrap fee/SMA clients. The investment management firm typically has knowledge of only the fees it receives for its investment management services.
    - The GIPS standards require investment management firms to deduct trading expenses from all performance. Because the total fee charged to wrap fee/SMA portfolios is determined by the sponsor, a wrap fee is difficult, if not impossible, for the investment management firm to separate into parts in order to identify which portion is attributable to a specific service (e.g., 20% of the wrap fee is attributable to custody fees, 60% of the wrap fee is attributable to management fees, 5% is attributable to trading costs, 5% is attributable to client reporting, etc.).

- The investment management firm typically does not have a direct relationship with the end user of its wrap fee/SMA investment management services, although these portfolios are considered discretionary assets of the investment management firm. Instead, multiple parties (at least an investment management firm, a broker or sponsor, and an end user) are involved in this business model, with the wrap fee/SMA sponsor serving as the intermediary between the investment management firm and the end user of the investment services.
    - Investment management firms must have records to support performance presented to satisfy law and regulations as well as the requirements of the GIPS standards; however, wrap fee/SMA sponsors typically maintain underlying portfolio records and investment management firms may not have access to those records.
    - The investment management firm provides investment performance presentations to wrap fee/SMA sponsors which may or may not be used by the wrap fee/SMA sponsor for presenting to wrap fee/SMA prospects.
    - The investment management firm provides investment performance and other information to prospective wrap fee/SMA sponsors that is used by the sponsor to evaluate the investment management firm. The wrap fee/SMA sponsor typically requires specific information from the investment management firm that may or may not comply with the GIPS standards.

[1]For purposes of this guidance, the combined term "wrap fee/SMA" is used to describe these relationships and portfolios.

Scope of Guidance Statement on Wrap Fee/SMA Performance

This Guidance Statement clarifies and interprets the broader GIPS provisions, specifically addressed from the perspective of the wrap fee/SMA investment management firm, and is applicable to those GIPS-compliant investment management firms which have discretionary portfolio management responsibility for wrap fee/SMA portfolios. This Guidance Statement is not applicable to those investment management firms that provide model portfolios to wrap fee/SMA sponsors, but have no discretionary portfolio management responsibility for individual wrap fee/SMA portfolios. Similarly, an overlay manager in a Multiple Strategy Portfolio (MSP) may also be excluded from this Guidance Statement if they do not have discretionary management. This Guidance Statement is only applicable to those firms that manage wrap fee/SMA portfolios; it is not applicable to those firms that manage portfolios defined as other types of Bundled Fee portfolios. (See Appendix B.)

While there are different types of wrap fee/SMA structures, this guidance is applicable to all wrap fee/SMA portfolios where the fees are bundled and the wrap fee/SMA sponsor serves as an intermediary between the investment management firm and the end user of the investment services. This guidance does not impose any specific, additional requirements for an investment management firm to monitor the use of their performance information once it has been provided to a third party; however, as in all situations where the performance information of the investment management firm is distributed by a third party, the firm should take appropriate measures to ensure that their performance is not misrepresented or used in a misleading fashion.

Key GIPS Provisions Specifically Applicable to Wrap Fee/SMA Performance

1.A. Input Data — Requirements

1.A.1. All data and information necessary to support a firm's performance presentation and to perform the required calculations must be captured and maintained.

2.A. Calculation Methodology — Requirements

2.A.5. All returns must be calculated after the deduction of the actual trading expenses incurred during the period. Estimated trading expenses are not permitted.

2.A.7. If the actual direct trading expenses cannot be identified and segregated from a bundled fee:

a. when calculating Gross-Of-Fees Returns, returns must be reduced by the entire Bundled Fee or the portion of the Bundled Fee that includes the direct Trading Expenses. The use of estimated trading expenses is not permitted.

b. when calculating Net-Of-Fees Returns, returns must be reduced by the entire bundled fee or the portion of the Bundled Fee that includes the direct Trading Expenses and the Investment Management Fee. The use of estimated trading expenses is not permitted.

3.A. Composite Construction — Requirements

3.A.2 Composites must be defined according to similar investment objectives and/or strategies. The full composite definition must be made available upon request.

4.A. Disclosures — Requirements

4.A.6. Firms must clearly label returns as Gross-Of-Fees or Net-Of-Fees.

4.A.12. Firms must disclose the fee schedule appropriate to the presentation.

4.A.13. If a composite contains portfolios with bundled fees, firms must disclose for each annual period shown the percentage of composite assets that is bundled fee portfolios.

4.A.14. If a composite contains portfolios with Bundled Fees, firms must disclose the various types of fees that are included in the bundled fee.

4.A.15. When presenting gross-of-fees returns, firms must disclose if any other fees are deducted in addition to the direct trading expenses.

4.A.16. When presenting net-of-fees returns, firms must disclose if any other fees are deducted in addition to the investment management fee and direct trading expenses.

Guiding Principles

It is important for investment management firms managing wrap fee/SMA portfolios to consider the following guiding principles when determining the manner in which to apply the GIPS standards to wrap fee/SMA portfolios:

- As specified in the GIPS standards (Introduction I.D.10.i.), firms are required to comply with all applicable local laws or regulations. This includes the laws and regulations relating to record keeping (e.g., having records to substantiate the performance record), which can be difficult to satisfy for some wrap fee/SMA investment management firms.
- The GIPS standards require the presentation of performance after the deduction of actual trading expenses. The wrap fee itself may be difficult to segregate into its component parts; however, the GIPS standards require the presentation of performance after the deduction of the actual trading expenses.
- Firms may wish to calculate performance history for presentation to wrap fee/SMA prospects using the gross-of-fees performance results for non-wrap fee/SMA portfolios managed to the same strategy reduced by the highest wrap fee applicable to that product. This performance history can be presented in compliance with the Standards since the performance of the investment strategy presented is based on actual assets under the firm's management and satisfies the underlying principles of fair representation and full disclosure.
- The firm must not exclude the performance of actual wrap fee/SMA portfolios when presenting performance to wrap fee/SMA prospects.

Definition of Firm

For purposes of claiming compliance, the GIPS standards define a firm as an investment firm, subsidiary or division held out to the public (clients or potential clients) as a distinct business entity. This entity is a unit, division, department, or office that is organizationally and functionally segregated from other units, divisions, departments, or offices, retains discretion over the assets it manages and should have autonomy over the investment decision-making process. Possible criteria that can be used to determine this include:

- Being a legal entity,
- Having a distinct market or client type (e.g., institutional, retail, private client, etc.),
- Using a separate and distinct investment process

Organizations that have both a non-wrap fee/SMA division (e.g., institutional, private client, mutual fund, etc.) and a wrap fee/SMA division should examine the alternatives for defining the firm according to the above definition. These alternatives apply both to organizations that are just entering into the investment management industry as well as to those that are simply expanding their operations to now incorporate wrap fee/SMA products.

There are benefits and drawbacks that must be considered for each alternative definition. Possible scenarios include:

1. *Define the Entire Organization as the Firm and the Firm Claims Compliance with the GIPS standards, or*
2. *Define the Divisions Separately with either*
   (a) *The Non-Wrap Fee/SMA Division and the Wrap-Fee /SMA Division are Defined as Separate Firms, and both claim compliance with the Standards, or*
   (b) *The Non-Wrap Fee/SMA Division and the Wrap-Fee /SMA Division are Defined as Separate Firms, and only one division claims compliance with the Standards*

1. *Define the Entire Organization as the Firm and the Firm Claims Compliance with the GIPS standards*

The Standards recommend that investment management firms adopt the broadest, most meaningful definition of the firm. If both the wrap fee/SMA and non-wrap fee/SMA divisions are held out to the public as one entity, in order to meet the objectives of fair representation and full disclosure, it is recommended that the entire organization, including both non-wrap fee/SMA and wrap fee/SMA divisions, be defined as the as the firm for purposes of compliance. The organization will likely benefit from this broad definition, since:

- Both the non-wrap fee/SMA and wrap fee/SMA portfolios are included in and increase the firm's total assets under management.
- The firm has the option to combine wrap fee/SMA and non-wrap fee/SMA portfolios managed to similar investment objectives and/or strategies in the same composite provided additional required calculations and disclosures are made.
- Prior to the firm acquiring actual wrap fee/SMA portfolios, the firm can use the historical, non-wrap fee/SMA gross-of-fees performance history, adjusted to deduct the highest total wrap fee charged to the end user by the wrap fee/SMA sponsor, in order to calculate a wrap fee/SMA performance history.

However, the firm should also consider the following potential disadvantage of defining the entire organization as the firm: If the firm includes wrap fee/SMA portfolios in a composite that is presented to clients other than wrap fee/SMA prospects or wrap fee/SMA clients, the firm must deduct the entire wrap fee from the performance of the wrap fee/SMA portfolios, unless the firm is able to identify and deduct either actual trading expenses charged to wrap fee/SMA portfolios or the portion of the wrap fee that includes actual trading expenses charged to wrap fee/SMA portfolios.

2. *Define the Divisions Separately*

Organizations that choose to hold the divisions out to the public as separate and distinct entities must define the divisions as separate firms for purposes of compliance. The claim of compliance with the Standards may be made solely by either division or both divisions may make the claim of compliance independent of the other. Firms claiming compliance with the Standards may not show assets or performance of another firm except as supplemental information to an appropriate compliant presentation of the firm.

It is possible that the divisions of an organization may not be organizationally and functionally separate or independent of each other, but because:

- their operations and functions are distinct within the organization, and
- the divisions are held out to the public as distinct entities,

the organization would be permitted to define one or both of the divisions as separate firms for purposes of compliance.

Underlying Records

Firms have options for satisfying GIPS provision 1.A.1. *"All data and information necessary to support a firm's performance presentation and to perform the required calculations must be captured and maintained."*

Some firms do not maintain or have access to the data necessary to substantiate portfolio-level performance. In order to satisfy the requirement of the GIPS standards, firms may choose to:

- Place reliance on the performance calculated and reported by the wrap fee/SMA sponsor. This can be done on either the aggregate level, effectively viewing the wrap fee/SMA sponsor as a single portfolio, or on the underlying wrap fee/SMA portfolio level. When relying on information provided by a third party (in this instance the wrap fee/SMA sponsor), the firm claiming compliance with the Standards must take the necessary steps to satisfy that the information provided by the wrap fee/SMA sponsor can be relied on to meet the requirements of the Standards.

- Utilize "shadow accounting"[2] to track the wrap fee/SMA portfolios on their in-house performance measurement systems.
- Exclude the wrap fee/SMA division from the definition of the firm (see above).

A firm claiming compliance with the Standards is responsible for its claim of compliance and is responsible, as well, for reporting information in compliance with the Standards to prospective clients. The firm must be sure that the performance provided by the wrap fee/SMA sponsor can be used by the firm to satisfy the requirements of the GIPS standards or the firm must maintain separate/duplicate records at the firm level (which meet the requirements of the Standards). Further, if the firm undertakes the verification process, the wrap fee/SMA portfolios are subject to the same level of testing as all other portfolios within the firm.

For periods beginning 1 January 2006, the firm must maintain or have access to supporting records for all portfolios included in a composite. The lack of records is not a reason to classify these portfolios as non-discretionary.

Constructing and Maintaining Composites for Wrap Fee/SMA Portfolios

While the same investment strategy can be employed by the investment management firm for wrap fee/SMA and non-wrap fee/SMA portfolios, the delivery of information about the strategy to the end user is what distinguishes wrap fee/SMA portfolios and necessitates additional guidance for creating and maintaining composites that include wrap fee/SMA portfolios.

In order for a firm claiming compliance with the GIPS standards to present results for a specific strategy to wrap fee/SMA prospects that the firm historically managed for only non-wrap fee/SMA portfolios, the firm must satisfy the following:

(1) the firm definition must include both the wrap fee/SMA and non-wrap fee/SMA assets,

(2) there were no wrap fee/SMA portfolios under management for the particular strategy during the time periods for which the firm compiles the wrap fee/SMA performance using only non-wrap fee/SMA portfolios, and

(3) for all wrap fee/SMA composite presentations that include periods prior to the composite containing an actual wrap fee/SMA portfolio, the firm must disclose, for each period presented, that the composite does not contain actual wrap fee/SMA portfolios (i.e., that 0% or none of the composite portfolios/assets are wrap fee/SMA portfolios). This disclosure will be used by the firm prior to the implementation of GIPS provision 4.A.13., which will be required once the composite contains a wrap fee/SMA portfolio.

The firm may calculate a wrap fee/SMA performance history for a specific strategy by using that strategy's gross-of-fees, non-wrap fee/SMA composite history reduced by the highest total wrap fee charged to the client (end user) by the wrap fee/SMA sponsor for the strategy (product), resulting in net-of-fees wrap fee/SMA performance.

It is up to the firm to determine the appropriate highest wrap fee to deduct. This highest wrap fee should be obtained from the prospective wrap fee/SMA sponsor and should be comparable for the investment style or strategy of the wrap fee/SMA composite. "Pure" gross-of-fees performance (i.e., gross of all expenses, including trading expenses) is only permitted as supplemental information to a compliant presentation. It is recognized that when starting with the gross-of-fees, non-wrap fee/SMA composite history, the gross-of-fees performance already reflects the deduction of actual trading expenses incurred. By then reducing the composite performance by the highest total wrap fee, which includes a portion attributable to trading expenses, performance will reflect the deduction of trad-

[2] "Shadow accounting" is considered the process of maintaining investment performance records for each account that enables an investment management firm to determine beginning and end of reporting period values and cash flows.

ing expenses two times (actual and portion of highest wrap fee). If the firm can identify the portion of the highest total wrap fee attributable to trading expenses, the firm may first calculate performance reflecting the deduction of both actual trading expenses and the highest wrap fee; the firm may then increase this result by the identifiable portion of the wrap fee attributable to trading expenses in order to compute a net-of-fees return.

Beyond building an initial track record for presentation to wrap fee/SMA prospects, the investment management firm must consider whether it will revise its wrap fee/SMA composite history as it accumulates an actual wrap fee/SMA performance record. Once a firm acquires one or more wrap fee/SMA portfolios for management, the firm must include the performance of the actual wrap fee/SMA portfolio(s) in an appropriate composite in accordance with the firm's established portfolio inclusion policies. The firm must determine if it will combine wrap fee/SMA portfolios in a composite with non-wrap fee/SMA portfolios with the same strategy, or if it will have separate composites for non-wrap fee/SMA portfolios.

The firm has three options to consider:

1. Keep the calculated history, redefine the composite to include only actual wrap fee/SMA portfolios going forward, and include relevant disclosures;
2. Continue to include the ongoing performance of the non-wrap fee/SMA portfolios and combine this with actual wrap fee/SMA portfolios; or,
3. Create a new composite to represent only actual wrap fee/SMA portfolios. The new composite will reflect a recent composite creation date. The non-wrap fee/SMA calculated composite will be discontinued, and must be shown as a discontinued composite on the firm's list of composites for at least five years after discontinuation.

The firm must not exclude the performance of actual wrap fee/SMA portfolios from the appropriate composite(s). When presenting wrap fee/SMA performance to wrap fee/SMA prospects, the firm must choose one of the three options listed above.

Firms must not redefine a composite on a retroactive basis, according to the ***Guidance Statement on Composite Definition.*** Once the firm includes non-wrap fee/SMA portfolios in the wrap fee/SMA composite history, the firm must not retroactively strip those portfolios out of the composite in order to create a "Wrap Fee/SMA Only" composite history.

Performance Presentation

Depending on the recipient of the presentation, the Standards have different requirements for presenting wrap fee/SMA performance results. Specifically, most wrap fee/SMA sponsors need different statistics and disclosures than retail investors. These differences result in separate requirements depending on the audience being presented the composite results. The investment management firm may provide its performance to wrap fee/SMA prospects to generate new business or may provide its performance to existing wrap fee/SMA sponsors to generate additional business.

Wrap Fee/SMA Results for Wrap Fee/SMA Prospects (the 1st time the firm presents performance to a wrap fee/SMA prospect to obtain new business)

When presenting performance to a wrap fee/SMA prospect, performance must be shown net-of-fees (i.e., the entire wrap fee). Firms may also present gross-of fees and/or "pure" gross-of-fees returns as additional and/or supplemental information.[3]

The GIPS standards require firms to define composites according to similar investment objectives and/or strategies. In order to facilitate the comparability of performance results and prevent firms from cherry-picking their best performing portfolios for presentation, investment management firms must group all appropriate wrap fee/SMA portfo-

[3]See the ***Guidance Statement on the Use of Supplemental Information*** at www.cfainstitute.org.

lios in a composite according to the same investment style or strategy (creating a style-defined composite) regardless of the wrap fee/SMA sponsor.[4] If the firm has no actual wrap fee/SMA portfolios under management for the specified strategy, this style-defined composite will be composed of only non-wrap fee/SMA portfolios managed to the specified strategy, using the gross-of-fees performance results reduced by the highest wrap fee applicable to that strategy.

Once the firm has actual wrap fee/SMA portfolios under management, the firm has two options for composite construction.

1. If the firm chooses to define its composites to include only actual wrap fee/SMA portfolios going forward, the style-defined composite will consist of portfolios from all wrap fee/SMA sponsors that are managed to the specified strategy.
2. If the firm chooses to continue to combine the ongoing performance of the non-wrap fee/SMA portfolios and actual wrap fee/SMA portfolios in the same composite, the style-defined composite will consist of the continuing non-wrap fee/SMA portfolios as well as all wrap fee/SMA portfolios managed to the specified strategy, regardless of the wrap fee/SMA sponsor.

Regardless of the firm's composite construction choice, this style-defined composite must be presented to wrap fee/SMA prospects in order to demonstrate a full and fair picture of the firm's ability to manage wrap fee/SMA portfolios in the defined style. Firms may choose to present additional and/or supplemental information demonstrating the firm's ability to manage portfolios for a specific wrap fee/SMA sponsor or group of wrap fee/SMA sponsors.

When an investment management firm that claims compliance with the GIPS standards prepares a performance report to be provided to prospective wrap fee/SMA clients (either directly by the investment management firm or through the wrap fee/SMA sponsor) performance must be prepared net-of-fees reflecting the actual wrap fee or the highest wrap fee charged to clients by the wrap fee/SMA sponsor. The investment management firm may prepare additional information as requested by the wrap fee/SMA sponsor consistent with the ethical principles of the Standards.

Wrap Fee/SMA Results for Existing Wrap Fee/SMA Sponsors For the Purpose of Generating Additional Business (once an agreement is established with a wrap fee/SMA sponsor)

When reporting performance to an **existing** wrap fee/SMA sponsor for the purpose of generating additional investment management business, the firm may choose whether to show returns on a gross-of-fees or net-of-fees basis. (Firms may also present "pure" gross-of-fees returns as supplemental information.) However, as described above, all presentations that are prepared by the investment management firm and will be provided to **prospective** wrap fee/SMA clients must be presented net-of-fees reflecting the actual wrap fee or the highest wrap fee charged to clients by the wrap fee/SMA sponsor.

When an investment management firm is reporting the performance of a wrap fee/SMA program to an existing wrap fee/SMA sponsor, there is a need to report how the firm has performed managing a particular program or "product" for that individual wrap fee/SMA sponsor. The investment management firm may report the performance of the composite that includes only the portfolios managed for that wrap fee/SMA sponsor. Similar to the concept of existing client reporting, an investment management firm may choose to create a smaller "composite" consisting only of the portfolios managed for the wrap fee/SMA sponsor in order to present to that sponsor the performance of their own wrap fee/SMA product. Provided all the requirements of the Standards are met on a firm-wide basis, the sponsor-specific "composite" presentation may include the claim of compliance. The investment management firm must reflect the name of the existing wrap fee/SMA spon-

[4]The Standards require firms to include all fee-paying discretionary portfolios in at least one composite. In this way, firms cannot "cherry-pick" their best performing portfolios to present to prospective clients.

sor in the sponsor-specific compliant presentation. Further, if the presentation does not include net-of-fees returns, the investment management firm must include a prominent disclosure stating that the sponsor-specific composite presentation is only for the use of the named wrap fee/SMA sponsor.

The Use of Aggregate Information

The use of aggregate information for performance and performance-related reporting purposes is permitted. A firm may choose to rely on and report aggregate information obtained from the wrap fee/SMA sponsor, effectively viewing the sponsor as a single portfolio. For example, at year-end, if a firm is managing 1,000 underlying wrap fee/SMA portfolios for one sponsor, and the firm effectively views the sponsor as a single portfolio, the firm may choose to report "1" or "≤5" for the number of portfolios in the composite. The Standards provide that the firm is not required to disclose the number of portfolios if there are five or fewer portfolios in the (wrap fee/SMA) composite.

Alternatively, the firm may chose to rely on the underlying portfolios of each sponsor, and the performance and performance-related information presented will reflect the individual wrap fee/SMA portfolios (end users). Using the example above, the firm will report "1000" for the number of portfolios in the composite.

Calculating Gross-of-Fee and Net-of-Fee Returns for Wrap Fee/SMA Composites

The Standards require that performance is to be calculated net of actual trading expenses. For wrap fee/SMA portfolios, this concept is not so easily applied, because the wrap fee itself may be difficult, if not impossible, to segregate into its component parts. In some cases, the actual fees charged to each wrap fee/SMA portfolio are not available. See examples of calculations in Appendix C.

Calculating Performance For Composites That Include Wrap Fee/SMA Portfolios To Be Presented To a Wrap Fee/SMA Prospect (the 1st time performance is shown to obtain new business)

When calculating performance to be presented to a wrap fee/SMA prospect, performance must be reduced by the entire wrap fee in order to compute a net-of-fees return. This reduction is applicable to all wrap fee/SMA portfolios in the composite as well as any non-wrap fee/SMA portfolios in the composite. The net-of-fees requirement for *Wrap Fee/SMA Prospects* is applicable regardless of whether the firm can determine the portion of the wrap fee that includes trading expenses.

Calculating Performance For Composites That Include Wrap Fee/SMA Portfolios To Be Presented To Existing Wrap Fee/SMA Sponsors For the Purpose of Generating Additional Business (once an agreement is established with a wrap fee/SMA sponsor)

When calculating performance to be presented to an existing wrap fee/SMA sponsor, performance can be calculated (and presented) either gross- or net-of-fees. These calculations can be difficult to compute for wrap fee/SMA portfolios because the wrap fee cannot be broken into its components.

Therefore, in cases where the trading expenses cannot be identified and segregated from a total wrap fee, either the entire wrap fee or the portion of the wrap fee containing the trading expenses must reduce the gross-of-fees and net-of-fees returns. In these cases, custody and other administrative fees might be included in (reduce) the gross-of-fees and net-of-fees returns. Firms may find that the gross-of-fees return is equal to the net-of-fees return.

If firms can identify these other fees and expenses, firms are permitted to add back any fees and expenses except for the trading expenses for gross-of-fees returns and any may add back any fees and expenses except for the trading expenses and investment management fees for net-of-fees returns.

In order to assist prospective clients and their understanding of the fees charged in these situations, when presenting gross-of-fees returns, firms must disclose if other fees are deducted in addition to the direct trading expenses. When presenting net-of-fees returns, firms must disclose if any other fees are deducted in addition to the investment management fee and trading expenses.

Calculating an Internal Risk Measure for a Wrap Fee/SMA Composite

The GIPS standards require all presentations to include a measure of dispersion of portfolio returns, considering only those portfolios that have been included in the composite for the full year. Firms are encouraged to maintain the individual (end user) portfolio-level returns, which will facilitate the computation of the required measure of dispersion (and number of portfolios within the composite).

An investment management firm may choose to view the aggregate performance information reported by a wrap fee/SMA sponsor as a single portfolio. This measure of dispersion considers the sponsor-level returns, not the portfolio-level returns that are consolidated in the sponsor-level returns. The Standards provide that the firm is not required to disclose a measure of composite dispersion if there are five or fewer portfolios in the (wrap fee/SMA) composite.

Supplemental/Additional Information

The GIPS standards recommend that firms present information that supplements the required compliant presentation that will assist clients to interpret the record. With regard to presenting wrap fee/SMA performance to wrap fee/SMA prospects, firms are required to show net-of-fees performance results; however, they are permitted to show "additional information" in the form of gross-of-fees results (i.e., reduced by trading expenses) as well as "supplemental information" in the form of "pure" gross-of-fees results (i.e., gross of all expenses, including trading expenses). See the Guidance Statement on the Use of Supplemental Information as well as the sample presentations provided in Appendix A.

Effective Date

The Effective Date of this Guidance Statement is 1 January 2006. Firms currently coming into compliance are encouraged to apply this guidance to all periods. Firms are also encouraged to apply this guidance prior to the effective date; however, this guidance must be applied for all performance periods beginning 1 January 2006.

For periods prior to the effective date of 1 January 2006, the firm may link non-compliant performance to their ongoing performance record, provided the firm discloses the periods of non-compliance and explains how the presentation is not in compliance with the GIPS standards. As with all aspects of complying with the GIPS standards, a firm must meet any regulatory requirements, including those related to recordkeeping.

Applications

1. *The Standards require the disclosure of a fee schedule that is appropriate to the presentation. As an investment management firm managing wrap fee/SMA portfolios, we maintain a fee schedule that is between us and the SMA sponsor. The SMA sponsor has a fee schedule that is between the SMA sponsor and the end client. Which fee schedule should be presented?*

In all instances, if the composite presentation will or may be presented to a prospective client that is an end user of investment management services, the appropriate fee schedule to present is the one that reflects the total wrap fee that will be charged by the SMA sponsor to the end user.

If the composite presentation is provided only to a prospective SMA sponsor (and will not be used to market to an end user), the fee schedule may reflect the investment management firm's portion of the total wrap fee (the fee schedule between the investment management firm and the SMA sponsor). Additional information about other fee schedules may be presented as supplemental information.

2. *When reporting performance to a specific wrap fee/SMA sponsor with whom our firm has entered into a sponsor agreement, we report the performance of that sponsor's portfo-*

lios (managed to the same strategy) since the inception of our relationship with the sponsor in a composite. May we link the performance of the sponsor-specific results to our historical, style-defined wrap fee/SMA composite track record, which includes the combined historical performance of all wrap fee/SMA portfolios managed in the same style, regardless of sponsor?

Yes, sponsor-specific wrap fee/SMA composite results may be linked to the historical performance of a style-defined composite (which could also include the performance of non-wrap fee/SMA portfolios managed in the same style reduced by the highest total wrap fee).

3. *When reporting performance to a wrap fee/ SMA prospect, may we present sponsor-specific composite performance from an existing wrap fee/SMA sponsor?*

When presenting performance to a wrap fee/SMA prospect, the firm must present a style-defined composite in order to demonstrate a full and fair picture of the firm's ability to manage all wrap fee/SMA portfolios in the defined style. Firms may choose to present additional and/or supplemental information demonstrating the firm's ability to manage portfolios for a specific wrap fee/SMA sponsor or group of wrap fee/SMA sponsors.

4. *Does this guidance mean we have to control how a wrap fee/SMA sponsor uses our firm's presentations? What if the sponsor delivers our sponsor-specific wrap fee/SMA gross-of-fees composite performance to a wrap fee/SMA prospect?*

No; this guidance does not impose any specific, additional requirements for an investment management firm to monitor the use of their performance information once it has been provided to the wrap fee/SMA sponsor; however, as in all situations where the performance information of the investment management firm is distributed by a third party, the firm should take appropriate measures to ensure that their performance is not misrepresented or used in a misleading fashion.

5. *Our firm manages both institutional and SMA portfolios. As of 1 January 2000, we began to claim compliance with the GIPS standards for our institutional portfolios. Given the guidance provided for wrap fee/SMA portfolios, we do not believe we can currently meet the requirements of the GIPS standards for our wrap fee/SMA portfolios. Can we continue to exclude our wrap fee/SMA portfolios from our GIPS-compliant firm, so we may continue to claim compliance for our institutional portfolios?*

The answer depends on how the firm holds itself out to the public. For purposes of claiming compliance, the GIPS standards define a firm as an investment firm, subsidiary or division held out to the public (clients or potential clients) as a distinct business entity. This entity is a unit, division, department, or office that is organizationally and functionally segregated from other units, divisions, departments, or offices and retains discretion over the assets it manages and should have autonomy over the investment decision-making process. Possible criteria that can be used to determine this include:

- Being a legal entity,
- Having a distinct market or client type (e.g., institutional, retail, private client, etc.),
- Using a separate and distinct investment process

In the situation described, provided the non-wrap fee/SMA division satisfies the definition of the firm guidance above, it is possible for the organization to separately define its institutional division as a distinct business entity that excludes its wrap fee/SMA division from its claim of compliance. This would not automatically jeopardize the organization's claim of compliance with the GIPS standards. If the non-wrap/SMA (institutional) portfolio managers also manage the wrap fee/SMA portfolios, this structure would not necessarily prevent the firms from being separately defined. The firm should consider that it may not show performance from the wrap fee/SMA division (except as supplemental information to its institutional track record). For more information on supplemental information, please review the *Guidance Statement on the Use of Supplemental Information*.

6. *We manage SMA portfolios for approximately 45 SMA sponsors. We are able to maintain satisfactory supporting records for 44 of those 45 SMA sponsors. For one SMA sponsor, we are not able to obtain what we consider to be adequate supporting records. We intend to exclude them from our firm's assets and definition of the firm, and claim compliance for the remainder of our SMA business (the other 44 SMA sponsors). Can we do so?*

The concept of compliance with the GIPS standards must be applied on a firm-wide basis. While there is some flexibility in defining a firm, an organization may not choose to exclude a portion of its assets from its firm definition simply because it cannot satisfy the recordkeeping requirements of the Standards.

That said, one troublesome wrap fee/SMA sponsor would not, in all cases, prevent the firm from claiming compliance. The firm should consider the records that are available for that wrap fee/SMA program and assess whether the firm can place reliance on the records that are maintained. In many instances, some records are available for all portfolios — such as trading records and summary information — regardless of wrap fee/SMA sponsor. Acknowledging that the level of detail may not be ideally what the firm would like to have, the firm may be able to determine that the minimal records available are enough to satisfy the firm's recordkeeping requirements, enabling it to meet the GIPS standards.

7. *Our firm currently manages wrap fee/SMA accounts. We will not be able to comply with the GIPS standards for SMA portfolios as of 1 January 2006. We believe we will be able to comply with GIPS for our SMA portfolios as of 1 January 2008. Can we begin to claim compliance with GIPS for our SMA portfolios as of 1 January 2008?*

Firms that manage SMA portfolios and wish to claim compliance with the GIPS standards must comply with the GIPS standards as of 1 January 2006, at a minimum. If the investment management firm is not able to claim compliance as of this date, they must wait until they have a minimum 5-year track record which complies with the GIPS requirements before claiming compliance.

8. *We manage small cap portfolios for three sponsors, using the same strategy. We place reliance on each sponsors' aggregate information effectively viewing each sponsor as a single portfolio. When reporting performance of the style-defined composite, how should we report number of accounts and the measure of internal dispersion?*

If the firm is relying on the three sponsors' aggregate information for disclosure and performance reporting purposes, the number of accounts could be reported either as 3 or five or fewer (≤ 5). The firm could report a measure of dispersion using the annual returns from each of the three sponsors, or could choose to not present the disclosure and report five or fewer portfolios (≤ 5) in the composite.

9. *I would like to present gross-of-fees returns for a sponsor-specific composite which contains only actual wrap fee/SMA portfolios to an existing wrap fee/SMA sponsor. I know the entire wrap fee (150 Basis Points) as well as the investment management fee (50 Basis Points) that is included in the wrap fee. This leaves the "portion of the bundled fee containing trading expenses" equal to 100 Basis Points. Can I add back the 50 basis points (investment management portion of the total wrap fee) to calculate a more accurate gross-of-fees return?*

The guidance provides that when calculating gross-of-fees performance for composites that include wrap fee/SMA portfolios to be presented only to existing wrap fee/SMA clients, firms may add back any fees and expenses they can identify within the wrap fee except for the trading expenses. When presenting gross-of-fees returns, the GIPS standards require firms to disclose if other fees are deducted in addition to the trading expenses. (See GIPS provision 4.A.15.) The investment management firm must also reflect the name of the existing wrap fee/SMA sponsor in the sponsor-specific compliant presentation. Further, if the presentation does not include net-of-fees returns, the investment management firm must include a prominent disclosure stating that the sponsor-specific composite presentation is only for the use of the named wrap fee/SMA sponsor.

In this situation, the firm should start with a net-of-fees performance return (which reflects or is reduced by the total wrap fee of 150 basis points). Because 50 basis points of the total 150 basis point wrap fee are attributable to the investment management fee, the remaining 100 basis points includes among other expenses, those directly attributable to trading expenses. The firm may add back the 50 basis point investment management fee to the net-of-fees performance results to compute a gross-of-fees performance return.

APPENDIX A

Sample 6 Investments
Large Cap SMA Composite
1 January 1993 through 31 December 2003

Year	Net Return (%)	"Pure" Gross Return* (%)	XYZ Index Return (%)	Internal Dispersion (%)	As of 31 December: Number of Portfolios	Composite Assets ($ millions)	% of Firm Assets (%)	% of SMA Portfolios
2003	13.89	16.42	15.99	0.7	1,834	2,125	14	100
2002	-16.77	-14.22	-21.51	1.1	1,730	2,130	15	100
2001	-12.00	-9.45	-11.71	1.0	1,631	2,141	14	100
2000	4.59	7.12	6.08	1.2	1,532	2,127	14	100
1999	11.63	14.22	12.75	0.9	1,428	2,116	11	100
1998	14.45	17.01	14.68	0.8	35	1,115	12	0
1997	25.48	28.02	29.98	1.0	32	1,110	13	0
1996	20.47	23.00	21.99	1.1	26	990	12	0
1995	38.39	41.01	37.01	0.9	24	975	15	0
1994	-2.67	-0.11	-0.62	0.8	18	870	14	0
1993	16.47	19.02	18.64	0.7	17	766	16	0

*Beginning 1 January 1999, "pure" gross-of-fees returns do not reflect the deduction of any expenses, including trading costs. "Pure" gross-of-fees returns are supplemental to net returns. See note 3.

Sample 6 Investments has prepared and presented this report in compliance with the Global Investment Performance Standards (GIPS®).

1. Sample 6 Investments is an independent investment advisor registered under the Investment Advisers Act of 1940.

2. Beginning 1 January 1999, the Large Cap SMA Composite (Composite) includes all separately managed (wrap) portfolios benchmarked to the XYZ Index. Performance results from 1993 through 1998 are those of the Large Cap Institutional Composite. The Composite was created in December 1998. A complete list and description of firm composites is available upon request.

3. Portfolio returns are calculated monthly, using the Modified Dietz method. Portfolios are revalued for any cash flow that exceeds 10% of the portfolio's market value. Pure gross returns from 1999 through 2003 do not reflect the deduction of any trading costs, fees or expenses. "Pure" gross returns from 1993 through 1998 reflect the deduction of trading costs. The SMA fee includes all charges for trading costs, portfolio management, custody, and other administrative fees. Net returns are calculated by subtracting the highest applicable SMA fee (2.50% on an annual basis, or 0.625% quarterly) on a quarterly basis from the gross Composite quarterly return. Monthly Composite returns are calculated by weighting each account's monthly return by its relative beginning market value. All returns are expressed in U.S. dollars. Additional information regarding policies for calculating and reporting returns is available upon request.

4. The XYZ Index returns are provided to represent the investment environment existing during the time periods shown. For comparison purposes, the index is fully invested and includes the reinvestment of income. The returns for the index do not include any trading costs, management fees or other costs.

5. The dispersion of annual returns is measured by the equal weighted standard deviation of portfolio returns represented within the Composite for the full year.

6. Past performance is not an indicator of future results. The standard fee schedule in effect is as follows: 2.50% on total assets.

Supplemental Information

Year	"Pure" Gross Return (%)	Net Return (%) Assuming 3% SMA Fees	Net Return (%) Assuming 2% SMA Fees
2003	16.42	13.45	14.39
2002	-14.22	-17.20	-16.19
2001	-9.45	-12.47	-11.44
2000	7.12	4.02	5.12
1999	14.22	11.11	12.12
1998	17.01	13.98	14.99
1997	28.02	24.95	26.03
1996	23.00	20.01	20.99
1995	41.01	37.99	39.02
1994	-0.11	-3.21	-2.10
1993	19.02	16.01	17.00

Sample 7 Asset Management Company
Small Cap SMA Composite
January 1, 1993 through December 31, 2004

					As of December 31		
Year	Net Return (%)	Small-Cap Index Return (%)	Internal Dispersion (%)	Number of Portfolios	Composite Assets ($ millions)	% of Firm Assets (%)	% of SMA portfolios
2004	10.0	8.9	0.8	583	1432	17	100
2003	-8.9	-15.4	0.7	573	1324	14	100
2002	6.7	7.6	1.1	563	1243	15	100
2001	-4.5	3.5	1.0	553	976	14	100
2000	11.0	2.6	1.2	503	890	14	100
1999	14.6	14.9	0.9	433	789	11	50
1998	-3.7	-7.3	0.8	333	654	12	40
1997	14.6	10.9	1.0	233	633	13	30
1996	19.1	14.3	1.1	133	300	12	25
1995	2.3	3.7	0.9	23	162	15	20
1994	-1.6	0.7	0.8	13	120	14	0
1993	12.7	13.4	0.7	3	25	16	0

Sample 7 Asset Management Company has prepared and presented this report in compliance with the Global Investment Performance Standards (GIPS®).

1. Sample 7 Asset Management Company is an independent investment advisor registered under the Investment Advisers Act of 1940.

2. Beginning January 1, 2000, the Small Cap SMA Composite (Composite) includes all separately managed (wrap) portfolios benchmarked to the XYZ Index and sponsored by Sparky Sponsor, Inc. Performance results from 1995 through 1999 are those of Sample 7's Small Cap Institutional Composite and small-cap wrap portfolios managed for Sparky Sponsor. Performance results from 1993 and 1994 are the Small Cap Institutional Composite. The Composite was created in August, 2000. A complete list and description of firm composites is available upon request.

3. Portfolio returns are calculated monthly, using the Modified Dietz method. Portfolios are revalued for any cash flow that exceeds 10% of the portfolio's market value. The SMA fee includes all charges for trading costs, portfolio management, custody, and other administrative fees. Net returns are calculated by subtracting the highest applicable SMA fee (2.50% on an annual basis, or 0.625% quarterly) on a quarterly basis from the gross quarterly return. Monthly Composite returns are calculated by weighting each account's monthly return by its relative beginning market value. All returns are expressed in U.S.

dollars. Additional information regarding policies for calculating and reporting returns is available upon request.

4. The XYZ Index returns are provided to represent the investment environment existing during the time periods shown. For comparison purposes, the index is fully invested and includes the reinvestment of income. The returns for the index do not include any trading costs, management fees or other costs.

5. The dispersion of annual returns is measured by the equal weighted standard deviation of portfolio returns represented within the Composite for the full year.

6. Past performance is not an indicator of future results. The standard fee schedule in effect is as follows: 2.50% on total assets.

APPENDIX B

Excerpt from GIPS Glossary:

Bundled Fee A fee that combines multiple fees into one "bundled" fee. Bundled Fees can include any combination of management, transaction, Custody, and other Administrative Fees. Two specific examples of Bundled Fees are the wrap fee and the all-in fee.

All-in Fee Due to the universal banking system in some countries, asset management, brokerage, and Custody are often part of the same company. This allows banks to offer a variety of choices to customers regarding how the fee will be charged. Customers are offered numerous different fee models in which fees may be bundled together or charged separately. All-in fees can include any combination of Investment Management, Trading Expenses, Custody, and other Administrative Fees.

Wrap Fee Wrap fees are specific to a particular investment product. The U.S. Securities and Exchange Commission (SEC) defines a wrap fee account (more commonly known as a Separately Managed Account) as "any advisory program under which a specified fee or fees not based upon transactions in a client's account is charged for investment advisory services (which may include portfolio management or advice concerning the selection of other investment advisers) and execution of client transactions". A typical separately managed account has a contract or contracts (and fee) involving a sponsor (usually a broker or independent provider) acting as the investment advisor, an investment management firm typically as the sub-advisor, other services (custody, consulting, reporting, performance, manager selection, monitoring, and execution of trades), distributor, and the client (brokerage customer). Wrap fees can be all-inclusive, asset-based fees (which may include any combination of management, transaction, custody, and other Administrative Fees).

APPENDIX C

Examples of Gross-of-Fees and Net-of-Fees Calculations

Non-Wrap	Presenting to Current Wrap Fee/SMA Sponsors and Clients (Can and choose to unbundle wrap fee)	Presenting to Prospective Wrap Fee/SMA Sponsors and Clients
Return on Assets – Trading Expenses	Return on Assets ("Pure Gross")** – Portion of Wrap Fee that includes Trading Expenses that can be segregated	Return on Assets ("Pure Gross")**
Gross-of-Fees Return – Investment Management Fee	**Gross-of-Fees Return** – Portion of Wrap Fee that includes IM Fee that can be segregated-	– Highest Wrap Fee Or – Actual Wrap Fee
Net-of-Fees Return – Administrative Fee	**Net-of-Fees Return** – Remaining portion of wrap fee (if any)	
Client Return*	Client Return*	**Gross-of-Fees Return and Net-of-Fees Return** and Client Return *

* The Client Return is not required by the GIPS standards and is presented here as additional information that may be helpful for existing clients.

** While the "pure gross" return is not required or recommended by the GIPS standards, it can be shown as supplemental information.

4-13

QUESTIONS AND ANSWERS ON THE REVISED GIPS STANDARDS (EFFECTIVE 1 JANUARY 2006)

Effective Dates and Implementation

1. We currently comply with the GIPS standards. Please explain when we must comply with the revised version of the GIPS standards (adopted February 2005).

A firm that claims compliance with the GIPS standards must comply with all of the requirements of the revised version of the GIPS standards by their effective date – 1 January 2006. Earlier adoption of the revised version of the GIPS standards is encouraged. All presentations that include performance results for periods after 31 December 2005 must meet all the requirements of the revised version of the GIPS standards. Performance presentations that include results only up to 31 December 2005 may be prepared in compliance with the previous version of the GIPS standards.

2. We have claimed compliance with the GIPS standards since 2000. Do we need to disclose which version of the GIPS standards we complied with, and for which periods?

The GIPS standards are not a static set of requirements and recommendations. The GIPS standards will evolve over time and are scheduled for revision every 5 years. However, the Standards will always be known as the "GIPS standards." There is no need to refer to which version of GIPS standards the firm has followed throughout time.

Reciprocity

3. We currently claim compliance with the AIMR-PPS standards and first claimed compliance in 1993. How do we take advantage of the historical reciprocity and claim compliance with the GIPS standards? Must we make any disclosures concerning our prior compliance with the AIMR-PPS standards?

No additional disclosures are required. Any firm that previously claimed compliance with an IPC-endorsed Country Version of GIPS (CVG) may consider CVG compliance to equal GIPS compliance for all periods prior to 31 December 2005. To continue to claim compliance with the GIPS standards a firm must comply with the revised version of the GIPS standards (February 2005) beginning 1 January 2006. Early adoption of the changes is encouraged.

4. We currently claim compliance with the AIMR-PPS standards. We will claim AIMR-PPS compliance until 31 December 2005, and will then claim compliance with the GIPS standards. We are planning to have our yearly verification done in March 2006. Should the verification report refer to compliance with the AIMR-PPS standards or the GIPS standards?

The verification report covering periods up to 31 December 2005 should make reference to the AIMR-PPS standards. Once the firm has claimed compliance with the GIPS standards under the reciprocity allowance for CVGs, the subsequent verification report should make reference to the GIPS standards.

5. We have been verified for compliance with the AIMR-PPS standards through 31 December 2004. We are planning to comply with the GIPS standards as of 1 July 2005. We are planning to have our yearly verification done in March 2006. Should the verification report refer to standards for all periods or to GIPS standards for some periods and AIMR-PPS standards for others?

Once a firm has taken advantage of the reciprocity allowance for CVGs, all future references should be to the GIPS standards, and not to the AIMR-PPS standards or another CVG.

6. We have complied with the AIMR-PPS standards since 1990 and have recently transitioned to complying with the revised GIPS standards. We make no reference to complying with the AIMR-PPS standards and only refer to the GIPS standards. Although the AIMR-PPS stan-

dards no longer exist, RFPs and others continue to ask whether we comply with the AIMR-PPS standards. How should we respond?

CFA Institute and the IPC continue to spread the word about the elimination of CVGs and the convergence to one global standard, the GIPS standards. However, some RFPs and other requests for information incorrectly continue to ask about CVG compliance and verification. If a firm previously claimed compliance with a CVG, they may respond that they are CVG compliant and verified (if true), solely for the purpose of responding to requests for information. The firm may not, unprompted, positively assert that they are in compliance with a CVG. The firm must also attempt to explain to the requestor why the questions concerning the CVG are incorrect.

7. *We have claimed compliance with the UK Investment Performance Standard and have a 7 year compliant track record. We intend to comply with the revised version of the GIPS standards as of 1 January 2006. Because the GIPS standards require an initial 5 year compliant track record, we plan to present only 5 years of history initially and claim compliance with the GIPS standards. May we do so?*

No. A firm that previously complied with a CVG is not permitted to eliminate previously reported CVG-compliant periods. Since the GIPS standards require firms to show five years of compliant track record building to ten years, the firm that previously complied with a CVG must continue to show their historical performance, building up to ten years, or since composite inception. In this specific example, the firm with 7 years compliant history must present all 7 years track history.

Specific Changes to GIPS Standards

8. *The upcoming release of the GIPS standards appears to have changed the options for defining a firm and the legal registration option is no longer available. Please explain how this change will affect firms that currently define themselves according to legal registration.*

The revised GIPS standards specify that firms must be defined according to how the firm, subsidiary, or division is held out and marketed to clients and should be a distinct business entity. It further clarifies in the glossary that a distinct business entity is a unit, division, department, or office that is organizationally and functionally segregated from other units, divisions, departments or offices and retains discretion over the assets it manages and should have autonomy over the investment decision-making process. It goes on to provide several criteria that should be considered when defining the firm. One of those criteria is how the firm is legally registered and defined. Other considerations include defining a firm by a distinct market or client type (e.g. institutional, retail, private client, etc.) or a separate and distinct investment process. In most cases, the change in the firm definition requirement will not affect how firms are defined. However, the change emphasizes that the key to defining a firm is how it is marketed and held out to the investing public.

9. *Please elaborate on the provision requiring firms to provide 'prospective clients' with a GIPS standards complaint presentation. Can we choose which potential clients to provide a compliant presentation?*

Once a firm claims compliance with the GIPS standards, it must present all potential clients with a presentation that complies with all the requirements of the Standards. This does not preclude the firm from showing additional and/or supplemental information to help the prospective client interpret the performance information. However, the firm may not pick and choose when to market their claim of compliance. Instead, this requirement ensures that once a firm represents to the investing public that it complies with the GIPS standards, it shows all prospective clients a compliant presentation.

10. *From time to time our firm does not have an appropriate composite that specifically meets the investment strategy a prospective client would like our firm to present. What information is our firm required to provide?*

If the firm does not have a composite appropriate to present to a prospective client, the firm is exempt from this requirement. However, the firm must disclose that it does not currently manage the specific style or strategy appropriate for the prospective client. The firm must be able to clearly demonstrate the strategies and investment products the firm currently manages and must make a list and description of all firm composites available to the prospective client. The firm is not prohibited from providing any information the prospective client specifically requests. Also, supplemental information can always be provided in addition to the firm's existing composites.

11. *Our firm manages private equity strategies and it is not clear how to provide a fee schedule appropriate to the composite. Fund-of-funds do not have their 'own' fee schedule, what are we required to provide?*

Within the fund-of-funds structure, there are two levels of fees. The fund-of-funds manager normally charges fees within the fund according to a schedule. This is the schedule that must be disclosed under the GIPS requirement. In addition, the underlying funds charge fees within their funds which vary according to the funds' strategy and size and include a performance element. These fees on underlying funds would be very difficult to separate out for a composite, but are fully taken into account in the fund-of-funds performance.

12. *Required disclosure 4.A.19 states a firm must disclose all significant events that would help a prospective client interpret the performance record. Please elaborate.*

Any and all events that impact the firm's operations and/or investment process (e.g., change in ownership, merger or acquisition, departure of key investment professional, etc.) are examples of events that must be disclosed.

13. *What information must we include in our GIPS-compliance policies and procedures?*

A firm must document all the policies and procedures it follows for meeting the requirements of the GIPS standards. Items that should be considered include, but are not limited to:

— criteria used to define the firm
— criteria for defining discretion
— valuation policies
— calculation methodologies
— how the firm handles large cash flows
— how it handles new and terminated portfolios
— policies for using a minimum portfolio size

14. *In the revised version of the GIPS standards, it states that some disclosures may not be required in all situations. Please elaborate.*

If a situation described in a disclosure requirement does not exist at a firm, or is not applicable to a specific composite, no disclosure is required. Not all disclosures are necessary for all firms, only those applicable specific to the firm. For example, the GIPS standards require that firms disclose if a composite's name has changed. When preparing a presentation for a composite that has not had a name change, no disclosure is needed with regard to this provision. The firm does not need to disclose that the composite has not changed names. No "negative assurance" language is needed for non-applicable disclosures.

15. *The GIPS standards and the GIPS Advertising Guidelines recommend that a firm disclose its verification status. Do you have suggested language?*

The GIPS standards recommend that firms undertake verification. A firm that has been verified may add a disclosure to composite presentations or advertisements stating that the firm has been verified. The firm must disclose the periods of verification if the composite presentation includes results for periods that have not been subject to firm-wide verification. The firm is not required to disclose the name of the verification firm. If the firm wishes to include the name of the verification firm, the firm should discuss this disclosure with their verifier. Sample disclosure language could be: "ABC Company has been verified for the periods from 1 January 1999 through 31 December 2004 by XYZ Verification Inc. A copy of the verification report is available upon request."

16. *We provide a compliant presentation to all prospective clients when we first meet with them. However, we often are in discussions with large prospective clients for many months, if not years. We send them updated composite information quarterly. Must the quarterly updates include all required disclosures?*

No. Provided the firm has given a compliant presentation to a prospective client within the past 12 months, the firm may present additional information that does not meet the requirements of the GIPS standards. A reference should be made that a composite presentation in compliance with the GIPS standards is available upon request. If the prospective client is receiving investment results for the first time, the presentation must meet the requirements of the Standards.

17. *Please explain the difference between a "description" and a "definition." For example, the GIPS standards now require firms to disclose the description of the composite being presented; however, there is a guidance statement outlining Composite Definition.*

A description is more abbreviated than a definition, but it includes key facts and salient features. A composite description includes the strategy for the composite and any special characteristics as to which portfolios are included in that composite. For example, a composite description might state "the Large Cap Composite includes all non-taxable portfolios with at least a 90% allocation to large cap stocks. We define large cap stocks as those securities with a capitalization of €5 billion or above." A composite definition would include additional factors concerning the characteristics of the portfolios included in the composite. Other factors might include the new portfolio inclusion policy, the closed portfolio exclusion policy, and the details concerning how large external cash flows are handled.

18. *We have five terminated composites on our list and description of composites. GIPS 0.A.13. says we have to provide a compliant presentation for any composite on the list, upon request. Does that include terminated composites?*

Yes. If requested, a firm must provide a compliant presentation for a terminated composite. One objective of the GIPS standards is to ensure the fair representation of a firm's investment performance track record. This includes not only currently managed strategies, but also those that the firm previously maintained.

19. *Please provide clarification concerning what is and is not considered an external cash flow.*

When considering a total portfolio, an external cash flow is a flow of cash and/or securities (capital additions or withdrawals) that is client initiated. Expense payments are also considered external cash flows. Income receipts are not cash flows. The "cash flow" may be defined by the firm as a single flow or an aggregate of a number of flows within a stated period of time. When considering sub-portfolios of a multiple asset portfolio, a manager-directed reallocation of assets between segments could also be considered an external cash flow for that segment.

20. *What factors should we consider when determining what is a large external cash flow?*

Instead of defining a specific percentage or dollar amount, the firm must determine in advance what is considered to be a large cash flow. The definition of "large" may be influenced by the characteristics of the asset class(es) within the strategy, such as asset market liquidity, market volatility, and/or by the trading capabilities of the investment manager.

21. *Please explain the difference between composite inception date and composite creation date.*

The composite creation date is the date on which the firm first groups the portfolios to create a composite. The composite inception date is the earliest date for which performance is reported for the composite - the initial date of the performance record.

22. *We do not include non-fee paying portfolios in our composites. Do we have to include non-fee-paying portfolios in our firm assets?*

All portfolios must be included in total firm assets. This includes both discretionary and non-discretionary portfolios, as well as fee-paying and non-fee paying portfolios.

23. Please clarify how to calculate the required internal dispersion measure.

The internal dispersion is a measure of the variability of portfolio-level returns for only those portfolios that are included in the composite for the full year. First, the firm must identify which portfolios were in the composite for the full year. Second, the firm must calculate the annual return for each of the portfolios that were included in the composite for the full year. The internal dispersion measure is then calculated using these portfolio-level annual returns. The specific measure of dispersion presented is a required disclosure. If the firm has five portfolios or less in a composite, a measure of dispersion is not required.

24. How do we determine what is considered a non-fee paying portfolio?

If a portfolio pays no management fee, it is considered a non-fee paying portfolio. Some firms may manage portfolios that have a minimal management fee that is meant to cover operating or transaction costs. If a portfolio has a very minor management fee which is not representative of a management fee a client portfolio would pay, the firm should consider such accounts as non-fee paying accounts.

PROPOSED GUIDANCE STATEMENT ON ERROR CORRECTION

The Investment Performance Council (IPC) and CFA Institute seek comment on the proposals set forth below regarding the addition of a GIPS Guidance Statement to address the correction of errors in performance-related information. For information on the Guidance Statement process, please see http://www.cfainstitute.org/standards/pps/process.html.

Comments must be submitted in writing and be received by CFA Institute no later than 28 February 2005. All comments and replies will be put on the public record unless specifically requested. It is preferable that comments be submitted in electronic form with settings that do not restrict the ability to 'cut-and-paste' text from the comment letter. Comments are also accepted in hardcopy and should be addressed to:

CFA Institute
CFA Centre for Financial Market Integrity
Reference: Guidance Statement on Error Correction
P.O. Box 3668
Charlottesville, Virginia 22903
Fax: 434-951-5320
E-mail: standardsetting@cfainstitute.org

Effective Date

This guidance statement will apply to all firms from the Effective Date forward. The proposed Adoption Date for this Guidance Statement is September 2005 and proposed Effective Date is 1 January 2006.

Executive Summary

The GIPS standards do not currently address the issue of accuracy; however, even with the tightest of controls, errors will occur. Firms that claim compliance with the Standards are faced with addressing situations where errors are discovered and specifically addressing the adjustments that should be made to prior period returns and previously reported GIPS-compliant presentations. Firms should consider the principles outlined in the Error Correction Guidance Statement when determining how to handle all types of errors.

Comment Requested

CFA Institute seeks public input on the proposals set forth in this document. Issues to consider in conjunction with this proposal include:

1. Do you support CFA Institute's effort to develop provisions to be added to the GIPS standards addressing the guidance of error correction?
2. Do you agree that the guidance should be applied to all types of errors?
3. Do you agree with firms not making retrospective changes to previously presented information?
4. Should the GIPS standards require firms to have documented policies and procedures for correcting errors?
5. Do you agree with the guiding principles provided to firms when determining how to handle errors?
6. Do you agree with the application questions and responses provided?

If commentators put forward other proposals, CFA Institute requests they explain how their proposals satisfy these objectives.

Proposed Adoption Date: September 2005
Proposed Effective Date: 1 January 2006
Retroactive Application: No
Public Comment Period: Oct 2004 – Feb 2005

PROPOSED GUIDANCE STATEMENT ON ERROR CORRECTION

Introduction

The GIPS standards do not currently specifically address the issue of accuracy; however, even with the tightest of controls, errors will occur. Firms that claim compliance with the Standards are faced with addressing situations where errors are discovered and specifically addressing the adjustments that should be made to prior period returns and previously reported GIPS-compliant presentations.

Background

Clearly, investment management firms use their portfolio accounting data as the basis for the rates of return they publish and report. Typically, prior to initiating the reporting cycle a reconciliation process is initiated against the "official books and records." These records are normally maintained by the custodian, who is responsible for the integrity of the data. In some instances, the investment management firm also serves as the custodian. In other instances, the investment management firm and custodian are hired separately by the client. In either instance, normal practice is to reconcile between the investment manager's and custodian's records, at least monthly, if not more frequently.

For a variety of reasons, reconciliation differences (errors) are discovered that could result in an erroneous calculation of the rate of return for a specific portfolio which in turn results in an error in the composite return. Errors can be caused by, but are not restricted to:

- *Missed trades:* Perhaps a trade was processed against the wrong account or wasn't correctly registered on either system.
- *Mishandling of corporate actions:* On occasion, a corporate action may have been missed completely or simply not processed correctly.
- *Missed cash flows*
- *Pricing problems:* A particular problem for securities that aren't actively traded or for which market prices aren't available and for which manual prices are entered.
- *Exchange rate problems*

Other types of errors include, but are not limited to:

- Incorrect allocation of portfolios to composites;
- Index returns, customized or externally published, presented incorrectly;
- Misstated composite assets, composite dispersion, or other disclosures, and/or presentation statistics.

Although this guidance statement is targeted to calculation errors, the concepts provided should be applied to all types of errors.

Once the investment management firm becomes aware of any error, they must decide what to do from a reporting standpoint. They must decide whether the firm should recalculate the previously reported performance and inform any and all recipients of the GIPS compliant presentation

This guidance statement is concerned only with error correction for GIPS compliant presentations; however, firms should consider whether they require similar controls for specific client reports.

Some firms will determine not to make retrospective changes to previously presented information:

- Often they don't want to inform current and prospective clients of retrospective changes. They feel this will suggest that the firm doesn't have the correct controls in place and that any adjustments will raise concerns about processing and the information about changes will have little benefit to the client. This response, however, is not justified. Clients need to be aware that there will be occasions when prior period results will change and should be pleased that the investment management firm is willing to go back and make the necessary adjustments to insure the highest quality and accuracy of reported data.
- The correction will have little or no impact on the previously reported numbers. Changes that may be considered "immaterial" may not be worth changing.
- The error will be captured and corrected in a subsequent reporting period. This may often occur; however, this will impact any risk statistics derived from performance returns, and valuation errors - particularly if cash flows have taken place - may result in a permanent change in performance that is not corrected in subsequent periods. Materiality should still be considered

Guiding Principles

The firm should consider the following Guiding Principles when determining how to handle errors:

- Develop written policies and procedures
- Proactively define materiality
- Develop and follow an error correction process

Written Policies and Procedures

Firms must have written policies and procedures on how they handle prior period adjustments. These policies should be strictly adhered to. The presence of administrative controls is of utmost importance, as they will help minimize the need to make adjustments.

Firms may decide it is appropriate to issue GIPS compliant presentations only after the reconciliation process is complete.

If presentations are published prior to reconciliation, they should carry notation such as "preliminary numbers; changes may occur as a result of reconciliation (or "subject to change")" to alert the recipients that the numbers haven't been finalized; however, firms are reminded that all GIPS requirements remain in force for preliminary presentations

The written policies and procedures should include guidance on how quickly errors should be reported, and to whom, and should also include a definition of materiality.

Definition of Materiality

A decision to change or notify recipients of errors should be linked to the materiality of the correction.

Firms must define on an ex ante basis the size and impact of an error that would require a restatement (i.e., adjustment to prior periods without republishing to prior recipients) or republishing of previously presented information.

The size and impact of the error defined may vary for different asset types (e.g., equities, fixed income, emerging markets), reporting periods (e.g., monthly, quarterly, or annual returns) and time periods (e.g., prior to a specific date, more than 5 years ago, or in a "frozen" time period).

Firms should disclose that their policies and procedures on error correction are available on request.

Erroneous disclosure notes may also require the firm to consider republishing compliant presentations.

Error Correction Process

A firm should strive to create an unambiguous process including specific steps followed to not only discover errors but also to correct errors and how that information will be disseminated to all interested parties. For example a simplistic process may include the following steps:

- Recalculate the returns.
- Determine if the error is material.
- Decide what action to take. Document the original figure, the corrected figure, and the action taken.

Reporting of errors (republishing) to prospective clients

All firms must have a policy and procedure in place to proactively report material corrected errors not only to their existing clients but to ANY prospective client that the firm believes relied upon the incorrect information, including consultants and verifiers. As mentioned above the firm's materiality threshold should determine whether the firm merely restates performance or if republishing is necessary. Republishing is defined as making certain that ANY prospective client that the firm believes relied upon the incorrect information is updated with the correct information; a disclosure must also be provided to ensure that the prospective client fully understands the change. Restating is defined as correcting the error but due to the lack of materiality there is no requirement to inform prospective clients.

Effective Date

This Guidance Statement is proposed to take effect 1 January 2006. Firms currently coming into compliance should apply this guidance to all periods. Firms are encouraged, but not required to apply this guidance prior to the Effective Date.

Applications:

1. *We recently determined that our total firm assets disclosure for the past two years has been incorrectly reported in our GIPS compliant presentations, but the rest of the information in our presentations is correct. Does this qualify as an error?*

The concept of correcting for an error applies to all information included in a compliant presentation and not simply the composite returns. If the amount of firm assets was misstated by a material amount, considering your firm's definition of materiality, you should treat this as the correction of an error and report the correction to those prospective clients that received the incorrect information.

2. *Our firm has claimed compliance with the GIPS standards for approximately 5 years. We have just taken a fresh look at our composite presentations and realized that we inadvertently excluded one of the required disclosures concerning the composite's creation date. We have corrected our presentations, and would like some guidance on whether a missing disclosure qualifies as an error.*

The lack of a required GIPS disclosure would be considered a material error. All firms must have a policy and procedure in place to proactively report corrected errors not only to their existing clients but to ANY prospective client that the firm believes relied upon the incorrect information, including consultants and verifiers.

3. *We realized that an account had been included in the wrong composite for the past 5 years. We have corrected the account's composite assignment and recalculated the composite's return and related disclosures. While the annual composite gross returns changed by an immaterial amount for each year, the composite's net annual returns changed quite a bit, as this account was a non-fee-paying account. Does this qualify as an error?*

PROPOSED

Firms must have written policies and procedures on how they handle prior period adjustments. Assuming the change in the composite's net annual returns is considered material — based on the firm's definition of materiality — the firm should treat this as the correction of an error and report the correction to those prospective clients that received the incorrect information.

Further, erroneous disclosure notes may also require the firm to consider republishing compliant presentations. The GIPS standards require firms to disclose whether non-fee-paying portfolios have been included in the composite and the percentage of composite assets that are non-fee-paying. Depending on whether the firm had other non-fee-paying portfolios in this composite, the firm would need to determine whether:

- the required GIPS disclosure was missing, which would result in a material error), or
- whether the disclosure was misstated which may or may not result in a material error.

4. *While undergoing our first verification, we noted that we had not consistently calculated asset weighted standard deviation for our internal risk measure. In two of the past 5 years we had calculated an equal weighted standard deviation. We intend to restate all amounts to reflect the asset weighted standard deviation. Does this qualify as an error?*

First, it is important to recognize the GIPS standards require firms to present "a measure of dispersion of individual component portfolio returns around the aggregate composite return." The GIPS standards do not specify that firms use a specific measure of dispersion and leave the choice of which measure to present up to the firm.

Depending on the firm's policy for handling error correction, there are many potential solutions to the above situation, two of which are: (1) If the restatement of the two years to an asset-weighted standard deviation measure did not result in a material change, the firm should restate the dispersion information on the performance presentation; or (2) If the restatement results in a material correction, the firm should republish the presentation, making certain that ANY prospective client that the firm believes relied upon the incorrect information is updated with the correct information. A disclosure must also be provided to ensure that the prospective client fully understands the change.

5. *We recently determined that our list and description of composites inadvertently excluded 5 of our cash management composites. We have supplied this list to hundreds of prospective clients over the past few years. Does this qualify as an error?*

Firms must have written policies and procedures on how they handle prior period adjustments. In the situation described, the omission of five of the firm's composites from the required list and description of firm composites is considered an error; however, the firm must determine whether this is considered a material error and necessitates further action (such as republishing the list to all prospective clients that relied on the incorrect information provided). The firm must evaluate their error correction policies and procedures to make a determination as to whether any further steps are necessary.

6. *Our firm had a software problem that went unnoticed for several months. We recently became aware of the issue and have corrected our composite returns and updated our presentations. We have attempted to identify everyone who received an incorrect GIPS compliant presentation and have provided updated presentations to them. However, we believe there may be others that we are not aware of, and/or may have obtained our presentations on the website. How do we handle this?*

Given that the firm has deemed this error "material" according to their policies and has decided to republish the presentation for all prospective clients that relied on the information, the firm should consider taking additional steps to ensure that clients that relied on the erroneous information are informed. The firm should include a disclosure on all presentations that indicates the presentation has been changed due to an error on a specified date and that the information provided may differ from previous presentations. This disclosure should remain on the presentation a minimum of twelve months.

PROPOSED GUIDANCE FOR PERFORMANCE EXAMINATIONS

The Investment Performance Council (IPC) and CFA Institute seek comment on the proposed Guidance Statement addressing Performance Examinations set forth below. For information on the Guidance Statement process, please see www.cfainstitute.org/standards/pps/process.html.

Comments must be submitted in writing and be received by CFA Institute no later than 31 December 2005. All comments and replies will be put on the public record unless it is specifically requested not to. It is preferable that comments be submitted in electronic form with settings that do not restrict the ability to 'cut-and-paste' text from the comment letter. Comments are also accepted in hardcopy and should be addressed to:

CFA Institute
CFA Centre for Financial Market Integrity
Reference: Guidance Statement on Verifier Independence
P.O. Box 3668
Charlottesville, Virginia 22903
Fax: 434-951-5320
E-mail: standardsetting@cfainstitute.org

Effective Date

This guidance statement will apply to all firms from the Effective Date forward. The proposed Adoption Date for this Guidance Statement is 1 March 2006 and the proposed Effective Date for this Guidance Statement is 1 April 2006.

Executive Summary

A verification of an investment firm's claim of compliance with GIPS provides substantial benefit not only to the investment management firm that has its policies and processes examined, but also to the prospective investor relying on the performance information.

In addition to a verification, investment firms may choose to have a more extensive, specifically focused examination (or performance audit) of a specific composite and its presentation by an independent third-party verifier, termed a Performance Examination (or Performance Audit) under the GIPS standards. It is a secondary level of testing that cannot be completed without a Verification. This Guidance Statement provides clarification on the processes to be followed for a GIPS Performance Examination.

After much discussion at the September 2004 IPC meeting, the Verification Subcommittee recommended that the IPC should attempt to standardize the procedures used for conducting Performance Examinations under the GIPS standards. The Subcommittee surveyed all Country Sponsors and discovered that certain parts of the industry demand GIPS Performance Examinations. Without guidance on what a Performance Examination entails, the quality and consistency of Performance Examinations vary widely.

Furthermore, the Subcommittee believed providing guidance would not create demand for Performance Examinations where it does not already exist. It would simply ensure the quality of the services already being provided. The IPC agreed with the approach and requested the Verification Subcommittee create a Guidance Statement for Performance Examinations.

It is neither a requirement nor a recommendation of the Standards that a composite have a performance examination.

It is important to understand that a verification tests firm-wide compliance with the composite construction requirements of the Standards as well as the design of firm-wide processes and procedures to calculate and present performance results in compliance with the Standards. The verification does not focus on single composites of the firm: it tests the implementation of processes and procedures specified at the firm-wide level. The

PROPOSED

Performance Examination is a specifically-focused examination of each element used in the specified composite's construction, calculation and presentation of performance.

Comment Requested

CFA Institute seeks public input on the proposals set forth in this document. Issues to consider in conjunction with this proposal include:

1. Do you agree with the scope and purpose of the Guidance Statement?
2. Do you agree with the processes established in the Guidance Statement?
3. Are there other elements involved in a performance examination that are not included?
4. Do you agree with the Applications?
5. Do you agree with the proposed Effective Date?

If commentators suggest other proposals, CFA Institute requests that they explain the rationale behind their proposal.

Proposed Adoption Date: 1 March 2006
Proposed Effective Date: 1 April 2006
Retroactive Application: Not Required
Public Comment Period: Nov-Dec 2005

PROPOSED GUIDANCE FOR PERFORMANCE EXAMINATIONS

Introduction

Separate from a Verification as defined in the GIPS standards, a firm may choose to have a detailed examination of any of its composites. This further, more extensive, specifically focused examination (or performance audit) of a specific composite and its presentation by an independent third-party verifier is termed a Performance Examination (or Performance Audit) under the GIPS standards. The Performance Examination may be performed concurrently with or upon completion of a Verification. Examinations of this type are unlikely to become a requirement of the Standards or become mandatory. However, certain parts of the investment industry demand composite-specific examinations to provide additional and specific assurance that a specific composite has been calculated and presented in accordance with the GIPS standards. In order to ensure consistency of the procedures that should be followed for a GIPS Performance Examination, the following guidance has been developed.

Scope and Purpose of Performance Examination

1. A Performance Examination is the review of a specific composite by an independent third-party verifier. A Performance Examination tests, for a specific composite:
    - A. Whether the firm has constructed and calculated the composite in compliance with the GIPS standards, and
    - B. Whether the firm presents the composite in compliance with the GIPS standards.

A Performance Examination Report is issued only with respect to the single composite examined by the verifier and does not attest to the accuracy of a performance presentation for any other composite.

2. A Performance Examination requires that:
    - A. The investment firm has a Verification Report(s) stating that the firm has complied with all the composite construction requirements of the GIPS standards on a firm-wide basis, and the firm's processes and procedures are designed to calculate and present performance results in compliance with the GIPS standards for a specified time period(s).
        - i. A principal verifier may accept the work of a local or previous verifier as part of the basis for satisfying that a firm has previously received a Verification Report. The verifier must use discretion when placing reliance on others' Verification Reports.
        - ii. It is expected that the time periods covered by the firm's Verification Report(s) includes the Performance Examination time period. If the firm has a Performance Examination performed concurrently with a Verification, and the period covered for the Performance Examination is within the ongoing Verification, the Performance Examination report may not be issued prior to the Verification Report.

iii. If the firm's Verification Report(s) does not include a time period to be covered in the Performance Examination, the Performance Examination may not include any time periods extending beyond twelve (12) months of the end date of the most recent time period covered by a Verification Report. This situation is expected to be an unusual, infrequently-occurring situation (for example, at the specific request of a client of the investment firm) and is not expected to be an ongoing practice at the firm.

B. The verifier performs procedures to confirm that the specific composite being examined has been constructed, calculated and presented in compliance with the GIPS standards.

3. A Performance Examination Report must include the following information:
   A. The report is for a Performance Examination of the named composite.
   B. The time period covered by the report.
   C. The verifier completed the Performance Examination in accordance with the GIPS Guidance for Performance Examinations.
   D. The verifier's opinion that the composite presentation is in compliance with the GIPS standards.
   E. If the Performance Examination extends beyond the most recent time period covered by a Verification Report

Without the Performance Examination Report from the verifier, the firm cannot state that the composite has been examined with respect to the GIPS standards. The underlying composite presentation examined is to be part of or attached to the Performance Examination Report.

4. After completing the Performance Examination procedures, the verifier may conclude that the presentation does not comply with the GIPS standards or that the records of the firm cannot support the composite's construction or calculation methodologies. In such situations, the verifier must provide to the investment management firm the reason(s) why it was not possible to provide a Performance Examination report. The verifier and the investment management firm must also consider the impact on total firm compliance of the verifier's inability to provide the Performance Examination report.

Procedures for Performance Examinations

When conducting a Performance Examination of a specific composite presentation, the verifier should consider the following presumptions, bearing in mind that they are not mutually exclusive and may be subject to important exceptions:

- Information obtained from independent sources outside the client firm provides greater assurance than information secured solely from within the client firm.

- Information obtained from the verifier's direct personal knowledge (such as through tangible documentation, observation, computation, operating tests, or inspection) is more persuasive than information obtained indirectly.

- The more effective the controls over the subject matter, the more assurance they provide about the subject matter or the assertion.

In performing a Performance Examination, the verifier's objective is to accumulate sufficient evidence and perform appropriate procedures such that the risk of not detecting errors in the composite presentation during the examination is mitigated to an acceptably low level of risk.

The extent to which the examination procedures will be performed should be based on the verifier's consideration of

a) the nature and materiality of the information to be tested,
b) the likelihood of misstatements,

c) knowledge obtained during current and previous engagements,
d) the extent to which the information is affected by judgment, and
e) inadequacies in the underlying data.

Required Performance Examination Procedures

The following are the minimum procedures required when conducting a performance examination. Verifiers must follow these procedures prior to issuing a Performance Examination Report to the firm.

Pre-Performance Examination Procedures (if not fulfilled during Pre-Verification Procedures):

1. Knowledge of the Firm: Verifiers must obtain the relevant Verification Report(s) and the Composite Presentation(s) to be examined, as well as any other available information regarding the firm to ensure appropriate knowledge of the firm.
2. Knowledge of the GIPS standards: Verifiers must understand all the requirements and recommendations of the GIPS standards.
3. Knowledge of applicable country-specific laws and regulations for Performance Standards: Verifiers must be knowledgeable of country-specific laws and regulations applicable to the firm and must determine any differences between the GIPS standards and the country-specific laws and regulations.
4. Knowledge of Firm Policies: Verifiers must obtain the firm's policies and procedures used for the composite when establishing and maintaining compliance during the period to be examined.

Performance Examination Procedures:

1. *Sample Account Selection:* Objective: to ensure the proper accounts are included in the examined composite. Verifiers may check compliance with the GIPS standards using a selected sample of the composite's accounts.
   A. Obtain a list of open and closed accounts for the composite for the years under examination and ensure composite inclusion policies and procedures were appropriately implemented;
   B. Ensure the composite includes all accounts that meet the definition of the composite for the years under examination; and
   C. Consider the following criteria when selecting the sample accounts for examination:
      - number of accounts in the composite,
      - strategy of the composite
      - total assets of the composite relative to total firm assets
      - internal control structure at the firm
      - number of years under examination
      - use of technology and external service providers
2. *Cash Flows:* Objective: to determine whether capital contributions and withdrawals:
   A. are recorded in the proper accounts,
   B. at the right amounts, and
   C. on a timely basis, consistent with the established policies.

The following procedures should be considered and performed at a level such that the verifier is satisfied that:

- cash flows reflect appropriate supporting documentation, such as custody statements or internal records,
- contributions or withdrawals of securities reflect proper valuation and timely recording, and

PROPOSED

- the methods used to account for cash flows, contributions, and withdrawals are reasonable and consistently applied.

3. *Income and Expenses:* Objective: to determine that income and expenses are:

   A. recorded in the proper accounts,
   B. at the right amounts, and
   C. on a timely basis.

The following procedures should be considered and performed at a level such that the verifier is satisfied that:

- income and expenses reflect supporting documentation such as custody statements,
- the methods used to record income and expenses are reasonable and consistently applied, and
- the calculation and use of accrued income is reasonable and appropriate.

4. *Portfolio Trade Processing:* Objective: to determine that purchases and sales of securities have been:

   A. recorded in the proper accounts,
   B. at the correct amounts, and
   C. on the appropriate dates.

The following procedures should be considered and performed at a level such that the verifier is satisfied that:

- trading activity is supported by documentation such as custody statements,
- end-of-period portfolio positions are supported by documentation such as custody statements, and
- the portfolio trade processing processes and procedures are reasonable.

5. *Portfolio Valuation:* Objective: to determine whether the end-of-period valuations of security positions are:

   A. appropriate, and
   B. that valuation policies are consistently applied.

The following procedures should be considered and performed at a level such that the verifier is satisfied that:

- end-of-period security valuations are supported by an independent pricing source,
- foreign currency exchange rates are supported by an independent pricing source, and
- the portfolio valuation methodologies are reasonable.

6. *Performance Measurement Calculation:* Objective: to determine that the returns have been calculated in accordance with the requirements contained in the GIPS standards on a consistent basis.

The following procedures should be considered and performed at a level such that the verifier is satisfied that:

A. computations of account returns use appropriate return calculations, as specified in the Standards,
B. computations of the composite's returns use the appropriate asset-weighted return calculations, and
C. application of the performance measurement calculation at both the account and composite levels presents performance fairly and is consistently applied as defined within the requirements of the Standards.

7. *Disclosures and Data:* Objective: to determine whether all required disclosures and data:

    A. have been properly presented in the examined composite's performance presentation, and
    B. are appropriately supported by available documentation.

The following procedures should be considered and performed at a level such that the verifier is satisfied that:

- all of the required disclosure requirements and presentation of required data have been adequately satisfied,
- tests of required calculations are performed as deemed necessary. These tests could involve agreeing to supporting documentation, analytical procedures, recomputations, or inquiry as appropriate, and
- the application and inclusion of the required disclosures and data are appropriate, reasonable and consistent.

8. *Maintenance of Records:* The verifier must maintain sufficient information to support the performance examination report.

Prior to issuing the Performance Examination report, the verifier must obtain a representation letter from the client firm confirming that the composite being examined, and its accompanying presentation, has been calculated and presented in accordance with the GIPS standards. The management representation letter should also confirm any other specific representations made to the verifier during the examination.

Effective Date

All firms choosing to have a performance examination of a specific composite on or after 1 April 2006 must apply this guidance. This guidance must be applied to all performance examinations commencing on and after 1 April 2006. If firms have had a performance examination on a composite prior to 1 April 2006, firms are not required to have the composite reexamined using this guidance: retroactive application of this guidance is not required.

Applications:

1. *Our most recent firm-wide verification covered the period from 1 January 2000 through 31 December 2004. A prospective client requested that the firm have a performance examination on one composite, the Large Cap Composite, for the period from 1 January 2000 through 30 June 2005. Must the firm-wide verification report be updated through 30 June 2005 before the performance examination for the Large Cap Composite can be completed?*

It would be expected that the periods covered by a verification be consistent with the periods covered by the performance examination. However, there are circumstances where a performance examination could cover longer periods. Both the firm and the verifier would need to consider the firm's policies and procedures, including the controls surrounding the application of those policies and procedures to future periods. The verifier may conclude that they can issue a performance examination report for a longer period, which must not exceed twelve months.

2. *Our firm recently completed our annual verification and then hired a different verification firm to conduct performance examinations on selected composites. During the verification, several issues were identified that might be important for the performance examination verifier to know. What is our responsibility to report such information?*

It is the responsibility of the investment firm to fully disclose any information that might impact the work of the verifier who is performing the performance examinations. Although permitted by the Standards, it is not required that the principal verifier accept the work of a previous verifier as part of the basis of the firm's opinion for the performance examinations. Investment firms should carefully consider the costs and consequences of having different verifiers perform the verification and the performance examinations.

P R O P O S E D

3. *We are a verification firm and we have been hired to conduct a GIPS verification for Acme Asset Manager. In addition to the verification, we have also been hired to conduct a performance examination on the Large Cap Composite. What language must be included in our performance examination report?*

There are several options, but a commonly used report makes reference to both the firm-wide verification and the performance examination. The firm could consider using the language provided in the following sample report, and should also add references to any professional standards.

Acme Asset Manager
20 Main Street
Small Town, USA

We have verified whether Acme Asset Manager Inc. (the Company)

(1) complied with all the composite construction requirements of the Global Investment Performance Standards (GIPS®) on a firm-wide basis for the periods from 1 January 2000 through 31 December 2004 and

(2) designed its processes and procedures to calculate and present performance results in compliance with the GIPS standards as of 31 December 2004.

We have also performed a performance examination of the Company's Acme Large Cap Composite for the periods from 1 January 2000 through 31 December 2004. The Company's management is responsible for compliance with the GIPS standards and the design of its processes and procedures and for the Acme Large Cap Composite's performance presentation. Our responsibility is to express an opinion based on our verification and performance examination.

We completed this verification in accordance with the verification procedures set forth in the GIPS standards. We completed this performance examination in accordance with the performance examination procedures set forth in the *GIPS Guidance Statement on Performance Examinations.*

In our opinion, Acme Asset Manager Inc. has, in all material respects:

- Complied with all the composite construction requirements of the GIPS standards on a firm-wide basis for the periods from 1 January 2000 through 31 December 2004, and

- Designed its processes and procedures to calculate and present performance results in compliance with the GIPS standards as of 31 December 2004.

Also, in our opinion, the accompanying performance presentation of the Company's Acme Large Cap Composite for the periods from 1 January 2000 through 31 December 2004 is presented, in all material respects, in compliance with the GIPS standards.

This report does not attest to the accuracy of any composite presentation of the Company other than the Company's Acme Large Cap Value Equity Composite.

Value Verification Company
15 March 2005

PROPOSED GUIDANCE STATEMENT ON PORTFOLIO RECORDKEEPING REQUIREMENTS

The Investment Performance Council (IPC) and CFA Institute seek comment on the proposed GIPS Guidance Statement addressing Portfolio Recordkeeping Requirements set forth below. For information on the Guidance Statement process, please see www.cfainstitute.org/standards/pps/process.html.

Comments must be submitted in writing and be received by CFA Institute no later than 31 December, 2004. All comments and replies will be put on the public record unless specifically requested. It is preferable that comments be submitted in electronic form with settings that do not restrict the ability to 'cut-and-paste' text from the comment letter. Comments are also accepted in hardcopy and should be addressed to:

CFA Institute
CFA Centre for Financial Market Integrity
Reference: Guidance Statement on Portfolio Recordkeeping Requirements
P.O. Box 3668
Charlottesville, Virginia 22903
Fax: 434-951-5320
E-mail: standardsetting@cfainstitute.org

Effective Date

This guidance statement will apply to all firms from the Effective Date forward. The proposed Adoption Date for this Guidance Statement is June 2005 and proposed Effective Date is 1 January 2006.

Executive Summary

This guidance relates only to records necessary to satisfy the recordkeeping requirements of the GIPS standards. In all instances, either paper (hard-copy) records or electronically stored records will suffice. If records are stored electronically, the records must be easily accessible and printable if needed. Although most firms are looking for a very precise list of the minimum supporting evidence that must be maintained in order to be able to recreate the firm's performance history, there is not a single list of records that will suffice in all situations.

Comment Requested

CFA Institute seeks public input on the proposals set forth in this document. Issues to consider in conjunction with this proposal include:

1. Do you agree with the principles established in the Guidance Statement?
2. Are there other elements involved in portfolio recordkeeping that are not included?
3. Do you agree with the guiding principles provided to firms when determining which records are necessary to support their performance track record?
4. Do you agree with the proposed Effective Date?

If commentators suggest other proposals, CFA Institute requests that they explain the rationale behind their proposal.

P R O P O S E D

Proposed Adoption Date: June 2005
Proposed Effective Date: 1 January 2006
Retroactive Application: No
Public Comment Period: Oct – Dec 2004

PROPOSED GUIDANCE STATEMENT ON PORTFOLIO RECORDKEEPING REQUIREMENTS

Introduction

The following guidance relates only to records necessary to satisfy the recordkeeping requirements of the GIPS standards. In all instances, either paper (hard-copy) records or electronically stored records will suffice. If records are stored electronically, the records must be easily accessible and printable if needed. Although most firms are looking for a very precise list of the minimum supporting evidence that must be maintained in order to be able to recreate the firm's performance history, there is not a single list of records that will suffice in all situations.

GIPS provision 1.A.1 states "All data and information necessary to support a firm's performance presentation and to perform the required calculations must be captured and maintained."

Guiding Principles

1. Above all else, a firm must meet any and all regulatory requirements concerning records that must be maintained.
2. A firm must maintain sufficient records that allow for the recalculation of account-level returns. Depending on the system and methods used for calculating account-level returns, one firm may need different records than another. For each period, records to support those returns might include a combination of the following (this list is not meant to be an exhaustive list):
    - Associated bank/custodial statements and reconciliations.
    - Investment portfolio listing and valuations, including pricing calculations for non-market traded or illiquid securities
    - Portfolio transactions reports
    - Outstanding trade reports
    - Corporate action reports
    - Income received/earned reports
    - Accrued income reports
    - Tax reclaim reports
    - Cash flow/weighted cash flow reports
    - Fee information
3. A firm must maintain records that allow for the recalculation of composite-level returns. For each period, records to support those returns must include
    - The accounts that are included in the composite;
    - When each portfolio entered (and/or exited) the composite;
    - The portfolio performance return for each account;
    - The market value used to weight each account (BMV or BMV plus weighted cash flows);
    - Fee information, if model fees are used;

4. A firm must maintain records to support why an account was assigned to a specific composite, or was excluded from all composites. Supporting records might include:
    - Investment management agreements and amendments thereto;
    - Email/other correspondence with clients regarding investment management strategy amendments

5. A firm must maintain records to support their claim of compliance on a firm-wide basis. Information should be maintained to establish:
    - Total firm assets under management
    - Excluded accounts (non-discretionary, e.g.)
    - Complete list and description of the firm's composites;
    - Compliant presentations, and supporting information for all composites

6. A firm should maintain all policies and procedures manuals (both current and previous versions) that support the claim of compliance.

7. Firms are encouraged to ensure that they have adequate service-level agreements with third-party administrators to provide the records necessary for verification, both currently and at a date in the future.

8. A firm should maintain certain other specific records necessary to support a claim of compliance, such as (but not limited to):
    - Client reports;
    - Attribution information; if utilized to determine account composite assignment;
    - Marketing output/RFPs responses;
    - Third party performance data;
    - Externally reviewed system and control reports (such as accounting reports or other internal controls/compliance reports for the client and/or custodians);
    - Third party sub-advisory agreements;
    - Board, Investment Committee or Composite/GIPS Compliance Committee minutes;
    - Assets under management reconciliations (AUM per GIPS reports to AUM per regulatory returns);
    - Client fee schedules/agreements;
    - Custody fees data;
    - Systems manuals especially for the systems that generate the composite reports (including returns and additional disclosures/statistics);
    - A list of recipients of compliant presentations.

9. Subject to local regulatory requirements, once a firm has been verified, a firm may be able to reduce the amount of records stored. For example, an annual account transaction report may be maintained instead of individual monthly detail reports. The summary report could be used to recreate period-specific information if needed. Microfiche or electronically-stored reports are acceptable. However, all records deemed necessary must be maintained for each year that is presented in a GIPS-compliant presentation.

Effective Date

This Guidance Statement is proposed to take effect 1 January 2006. Firms currently coming into compliance should apply this guidance to all periods. Firms are encouraged, but not required to apply this guidance prior to the Effective Date.

Applications:

1. *We have custodial records, trade confirmations, portfolio holdings and valuations, transactions reports, corporate action reports, income received/earned reports, accrued income reports, and cash flow/weighted cash flow reports. Must we maintain all these records for all portfolios (both discretionary and non-discretionary) in order to satisfy GIPS 1.A.1?*

5-3

PROPOSED

No. The firm must maintain sufficient records to support the firm's performance record. This might include a combination of the types of records listed. The firm must determine which records would suffice and maintain these records for all portfolios/composites for each period of performance presented.

2. *How long must I keep the records? For example, we show a 25-year track record for our Large Cap Value Equity strategy. Must we still maintain the records?*

Yes. The firm must maintain records to support performance presentations for as long as the particular period is being presented. For example, a firm with a 25 year track record of their Large Cap Value Equity strategy would need to maintain sufficient records for the full 25 year period.

3. *I have a group of portfolios that I don't use for advertising or marketing purposes. Must I keep the records for these accounts, even if I don't market their performance?*

Yes; the firm must maintain sufficient records that allow for the recalculation of account-level and composite level returns regardless of whether the accounts are used for marketing or not.

4. *Certain types of records (e.g. thermal printed faxes) have a limited life and in many cases such documents more than 10 years old. What happens if these records begin to disintegrate and are no longer readable?*

Individual documents are not required, summary documents are acceptable. With the advent of technology, firms can rely on electronic scans of paper documents in order to satisfy the record-keeping requirements.

5. *Do we have to keep trade tickets?*

The determination of which records are necessary to support the performance record is left up to the firm. In certain cases, the trade tickets may prove a useful resource to capture and maintain some of the data needed to support the record. In other cases, this data may be captured elsewhere. Since records capturing duplicate information isn't necessary, the firm must make the determination of which records to maintain.

6. *I have records to support my performance; however, the records are stored in a system that is not operable and I do not have access to the records. Is this acceptable?*

Records stored in a system that is not operable will not satisfy the requirements of the GIPS standards to maintain data and information necessary to support the firm's performance presentation.

7. *I have a question that has not been answered directly by this Guidance Statement on the record-keeping requirements. What should I do?*

Temporarily, the firm should maintain as much data as possible and seek legal counsel to consult on the most appropriate data to keep.

PROPOSED GUIDANCE STATEMENT ON THE USE OF LEVERAGE AND DERIVATIVES

The Investment Performance Council (IPC) and CFA Institute seek comment on the proposed GIPS Guidance Statement addressing the Use of Leverage and Derivatives set forth below. For information on the Guidance Statement process, please see www.cfainstitute.org/standards/pps/process.html.

Comments must be submitted in writing and be received by CFA Institute no later than 31 December 2004. All comments and replies will be put on the public record unless specifically requested. It is preferable that comments be submitted in electronic form with settings that do not restrict the ability to 'cut-and-paste' text from the comment letter. Comments are also accepted in hardcopy and should be addressed to:

CFA Institute
CFA Centre for Financial Market Integrity
Reference: Guidance Statement on the Use of Leverage and Derivatives
P.O. Box 3668
Charlottesville, Virginia 22903
Fax: +1-434-951-5320
E-mail: standardsetting@cfainstitute.org

Effective Date

This guidance statement will apply to all firms from the Effective Date forward. The proposed Adoption Date for this Guidance Statement is June 2005 and proposed Effective Date is 1 January 2006.

Executive Summary

Strategies that utilize derivative instruments and/or leverage (gearing) are often very complex. These strategies tend to behave differently than traditional strategies and generally have additional risks associated with them. As a result, prospective clients that invest in strategies that materially employ leverage and/or derivatives need additional information. It is difficult to identify specific measures that are relevant and meaningful in all situations. The objective is to provide prospective clients with the crucial data to aid in a better understanding of the firm's strategy, performance history, and risk profile.

Comment Requested

CFA Institute seeks public input on the proposals set forth in this document. Issues to consider in conjunction with this proposal include:

1. Do you agree with the principles established in the Guidance Statement?
2. Are there other elements involved in the use of leverage and derivatives that are not included?
3. Do you agree with the guiding principles provided to firms employing leverage and/or derivatives?
4. Do you agree with the proposed Effective Date?

If commentators suggest other proposals, CFA Institute requests that they explain the rationale behind their proposal.

Proposed Adoption Date: June 2005
Proposed Effective Date: 1 January 2006
Retroactive Application: No
Public Comment Period: Oct 2004 – Dec 2004

5-4

PROPOSED

PROPOSED GUIDANCE STATEMENT ON THE USE OF LEVERAGE AND DERIVATIVES

Introduction

Strategies that utilize derivative instruments and/or leverage (gearing) are often very complex. These strategies tend to behave differently than traditional strategies and generally have additional risks associated with them. As a result, prospective clients that invest in strategies that *materially* employ leverage and/or derivatives need additional information. It is difficult to identify specific measures that are relevant and meaningful in all situations. The objective is to provide prospective clients with the crucial data to aid in a better understanding of the firm's strategy, performance history, and risk profile.

Because asset classes such as real estate and private equity utilize leverage and/or derivatives differently than traditional asset classes, they are not subject to this guidance statement. Instead, leverage and derivatives for private equity and real estate are addressed through other GIPS guidance.

Guiding Principles

This guidance can be separated into three major guiding principles (as listed below) followed by three appendixes incorporating calculation guidance.

1. Creation of a Leverage Policy
2. Composite Construction for Portfolios Utilizing Leveraged Strategies
3. Risk Measure Disclosure and Reporting

Creation of a Leverage Policy

In general, a portfolio is considered to be leveraged if certain instruments or strategies are implemented to *materially* alter the return impact that a unit move in certain underlying securities markets will have on the portfolio to an extent otherwise unachievable without the use of such instruments or strategies. Some examples of instruments or strategies that might apply leverage include financing assets through liabilities or using futures, options, or other derivative instruments.

Since each firm's definition of leverage will most likely be different it should rest with each firm to create its own ex ante *leverage policy*. This policy should discuss in detail the types of leveraged strategies implemented across the firm and more importantly discuss what constitutes materiality for each strategy/composite. Materiality should be thought of as the threshold that a firm sets to distinguish when a strategy/composite is considered leveraged. (i.e. in a growth equity composite portfolios may use derivative instruments; in regard to a portfolio's investment policy, a 120% or greater exposure to the S&P 500 undeniably constitutes materiality). It is sensible for firms to establish in advance certain criteria to identify at what point the risk/return profile for a composite becomes materially altered and to establish and document policies as to what disclosures must be made for the composite.

Composite Construction for Portfolios Utilizing Leveraged Strategies

While there are a wide variety of strategies that involve leverage and the risk profiles of those portfolios are complex, calculation of returns for leveraged portfolios doesn't need case-by-case methodology and is basically the same as for non-leveraged portfolios.

(Please see Appendix A for calculation examples of returns)

The GIPS standards require that firms construct composites based on investment strategy or style. Further, the Guidance Statement on Composite Definition states "In general, portfolios that use derivatives, leverage and/or hedging have a unique investment strategy from those portfolios that do not utilize these techniques or instruments. Accordingly, firms should consider whether portfolios that use leverage, derivatives, and/or hedging should be included in separate composites from portfolios that are restricted from using such instruments or strategies."

If the nature of the mandated usage of derivatives and margin borrowing is such that the firm does not have the ability to implement its intended strategy, then the respective portfolio might be considered non-discretionary and therefore must not be included in a composite.

Risk Measure Disclosure and Reporting

Disclosing proper risk measures is crucial for capturing the altered risk/return profile that a leveraged portfolio contains when compared with a traditional strategy. Presenting the prospective client with the risk measure that best captures a leveraged portfolio's altered risk/return profile must be stressed. At the composite level, the range and median value for the constituent portfolio risk measures will provide a prospective client with valuable insight into the overall composite's risk/return profile. Useful risk measures and information for leveraged strategies include the exposure, Value at Risk, the tracking error and the volatility of a composite, the percentage of composite assets which are not traded on a stock exchange or equivalent, the percentage of composite assets held in short positions and overlay assets of overlay strategy.

The following are descriptions of some recommended risk measures for leveraged strategies. In these descriptions some calculation methodologies are shown but are not necessarily definitive. Alternative methodologies can be used. Firms should disclose the methodology and/or system that is used to calculate the risk measure and information.

Exposure

Firms may present minimum, average, and maximum levels of exposure for each period. Exposure could be defined as the expected unit move in the portfolio divided by the unit move in the market. This information gives prospective clients an indication of the range of leverage that is employed during the period. The minimum, average, and maximum exposure should be calculated based on monthly (or daily if available) data points. Firms with leveraged multi-asset strategies should indicate which segments within the multi-asset strategy use leverage. Firms may also present the total exposure, which could be calculated as the sum of the weight of each segment multiplied by its respective exposure. While this aggregation of exposures is not a precise technical measurement it is a useful approximation of the total exposure. It would be more precise to present each of the segment's exposure relative to the underlying market (e.g., the stock segment relative to the stock market), but this would require the presentation of a great number of data points, particularly for composites with several segments. Firms are encouraged to present the exposure of each of the individual segments as supplemental information.

(Please see Appendix B for calculation examples of exposure)

Value at Risk

Firms may present the minimum, average, and maximum Value at Risk (VaR) ratio for the composite and the composite benchmark for each period presented. The VaR ratio is calculated as the weighted-average of the VaR ratios of the individual portfolios within a composite divided by the composite assets. Firms should base the VaR on the 95% confidence interval and one month (or daily, if appropriate) time horizon for comparison among composites. The firm can also present additional VaR ratios based on other parameters. The firm should also disclose the methodology or system that is used to calculate the VaR.

(Please see Appendix C for calculation examples of Value at Risk)

Tracking Error

Tracking error for the most recent three, five, and ten year (or since inception if inception is less than ten years) periods can be used to demonstrate a portfolio's variability to a benchmark. Due to the small number of data points, composites with less than three years of performance history should not disclose the tracking error. The tracking error is computed as the annualized standard deviation of the arithmetic or geometric difference between the monthly composite return and the composite benchmark return. While it is potentially problematic to annualize the standard deviation of leveraged returns, the use of an annualized figure allows for comparability with the other annual disclosures. When there is more than one portfolio in a composite, using the composite return and composite benchmark return will tend to under-estimate the tracking error of a typical portfolio in the composite because of the diversification effect. While it would be more suitable to calculate the weighted-average of the tracking errors of the individual portfolios within the composite to calculate the composite tracking error, problems can arise when portfolios are not included in the composite for the entire period. The use of the composite return and composite benchmark return is still meaningful, avoids the problem of portfolios moving into and out of composites, and is generally very easy for firms to calculate. It should be noted that when the dispersion of portfolio returns within a composite is higher, the tracking error of a typical portfolio in the composite will tend to be more under-estimated.

Overlay Strategy Discussion

Firms with overlay strategies should disclose the overlay assets in addition to composite assets for the overlay composite. For example, if a firm is hired to implement an overlay strategy on an underlying portfolio of €100 million and is given €10 million to implement the strategy (e.g., for margin requirements), then the €10 million is included in the composite assets and the €100 million is also reported as overlay assets.

Effective Date

This Guidance Statement is effective 1 January 2006. Firms currently coming into compliance should apply this guidance to all periods. Firms are encouraged, but not required to apply this guidance prior to the Effective Date.

APPENDIX A
CALCULATING RETURNS FOR PORTFOLIOS THAT UTILIZE LEVERAGE

Standard 2.A.1 requires that a "total return, including realized and unrealized gains plus income, must be used." In addition, Standard 2.A.2 requires that "time-weighted rates of return that adjust for cash flows must be used. Period returns must be geometrically linked. Time weighted rates of return that adjust for daily weighted cash flows must be used for periods beginning 1 January 2005. Actual valuations at the time of external cash flows will likely be required for periods beginning 1 January 2010." A cash flow is defined as an external flow of cash and/or securities (capital additions or withdrawals) that is client initiated.

In general, calculating returns for portfolios that use leverage and/or derivatives is the same as calculating returns for non-leveraged portfolios. Returns are calculated by dividing the change in market value of the portfolio by the beginning market value of the portfolio. The market value of the actual client assets is used in the denominator. The return for the period is:

$$R = \left(\frac{x_1 - x_0}{x_0} \right)$$

where x_0 is the portfolio beginning market value and x_1 is the portfolio ending market value = $(x_0 + \Delta x)$.

The market value includes the value of all current holdings including any accrued income and unrealized gains or losses. The market value of the portfolio can also be thought of as the cash value if all positions were liquidated (assuming zero transaction costs) including accrued income. The notional value of the derivative securities is not used to calculate the market value.

Example 1: Stock portfolio with long futures
At the beginning of the period portfolio consists of $90 long stocks, $10 margin deposited for futures and long futures position with $60 notional value. At the end of the period the value of long stocks is $96 and notional value of futures is $63. Interest received from the deposited margin is $0.02. Total value of the portfolio changes from $100 (= $90 + $10) to $109.02 (= $96 + $10 + $63 - $60 + $0.02).

$$R = \left(\frac{109.02 - 100}{100} \right) = 9.02\%.$$

Example 2: Stock portfolio with short futures – full hedge case
At the beginning of the period the portfolio consists of $90 long stocks, $10 margin deposited for futures and a short futures position of $90 notional value. At the end of the period the value of long stocks is $84 and notional value of futures is $83.60. Interest received from the deposited margin is $0.02. Total value of the portfolio changes from $100 (= $90 + $10) to $100.42 (= $84 + $10 + $90 - $83.60 + $0.02).

$$R = \left(\frac{100.42 - 100}{100} \right) = 0.42\%.$$

Example 3: Stock portfolio with options
Portfolio consists of $90 stocks and $10 call options at the beginning of the period. Valuations of the stocks and options are $95 and $25 respectively at the end of the period. Total value of the portfolio changes from $100 (= $90 + $10) to $120 (= $95 + $25).

$$R = \left(\frac{120 - 100}{100} \right) = 20.0\%.$$

Example 4: Stock portfolio with short options

Portfolio consists of \$110 stocks and \$10 short call options at the beginning of the period. Valuations of the stocks and options are \$117 and \$15 respectively at the end of the period. Total value of the portfolio changes from \$100 (= \$110 - \$10) to \$102 (= \$117 - \$15).

$$R = \left(\frac{102 - 100}{100} \right) = 2.0\% .$$

Example 5: Stock portfolio with partially short position

At the beginning of the period the portfolio consists of \$130 long stocks and \$30 short stocks. Then beginning market value of the total portfolio is \$100 (=\$130 - \$30). If long stocks become \$142 and short stocks become \$27 at the end, then ending market value of the total portfolio is \$115 (= \$142 - \$27).

$$R = \left(\frac{115 - 100}{100} \right) = 15.0\% .$$

Example 6: Stock portfolio with margin borrowing

Portfolio consists of \$100 long stocks and additional \$50 long stocks bought on margin. Valuation of long stocks is \$170 at the end of the period. Interest paid for margin borrowing is \$0.20. Value of the portfolio that belongs to client at the beginning of the period is \$100 (= \$150 - \$50). It becomes \$119.80 (= \$170 - \$50 - \$0.20) at the end of the period.

$$R = \left(\frac{119.8 - 100}{100} \right) = 19.8\% .$$

Example 7: Market neutral strategy

A client provided a hedge fund manager with capital of \$100 at the beginning of the first month. The hedge fund manager deposited \$100 with a prime broker and constructed positions of \$100 long stocks and \$100 short stocks. At the end of the first month market values of long stocks and short stocks are \$109 and \$107 respectively. The fund manager received interests of \$0.30 (annual rate of 3.6%) from the prime broker. The value of the total portfolio changes from \$100 (= \$100 + \$100 - \$100) to \$102.30 (= \$100 + \$109 - \$107 + \$0.30).

$$R = \left(\frac{102.3 - 100}{100} \right) = 2.3\% .$$

Overlay Strategies

Currency and asset overlay strategies are unique, but are treated similarly. In general, returns on overlay strategies are based on the gain or loss on the overlay assets (typically futures or forwards) divided by the assets of the underlying portfolio.

Example 8:

A client hires Manager A to implement a tactical asset allocation futures overlay on \$100 million. Manager A is given \$10 million to implement the overlay strategy.

Basis of the overlay strategy = \$100 million
Overlay gain/loss for the period = + \$500,000

$$R = \left(\frac{500{,}000}{100{,}000{,}000} \right) = 0.50\% \cdot$$

The firm should include the \$10 million in the composite assets and the \$100 million should also be reported as overlay assets.

APPENDIX B
CALCULATING EXPOSURE

Exposure is one of the most important risk measures for leveraged portfolios because it defines the degree of leverage and is the basic of the judgment of "materiality". Exposure could be defined as the expected unit move in the portfolio divided by the unit move in the market. For example, if a portfolio is expected to increase in value by 1.5% for a 1% increase in the market, the exposure would be 150%. Although exposure could be defined differently, in this appendix we show examples of exposure calculations according to the definition above. Some of the examples, such as Example 5 and Example 6 might be disputable and the subcommittee hopes the concept of exposure and methodology of calculating exposures will be enhanced through fruitful discussions with the industry.

In order to calculate exposure, firms should identify the "markets" against which the exposure is calculated. It is expected that the markets used to calculate exposure will be consistent with the investment strategy and benchmark. In the case of simple single asset-class strategy, the market will be a broad index that represents the asset-class, such as the S&P 500, FTSE 100, TOPIX, etc. In the case of a market neutral strategy, the strategy is usually employed relative to a single asset market, such as the U.S. stock market. The exposure to U.S. stock market would be expected to be around zero for a market neutral strategy, so the exposure information provides a useful way to confirm the degree of market neutrality.

General Formula

Let I and V be the market level and portfolio value, respectively. The portfolio value changes ΔV if the market changes ΔI. In general, the following formula can be used to calculate exposure:

$$\frac{\frac{\Delta V}{V}}{\frac{\Delta I}{I}} = \frac{\sum_{i=1}^{n}\frac{\Delta V_i}{V}}{\frac{\Delta I}{I}} = \frac{\sum_{i=1}^{n}\frac{V_i}{V}\times\frac{\Delta V_i}{V_i}}{\frac{\Delta I}{I}} = \sum_{i=1}^{n}\frac{V_i}{V}\times\frac{\frac{\Delta V_i}{V_i}}{\frac{\Delta I}{I}} = \sum_{i=1}^{n} w_i \times \frac{\frac{\Delta V_i}{V_i}}{\frac{\Delta I}{I}},$$

where i is an instrument or strategy within the portfolio and w_i is the weight of the instrument or strategy in the portfolio (i.e., $w_i = \frac{V_i}{V}$).

Exposure of Stocks

In the case of a non-leveraged stock portfolio, the exposure of the stocks is calculated as follows:

$$\frac{\frac{\Delta V}{V}}{\frac{\Delta I}{I}} = \frac{\beta\times\frac{\Delta I}{I}}{\frac{\Delta I}{I}} = \beta,$$

where β is the portfolio's sensitivity to changes in the stock market. Firms should use a β of 1, but may also present the exposure calculated using a different β, based on an estimate from a risk model (e.g. forecast beta) or historical β, if it determines that this is appropriate. The beta of the portfolio is calculated as an asset-weighted average of each stock's sensitivity to changes in the stock market. If the firm presents the exposure based on a β other than 1, the firm should disclose how the β is determined. Using a β of 1 improves comparability (otherwise two firms could estimate the β of the same portfolio differently, leading to two different exposure figures for the same portfolio).

The exposure of the total portfolio is therefore the percentage of stocks times the β. For example, if the portfolio holds 95% stocks and 5% cash, the exposure would be 95% times β. Since it is recommended that firms use a β of 1, the exposure is simply the percentage of stocks in the portfolio.

P R O P O S E D

Exposure of Bonds

In the case of a bond portfolio, the portfolio's modified duration is used instead of β. The price sensitivity of a bond and/or a bond portfolio versus a unit change in interest rates is expressed by modified duration as below:

$$D = -\frac{\Delta V}{\Delta y} \times \frac{1}{V},$$

where D is the modified duration, V is the price level of a bond, and Δy is the unit change in interest rates.

Portfolio duration (D_p) and benchmark index duration (D_I) are expressed as follows:

$$D_p = -\frac{\Delta V}{\Delta y} \times \frac{1}{V}, \quad D_I = -\frac{\Delta I}{\Delta y} \times \frac{1}{I}.$$

Rearranging these formulas leads to the following:

$$\frac{\Delta V}{V} = -D_p \times \Delta y, \quad \frac{\Delta I}{I} = -D_I \times \Delta y.$$

From these equations the exposure of the bond portion of the portfolio is calculated as follows:

$$\frac{\frac{\Delta V}{V}}{\frac{\Delta I}{I}} = \frac{-D_p \times \Delta y}{-D_I \times \Delta y} = \frac{D_p}{D_I}.$$

If portfolio duration (D_p) is equal to the benchmark index duration (D_I), then the exposure is 100%. If D_p is larger than D_I, then the exposure exceeds 100%. As with the stock portfolio, the exposure of the total portfolio is equal to the percentage of bonds in the portfolio times the exposure of the bonds. For example, if the portfolio is 97% bonds and 3% cash and the exposure of the bonds is 105%, then the exposure of the total portfolio is 97% times 105%, or 101.85%.

While the use of the portfolio's effective duration is better to use in theory, the use of modified duration is simpler and does not depend on an underlying pricing model to estimate spot rates. Firms are allowed to use the effective duration instead of the modified duration, but should disclose the pricing model methodology used.

Exposure of Options

In the case of options, the delta-weighted exposure should be used. The option delta (δ), which is the first derivative of the option price relative to a change in the price of the underlying security, is used rather than β. The option premium changes ΔV if the stock market changes ΔI. In this case, exposure is calculated as

$$\frac{\frac{\Delta V}{V}}{\frac{\Delta I}{I}} = \frac{\frac{I}{V} \times \frac{\Delta V}{I}}{\frac{\Delta I}{I}} = \frac{\frac{I}{V} \times \delta \times \frac{\Delta I}{I}}{\frac{\Delta I}{I}} = \frac{I}{V} \times \delta.$$

If the option is an at-the-money call option, δ is approximately 0.5. The option premium V depends on stock market level (I), volatility of the stock market, execution price, time to maturity, and the risk-free interest rate. A typical example could be I=$100, V=$8 and δ=0.5. The exposure would be calculated as follows:

$$\frac{\frac{\Delta V}{V}}{\frac{\Delta I}{I}} = \frac{I}{V} \times \delta = \frac{100}{8} \times 0.5 = 6.25.$$

Thus, the exposure is 625% for this at-the-money call option.

Multi-Asset Composites

In the case of multi-asset composites that use leverage, firms should indicate which segments within the multi-asset strategy use leverage. Firms may also present the total exposure, which could be calculated as the sum of the weight of each segment multiplied by its respective exposure. While this aggregation of exposures is not a precise technical measurement it is a useful approximation of the total exposure. It would be more precise to present each of the segment's exposure relative to the underlying market (e.g., the stock segment relative to the stock market), but this would require the presentation of a great number of data points, particularly for composites with several segments. Firms are encouraged to present the exposure of each of the individual segments as supplemental information.

Example 1: Stock portfolio with long futures
At the beginning of the period the portfolio consists of \$90 long stocks, \$10 margin deposited for futures, and a long futures position with \$60 notional value.

$$\frac{\frac{\Delta V}{V}}{\frac{\Delta I}{I}} = \sum_{i=1}^{2} \frac{V_i}{V} \times \frac{\frac{\Delta V_i}{V_i}}{\frac{\Delta I}{I}} = \left(\frac{90}{100} \times \frac{\frac{\Delta V_1}{V_1}}{\frac{\Delta I}{I}} \right) + \left(\frac{10}{100} \times \frac{\frac{\Delta V_2}{V_2}}{\frac{\Delta I}{I}} \right) = \left(\frac{90}{100} \times \beta \right) + \left(\frac{10}{100} \times \frac{\frac{V_{2n}}{V_2} \times \frac{\Delta V_2}{V_{2n}}}{\frac{\Delta I}{I}} \right) = \left(\frac{90}{100} \times \beta \right) + \left(\frac{10}{100} \times \frac{\frac{\Delta V_2}{V_{2n}}}{\frac{\Delta I}{I}} \times \frac{V_{2n}}{V_2} \right).$$

Assume that V_2 is deposited margin for futures and is equal to \$10, V_{2n} is a notional value of futures position and is equal to \$60, β is 1, and $\frac{\frac{\Delta V_2}{V_{2n}}}{\frac{\Delta I}{I}} = 1$. Then the exposure is calculated as:

$$\frac{\frac{\Delta V}{V}}{\frac{\Delta I}{I}} = \left(\frac{90}{100} \times \beta \right) + \left(\frac{10}{100} \times \frac{\frac{\Delta V_2}{V_{2n}}}{\frac{\Delta I}{I}} \times \frac{V_{2n}}{V_2} \right) = \left(\frac{90}{100} \times \beta \right) + \left(\frac{10}{100} \times 1 \times \frac{V_{2n}}{V_2} \right) = \left(\frac{90}{100} \times 1 \right) + \left(\frac{10}{100} \times \frac{60}{10} \right) = 1.5.$$

Thus an exposure against the stock market is 150%.

Example 2: U.S. equity market neutral strategy
At the beginning of the period \$100 is deposited margin to a primary broker and the portfolio consists of \$94 long stocks and \$96 short stocks. The market value of the total portfolio is \$98 (= \$100 + \$94 - \$96). Exposure against U.S. stock market is calculated as follows:

$$\frac{\frac{\Delta V}{V}}{\frac{\Delta I}{I}} = \sum_{i=1}^{3} \frac{V_i}{V} \times \frac{\frac{\Delta V_i}{V_i}}{\frac{\Delta I}{I}} = \left(\frac{100}{98} \times 0 \right) + \left(\frac{94}{98} \times 1 \right) + \left(\frac{-96}{98} \times 1 \right) = -0.0204.$$

The first term relates to the margin deposit and is assumed to have zero sensitivity to the stock market. The second term and third terms relate to the long and short positions respectively and are assumed to have a β of 1. The exposure of –2.04% is small but it is useful information because prospective clients would like to know the actual level of neutrality.

Example 3: Stock portfolio with index options
A portfolio consists of \$90 stocks and \$10 call options at the beginning of the period. Using a β of 1 and option exposure of 6.25 (from the example above), the exposure is calculated as:

$$\frac{\frac{\Delta V}{V}}{\frac{\Delta I}{I}} = \sum_{i=1}^{2} \frac{V_i}{V} \times \frac{\frac{\Delta V_i}{V_i}}{\frac{\Delta I}{I}} = \left(\frac{90}{100} \times \frac{\frac{\Delta V_1}{V_1}}{\frac{\Delta I}{I}} \right) + \left(\frac{10}{100} \times \frac{\frac{\Delta V_2}{V_2}}{\frac{\Delta I}{I}} \right) = \left(\frac{90}{100} \times \beta \right) + \left(\frac{10}{100} \times \frac{I_2}{V_2} \times \delta \right)$$

$$= (0.9 \times 1.0) + (0.1 \times 6.25) = 1.525.$$

Thus the exposure relative to the stock market is 152.5%.

Example 4: Portfolio consisting of options of individual stocks
A portfolio consists of many options of individual stocks. For example, a call option of General Electric, a call option of IBM, and a put option of General Motors, etc.

$$\frac{\frac{\Delta V}{V}}{\frac{\Delta I}{I}}=\sum_{i=1}^{n} w_i \times \frac{\frac{\Delta V_i}{V_i}}{\frac{\Delta I}{I}}=\sum_{i=1}^{n} w_i \times\left(\frac{\frac{\Delta V_i}{V_i}}{\frac{\Delta S_i}{S_i}} \times \frac{\frac{\Delta S_i}{S_i}}{\frac{\Delta I}{I}}\right)=\sum_{i=1}^{n} w_i \times\left(\frac{S_i}{V_i} \times \delta_i \times \beta_i\right),$$

where S_i is the price of stock i, V_i is premium of option i, δ_i is the delta of option i, and β_i is the beta of stock i.

Assuming β_i is 1, the formula simplifies to the following:

$$\frac{\frac{\Delta V}{V}}{\frac{\Delta I}{I}}=\sum_{i=1}^{n} w_i \times\left(\frac{S_i}{V_i} \times \delta_i\right).$$

Example 5: Multi-Asset portfolio with tactical asset allocation strategy
A portfolio consists of stocks (s), bonds (b), and short term instruments including cash (c), and the benchmark consists of 60% stock index and 40% bond index. Let I be the stock market or bond market. The total exposure for the composite is calculated as the weight of the stock segment multiplied by the stock exposure, plus the weight of the bond segment multiplied by the bond exposure. The exposure of the cash segment is assumed to be zero.

Assume stock futures have a short position and bond futures have a long position. Let sm correspond to the margin for stock futures, bm correspond to the margin for bond futures, sn correspond to the notional value of stock futures, and bn correspond to the notional value of the bond futures.

$$\frac{\frac{\Delta V}{V}}{\frac{\Delta I}{I}}=\left(\left(w_s \times \frac{\frac{\Delta V_s}{V_s}}{\frac{\Delta I}{I}}\right)+\left(w_{sm} \times \frac{\frac{\Delta V_{sm}}{V_{sm}}}{\frac{\Delta I}{I}}\right)\right)+\left(\left(w_b \times \frac{\frac{\Delta V_b}{V_b}}{\frac{\Delta I}{I}}\right)+\left(w_{bm} \times \frac{\frac{\Delta V_{bm}}{V_{bm}}}{\frac{\Delta I}{I}}\right)\right)+\left(w_c \times \frac{\frac{\Delta V_c}{V_c}}{\frac{\Delta I}{I}}\right). \quad (5\text{-}1)$$

Let I_s be the stock market and ΔI_s be a change of the stock market. The portion of the equation related to stocks is as follows:

$$\left(w_s \times \frac{\frac{\Delta V_s}{V_s}}{\frac{\Delta I_s}{I_s}}\right)+\left(w_{sm} \times \frac{\frac{\Delta V_{sm}}{V_{sm}}}{\frac{\Delta I_s}{I_s}}\right)=\left(w_s \times \frac{\frac{\Delta V_s}{V_s}}{\frac{\Delta I_s}{I_s}}\right)+\left(w_{sm} \times \frac{\frac{V_{sn}}{V_{sm}} \times \frac{\Delta V_{sm}}{V_{sn}}}{\frac{\Delta I_s}{I_s}}\right) \quad (5\text{-}2)$$

$$=\left(w_s \times \beta_s\right)+\left(w_{sm} \times \frac{V_{sn}}{V_{sm}}\right)=\left(w_s \times \beta_s\right)+\frac{V_{sn}}{V}.$$

The second term is the ratio of nominal value of stock futures to portfolio total value and because the futures are short, the numerator will have a negative sign in this case.

The bond segment is calculated as follows:

$$\left(w_b \times \frac{\frac{\Delta V_b}{V_b}}{\frac{\Delta I_s}{I_s}}\right)+\left(w_{bm} \times \frac{\frac{\Delta V_{bm}}{V_{bm}}}{\frac{\Delta I_s}{I_s}}\right)=\left(w_b \times \frac{\frac{D_p}{D_I} \times \frac{\Delta I_b}{I_b}}{\frac{\Delta I_s}{I_s}}\right)+\left(w_{bm} \times \frac{\frac{V_{bn}}{V_{bm}} \times \frac{\Delta V_{bm}}{V_{bn}}}{\frac{\Delta I_b}{I_b}} \times \frac{\frac{\Delta I_b}{I_b}}{\frac{\Delta I_s}{I_s}}\right) \quad (5\text{-}3)$$

$$=\left(\left(w_b \times \frac{D_p}{D_I}\right)+\frac{V_{bn}}{V}\right) \times \frac{\frac{\Delta I_b}{I_b}}{\frac{\Delta I_s}{I_s}}.$$

Since the sensitivity of bond market relative to the stock market is generally expressed as:

$$\frac{\frac{\Delta I_b}{I_b}}{\frac{\Delta I_s}{I_s}} = \frac{Cov(I_b, I_s)}{Var(I_s)} = \frac{\sigma_b \times \sigma_s \times \rho_{bs}}{\sigma_s^2} = \frac{\sigma_b}{\sigma_s}\rho_{bs}. \qquad (5\text{-}4)$$

$\sigma_b \sigma_s \rho_{bs}$ are the bond market volatility, the stock market volatility, and the correlation between bond and stock market respectively. The last term of equation (5-1) should be zero because it is assumed that ΔV_c is not correlated with ΔI_s. From these considerations equation (5-1) becomes as follows:

$$\frac{\frac{\Delta V}{V}}{\frac{\Delta I_s}{I_s}} = \left((w_s \times \beta_s) + \frac{V_{sn}}{V} \right) + \left(\left(\left(w_b \times \frac{D_p}{D_I} \right) + \frac{V_{bn}}{V} \right) \times \frac{\sigma_b}{\sigma_s}\rho_{bs} \right). \qquad (5\text{-}5)$$

To facilitate comparability among firms, the β_s is recommended to be equal to 1 and the correlation is zero. However, firms may use a different β, based on an estimate from a risk model (e.g., forecast beta) or historical β, if it determines that this is appropriate. This results in the following equation:

$$\frac{\frac{\Delta V}{V}}{\frac{\Delta I_s}{I_s}} = w_s + \frac{V_{sn}}{V}. \qquad (5\text{-}6)$$

Therefore, the exposure of the multi-asset portfolio versus the stock market is simply the sum of the ratio of the stocks in the portfolio plus the ratio of nominal value of stock futures in the portfolio. As stated earlier, because the futures are a short position, the numerator of the second term will be negative. Note that the assumption of a zero correlation leads to an underestimation of the exposure. As the correlation increases, the exposure increases.

The calculation of the exposure against the bond market is calculated similarly as the stock exposure and the next equation corresponds to equation (5-5).

$$\frac{\frac{\Delta V}{V}}{\frac{\Delta I_b}{I_b}} = \left(\left((w_s \times \beta_s) + \frac{V_{sn}}{V} \right) \times \frac{\sigma_s}{\sigma_b}\rho_{bs} \right) + \left(\left(w_b \times \frac{D_p}{D_I} \right) + \frac{V_{bn}}{V} \right). \qquad (5\text{-}7)$$

As stated above, assuming a zero correlation between stock and bond markets, the following equation results:

$$\frac{\frac{\Delta V}{V}}{\frac{\Delta I_b}{I_b}} = \left(w_b \times \frac{D_p}{D_I} \right) + \frac{V_{bn}}{V}. \qquad (5\text{-}8)$$

The exposure of the total portfolio should be calculated as the sum of equation (5-6) and (5-8). In addition, the firm should indicate which segments use leverage.

Example 6: Global Equity portfolio with tactical country allocation
Let us consider the case of multiple underlying equity indexes. In this example the benchmark is constructed as, for example, 40% S&P 500, 40% MSCI Europe, and 20% MSCI Japan and a manager is permitted to use stock futures to change country allocation for the purpose of generating active returns. The actual portfolio consists of U.S. stocks, European stocks, Japanese stocks, stocks of other regions/countries, and cash. The portfolio has positions of long or short stock futures. The suffix m corresponds to

PROPOSED

the margin for futures position. Portfolio sensitivity relative to the "market" (I) is expressed as follows.

$$\frac{\frac{\Delta V}{V}}{\frac{\Delta I}{I}} = \sum_{i=1}^{4}\left(\left(w_i \times \frac{\frac{\Delta V_i}{V_i}}{\frac{\Delta I}{I}}\right) + \left(w_{im} \times \frac{\frac{\Delta V_{im}}{V_{im}}}{\frac{\Delta I}{I}}\right)\right) + \left(w_c \times \frac{\frac{\Delta V_c}{V_c}}{\frac{\Delta I}{I}}\right). \qquad (6\text{-}1)$$

Please note that $\sum_{i=1}^{4}$ corresponds to the various markets (U.S., Europe, Japan, and others). The last term should be zero because it is cash. The second term of the parenthesis corresponds to stock futures. The first and second terms would be converted in the same way as equation (5-2).

$$\frac{\frac{\Delta V}{V}}{\frac{\Delta I}{I}} = \sum_{i=1}^{4}\left(\left(w_i \times \frac{\frac{\Delta V_i}{V_i}}{\frac{\Delta I}{I}}\right) + \left(w_{im} \times \frac{\frac{\Delta V_{im}}{V_{im}}}{\frac{\Delta I}{I}}\right)\right) = \sum_{i=1}^{4}\left(\left(w_i \times \frac{\frac{\Delta V_i}{V_i}}{\frac{\Delta I_i}{I_i}}\right) + \left(w_{im} \times \frac{\frac{\Delta V_{im}}{V_{im}}}{\frac{\Delta I_i}{I_i}}\right)\right) \times \frac{\frac{\Delta I_i}{I_i}}{\frac{\Delta I}{I}} \qquad (6\text{-}2)$$

$$= \sum_{i=1}^{4}\left(\left(w_i \times \beta_i\right) + \frac{V_{in}}{V}\right) \times \frac{\frac{\Delta I_i}{I_i}}{\frac{\Delta I}{I}}.$$

The sign of V_{in} is plus if the futures position is long and is minus if the futures position is short. If I is assumed to be the "global stock market" (i.e., including exposure to markets outside of the benchmark), it might be assumed that $\frac{\frac{\Delta I_i}{I_i}}{\frac{\Delta I}{I}} = 1$ for each i. Theoretically these assumptions are not necessary correct and more accurate estimations are possible. Those estimations, however, would reduce the comparability among firms. The exposure is calculated as:

$$\frac{\frac{\Delta V}{V}}{\frac{\Delta I}{I}} = \sum_{i=1}^{4}\left(\left(w_i \times \beta_i\right) + \frac{V_{in}}{V}\right). \qquad (6\text{-}3)$$

Firms are reminded that Standard 4.A.10 requires firms to disclose the percentage of the composite invested in countries or regions outside of the benchmark.

Again, assuming the β within each market is equal to 1 for simplicity and comparability among firms, inserting 1 into equation 6-3 leads to the final exposure figure. Firms should report the result of equation (6-3). Firms are also encouraged to report as supplemental information the exposure against particular stock markets, for example U.S. stock market, if it characterizes the investment strategy and has a prominent effect to the portfolio returns. Exposure against the U.S. stock market is calculated from equation (6-2) by defining I as U.S. stock market, $\frac{\frac{\Delta I_1}{I_1}}{\frac{\Delta I}{I}} = 1$, and $\frac{\frac{\Delta I_i}{I_i}}{\frac{\Delta I}{I}} = 0$ for $\sum_{i=2}^{4}$. Assuming the β of the U.S. stock portfolio is 1 leads to the following equation:

$$\frac{\frac{\Delta V}{V}}{\frac{\Delta I_{US}}{I_{US}}} = \left(w_{US} \times \beta_{US}\right) + \frac{V_{USn}}{V} = w_{US} + \frac{V_{USn}}{V}. \qquad (6\text{-}4)$$

APPENDIX C

Calculation of Composite Value at Risk

The Value at Risk (VaR) ratio is the ratio of the value of possible loss to total assets. The composite VaR ratio is the asset-weighted average of individual portfolio VaR ratios.

The composite VaR ratio should be calculated on a monthly basis. The firm should present the minimum, average, and maximum of the 12 monthly composite VaR ratios for each annual period reported. If the strategy assumes frequent change of leveraged positions, these calculation should be performed based on daily data.

Example 1

Composite C has three portfolios, X, Y, and Z. Assume that asset values and VaRs for January are as follows:

	Asset Value	VaR	VaR Ratio
Portfolio X	$100	$8.5	8.5%
Portfolio Y	$200	$18	9%
Portfolio Z	$40	$3	7.5%
Composite	$340		8.68%

The composite VaR ratio of 8.68% is the asset-weighted average of the individual portfolio VaR ratios. Assume the same calculations are performed each month with the following results:

	Composite VaR Ratio (%)
January	8.68
February	8.98
March	8.33
April	8.09
May	8.16
June	7.84
July	8.11
August	7.78
September	7.72
October	7.51
November	7.88
December	8.03

The firm would present 7.51%, 8.09%, and 8.98% as the minimum, average, and maximum composite VaR ratios for the year. From these three figures, a prospective client should anticipate that their average value at risk is the value of their portfolio times 8.09% and they should expect that their value at risk ranges from 7.51% to 8.98% times their portfolio value.

6-1

COUNTRY SPONSORS OF THE GIPS STANDARDS

(as of 1 November 2005)

About the Country Sponsors of the GIPS Standards:

Although the CFA Centre funds and administers the activities of the GIPS standards, their success is the result of an alliance among experts from a variety of fields within the global investment industry. The following key industry groups have been involved in and contributed significantly to promoting and developing the GIPS standards:

Australia
Performance Analyst Group of Australia

Austria
Österreichischen Verreinigung für Finanzanalyse und Asset Management und der Vereinigung Österreichischer Investmentgesellschaften

Belgium
Belgian Association for Pension Institutions

Denmark
The Danish Society of Investment Professionals, The Danish Society of Financial Analysts

France
Société Francaise des Analystes Financiers and Association Francaise de la Gestion Financière

Germany
BVI Bundesverband Investment und Asset Management e.V., Deutsche Vereinigung für Finanzanalyse und Asset Management, and German CFA Society

Hong Kong
The Hong Kong Society of Financial Analysts

Hungary
Hungarian Society of Investment Professionals

Ireland
Irish Association of Investment Managers

Italy
Italian Investment Performance Committee

Japan
The Security Analysts Association of Japan

Luxembourg
Association Luxembourgeoise des Fonds d'Investissement and Association Luxembourgeoise des gestionnaires de portefeuilles et analystes financiers

Netherlands
Beroepsvereniging van Beleggingsdeskundigen

New Zealand
CFA Society of New Zealand

Norway
The Norwegian Society of Financial Analysts

Poland
Polski Komitet Wyników Inwestycyjnych

Portugal
Associação Portuguesa de Analistas Financeiros

Singapore
Investment Management Association of Singapore

Spain
CFA Spain

South Africa
Investment Management Association of South Africa

Sweden
Swedish Society of Financial Analysts

Switzerland
Swiss Bankers Association

United Kingdom
National Association of Pension Funds Ltd

United States and Canada
CFA Institute

CORRECTIONS TO GIPS STANDARDS

Last updated 31 October 2006

6-2

Provision	Original	Correction
II. Provisions of the Global Investment Performance Standards (page 6)	2. Calculation Methodology: Achieving comparability among firms' performance presentations REQUIRES...	2. Calculation Methodology: Achieving comparability among firms' performance presentations requires...
2.A.1	TOTAL RETURN, including realized and unrealized gains and losses plus income, MUST be used.	Total return, including realized and unrealized gains and losses plus income, MUST be used.
5.A.1.c	. . .If the COMPOSITE contains less than 5 PORTFOLIOS, the number of PORTFOLIOS is not REQUIRED.	. . .If the COMPOSITE contains 5 PORTFOLIOS or less, the number of PORTFOLIOS is not REQUIRED.
5.A.1.d	. . .If the COMPOSITE contains less than 5 PORTFOLIOS for the full year, a measure of DISPERSION is not REQUIRED.	. . .If the COMPOSITE contains 5 PORTFOLIOS or less for the full year, a measure of DISPERSION is not REQUIRED.
5.A.6	The TOTAL RETURN for the BENCHMARK (or BENCHMARKS) that reflects...	The total return for the BENCHMARK (or BENCHMARKS) that reflects...
5.B.2	. . . over time of the COMPOSITE and BENCHMARK returns.	. . . over time of the COMPOSITE and BENCHMARK ~~returns~~.
6. Real Estate	...all the required and recommended elements of the GIPS standards (outline in Section II.1 through Section II.5.), ...	...all the required and recommended elements of the GIPS standards (outline in Section II.0 through Section II.5.), ...
6.A.3.a	. . .(1) calculated separately using chain-linked TIME-WEIGHTED RATE OF RETURN, (2) adjusted such that the sum of THE INCOME RETURN and the CAPITAL RETURN is equal to the TOTAL RETURN, or (3) income cash recognition mode,	. . .(1) calculated separately using chain-linked TIME-WEIGHTED RATE OF RETURN, or (2) adjusted such that the sum of THE INCOME RETURN and the CAPITAL RETURN is equal to the TOTAL RETURN, ~~or (3) income cash recognition mode,~~
6.A.3.f	The percent of total MARKET VALUE of COMPOSITE assets (asset weighted not equally weighted) total REAL ESTATE assets valued by an EXTERNAL VALUATION for each period, and	The percent of total MARKET VALUE of COMPOSITE assets (asset weighted not equally weighted) to total REAL ESTATE assets valued by an EXTERNAL VALUATION for each period, and

6-2

7. Private Equity	...all the required and recommended elements of the GIPS standards (outline in Section II.1 through Section II.5.), ...	...all the required and recommended elements of the GIPS standards (outline in Section II.0 through Section II.5.), ...
Appendix A Example 4: Private Equity Partners Disclosures	The required fee schedule disclosure is inadvertently omitted	Include sample disclosure text: The standard fee schedule currently in effect is as follows: 1.00% of assets under management. In addition, there is a 20% incentive fee for all assets. The incentive fee is applied to the value added in excess of fees, expenses, and the return of the GP-BO Index.
Glossary, definition of DISTINCT BUSINESS ENTITY	A unit, division, department, or office that is organizationally and functionally segregated from other units, divisions, departments, or office and retains discretion over the assets it manages and autonomy over the investment decision-making process.	A unit, division, department, or office that is organizationally and functionally segregated from other units, divisions, departments, or office and assets retains discretion over the it manages and should have autonomy over the investment decision-making process.
Glossary, definition of FEE SCHEDULE	. . .This schedule is typically listed by asset level ranges and ~~SHOULD~~ be appropriate to the particular prospective client.	. . .This schedule is typically listed by asset level ranges and ~~MUST~~ should be appropriate to the particular prospective client.
Glossary, definition of MARKET VALUE	The current listed price at which investors buy or sell securities at a given time.	The current ~~listed~~ price at which investors buy or sell securities at a given time.
Glossary, definition of OPEN MARKET VALUE (PRIVATE EQUITY)	Open Market Value (~~PRIVATE EQUITY~~)	Open Market Value (REAL ESTATE)

INTERPRETATIONS SUBCOMMITTEE ROSTER (2005-2006)

Carl R. Bacon, ***Chair***
Chairman
Statpro Group Plc.
United Kingdom

Hiroshi Fujibayashi
Senior Researcher
Sumitomo Trust and Banking Co., Ltd.
Japan

Brian Henderson
Investment Consultant
Hymans Robertson
United Kingdom

Stefan Illmer
Custody & Transaction Services Client Reporting, UXD
Credit Suisse
Switzerland

Michaela Krahwinkel
Head of Performance Analysis
Union Asset Management Holding AG
Germany

Neil E. Riddles, CFA
COO
Hansberger Global Investors, Inc.
United States

Timothy M. Simons, CFA
Partner
Ashland Partners & Company LLP
United States

David Spaulding
President
The Spaulding Group Inc.
United States

Karyn D. Vincent, CFA
President
Vincent Performance Services, LLC
United States

Alexandre Zannoni
Vice President/Head of Performance Risk Analysis
Banque Cantonale Vaudoise
Switzerland

7. Index

7

LaVergne, TN USA
11 February 2010
172772LV00001B/1/P